Geographies of Development in the 21st Century

Geographies of Development in the 21st Century

An Introduction to the Global South

Sylvia Chant

Professor of Development Geography, London School of Economics and Political Science, UK

Cathy McIlwaine

Reader in Human Geography, Queen Mary, University of London, UK

Edward Elgar

Cheltenham, UK • Northampton, MA, USA

Published by
Edward Elgar Publishing Limited
The Lypiatts
15 Lansdown Road
Cheltenham
Glos GL50 2JA
UK

Edward Elgar Publishing, Inc.
William Pratt House
9 Dewey Court
Northampton
Massachusetts 01060
USA

A catalogue record for this book
is available from the British Library

Library of Congress Control Number: 2008935952

PEFC
PEFC/16-33-111
CATG-PEFC-052
www.pefc.org

ISBN 978 1 84720 965 8 (hardback)
     978 1 84720 966 5 (paperback)

Printed and bound in Great Britain by MPG Books Ltd, Bodmin, Cornwall

Contents

Acknowledgements

This book grew out of a fully updated Subject Guide on 'geographies of development' completed for external students at the University of London in 2008. We are extremely grateful to the External Office for granting us permission to work the guide into book form, and one which we hope is accessible not only to undergraduate students, but to advanced A-level candidates. In particular we owe thanks to a number of individuals involved in various stages of the process of initial preparation of the Subject Guide, to its present incarnation as a book. These are (in alphabetical order): Katherine Barker, Gwendolyn Beetham, Sarah Bradshaw, Sam Carpenter, Caroline Cornish, Vandana Desai, Bouke de Jong, Katja Jassey, Ralph Kinnear, Christina Koziel-Webster, Tiziana Leone, Emma Meldrum, Mina Moshkeri, Suelle Nachif, Ed Oliver, Felicity Plester, Rob Potter, Silvia Posocco, David Satterthwaite, Nigel Spence, Penny Vera-Sanso, Melissa Weir, Jenny Wilcox and Ailsa Winton. We also thank students who have taken our various undergraduate and postgraduate courses relating to development at the London School of Economics and Queen Mary, University of London for feedback that has enabled us to think about ways to update and improve course content and presentation, as well as our colleagues who have also helped shape our ideas over the years. Last, but not least, both of us have greatly benefited from the participation of people as assistants, participants and respondents in first-hand research we have conducted jointly or independently in the following countries: Botswana, The Gambia, Colombia, Costa Rica, El Salvador, Guatemala, Mexico and the Philippines. Contributions from the 'grassroots' in these diverse parts of the Global South have been the bedrock of our knowledge of development, and a source of continued inspiration and enrichment for nearly three decades. For this we remain eternally indebted.

Sylvia Chant
Cathy McIlwaine

Abbreviations

ADHD	Attention-Deficit Hyperactivity Disorder
AIDS	Acquired Immunodeficiency Syndrome
ART	Anti-Retroviral Therapy
ANGO	Advocacy-oriented non-governmental organisation
ASEAN	Association of Southeast Asian Nations
AWID	Association for Women's Rights in Development
BINGO	Big international NGO
BPFA	Beijing Platform for Action
BWI	Bretton Woods Institutions
CBO	Community-based organisation
CCC	Clean Clothes Campaign
CCT	Conditional Cash Transfer (programmes)
CDD	Community-driven development
CEDAW	Convention on the Elimination of all Forms of Discrimination Against Women
CI	Communication Initiative
CIDA	Canadian International Development Agency
CIS	Commonwealth of Independent States
CMD	Common Mental Disorder
CODI	Community Organisations Development Institute
CPE	Complex Political Emergency
CPRC	Chronic Poverty Research Centre
CSO	Civil society organisation
DAC	Development Assistance Committee (of OECD)
DALYs	Disability Adjusted Life Years
DAWN	Development Alternatives with Women for a New Era
DFID	Department for International Development (UK)
DONGO	Donor non-governmental Organisation (created and owned by donors)
DTM	Demographic Transition Model
EAP	Economically active Population (with reference to employment) or East Asia and the Pacific (with reference to region)
EBAIS	Basic Comprehensive Health Team (Costa Rica)

ECA	Europe and Central Asia
ECLA/ECLAC	Economic Commission for Latin America and the Caribbean
EFF	Extended Fund Facility
EOI	Export-oriented Industrialisation
EPZ	Export Processing Zone
ERP	Economic Recovery Programme
ESF	Emergency Social Fund
ESAF	Enhanced Structural Adjustment Facility
ETI	Ethical Trading Initiative
EU	European Union
FARC	Revolutionary Armed Forces of Columbia
FDI	Foreign Direct Investment
FGM	Female Genital Mutilation
FLO	Fairtrade Labelling Organisations International
FPA	Family Planning Association
FWCW	Fourth World Conference on Women
FTZ	Free Trade Zone
G8	Group of Eight referring to seven of the world's leading industrialised nations (France, Germany, Italy, Japan, the UK, the USA and Canada) plus Russia
GAD	Gender and Development
GAMCOTRAP	Gambia Committee on Traditional Practices
GAP	Gender Action Plan
GATT	General Agreement on Tariffs and Trade
GBS	General Budget Support
GDI	Gender-related Development Index
GDP	Gross Domestic Product
GEM	Gender Empowerment Measure
GID	Gender, Institutions and Development (database)
GNI	Gross National Income
GNP	Gross National Product
GRO	Grassroots organisation
HAI	HelpAge International
HDI	Human Development Index
HIPC	Highly Indebted Poor Country
HIV	Human Immunodeficiency Virus
HLF	High Level Forum
HNP	Health, Nutrition and Population
HPI	Human Poverty Index
IADB	Inter American Development Bank

IBRD	International Bank for Reconstruction and Development
ICFTU	International Confederation of Free Trade Unions
ICPD	International Conference on Population and Development
ICT	Information and Communications Technology
IDA	International Development Association
IDP	Internally Displaced Person
IFC	International Finance Corporation
IFI	International Financial Institution
ILO	International Labour Organisation
IMF	International Monetary Fund
INGO	International non-governmental organisation
IPPF	International Planned Parenthood Federation
ISI	Import Substitution Industrialisation
IWTC	International Women's Tribune Centre
IWY	International Women's Year
LAC	Latin America and the Caribbean
LACAAP	Latin America, the Caribbean, Africa, Asia and the Pacific
LECD	Less Economically Developed Country
LGBT	Lesbian, Gay, Bisexual and Transgender
MDG	Millennium Development Goal
MDRI	Multilateral Debt Relief Initiative
MEDC	More Economically Developed Country
MENA	Middle East and North Africa
MHT	Gujarat Mahila Housing SEWA Trust
MIGA	Multilateral Investment Guarantee Agency
MNC	Multinational corporation (or company)
MONGO	My own non-governmental organisation (personal property of individual)
NAFTA	North American Free Trade Agreement
NAM	Non-Aligned Movement
NASVI	National Association of Street Vendors of India
NATO	North Atlantic Treaty Organisation
NGO	Non-governmental organisation
NIC	Newly industrialising country
NIDL	New International Division of Labour
NIE	New Institutional Economics
NNGO	Northern NGO or National NGO
NPM	New Public Management

ODA	Overseas Development Assistance/Official Development Assistance
OECD	Organisation for Economic Co-operation and Development
ONGO	Operational NGO
PAHO	Pan-American Health Organisation
PAMSCAD	Programme of Actions to Mitigate the Social Costs of Adjustment (Ghana)
PD	Paris Declaration
PHC	Primary Health Care
PPA	Participatory Poverty Assessment
PPP	Purchasing Power Parity
PQLI	Physical Quality of Life Index
PRGF	Poverty Reduction and Growth Facility
PRS	Poverty Reduction Strategy
PRSP	Poverty Reduction Strategy Paper
RBA	Rights-Based Approach
SA	South Asia
SADC	South African Development Community
SAP	Structural Adjustment Programme
SAPRIN	Structural Adjustment Participatory Review International Network
SARS	Severe Acute Respiratory Syndrome
SBA	Stand-By Arrangement
SDI	Shack/Slum Dwellers International
SEWA	Self-Employed Women's Association, India
SIGE	Standardised Indicator of Gender Equality
SIPRI	Stockholm International Peace Research Institute
SLF	Sustainable Livelihoods Framework
SNA	System of National Accounts
SPARC	Society for the Promotion of Area Resource Centres
SPHC	Selective Primary Health Care
SSA	Sub-Saharan Africa
STI	Sexually Transmitted Infection
SUF	Slum Upgrading Facility
SWAps	Sector-Wide Approaches
TLU	Textile Labour Union
TNC	Transnational corporation (or company)
UN	United Nations
UNCHS	United Nations Centre for Human Settlements
UNCTAD	United Nations Conference on Trade and Development

UNDP	United Nations Development Programme
UNDW	United Nations Decade for Women
UNFPA	United Nations Fund for Population Activities
UNICEF	United Nations Children's Fund
UNIFEM	United Nations Development Fund for Women
UNSD	United Nations Statistics Division
USAID	United States Agency for International Development
VAW	Violence Against Women
VCC	Voluntary Code of Conduct
VSO	Voluntary Service Overseas
WDM	World Development Movement
WEDO	Women's Environment and Development Organisation
WEF	World Economic Forum
WFM-IGP	World Federalist Movement – Institute for Global Policy
WHO	World Health Organisation
WID	Women in Development
WIEGO	Women in Informal Employment: Globalising and Organising
WLUML	Women Living Under Muslim Laws
WSO	World Summit Outcome
WTO	World Trade Organisation

Introduction

On a hot, dry day in 1989, together with another colleague and friend, Sarah Bradshaw, we found ourselves on a rickety former US school bus doing its hourly roundtrip to a *barrio* (low-income neighbourhood) called 'Independencia'[1] on the outskirts of Liberia, the capital of Guanacaste province in north-west Costa Rica. As we arrived we were greeted by children running around wanting to know who we were and what we were doing there. On that and subsequent days we got to know most residents of Independencia and gradually learned about their lives as individuals, as members of households, and as part of their community. Although we had worked in this and other places previously, it was the first time we had undertaken team-based fieldwork. Our shared experience of development and what it actually meant on the ground took another formative step during what stretched out as five months together in Costa Rica, and has since been shaped by experiences in many other contexts. We have learned about injustices, but also about hope. Although Independencia had no electricity, there was a water standpipe that served the nearly hundred households of the *barrio*. It had been secured by the residents' committee who had lobbied the local *presidente municipal* (municipal president) at election time until he gave in. But most people still lived in one-room shacks, made from discarded timber or corrugated iron, which were constantly polluted by woodsmoke used for cooking. Most of the women worked selling fruit, vegetables or cooked food, as home-based washerwomen or seamstresses or, for the lucky ones, as maids or restaurant workers in the centre of town. Few earned anything beyond what covered their basic survival needs. The men did not fare much better. Most worked as *jornaleros* (unskilled casual workers), clearing pasture or cutting sugarcane, often hired by the day and taken, like cattle, in trucks to outlying farms in the rural hinterlands to earn meagre wages. Many of these men also had to leave their families for up to nine months of the year in search of other opportunities such as in the banana plantations on the Pacific and Atlantic coasts. Yet, most of the children in Independencia went to school in pristine, freshly starched blue and white uniforms, and, until their teenage years at least, seemed hopeful about their futures. The adult residents were lobbying for land titles, to secure more infrastructure such as a sewerage system and to create a better place to live for themselves and their children. Independencia was a poor community in one of the richer and more developed countries of the Global South. Costa Rica is a democratic, middle-income country with relatively low levels of poverty and high levels of literacy.

Our mutual experiences in Independencia showed us that development was uneven, contradictory and complex. Although it is rooted in inequalities, these vary across place and space not only within the South as a whole, but also within a small country in Central America, and indeed within a smallish town. Development means something different to the residents of *barrios* such as Independencia, which is different again to the views of the local municipal council, civil society organisations, academics, or the national power brokers in central government who negotiate funding from the World Bank and the International Monetary Fund (IMF).

In light of our experiences in places such as Independencia, as well as through engagement with a host of other development actors, the aim of *Geographies of Development in the 21st Century* is to explore the immense social, cultural, political and economic variations among countries and in different places in the so-called 'Global South' – a vast constituency comprising Latin America, the Caribbean, Africa and Asia – to highlight how patterns of development differ. In turn, we attempt to examine how and why these differences occur, and to explore the interrelationships with social and economic inequalities within and between different places and across scales.

While a large body of conceptual and empirical work undertaken in Development Geography – and Development Studies more generally – seeks to understand why inequalities emerge and to evaluate their outcomes for people in the South, it is also a subject which intersects strongly with practice and policy. Not only does studying development require analysis of the nature and consequences of planned interventions, but a considerable body of development research has practical and policy implications. The importance of cross-fertilising ideas generated within both academic and policy arenas is such that scholars of development are often engaged in research, training, activism and advisory work commissioned by different organisations or in collaboration with them. This, in turn, feeds back into their conceptual and empirical endeavours. In our own cases, for example, we have undertaken a variety of consultancies for agencies such as the United Nations Development Programme (UNDP), the International Labour Organisation (ILO), the World Bank, the Inter-American Development Bank (IADB), the United Nations Children's Fund (UNICEF) and the Commonwealth Secretariat. In addition, we have worked and collaborated with smaller civil society and campaign organisations both in the South and in the UK. Although it is often hard to evaluate the actual impact of our involvement in these ventures, it has certainly informed our teaching and research, and through these varied experiences we have long shared an abiding hope to make some contribution to addressing core injustices in our contemporary world.

As indicated in the context of our opening vignette of fieldwork in Costa Rica, we suggest that geographies of development are arguably best understood through writing which emanates from firsthand knowledge. We have therefore attempted to draw as much as possible from our own experiences. Thus while the principal objective of *Geographies of Development in the 21st Century* is to provide a basic introduction to development and the contemporary Global South, and covers a range of topics typically taught in undergraduate courses, we have also made a deliberate choice to feature some of the issues with which we have personally been most closely engaged research- and policy-wise. These include gender and development, gender indicators, households, migration, poverty, employment, violence, housing, urbanisation and civil society. Similarly, a lot of the case study material on which we draw comes from countries in which we have had direct involvement (see Acknowledgements).

The organisation of *Geographies of Development in the 21st Century* is as follows. The first two chapters provide the foundation for the remainder of the book in respect of core concepts and theoretical background. Chapter 1 interrogates common meanings (and understandings) of the term 'development', and how these have changed over time. It examines the evolution of different constructions and categorisations of the so-called 'less developed' parts of the world, such as the 'Third World' and the 'Global South', and how development has been measured.

Chapter 2 deals with development theories, outlining the main perspectives which have emerged over the past 60 years, focusing in particular on modernisation, dependency and Latin American structuralism, coupled with more recent neoliberal and post-development approaches. In Chapter 2 we also touch upon some new themes of key relevance to the evolving field of Development Studies such as globalisation, conflict and everyday violence.

Moving on to more specialist themes, Chapter 3 is dedicated to major features of population growth and distribution, including rates of natural increase, fertility behaviour and management, trends in mortality, life expectancy and demographic ageing, and rural–urban migration. Chapter 4 progresses to a review of urbanisation, including the pace, scale and nature of urban growth in the Global South over the past six decades, and policies for more effective and/or equitable urban management and governance. This chapter also looks at evolving housing markets for the urban poor and changing policy approaches to low-income shelter.

In Chapter 5 we examine economic development strategies commonly found in developing countries, with a focus on industrialisation and trade.

In particular, Chapter 5 outlines the nature of export-oriented industriali-sation and its gender dimensions, the extent to which industrialisation is essential for development to occur, and issues around 'fair' and 'ethical' trade. Leading on from this, Chapter 6 considers specific types of employ-ment in cities of the Global South, with particular attention to activities falling under the rubric of the 'informal' economy. It covers the key acade-mic and policy debates on the role of the informal economy, as well as the character of livelihood strategies among the urban poor.

In Chapter 7, we deal with what is arguably one of the central defining characteristics of the Global South – poverty. Here we outline the chang-ing meanings and measurement of poverty, explore its causes and charac-teristics, and examine some of the strategies developed to alleviate poverty in developing countries.

Chapter 8 introduces the concept of gender and development, paying particular attention to its rising importance within the field of development analysis and policy over the past few decades, as evidenced, *inter alia*, by a United Nations (UN) Decade for Women and a dedicated Millennium Development Goal for 'empowering women and promoting gender equal-ity'. Since gender can rarely be abstracted from its construction and per-formance within households and families, Chapter 9 examines continuities and change in the configuration of households in developing societies. Linking in with Chapter 7, a major focus within the discussion is the 'fem-inisation' of household headship and its interactions with the so-called 'feminisation of poverty'.

Although policy and planning are important threads throughout the book, our last two chapters concentrate on these issues in their own right. In order to provide as comprehensive a review as possible, in Chapter 10 we have selected a single social development issue – health – in which a range of policy initiatives pertaining to a specific sector can be illustrated. Following a review of epidemiological diversity in the Global South which includes 'dis-eases of poverty', HIV/AIDS and common mental disorders (CMDs), Chapter 10 considers the nature of preventative and curative health-care interventions adopted and/or promoted by national and international agen-cies. In Chapter 11, a more dedicated review of the 'development community' itself is provided. Given the increasing importance of participatory develop-ment and civil society, attention is focused on the increasingly multi-centred and coalition-based nature of development policy and planning. This involves discussion not only of national and international players, but also of local stakeholders such as community based organisations (CBOs) and small-scale non-governmental organisations (NGOs).

While each chapter aims primarily to provide a comprehensive yet concise review of the main parameters of particular topics, we have also included a number of 'activities' in which you, as readers, can engage in order to enliven and enrich your understanding. A select list of annotated sources is given at the end of each chapter, which, in conjunction with consulting the general bibliography at the end of the book, will allow you to follow up and deepen your knowledge of chosen themes. These also provide pointers to many other readings which space constraints prevented us from citing. In order to improve your command of the subject matter, we have also included a short checklist of 'learning outcomes' in each chapter.

NOTE

1. 'Independencia' is a pseudonym for the settlement in order to protect its anonymity. Independencia means 'Independence', which is similar to many names given to communities in Costa Rica, and elsewhere, which originated through squatting or other forms of unauthorised land alienation. Residents frequently choose names of figures or events linked with political, historical, patriotic, and/or religious pride and sentiment. This is one small, but often proven, means of garnering tolerance, sympathy or solidarity from other urban inhabitants and the local authorities, and, in the process, helps to guard against summary eviction.

1. Defining, conceptualising and measuring development

INTRODUCTION

Defining the groupings of poorer countries in the world and the nature and processes of development has been subject to much debate by scholars and policy-makers alike. Development means different things to different people in different places, and even then, there is rarely agreement. With this in mind, the first part of this chapter outlines the spatial and conceptual limits of the so-called 'Third World', 'developing world' and 'Global South', highlighting how such terms originated, and have been contested in terms of their utility and appropriateness. The second part of the chapter focuses on development as a concept, outlining its various meanings and how it has been deployed to date. The final section briefly examines how development has been measured in relation to such indicators as Gross National Product (GNP) and Gross National Income (GNI), and the Human Development Index (HDI), together with a discussion of the importance of the Millennium Development Goals (MDGs).

WHAT ARE THE 'UNDERDEVELOPED WORLD', THE 'THIRD WORLD' AND THE 'GLOBAL SOUTH'?

The division of the world into different spatial zones according to levels of development, and especially economic wealth and growth, is usually said to date back to the end of the Second World War. In the context of post-war reconstruction and especially the emergence of the Cold War between the superpowers, the USA and the former Soviet Union (USSR), as well as the formation of the United Nations (UN), attention was increasingly paid to the 'underdeveloped' parts of the world. The term 'underdeveloped' was introduced in the inaugural address of US President Harry S. Truman in January 1949 in what is known as the 'Four Point Plan'.[1] While Points 1–3 outlined US support for the establishment of the United Nations, the continuity of the Marshall Plan for Europe (1947) and the formation of the North Atlantic Treaty Organisation

(NATO), Point 4 was reportedly introduced as a 'last minute' addition. In laying out a vision for development in the post-war context of decolonisation, Truman's speech drew a distinction between the 'underdeveloped' and 'prosperous' areas of the world. People in the former lived in what Truman noted as 'conditions approaching misery' characterised by poverty, disease, and a 'primitive and stagnant' economic life (cited in Rist, 1997: 71). His plan was to assist these 'underdeveloped' areas with Western capital and technology, as well as encouraging democracy, with the ultimate aim that they should emulate patterns of development spearheaded by the USA and Europe. Although the world had been previously divided into the colonisers and the colonised, this was the first time that, in theory at least, all countries were viewed as equal within the world system. It is important to emphasise however that this inherently political term became an emblem for the imposition of North American ideals on the rest of the world, and that being 'underdeveloped' somehow implied an undignified condition (Esteva, 1992). It also assumed that lack of development was the fault of the countries themselves and that Western knowledge was superior to local knowledge of people in the South (Illich, 1997).

Also with political origins was another common term for the 'underdeveloped' parts of the globe – the 'Third World'. This term was allegedly first coined in France in 1952 as '*Tiers Monde*' by a demographer called Alfred Sauvry. It derived from the French notion of the 'Third Estate' used to describe the disadvantaged position of the peasantry in pre-Revolutionary France. In turn, it was suggested that because the peasantry has succeeded in challenging the traditional dominance of the clergy and nobility in France as a 'Third Way', then Third World countries would emerge as a new political force. Despite attempts by the USA and the former USSR to steer countries towards either capitalist or communist regimes, some members of the 'Third World' created the Non-Aligned Movement (NAM) in 1961. The NAM aimed to avoid the politics of the Cold War and to promote alternative forms of development through creating, *inter alia*, an international voting bloc of countries which were recently independent and non-aligned. The NAM also reflected what is sometimes called 'Third Worldism', referring to the attempts of Third World countries to act together (Berger, 2004). Although the original meaning of the 'Third World' was political or, more accurately, geo-political (reflecting what Dodds [2008] calls a 'new geopolitical imagination'), by the 1960s it was commonly used as part of a division of global politics that also encompassed economic distinctions. This comprised the 'First World' of wealthy, capitalist, industrialised Western nations referring to the USA and its allies; the 'Second World' of centrally planned economies encompassing the former USSR, the Eastern Bloc and the rest of the communist world, and the 'Third World' made up of poorer, and mainly recently politically independent, former colonies in Africa, Latin America and Asia (ibid.; see also Figure 1.1).

CRITICISMS OF THE TERM 'THIRD WORLD'

Despite its popular usage up until the present day, the term 'Third World' has been heavily criticised. One of the most enduring criticisms is that the notion is much too singular to encapsulate the huge diversity of conditions found within the construct. For instance, at one end of the spectrum the 'Third World' includes the world's most impoverished countries in Africa, such as Ethiopia and Mozambique, as well as those deeply undermined by conflict and inequality in Central America and the Caribbean such as Nicaragua and Haiti. At the other end of the spectrum, the term has also extended to the oil-rich nations of the Middle East, as well as Venezuela and Nigeria, in addition to wealthy 'Newly Industrialising Countries' (NICs), such as South Korea, Hong Kong, Singapore and Taiwan. Moreover, not only are there huge variations between countries of the 'Third World', but also within individual countries. Thus, as a spatial as well as political term, and in focusing on places rather than people, 'Third World' often glosses over vast intra-national as well as international income inequalities. Indeed, this was one of the reasons why the terms 'Fourth World' and 'Fifth World' briefly made an appearance in the 1970s and 1980s (see Manuel and Posluns, 1974; Potter et al., 2008; Rigg, 2007).

Another criticism pertaining to the term 'Third World' is its anachronism in light of the collapse of communism in the former USSR and Eastern Bloc in late 1980s and early 1990s. In changing the world international economic and political order, and effectively 'disappearing the Second World', the 'Third World' stands as something of a meaningless entity. On top of this, many former 'Second World' countries have very similar socio-economic circumstances to those in the Third World, and in some cases are even worse off economically. In turn, a number of such nations, at least in the 1980s, were themselves under socialist rule (for example, Cuba, Tanzania and Vietnam). While, until the end of the 1990s, some argued for the continued use of the term 'Third World' on grounds that its abolition would render this area unimportant and because there are still distinctive issues relating to the 'Third World' (Thomas, 1999), it is now largely redundant (see Dodds, 2008).

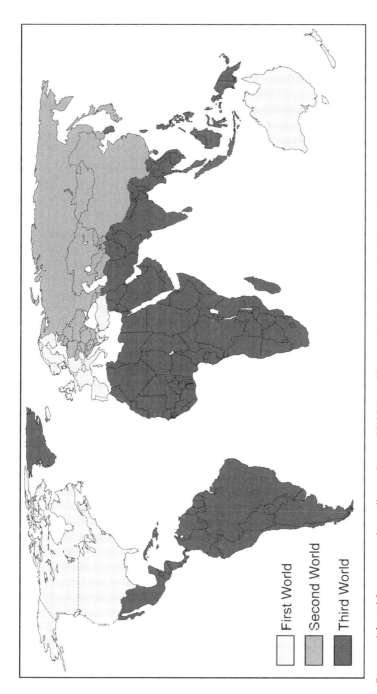

Source: Adapted from www.nationsonline.org/oneworld/third_world_countries.htm (accessed 5 February 2008).

Figure 1.1 Map of the 'First', 'Second' and 'Third' worlds

ALTERNATIVES TO THE TERM 'THIRD WORLD'

Even before the collapse of the 'Second World', there were several attempts to devise alternative nomenclature. One of the most important occurred as a result of the United Nations-sponsored Brandt Commission, whose publication *North–South: A Programme for Survival in 1980* (Brandt, 1980) distinguished between the industrialised nations of the rich, developed 'North' and the poor, developing, dependent 'South'. Although the Brandt Report did not explicitly identify the First, Second and Third Worlds, the 'South' broadly corresponded with the latter. Beyond this new terminology, it was also significant that the report recognised the interdependence of the world's nations (before the term 'globalisation' had been coined). However, use of the term the 'South' is also problematic given that there are countries with 'Northern' characteristics in the southern hemisphere, such as Australia and New Zealand, and those with 'Southern' characteristics in the northern hemisphere, such as China and Mongolia. Indeed, many criticisms similar to those levelled at the 'Third World', such as the fact that it glosses over pockets of poverty and inequality in rich nations, and wealth in poor nations (see Dodds, 2008; Power, 2003), can also be used against the 'South', which arguably has even less explanatory power (Potter et al., 2008).

Other alternatives for 'Third World' and 'South' include 'developing world' and 'developing countries'. Yet these also imply inferiority, together with normative assumptions that all countries should follow a similar path to that forged by the 'developed' nations, and/or that progress is being made even when it is not. Moreover, both these latter terms continue to conjure up an image of a rich/poor world binary and fail to recognise internal diversity within both continents and countries of the South and North alike. Similar criticisms are made of the terms 'less-developed', 'under-developed' and 'undeveloped' (see Willis, 2005). Another alternative, 'poor nations', has gained in popularity given that, despite variations, poverty tends to be geographically concentrated in Central America, sub-Saharan Africa, and parts of South, Southeast and Northeast Asia. Income is also used by the World Bank, which divides the world into 'low-income', 'middle-income' and 'high-income' countries. Yet while economic distinctions are to some extent useful, there are also a wide range of characteristics beyond poverty and income relevant to countries in the Global South (Rigg, 2007). Indeed, similar criticisms are applicable to the terms 'More Economically Developed Countries (MEDCs) and 'Less Economically Developed Countries' (LEDCs). Although the use of 'economic' in the term does not automatically imply that development is only related to the economy, they do suggest that economic factors are more important than social, cultural and political issues (Willis, 2005).

Coined by the *New Internationalist* magazine and reflecting the views of activists working towards global justice, another classification used in the last decade has been 'majority' and 'minority' world, with the former referring to the poorest countries and the latter the richest. The political message behind these terms is to show that despite being home to most of the world's population and countries (136 out of 192 recognised states), the majority world has limited power. It serves to remind people of the sheer scale of the South/Third World/Poor World, despite its apparent lack of importance in global affairs. Reflecting the significance of culture, another binary with some salience has been the 'Western'–'non-Western' distinction. Although this broadly corresponds with the North–South dyad, there are variations in terms of the social and economic position of Japan which in many ways can be described as 'non-Western' culturally, yet Northern geographically, not to mention being rich in monetary terms. Implicit in this is also the recognition that the West and/or Europe is taken as the cultural reference point for the world reflecting deep-seated Eurocentrism (Rigg, 2007; Willis, 2005).

Although there is a more neutral term, 'LACAAP' (to denote Latin America, the Caribbean, Africa, Asia and the Pacific), it is rarely used, leaving 'Global South' (and its counterpart 'Global North') as an increasingly favoured option. This is based on the earlier 'North–South' distinction of the 1980s, but the prefix 'Global' clarifies that this is not a geographical categorisation of the world. Rather, it is one based on economic inequalities albeit with some spatial resonance in terms of where the countries concerned are situated. In turn, the idea that the world is closely interconnected through a range of global processes is also reflected in this terminology (Rigg, 2007).[2]

It is also important to mention that the world is being increasingly divided into powerful trading blocs, some of which are exclusively located in the North such as the European Union (EU), while others straddle the so-called North–South divide such as the North American Free Trade Agreement (NAFTA) between the USA, Canada and Mexico. Perhaps most importantly, coalitions have also emerged within the South such as the Southern Africa Development Community (SADC) and the Association of Southeast Asian Nations (ASEAN). Similar to the NAM mentioned above, the wealthier countries in the South are also increasingly grouping together across regions. An example of this is the G20 of developing countries which emerged from the World Trade Organisation talks in Mexico in 2003 where nations such as Brazil, China, India and Nigeria came together to challenge the power of the USA and EU (Lawson, 2007). The significant point here is that global groupings are dynamic and shifting even though the poorest countries of the world are almost always the most disadvantaged politically and economically.

Leading on from this, whichever term is used to define the poorest parts of the world, Potter et al. (2008) remind us that all, in some form or other, point to persistent patterns of exploitation and inequality. For example, on one hand, the Global South contains the majority of the world's nations, the vast bulk of its population (around 80 per cent), and an increasingly large share of economic output, which by 2025 is anticipated to be around 60 per cent (Rigg, 2007). Yet, wealth and power remain concentrated in the Global North. For instance, 2.5 billion people living on less than $2 a day, most of whom live in the Global South, comprise 40 per cent of the world's population and account for 5 per cent of global income. In contrast, the richest 10 per cent, most of whom live in the Global North, account for 54 per cent (UNDP, 2005: 5). Furthermore, knowledge flows across the globe tend to move from North to South regardless of the content, quality and relevance of that knowledge. This is partly rooted in patterns of colonisation where countries of the North were more powerful than those of the South and where the values, ideals and knowledge of Southern countries were widely denigrated, a pattern which persists today (Power, 2003). Key to studying development, therefore, is not only how the poor of the South cope with adversity and disadvantage, but how global inequalities originate, are sustained, and frequently deepen over time.

Activity 1.1
Access President Harry S. Truman's inaugural speech either as a script from www.yale.edu/lawweb/avalon/presiden/inaug/truman.htm OR as an audio download from www.learnoutloud.com/Catalog/Politics/U.S.-Government/Harry-S-Truman-Inauguration-Speech-1949/6970#. Identify the sections relating to the division of the world into different political and economic areas. Assess the extent to which you think Truman was genuinely interested in the well-being of nations in the so-called 'underdeveloped world' and the degree to which this speech reflected an agenda of securing US interests through imposing its values on the rest of the world.

WHAT IS DEVELOPMENT?

Having discussed the terminology for describing the deprived parts of the world, it is now appropriate to think about what 'development' itself actually means. Popular understandings of development focus on making sure people have enough eat, have access to shelter, education, health care and jobs or as Wroe and Doney (2005: 13) in their *Rough Guide to a Better World* note: 'It's about making sure that the most basic things that we take for granted can also be taken for granted by everyone else in the world.' In other words, it is about having opportunities to fulfil personal and societal desires. However, while this interpretation is certainly valuable, development is more complex than this suggests. As Lawson (2007: 5) comments: ' "Development" itself is a complex, contradictory and powerful term that takes on particular meanings in the context of specific intellectual, institutional and political moments.'

Therefore, there is little consensus as to what development refers. The main problems with its definition include the issue of value judgements, and recognising that there are numerous divergences of opinion over its goals and objectives. This said, Thomas (2000a) outlines four key characteristics of development that can serve as an appropriately broad basis for its definition. The first is that development entails an all-encompassing change, and not just improvement in one particular element; second, development is a continuous and cumulative process of change; third, it implies change at both social and individual levels, and, fourth, developmental change is not always positive. Drawing on Cowen and Shenton (1996), Thomas (2000a) also distinguishes between different uses of the term focusing on the difference between 'immanent development', which is spontaneous and unconscious, 'intentional development', which involves deliberate policy and actions of the state, and 'progress', which is about improvement over time. Overall, then, development can be described as a vision of the state of being of a desirable society, as a historical process, and/or comprising deliberate improvement policies on behalf of various agencies and governments as well as changes that 'just happen' (Potter et al., 2008).

Although the assumption is that development is always for the better, it must also be recognised that it can also be conceived as having negative outcomes depending on its conception and implementation (Potter et al., 2008). In recent years, the role of interventionist development in particular has come under attack pioneered by the writings of Arturo Escobar (1995) who suggested that the Western development project, and especially those reflected in the policies of economists, have actually made life worse for many people of the South. This view has been most recently developed from a neo-conservative perspective by William Easterly (2006) in his book *The White Man's Burden* where he eloquently critiques the development aid industry and their inability to reduce poverty effectively despite their 'big plans' and good intentions. This critique is also linked with idea of ethnocentrism and racism within development thinking rooted in colonialism whether implicit or explicit. This is where people and places in the South are viewed as inferior and where they are stereotyped as ignorant, helpless and culpable in their own fate, thus reflecting a widespread racism that remains in much discourse today (Potter et al., 2008; Power, 2003; 2006).

In order to unpack these debates, it is arguably helpful to distinguish further between different types of development. Gillian Hart (2001) has created a useful division between what she calls big 'D' Development and little 'd' development. The former refers to the project of intervention in the post-Second World War era that entailed creating policies usually overseen by large organisations such as the World Bank as well as other actors to try to improve conditions for countries and people of the South. While this encompasses the notion of 'intentional development', the latter is much more akin to 'immanent development', which focuses on a range of economic, political, social and cultural processes that produce both improvements and setbacks depending on the place or the actors involved. As Hart (2001: 650) suggests, this is much more about the 'development of capitalism as a geographically uneven, profoundly contradictory set of historical processes'. Therefore, development is also about the ways in which certain ideas are grouped into a discourse or way of thinking that is influenced by a range of different political, economic and social positions that cohere in particular ways in different places.

While these definitions are very broad and rather esoteric, more specific versions have been elaborated. One of the most common which emerged in the 1950s, is that development is a synonym for economic growth. Yet although the latter remains an underlying factor in many contemporary definitions, it has been widely challenged. This has been mainly on social and/or cultural grounds in terms of development relating to adequate provision of health, education or nutrition, as well as more subjective elements such as self-respect, freedom of choice, and political agency (see, for example, Sen, 1999). In the case of political agency, for instance, it has been argued that development should entail free and fair elections, and people having the right to criticise their own states and governments without recrimination. These debates on expanding economic definitions underlie increasingly diverse attempts to measure development.

MEASURING DEVELOPMENT

Reflecting the 'intentional' or big 'D' approach to development, substantial efforts have been made to measure the level of development of specific countries. Although some argue that it is impossible to measure development in the first place, and that measurement reflects a very specific discourse about development, most agree that some form of approximation is necessary for policy-makers and governments as well as campaigning organisations (Willis, 2005). The categorisation of countries into global groupings, for example, conceivably allows targeting assistance and interventions more appropriately. Just as one of the most common definitions of development has been the level of economic growth, so the most widely used indicator to measure development since the 1950s has been Gross Domestic Product (GDP) or Gross National Product (GNP) if net income from abroad is included. Gross Domestic Product measures the size of the economy, whereas GNP is the total income available for private and public spending in a country. These terms are used to describe income per head (or per capita) by dividing the GDP or GNP by the estimated mid-year population in a given country. Economic growth is then measured by the increase in output of goods and services that a country produces over an accounting period (usually one year) (Thirlwall, 2008; Willis, 2005). More recently, GNP has been substituted by GNI per capita. This stands for Gross National Income, and is calculated by the sum of value added by all nationally resident producers (for example, through goods or services), plus net receipts of primary income (from labour and capital) from abroad, divided by the estimated mid-year population. While GNI is calculated in national currency but usually converted to US dollars, a new conversion process is used to minimise the vagaries caused by fluctuating exchange rates. More specifically, the so-called 'Atlas Method', developed by the World Bank, averages the exchange rate for the year of calculation together with those in the two preceding years, as well as adjusting for differences in rates of inflation between the country concerned and the G5 countries (the USA, the UK, Japan, France and Germany).

While the utility of the GDP and GNP/GNI lies in their ability to provide a snapshot of economies, and to act as a useful starting point for analysing and comparing the health of economies throughout the world – and for these reasons continue to be used – they are nonetheless blunt tools in assessing development, and have attracted criticism not only from academics but from the World Bank itself (Thirlwall, 2008). Measuring the size of an economy says little about the welfare of the country in terms of the distribution of income among the population or the composition of outputs such as education and health care. Other criticisms include the weak comparability of statistics calculated differently in different countries, as well as the systematic undervaluation of activities with no apparent economic value. This may include environmental degradation, domestic labour in the home (usually conducted by women), family labour involving subsistence farming (self-sufficiency), or illegal and informal activities of the economy that are not comprehensively registered in the System of National Accounts (SNA). Finally, GDP and GNP/GNI can imply that development can be achieved in straightforwardly measurable ways even if economic growth is only a very partial measure of the development of a country and is only a means to an end rather than an end in itself.

ALTERNATIVE MEASUREMENTS OF DEVELOPMENT

In light of the above, a number of alternative measures have been developed which aim to incorporate social and political dimensions, albeit still reflecting Development with a big 'D'. Many of these have drawn on the work of prominent thinkers such as the pioneer of development ethics, Denis Goulet, and Amartya Sen, a Nobel Laureate in Economics. Goulet (1971, cited in Thirlwall, 2008; see also Elliott, 2008), for instance, argues that three main components are central to the meaning and measurement of development:

1. Life sustenance in terms of basic needs.
2. Self-esteem related to self-respect and independence.
3. Freedom concerned with the ability of people to exercise freedom of choice over their own destiny.

Similarly, Sen argues that development should focus on people's 'entitlements' and 'capabilities', which refer to the opportunities and rights that people exercise in order to access resources in society and which invariably depend on power relations. More specifically, in his book, *Development as Freedom*, first published in 1999, Sen suggests that development entails the removal of 'unfreedoms' which constrain people's choices and opportunities. Freedom requires people to live lives free from starvation, undernourishment, morbidity, premature mortality, illiteracy and innumeracy (see also Potter et al., 2008).

Attempts to measure development in ways other than GDP have a fairly long history. One of the earliest alternatives measures was the Physical Quality of Life Index (PQLI) developed in 1979. This gave one-third weight each to life expectancy at year one, infant mortality and literacy. However, the most commonly used alternative measure is the Human Development Index (HDI) encompassing Sen's thinking on the capability approach. This was created by the UNDP in the late 1980s and published in 1990 in the first *Human Development Report* in an attempt to 'put people back at the centre of development'. Drawing on an understanding of development which expands people's choices, the HDI is based on:

1. Real GDP per capita to indicate living standards and a decent minimum level of income.
2. Adult literacy rate and gross enrolment ratios to indicate the attainment of knowledge.
3. Life expectancy at birth to reflect health and longevity.

These three measures are combined in a composite index ranging from 0 to 1 and then ranked. The higher the value, the higher the HDI. The HDI does not therefore measure absolute levels of human development, but ranks countries in relation to one another (Willis, 2005).

The HDI often produces very different results when compared with per capita income. For example, some countries may have low per capita GNPs/GNIs yet score highly on the HDI because they have invested heavily in welfare such as education and health care. In turn, other countries, especially the oil-rich states, have high per capita incomes but low HDI scores due to limited redistribution of wealth.

Criticisms of the HDI

As with all such measures, there are criticisms. One relates to the fact that the HDI is still premised on the notion of development as economic growth, thus reflecting a very narrow conception of well-being. It also assumes that it is possible to measure development in simple, quantitative ways when in fact development and deprivation are multidimensional and complex. In relation to this, others have critiqued the inclusion of specific variables outlining their drawbacks and the inappropriate ways they have been inserted into the HDI. Hicks (1997), for example, critiques the HDI on these grounds and suggests a revised version called the 'Inequality-Adjusted Human Development Index' that factors inequality into calculation of all the variables. More broadly, the HDI has been accused of ignoring both the situation within countries (although progress in measuring intra-national HDIs is now under way – see Chant, 2007a: ch. 6 on Costa Rica), as well as global power inequalities, and a host of other issues such as gender, ecology and sustainability. Thus, despite the proposed focus on a broader conception of people-centred development, the HDI continues to impose a particular view of the world from the point of view of the development professional rather than poor people experiencing life in poor nations (see Potter et al., 2008).

The UNDP itself openly admits that the HDI is a crude measure of development that must be complemented by others. This is one reason it has undertaken the creation of complementary indices such as the Human Poverty Index (HPI). Making its first appearance in the UNDP's *Human Development Report* of 1997, this brings together life expectancy over 40, adult literacy, and a deprivation index based on access to safe water and health services, and malnutrition among the under-5s (now divided into HPI-1 for developing countries and HPI-2 for selected Organisation for Economic Co-operation and Development [OECD] countries, with the cut-off point for life expectancy in the latter being 60 years). A slightly earlier addition (dating from 1995, and discussed further in Chapter 8, this volume) is the Gender-related Development Index (GDI), which is effectively the HDI discounted or adjusted for gender inequalities in overall development achievements. Related to this is the Gender Empowerment Measure (GEM) which measures gender inequality in relation to economic and political participation as well as earned income. More recently, the 2006 *Human Development Report* presented the HDI adjusted by income group in order to address some of the misgivings mentioned above in relation to measuring inequality (UNDP, 2006).

Although aggregate indices omit a lot of what development really means, they are still useful. As well as permitting a general glimpse of differences in well-being across the globe, some more specific advantages are, first, that the HDI and its associate indices turn the orientation away from measuring the means of development (via per capita GDP and GNP/GNI), to its ends, such as literacy, health and so on. Second, the HDI measures 'over-development' as well as underdevelopment (for example, there are diseases of affluence as well as poverty). Third, HDI, HPI and GDI make more sense when trying to reduce gaps between rich and poor and between men and women in literacy, life expectancy and so on, compared with income per capita.

In summary, no simple quantitative measure can accurately describe the nature and level of development in a country, especially since development is now widely accepted as comprising multidimensional advances in societal well-being, many of which defy precise determination. However, that measurement of factors beyond GNP/GNI is now established, not to mention subject to ongoing revision and refinement, is a welcome step towards a more holistic view of global development and inequality.

Activity 1.2
Consult the latest UNDP *Human Development Report*, available online at http://hdr.undp.org/en/reports/. From the section on Human Development Indicators, select five to ten developed and developing countries and compare their per capita income levels, their HDI, HPI-1 and HPI-2 and GDI. Write a short explanation of why you think variations between these indices might have occurred.

THE MILLENNIUM DEVELOPMENT GOALS

Despite enduring criticisms of the reduction of development to quantitative measures, the turn of the Millennium witnessed the creation of a set of development objectives and targets which have arguably reinforced a conceptualisation of development based on simplified measures. Again reflecting Development with a big 'D', these are encompassed within the Millennium Development Goals (MDGs) which have come to dominate development policy since 2000. With roots in earlier UN conferences such as the 1990 International World Summit on Children and the 1994 International Conference on Population and Development, the MDGs were developed at the UN Millennium Summit in 2000. They were subsequently set out in the UN Millennium Declaration and adopted by all 189 UN member countries (Rigg, 2008).

The MDGs are effectively a summary of the key issues affecting global development since the development project 'emerged' 60 years ago (although the baseline for targets is 2000). The goals were adopted following consensus of a team of experts from the UN Secretariat, IMF, OECD and the World Bank. They include a framework of 8 goals, 18 targets and 48 indicators. Under the overarching goal of reducing global poverty, specific quantified targets address income poverty, hunger, disease, shelter, exclusion, especially that related with gender inequality, as well as education and environmental sustainability (see Box 1.1). Underlying the series of goals and specific targets is a commitment to addressing basic human rights such as health, education, housing, and security.

The process by which these goals have begun to dominate the entire functioning of international development policy began with the UN Millennium Project established in 2002 in order to plan how the MDGs could be achieved. After wide consultation around the world, the independent advisory board published its findings and recommendations in a 2005 report called *Investing in Development: a Practical Plan to Achieve the Millennium Development Goals.*[3] Between 2005 and 2007 the Project worked on preparing countries' national development strategies based on the MDGs before shifting to the UNDP in January 2007 where work continues on assisting countries in meeting their goals.[4]

Challenging the MDGs

Although few would contest the desirability of fulfilling the broad aims of the MDGs in terms of eradicating poverty and hunger throughout the world, they have been the subject of much controversy. This has revolved around whether the goals can be met by 2015, and a critique of the goals themselves as reflecting an adequate agenda for change (Rigg, 2008).

With respect to the first issue, it is now widely accepted that many countries around the world will not meet the targets. According to the UN's *Millennium Development Goals Report* of 2007, only one of the eight regional country groupings is on track to meet the MDGs.[5] The greatest shortfalls will be in sub-Saharan Africa where, despite some progress in

BOX 1.1   MILLENNIUM DEVELOPMENT GOALS (AND TARGETS)

MDG 1. ERADICATE EXTREME POVERTY AND HUNGER
Target 1. Halve, between 1990 and 2015, the proportion of people whose income is less than $1 a day.
Target 2. Halve, between 1990 and 2015, the proportion of people who suffer from hunger.

MDG 2. ACHIEVE UNIVERSAL PRIMARY EDUCATION
Target 3. Ensure that, by 2015, children everywhere, boys and girls alike, will be able to complete a full course of primary schooling.

MDG 3. PROMOTE GENDER EQUALITY AND EMPOWER WOMEN
Target 4. Eliminate gender disparity in primary and secondary education, preferably by 2005, and in all levels of education no later than 2015.

MDG 4. REDUCE CHILD MORTALITY
Target 5. Reduce by two-thirds, between 1990 and 2015, the under-five mortality rate.

MDG 5. IMPROVE MATERNAL HEALTH
Target 6. Reduce by three-quarters, between 1990 and 2015, the maternal mortality ratio.

MDG 6. COMBAT HIV/AIDS, MALARIA AND OTHER DISEASES
Target 7. Have halted by 2015 and begun to reverse the spread of HIV/AIDS.
Target 8. Have halted by 2015 and begun to reverse the incidence of malaria and other major diseases.

MDG 7. ENSURE ENVIRONMENTAL SUSTAINABILITY
Target 9. Integrate the principles of sustainable development into country policies and programs and reverse the loss of environmental resources.
Target 10. Halve, by 2015, the proportion of people without sustainable access to safe drinking water and basic sanitation.
Target 11. Have achieved by 2020 a significant improvement in the lives of at least 100 million slum dwellers.

MDG 8. DEVELOP A GLOBAL PARTNERSHIP FOR DEVELOPMENT

Target 12. Develop further an open, rule-based, predictable, non-discriminatory trading and financial system (includes a commitment to good governance, development, and poverty reduction – both nationally and internationally).

Target 13. Address the special needs of the Least Developed Countries (includes tariff- and quota-free access for Least Developed Countries) exports, enhanced program of debt relief for heavily indebted poor countries [HIPCs] and cancellation of official bilateral debt, and more generous official development assistance for countries committed to poverty reduction).

Target 14. Address the special needs of landlocked developing countries and small island developing states (through the Program of Action for the Sustainable Development of Small Island Developing States and 22nd General Assembly provisions).

Target 15. Deal comprehensively with the debt problems of developing countries through national and international measures in order to make debt sustainable in the long term.

Target 16. In co-operation with developing countries, develop and implement strategies for decent and productive work for youth.

Target 17. In co-operation with pharmaceutical companies, provide access to affordable essential drugs in developing countries.

Target 18. In co-operation with the private sector, make available the benefits of new technologies, especially information and communications technologies.

Sources: www.unmillenniumproject.org/; www.undp.org/poverty/mdgsupport. htm (both accessed 16 April 2008).

some countries on specific targets, the main obstacles include lack of employment opportunities for young people, gender inequalities, rapid and unplanned urbanisation, deforestation, increasing water scarcity and high HIV prevalence (UN, 2007). Indeed, Clemens et al. (2007: 735–6) note that 42 out of a total of 47 African countries are 'off track' for meeting at least half of targets and 12 are 'off track' for meeting all the targets. They go on to assert that for most countries, meeting the goals will require more than doubling the rate of progress.

Given realisation that the goals will not be met, commentators have begun to ask why. Both the UN and other independent bodies invariably blame the countries of the Global North for failing to deliver on their commitments to the Official Development Assistance (ODA) target of 0.7 per

cent of gross national income by 2015, and for the G8 countries in particular to have failed in living up to their 2005 pledge to double aid to Africa
by 2010. Indeed, ODA appears to be falling rather than increasing (UN,
2007; see also Chapter 11, this volume). Clemens et al. (2007: 5) estimate
that between US$40–70 billion extra resources are needed each year until
2015 in order to meet targets.

There have also been growing criticisms of the entire conceptualisation
of the MDGs. In particular, many have questioned how each of the goals
is actually measured. For instance, there is little recognition of the widespread critique of income-based poverty lines as the most appropriate tool
of poverty assessment (see Chapter 7, this volume). Similarly, the assumption that gender inequality can be addressed and empowerment created by
focusing on education has been widely criticised (Saith, 2006; also Chapter
8, this volume). This reflects the fact that the MDGs tend to be monetar-
ily rather than movement driven – in terms of focusing on costing and
quantitatively measuring goals and neglecting social relations. In addition,
structural changes are often overlooked in favour of instrumental change
due to the latter's comparative ease of measurement. Often, conditions
that are beyond donor control are ignored despite being critical in meeting
the goals. The quality and accuracy of the data used have also been questioned, especially in countries where good quality data are notoriously
difficult to obtain. Other critiques focus on broader conceptual and political issues including the fact that the MDGs assume that development is
an essentially linear process which can only be achieved by following
neoliberal, capitalist dictates. Despite some recognition of the need to
work together across the South and North, development tends to be
viewed as a ghettoised issue with countries of the South being held responsible for meeting the targets. Finally, there have been concerns about the
calls for democratic governance in Southern countries when the world is
being ruled by small elites with no democratic mandate (Clemens et al.,
2007; Saith, 2006).

This said, the MDGs are associated with some positive breakthroughs.
First, they have been very good for advocacy. An example of this is the
'Make Poverty History' campaign which has mobilised around the MDGs
and has put pressure on the G8 country governments to honour their
pledges to reduce debt and poverty. Second, the MDGs arguably represent
a shift away from the extreme conservatism associated with the US presi-
dential administration of George Bush. Furthermore, they provide a basic
benchmark from which to negotiate with governments and agencies.
Ostensibly, this can act as a mechanism for channelling aid that can work,
as long as there are country-specific targets as well (Clemens et al., 2007).
Again, as with earlier criticisms of measuring development, the MDGs

continue the tendency to view development as uncontested and interventionist rather than complex and discursive.

Activity 1.3
Consult the website of the Make Poverty History campaign (www.makepovertyhistory.org/). Read the manifesto of the campaign and identify the aspects that relate to the Millennium Development Goals (www.makepovertyhistory.org/whatwewant/index.shtml).

LEARNING OUTCOMES

By the end of this chapter and relevant reading, you should be able to:

- Discuss the different terms used to describe the poorest countries of the world and explain the advantages and disadvantages of each one.
- Explain what the term 'development' means and recognise that it is contested.
- Describe the different measures of development focusing on per capita GNP/GNI and the HDI and assess their comparative merits and limitations.
- Outline the MDGs and identify the obstacles to their fulfilment across the Global South.

NOTES

1. For details of Truman's full inaugural address see www.yale.edu/lawweb/avalon/presiden/inaug/truman.htm (accessed 6 November 2007).
2. We use the terms 'Global South', 'South' and 'developing world/countries' interchangeably in this volume. In being arguably least value-laden, we also see these terms as preferential to some of the others identified.
3. Available at www.unmillenniumproject.org/reports/fullreport.htm (accessed 16 April 2008).
4. See www.unmillenniumproject.org/ (accessed 16 April 2008).
5. These groupings are defined as: developed regions, countries of the Commonwealth of Independent States (CIS), Northern Africa, sub-Saharan Africa, Southeastern Asia, Oceania, Eastern Asia, Southern Asia, Western Asia, and Latin America and the Caribbean (UN, 2007: 35).

FURTHER READING

Potter, Robert, Binns, Tony, Elliott, Jennifer A. and Smith, David (2008), *Geographies of Development*, 3rd edn, Harlow: Pearson Education.

Chapter 1 of this volume is probably the most comprehensive overview of debates about delineating the Global South and thinking about what development means. It provides case studies and examples to illustrate the points.

Rigg, Jonathan (2007), *An Everyday Geography of the Global South*, London and New York: Routledge.
Chapter 1 of this book outlines the different scales and geographies of development in the South with a particular focus on people themselves and how their lives are linked with broader processes of national and global change.

Thomas, Alan (2000), 'Meanings and views of development', in Tim Allen and Alan Thomas (eds), *Poverty and Development into the 21st Century*, Oxford: Oxford University Press, pp. 23–48.
This chapter provides a clear yet sophisticated overview of the conceptual debates about development.

Wroe, Martin and Doney, Malcolm (2005), *The Rough Guide to a Better World*, London: Rough Guides (downloadable from www.dfid.gov.uk/pubs/files/rough-guide/better-world.pdf).
This booklet, written in collaboration between the Department for International Development (DFID) and the Rough Guides travel books company, provides a popular account of the meanings and significance of development without the jargon.

USEFUL WEBSITES

www.un.org/millenniumgoals/ – website of the UN Millennium Development Goals
www.mdgmonitor.org/ – website of the MDG Monitor that shows how countries are progressing in achieving the MDGs
www.eldis.org/ – website of a gateway to development information on policy and research
www.developmentgateway.org/ – website of the Development Gateway Foundation, a portal on development information

2. Changing theoretical perspectives on development and newly emerging issues

INTRODUCTION

This chapter outlines the major development theories originated to explain differential patterns of development throughout the world since the 1950s. It summarises and explains the main approaches beginning with a consideration of modernisation theory, followed by an outline of dependency and world systems theory. These will provide a theoretical basis for the discussion of a more recent approach, notably neoliberalism, as well as its policy equivalent in the form, first, of Structural Adjustment Programmes (SAPs) and then Poverty Reduction Strategy Papers (PRSPs) as part of the Heavily Indebted Poor Countries (HIPC) initiative. The chapter then considers post-development before turning to some pressing issues of the day in relation to development in terms of globalisation, and the importance of war, conflict and everyday violence.

WHAT IS DEVELOPMENT THEORY?

As outlined in Chapter 1, thinking about development is characterised by debate and controversy, especially in relation to development theory. Theory refers to a way of organising a body of information into a coherent form in order to offer an explanation. A good theory should therefore make events more easily understandable as it attempts to explain the relationships between causes and consequences. Development theories, in turn, are sets of propositions which aim to explain how development has taken place in the past and how it might occur in the future. Development theory includes analyses of how development problems have come about and the best ways to deal with them. Yet, just as there is no fixed definition of development, there is no single theory of it. Instead, there are suggestions of what development should imply, or has implied, in different contexts. As discussed in Chapter 1, these are constantly redefined as understanding of the development process deepens and as new problems emerge (see Potter, 2008a).

Development theory is more concerned with change than is typical in conventional social science disciplines, and is highly interdisciplinary in nature, involving examination of transformations in politics, the economy, society and culture. Development theory has always been closely linked with development strategy in terms of the practical applications of theory in trying to solve a problem or bring about change. As well as academic thinking, development theories have also been influenced by the work of planners, administrators, politicians and activists, whether working for the state, international agencies, non-governmental or community-based organisations. In turn, ideologies have played a major role in constructions of development theory since politics, culture, religion and so on shape the nature of thinking about development (Potter et al., 2008).

Development theory was established following recognition that the problems of the South were different from those which Europe and the USA had historically undergone. In order to understand the problems and issues of developing countries, linked with the changing material conditions of the world post-1945, a vast body of theory on development emerged. Although there is no strict chronology in the emergence of development theories post-1945, with a high degree of overlap and contestation, it is still possible to identify several broad and overlapping phases (see also Willis, 2005):

1. *Modernisation theories* particularly influential in the 1940s and 1950s and still relevant until the 1960s.
2. *Dependency theories* important in the 1960s and 1970s.
3. *Neoliberalism and structural adjustment* emerging in the 1980s and continuing into the 1990s and 2000s.
4. *Post-development* in the 1990s and 2000s.

It is important to stress that although the earlier theories were less likely to overlap, today, several theories and approaches coexist and are expounded in different arenas. This effectively followed the so-called 'impasse' in development theory in the 1980s (Schuurman, 2008), reflecting disappointment at the lack of progress in addressing development problems as well as a shift towards accepting that no single theory of development was possible or desirable. Having said this, neoliberalism and the primacy of capitalism combine to represent the dominant perspectives for understanding the contemporary world, both North and South, despite many efforts that continue to challenge this hegemony from a poststructuralist stance among others (Lawson, 2007).

MODERNISATION THEORY

Although modernisation is usually referred to as a single theory, it is more accurately a school of thought or an approach that comprises a range of perspectives that follow the same basic argument, namely, that development is a positive and irreversible process through which all societies eventually pass. Development in the Global South in the second half of the twentieth century was not only anticipated to mirror that of the earlier evolution of Europe and the USA, but actively encouraged to do so. In the belief that 'West is best', and to counter a growing threat of communism, the diffusion of Western capital and technology and the adoption of Western values were widely promoted (Power, 2008).

Origins of Modernisation Theory I: Evolutionary Theory

Modernisation leant heavily on the European experience of development and relied on two main theoretical influences: evolutionary theory and diffusionist theory. In terms of the former, elements of nineteenth-century evolutionary theory formed the basis of early modernisation approaches. Evolutionary theories were characterised by an emphasis on the naturalness and inevitability of social change with 'blockages' in evolution needing to be problematised and explained, rather than the process of evolution itself. The intellectual roots of this theory lay in the work of nineteenth-century sociologists such as Max Weber and Emile Durkheim. Both drew on Darwin's theory of evolution in the natural world in their search for explanations for the shift from 'traditional' to 'modern' economies focusing on a need for change in a range of social and cultural institutions. Durkheim concentrated on new forms of social integration in 'modern societies', whereas Weber focused on the process of 'rationalisation' whereby a goal-orientated hard-working ethos displaced the predominance of leisure, recreation and culture in 'traditional societies'. Drawing on these distinctions, one of the main proponents of modernisation theory in the post-war period was sociologist, Talcott Parsons, who argued that changes in attitudes and values were critical to economic progress and development. Based on what he referred to as 'pattern variables', traditional societies would have to change their orientation away from family, local community, religion and superstition in order to become modern, rational and entrepreneurial. In other words, traditional cultures were regarded as inimical to development.

One of the first scholars to apply Parsons's pattern variables to problems of development was the economist, Bert Hoselitz (1952; 1995). Hoselitz tried to illustrate the ways in which economic, social and cultural factors interrelated and how patterns varied across societies depending on their stages of development. Most importantly, and echoing Parsons, he emphasised that most obstacles to development were internal to societies in the form of traditional attitudes and culture, which needed to be dismantled and reconstituted in order to emulate the European example (ibid.).

Origins of Modernisation II: Diffusionist Theories, Dualism and Unilinear Models

Hoselitz was also associated with another major conceptual influence on modernisation: diffusionist theory. This had earlier roots in classical-traditional approaches which highlighted the overarching role of economic growth and the freedom of the market in development processes, drawing on earlier ideas associated with Adam Smith (1723–90) and David Ricardo (1772–1823) (Potter et al., 2008; Sapsford, 2008; Willis, 2005). In development terms, diffusionist theories described the process of shifting from tradition to modernity through the spread of ideas, values and technology over space (rather than time). A key theme here was that underdeveloped nations were dualistic, comprising the coexistence of an advanced modern urban sector alongside a traditional rural sector. Economic growth and development would occur through the transmission of 'growth impulses' or a 'growth pole' of capital, technology, institutions and value systems from the advanced to the traditional sector. Over time, rural traditional society would be transformed economically, politically and socially in what has been referred to as the 'ink spot notion' denoting the way in which modernisation and growth spreads out from a centre or core. These ideas were incorporated in the notion of 'spread effects' coined by Gunnar Myrdal (1957), where economic growth in one region stimulated development in another neighbouring region. They were also linked with the 'trickle-down' effects identified by Albert Hirschman (1958) where economic inequalities were gradually evened out over time and space as development in the modern core filtered through to the 'backward' regions and generated growth (Binns, 2008). John Friedmann's (1966) 'core–periphery model' also incorporated ideas from both Myrdal and Hirschman. This model viewed cities and urban regions as the main engines for the development of nations. Growth would occur through the spatial diffusion of investment from the largest city (or 'core') through the urban hierarchy 'down' to the rural villages on the periphery (see Potter et al., 2008 for a review).

Some of this thinking was also encompassed within Walt Whitman Rostow's 'unilinear' or 'development stage' model of development which was also influenced by evolutionary theories. Published in 1960 in his book,

---

BOX 2.1   ROSTOW'S UNILINEAR MODEL OF DEVELOPMENT

Stage 1: *Traditional societies*
- Characterised by primitive nature of science or technology, people's values are fatalistic, production and trade based on custom and barter.

Stage 2: *Conditions for take-off*
- Characterised by development of entrepreneurship, capital investment, educational expansion, and centralisation of nation states.

Stage 3: *Take-off*
- Characterised by removal of traditional barriers to economic growth, increased investment, growth of economic elites, rapid economic growth, and commercialisation of agriculture. This is the most important stage when net investment and savings as a ratio to national income grow from 5 to 10 per cent which nominally facilitates industrialisation.

Stage 4: *Drive to maturity*
- Characterised by the economy taking its place in the international order, move away from heavy industry, diversification of industrial and agricultural sectors; investment increases to between 10 and 20 per cent of national income.

Stage 5: *Age of high mass consumption*
- Characterised by increasing importance of consumer goods and services and development of a welfare state.

Sources: Binns (2008); Potter et al. (2008); Willis (2005).

The Stages of Economic Growth: A Non-Communist Manifesto, Rostow likened the process of economic growth (rather than development per se) to an aeroplane on a runway until it reaches take-off and then soars into the sky. This identified not just two stages in economic development, but a number of intervening stages which countries would go through in the course of modernisation. Rostow set out five universal stages of economic development based on analysis of the British/European Industrial Revolution, assuming that all other societies would follow suit (Rist, 1997: 94–9; Willis, 2005: 39–42; see also Box 2.1).

Aside from its obvious Eurocentrism, criticisms of Rostow's model devolved upon the little empirical evidence that Western development had actually occurred through the stages he described, that there was any basis to assume that similar stages would occur in the South, and that emphasis lay on economic growth rather than non-economic gains (Binns, 2008). Moreover, despite some acknowledgement of the heterogeneity of experiences in different countries, all were shoehorned into one of the five stages of his universalising development model (Willis, 2005).

Main Characteristics of Modernisation

Bearing these theoretical foundations in mind, it is possible to outline some key characteristics of the modernisation approach. One was the need for nations to embrace industrialisation and the commercialisation of agriculture (from subsistence to cash-cropping), using the experience of the West as a blueprint for change and progress. Yet while modernisation could be speeded up by external forces in the form of Western ideas, technology and capital, and would thereby benefit from the development of mass media to disseminate information and values, it was also felt that the primary impetus for industrialisation and economic growth had to come from within. A prerequisite for these processes was the existence of middle-class entrepreneurs or 'change agents' who would form a 'modernising elite'. In order to sustain momentum for innovation, rationalisation of economic activity, and the accumulation of capital, social and attitudinal change among the population more generally was deemed vital. Since non-Western traditions and cultures were seen as barriers to development, this implied *inter alia*, the replacement of patterns of authority based on traditional loyalties by formal law and democracy, urbanisation based on the nuclear family unit (parents and children living independently – see Chapter 9, this volume), and educational growth and literacy (based on Western, meritocratic standards) (Potter et al, 2008).

In practical terms, the modernisation approach was extremely popular during the 1950s and early 1960s. At this time, modernisation views became the reference point for the majority of development projects and much aid to the Global South, especially by the US government and UN agencies. The focus here tended to urban-based industrialisation, projects to improve agricultural efficiency through the introduction of technology, and the implementation of large-scale infrastructure projects such as dam construction and road building (Willis, 2005). In addition, training middle-class elites in values and motivations relating to a free enterprise (Western) culture was encouraged and promoted. It is important to stress that there are different variations of modernisation approaches. Although the liberal approach based on the importance of the free market is the most common variant, there were also models that relied more closely on state intervention to bring about modernisation (Potter et al., 2008; see also Thomas, 2000a).

Criticisms of Modernisation

During the late 1960s, modernisation approaches began to be challenged on a number of grounds, mainly because policies formulated under this paradigm were not working as effectively as anticipated. In particular, there had been limited economic growth in developing countries, but instead a persistence of widespread poverty, and in many cases increased polarisation between rich and poor, which at the international scale paralleled a widening of the gap between most and least developed countries. This was further exacerbated by other world events leading to a questioning of free-market, capitalist development such as the Cuban Revolution of 1959 and the Vietnam War (1965–75). Indeed, many of the criticisms of modernisation came from the political Left, and formed the seeds of dependency theory which was to provide a direct challenge to modernisation (see later in this chapter).

Modernisation was criticised for viewing lack of development as the fault of developing countries due to the emphasis on internal factors, value systems and the importance of attitudinal change. As with the critiques of the Rostovian development model, modernisation was also charged with being ethnocentric in that it valued Western culture and denigrated traditional economies. This completely overlooked the diversity and sophistication of many ancient and contemporary non-Western societies. Indeed, in reality many developing nations had modernised while retaining several aspects of 'traditional' culture. Yet one of the most forceful criticisms of modernisation theory was that it neglected to take into account global historical development, and especially the history of colonialism. It failed to recognise that many countries of the South had little freedom to develop their own development goals and strategies beyond the dictates of colonial rule and, subsequently, of multinational companies and international organisations such as the IMF and the World Bank (see below).

Finally, there was little empirical evidence to back up the approach since, by the late 1960s, it was apparent that economic growth and poverty reduction remained limited. Moreover, a new class of Third-World elites had emerged who were reaping most of the benefits of policies informed by a modernisation ethos. It was partly the recognition of these criticisms that led to the formulation of dependency theory.

Activity 2.1
Read Ulrich Menzel's (2006) chapter on Rostow in David Simon's (ed.) *Fifty Key Thinkers on Development*. Consider how the evolution of Rostow's career was linked with the creation of his unilinear model and assess how important this model has been in understanding development processes.

DEPENDENCY THEORY

As with modernisation theory, there was not one dependency model, but rather a range of approaches. In general terms, however, dependency sought to overturn the views of modernisation from a Southern perspective and, more specifically, from a Latin American viewpoint. Indeed, it is often referred to as the '*dependencia* school' because most of the scholars (known as *dependistas*) were Latin American and therefore writing in Spanish.

The principal thrust of dependency theory was that lack of economic development and the persistence of widespread poverty in the Global South was caused by the exploitative influence of the industrialised, advanced nations. The *dependistas* argued that the growth of the advanced countries was only possible because of the active exploitation and underdevelopment of Southern countries (hence the fact that dependency theory is sometimes referred to as 'underdevelopment theory'). Unlike modernisation, dependency took the historical and global context, as well as colonialism into consideration (Conway and Heynen, 2008).

Origins of Dependency Theory I: Marxism and Neo-Marxism

Dependency emerged from a convergence of two major intellectual trends: Marxism/neo-Marxism together with Latin American structuralism. As far as the former is concerned, dependency theory drew on radical nineteenth-century thinkers such as Karl Marx and Freidrich Engels. Dependency theorists took the ideas of Marx and Engels and revised them from an international perspective, thereby creating what is known as 'neo-Marxism'. To put it crudely, they replaced classes by countries in their analyses. In essence, neo-Marxist theorists looked at the ways in which the South had been exploited over time through different stages of capitalist expansion. The most important phase was colonialism which involved political, legal and administrative control as well as economic exploitation by European nations over countries in the South. Neo-Marxists claimed that this laid the foundations for exploitation from which escape by developing countries was extremely difficult. Even when former colonies became independent nations, they were still exploited through a process of neo-colonialism where former colonial or other powers, especially multi-national corporations or international financial institutions (IFIs), continued to shape and/or dominate their development trajectories (Thomas, 2000a).

Origins of Dependency Theory II: Latin American Structuralism

The first major analysis of the situation of developing countries based on neo-Marxist ideas was from the Latin American structuralists. Structuralism refers to a strand of thought which argues that 'development involves changes in underlying social and economic structures' (Thomas, 2000a: 44). In the Latin American context, for example, it relates to phenomena such as the Great Depression of the 1930s when Latin American exporters of raw materials and agricultural products found themselves progressively less able to buy manufactured goods. Among the main reasons were Latin America's structural disadvantage in the world economy, their heavy dependence on European and North American markets, and competition from other primary producing regions – if Latin American countries set their prices for raw materials too high, then the West would go elsewhere for their coffee, bananas and so on.

These basic principles of structuralism were first put forward by a group of Latin American economists from the Economic Commission for Latin America (ECLA) (a UN agency based in Santiago, Chile – known as CEPAL in Spanish) under the direction of Raúl Prebisch, an Argentinian economist. Prebisch's main argument was that the international economic order was divided between an industrial core and an agrarian periphery whereby the colonising core countries dominated world trade and geopolitics, and systematically deprived colonised and/or ex-colonial peripheral nations. Through emphasis on comparative advantage, the global economic system condemned some countries to being exporters of raw materials and importers of manufactured goods in perpetuity. This created a cycle of poverty and disadvantage whereby poor countries always imported high-value goods without ever earning enough to pay for imports. As well as developing theoretical arguments, ECLA also propounded policy prescriptions. They suggested that the state should intervene in the economy through protectionism and Import Substitution Industrialisation (ISI) by which the import of consumption goods from the West could be replaced by domestic production (see Chapter 5, this volume). In this way, Latin American countries could withdraw from the global capitalist system. However, these import substitution policies, implemented during the 1950s, were seen to have failed by the 1960s due to a shortage of investment funds and foreign exchange (Conway and Heynen, 2008).

Main Characteristics of Classical Dependency

Also referred to as the 'American-Marxist tradition' (Vernego, 2006), classical dependency is most closely associated with Paul Baran and André Gunder Frank who brought the approach to North American and European audiences, and who were effectively the first to challenge the expectation that developing countries could, and should, develop along capitalist lines (Rist, 1997). Baran (1957), who has been called the 'father of dependency', argued that capitalist development had been disastrous for the developing world. He suggested that it was in the interests of capitalism to keep what he called the 'backward world' as an 'indispensable hinterland' to provide valuable raw materials and economic opportunities for the First World. The lack of dynamism in underdeveloped nations lay in their unequal insertion into the world economy. On top of this, in order to secure their interests, advanced economies formed special partnerships with the elites of the South, often helping either to create or prop up inequitable land distribution. This allowed small national elites to preside over plantation agriculture, to accumulate capital and to emulate the consumption patterns of developed countries.

Baran's work was further developed by Frank in his well-known critique of modernisation theory. Frank is one of the most frequently cited voices of the dependency school and regarded as one of the most influential figures in respect of converting dependency into a theoretical paradigm. In addition, he exemplified the radical Marxist protests of the time through his suggestion that genuine change for the developing world could only come about through de-linking from the West, and socialist revolution (Conway and Heynen, 2008). More specifically, Frank (1967; 1995) argued that development of the core (the West) depends on the exploitation and active underdevelopment of the periphery (Latin America). This process is perpetuated over time through the 'development of underdevelopment'. Although some countries at first appeared to be independent following decolonisation, Frank maintained that this was a fallacy given an active process of underdevelopment operating at international, national and regional scales. Frank conceptualised this process as one of 'metropolis–satellite' (North–South) relations through three key hypotheses:

1. There is a chain of metropolitan–satellite relations within and between countries, where resources and profits are channelled up to metropolis. As such, although large cities such as Buenos Aires or São Paulo

developed on the basis of the transfer of wealth from rural areas, they were still 'satellites' within the global economy and thereby underdeveloped by the leading world metropoli.

2. Satellites experience their greatest economic development when their ties with the metropolis are cut.

3. Regions which are the most underdeveloped are those which had the historically closest ties to the metropolis.

Criticisms of Classical Dependency

Despite the contributions made by Frank to unseating conventional wisdoms about the benign nature of capitalist economic development in the periphery, one key criticism of his work was that it was overgeneralised and oversimplified. Not only had Frank proposed a global theory on what was effectively the Latin American experience alone (although some attempts were made to examine African and Caribbean examples), but his approach tended to ignore huge differences within Latin America. Linked with this was that Frank's thesis was not always borne out in reality. For instance, it was not necessarily the case that those countries that had most extensive contact and interaction with the West were the most underdeveloped, as Mexico and Brazil testified (Conway and Heynen, 2008). This criticism is even more relevant today in the light of globalisation and increasing interrelations between countries (Potter et al., 2008; see below). Classical dependency approaches also fail to come up with specific causes of underdevelopment beyond the fact that they originate in the West and the functioning of the capitalist system. Furthermore, concepts such as core and periphery are little different from terms like traditional and modern (Rist, 1997: 120–21).

Another criticism is that while dependency theory might have struck some very relevant political chords and helped to bring about a much sharper and more critical awareness of the West's role in keeping the Third World in a subordinate position, workable policy measures were scant. Indeed, the only 'practical' solution put forward by Frank was effectively socialist revolution, which was not only arguably overambitious, but also creates its own dependencies. For example, while Cuba in 1959 was able to liberate itself from years of US domination, dependence on the US dollar was replaced to a very large degree by dependence on the Russian rouble.

Another key criticism was levelled at Frank's insistence that external relations of developing countries with the capitalist core led to poverty on the periphery, when there were also internal forces at stake. Particularly criticised was the failure to take class relations into consideration and instead to focus on market relations. Indeed, Frank was criticised for misinterpreting

Marx's notions of modes of production (Conway and Heynen, 2008). A final major criticism is that dependency is highly economistic, judging everything as the outcome of economic determinism (Potter et al., 2008). The oversimplification of world events in classical dependency accordingly led to variations on its basic principles.

Latin American Structuralist School

Drawing not only on intellectual criticisms of classical dependency but also the failure of ISI in Latin America, Latin American structuralists, spearheaded by Fernando Henrique Cardoso, a sociologist, who was subsequently twice elected President of Brazil (between 1995 and 2003), revised dependency approaches under the guise of 'dependent development' (Cardoso, 1995; Cardoso and Faletto, 1979). Cardoso's argument was that capitalist development on the periphery was possible. Dependency was not a relationship among commodity exporters and industrialised countries but, instead, among countries with varying degrees of industrialisation. Dependent development in association with foreign capital was possible, as indicated by the growing industrial might of Latin American nations such as Brazil, Argentina and Mexico (as well as several in East Asia). Internal political structures were also central to dependency relationships in that in some cases lack of development might be more accurately attributed to an inability on the part of nation states to generate domestic technological progress, to reorient patterns of consumption, and to diversify the capabilities and political will of entrenched domestic elites (Vernego, 2006). In short, Cardoso was a pragmatist who warned that it was incorrect to blame the North for all the problems of underdeveloped countries and that stagnation was not inevitable for Latin America (Velasco, 2002). However, it is also true that Latin American structuralists underestimated financial dependence, as shown in the debt crises of the 1970s and 1980s (see below).

Activity 2.2
Read the chapter by Marshall (2008) in Desai and Potter (eds) on the New World Group of Dependency Scholars. Also consult the website of the Cuba Solidarity Network, UK at www.cuba-solidarity.org/, especially the 'Cuba fact file'. Think about the nature of Fidel Castro's Cuba in the past, and how, in light of his recent relinquishment of the presidency, the future path of Cuba might unfold without him at the helm. Identify also ways in which a dependency perspective influenced not only the revolution in 1959, but also the subsequent development of the country.

BEYOND DEPENDENCY: WORLD SYSTEMS THEORY

World systems theory was developed during the mid-1970s to mid-1980s, at a time when a number of East Asian countries were experiencing rapid economic growth and spearheading an unprecedented departure from the classical dependency vision. The main proponent of world systems was Immanuel Wallerstein who developed the theory within broadly Marxist terms (see Wallerstein, 2004). The main difference between world systems and dependency theory was that underdevelopment was attributed to the global operation of capitalism, rather than the two-way interactions between poor countries and their former colonisers. World systems also incorporated the idea of dynamism: at different times certain regions rise and fall in terms of their development potential according to economic cycles called 'Kondratieff waves' (Klak, 2008). In general terms the world system is viewed as inherently unequal, with variations in the economic potential of countries and regions depending on capital accumulation. For the poorest, least industrialised, parts of the world, such as sub-Saharan Africa, the prospects for advancement looked (and still look) bleak. However, rather than a simple core–periphery divide, world systems proposed an additional category termed the 'semi-periphery', which, during the 1970s, housed the likes of fast-growing NICs in Latin America and Southeast Asia, such as Brazil, Argentina, South Korea, Hong Kong and Singapore. In these there was considerable scope for development, as well as the possibility of joining the core, as evidenced in the recent accession of Mexico and Korea to the OECD.

Yet despite the space opened up for the possibilities of dynamism and change in world systems, the approach has still attracted criticisms of over-generalisation. Many have also challenged the existence of Kondratieff cycles, suggesting instead that capitalism moves through different rather than similar phases. The difficulties in testing world systems theory have also been highlighted, together with its neglect of local conditions within individual countries. In light of these criticisms, Klak (2008) suggests that it is better to conceive of world systems as a 'perspective' rather than a full-blown theory. Nonetheless, debates around this perspective contribute to the view that integration into the world capitalist system is not always negative. Increasingly, there has been evidence that capitalist penetration in the developing world has resulted in economic growth, the most extreme form of which is neoliberalism.

NEOLIBERALISM

Neoliberal approaches began to dominate development theory during the 1980s, and have persisted to the present day. Known as the 'counter-revolution', this movement has had a profound effect on development policy at an international level through the implementation of what are known as Structural Adjustment Programmes. The essence of neoliberalism is that it seeks to deregulate markets as much as possible in order to promote free trade. Growing disillusionment in the North with the potential for the state to effectively manage economic and social life led to the increasing belief in the power of the market as an economic regulator. Minimal state involvement in the economy was thought to provide optimal conditions for economic prosperity and growth. The ideology was rapidly accepted in the Global North, and was then exported to the Global South in the form of aid and measures to address the debt crisis of the early 1980s (Simon, 2008).

Origins of Neoliberalism

Neoliberalism draws on the neoclassical economics of Adam Smith, as well as some elements of modernisation theory of the 1950s. While up to the 1970s development had been guided by Keynesian economics or development economics, which held that the state needed to intervene in the economies of developing countries in order to facilitate growth and development, the 1980s saw a return to the idea of capitalism as beneficial, and increased vilification of the state as it was seen to be failing to improve the position of poor countries. Market forces were deemed to be the primary stimulus for growth, with government interventions frequently acting as a hindrance.

The economists Friedrich Von Hayek (1978) and his student Milton Friedman (1962), known as the 'Chicago Boys', were the principal advocates of the neoliberal ideology of the so-called 'New Right', which gained increasing global influence through Thatcherism and Reaganism in the 1980s. The USA and the UK had controlling votes on the boards of the world's two most powerful financial agencies, the World Bank and the International Monetary Fund. These, in turn, had increasing influence on international development policy relative to other organisations such as the UN (see Chapter 11, this volume). Therefore, it is hardly surprising that free market views gathered momentum and gave rise to the so-called 'Washington Consensus', coined in 1989 by the World Bank's Chief Economist for South Asia, John Williamson. This prescribed heavy doses of neoliberal medicine to improve the economic health of the Global South (Lawson, 2007: 84–5).

Main Characteristics of Neoliberalism

On top of the argument that lack of development in the South is due to misguided policies on the part of governments and an over-concentration on domestic rather than global markets, the counter-revolution claimed that limited development owed to three main causes:

1. An overextended government and public sector apparatus associated with corruption and inefficiency.
2. A proliferation of state-sponsored distorting economic controls which inhibited the market.
3. The existence of 'traditional' non-market social relations which prevented the commodification of production (making a profit out of producing something) (Thomas, 2000a).

Leading on from this, the central proposals of neoliberalism are to permit free markets to flourish, to privatise state-owned enterprises, to promote free trade and expansion, to welcome foreign investors from the North, and to eliminate government regulations and protectionism. The role of the state becomes one of providing only those goods and services which would not otherwise be provided by the private sector. Underlying these proposals is a return to the importance of the individual, as in modernisation theory, whereby capitalist entrepreneurs are seen as the engine of economic growth and dynamism (Thomas, 2000a). Other similarities with modernisation include viewing tradition as an obstacle to development, together with perceived new risks such as monopolies and corruption, problems in the South as internal rather than external, and the equation of economic growth with development in general. While other development economists have tended to view development in the long term, neoliberals focus on the short term, in the belief that long-term prosperity will automatically follow (Hewitt, 2000).

NEOLIBERALISM IN PRACTICE: THE RISE OF STRUCTURAL ADJUSTMENT PROGRAMMES

The Debt Crisis

It was the debt crisis of the late 1970s and early 1980s which sparked the widespread implementation of neoliberal policies promoted by the IMF and the World Bank. The 1973 and 1979 oil crises saw sharp increases in oil prices. Oil-importing countries ran up huge import bills, and in turn, oil-exporting countries had massive build-ups of deposits in the international banking system. Because of the recession, banks could not lend to their previous customers in the industrial countries and so they turned to developing countries, many of which had not previously been creditworthy. Between 1973 and 1979 this process worked well, but the situation changed after 1979 when oil prices began again to escalate. International lending was still available, but Northern countries changed their economic policies in an attempt to reduce domestic inflation. As a result, real interest rates were raised to exceptionally high levels while commodity export prices declined drastically. This effectively spelt disaster for developing nations which had borrowed large amounts of money (Corbridge, 1993).

In August 1982 came the outbreak of the so-called 'debt crisis', when Mexico announced a moratorium on its foreign loan repayments, followed shortly by Brazil and other countries similarly unable to meet servicing deadlines. Defaulting on loan payments was thought to be the fault of the debtor countries, resulting from corrupt and overly bureaucratic governments rather than an uncontrollable economic climate (Corbridge, 1993; 2008). Most countries, however, sought to reschedule their loans in consultation with the World Bank and the IMF. The policy response of these IFIs was in the form of SAPs aimed to maximise the prospects for, and amounts of, repayments by debtor countries. Arguably, at this stage, they reflected little thought for the national repercussions of these repayments for heavily indebted nations (Simon, 2008; also Mohan et al., 2000).

STRUCTURAL ADJUSTMENT PROGRAMMES

The essence of SAPs was to reshape the economies of developing countries in favour of the free market, reducing overall government intervention in the economy. While governments were responsible for initiating adjustment, this was largely pushed by the IMF and the World Bank. Structural adjustment in practice meant that loans were granted, but with conditions of structural economic reforms attached, known as 'conditionalities' (Oxfam, 2006). The overall aim of adjustment programmes was to reduce the balance-of-payments deficit by increasing exports and reducing imports, in conjunction with economic restructuring to allow new growth. Structural adjustment programmes were based firmly on free-market principles, comprising deflation, devaluation, de-control and privatisation. There were two main types of measures, aspects of which remain in some policies today (see below). Initially, short-term stabilisation measures were implemented, usually associated with the IMF. These were intended to stop economic conditions from deteriorating further, such as public sector wage freezes, reduced government subsidies and currency devaluation. Acting as short, sharp shocks to the economy, these often resulted in temporary and sometimes protracted recession. Stabilisation was followed by long-term adjustment measures geared to improving economic efficiency through changing the structures within which transactions took place, and associated mainly with the World Bank. Such measures included export promotion (see Chapter 5, this volume), downsizing the civil service, economic liberalisation, privatisation and tax reductions (Hewitt, 2000; Willis, 2005). As SAPs were refined taking into account social development as well as economic needs, after three to four years they were followed up by Economic Recovery Programmes (ERPs). The main funding mechanism became the Enhanced Structural Adjustment Facility (ESAF) (Simon, 2008). The importance of these policies is reflected in the fact that by 1987, the World Bank had approved 52 structural adjustment loans and 70 sectoral adjustment loans. During 1980–90, 171 SAPs were implemented in sub-Saharan Africa alone (ibid.; also Mohan et al., 2000).

Outcomes and Effects of SAPs

Structural Adjustment Programmes have been the subject of intense controversy. The IMF, World Bank and many governments of developing countries saw adjustment as essential to ensure economic growth and the future welfare of their populations. Without adjustment, it was thought that countries would fall into greater poverty and economic stagnation, and it was claimed, at least initially, that adjustment did bring about economic growth and stabilisation especially in countries such as Ghana, which was one of the first to adjust (see Brydon and Legge, 1996). It has also been argued that SAPs appear to have reduced, if not reversed, urban bias, and that they have been associated with democratisation, especially in Africa where political reform in countries like Zambia, Kenya, Tanzania, Zaire and Malawi have addressed some aspects of state corruption. However, by the late 1990s, even the IMF was acknowledging that economic growth had been limited (Oxfam, 2006; see also SAPRIN, 2004).

Concerns that adjustment was an economic failure and even a cause of the poor economic performance of Southern countries, had already been expressed by a range of non-IFI development organisations and NGOs a decade earlier. Despite protestations on the part of the IFIs that it was impossible to measure the effects because the counterfactual situation could not be determined (that is, what would have happened if SAPs had not been implemented?), SAPs were seen as contributing to widespread dependence on the IFIs, and were criticised for addressing economic problems in only superficial ways. For instance, the instability of international

Table 2.1   The impact on poverty of IMF SAPs in Southern countries

Measure	3 years before	3 years after
GDP per capita (%)	−1.4	−1.4
% of population living on less than $1 a day	51.3	53.3
% of the population living on less than $2 a day	83.1	84.1

Source: Adapted from Oxfam (2006: 10).

financial markets, inequalities of the global trading system, and the weakness of social and economic structures dating back to colonial times were ignored, leading to unjustified blame on Southern countries for the cause of the debt crisis, for not managing their economies effectively, and for failing to implement adjustment programmes correctly (Mohan et al., 2000).

Wrapped-up in notion of the 1980s being the 'lost decade' of development because of the negative effects of SAPs on countries of the South, another major set of concerns related to the social costs of adjustment. Among the most influential criticisms came from a group of scholars linked with UNICEF in a publication entitled *Adjustment with a Human Face* (Cornia et al., 1987). This highlighted the effects of SAPs on health and education, and especially how women and children bore disproportionate burdens of SAPs (see below; also Chapter 6, this volume). The high social costs for the people of the South were related to increased unemployment, declining real wages, reduced public and social spending, and increased prices of basic commodities and foodstuffs (related to the lifting of subsidies). These processes combined to produce widespread increases in poverty. For example, an assessment by the United Nations Conference on Trade and Development (UNCTAD) of IMF and World Bank SAPs showed how poverty increased after the implementation of SAPs by measuring the proportion of the population living below the poverty line three years before SAPs were introduced and comparing this with three years after (see Table 2.1).

In general, it has also been shown that urban areas suffered more than rural areas, especially in the case of the urban poor and civil servants who lost their jobs or had their salaries eroded while having to pay more for goods and services. Yet the agricultural sector was also made vulnerable as a result of export-led reform. Food self-sufficiency was undermined as non-tradable production switched to cash crop (tradable) farming. In some cases this was disastrous, as in Sudan where the shift from the subsistence staple, maize, to cotton for export meant that when a dramatic fall in world cotton prices came about in the mid-1980s, famine was the result (Simon,

2008; see also Oxfam, 2006, on Mali). Those benefiting from SAPs have therefore generally been large traders and import–export merchants in rural areas, and national elites more generally (Simon, 2008).

Cutbacks in public spending associated with neoliberal restructuring have often led to deterioration in general welfare. Services have been cut and so-called user fees have been introduced, whereby people have to pay for health and education. Some of the results have included increased dropout rates from school (especially at secondary level), notable increases in malnutrition and disease, and the arrest of long-term declines in infant mortality. In Jamaica, for example, adjustment in the 1980s provoked a precipitous drop in government social sector expenditure – from 641 million Jamaican dollars in 1979–80 to only 372 by the mid-1980s. As a result, levels of infant malnutrition increased, education levels plummeted and the supply of new housing to the poor came to a standstill (Willis, 2005: 53–4). Women here and elsewhere were very adversely affected (see Baden, 1993; Cornia et al., 1987), as discussed further in Chapter 6.

Another major area of costs relates to the environment. The main problem arises from the creation of incentives to increase the exploitation of the natural environment to generate export revenues. As structural adjustment aims to increase agricultural crops for export, this usually involves increased use and exhaustion of mineral resources and land degradation (Simon, 2008). For example, in the Philippines, it has been noted that prawn farming introduced as part of SAP-induced export-orientated programmes had severe environmental consequences in that mangrove swamps were destroyed, along with the coastal breeding grounds for fish.

Just as women developed complex and innovative mechanisms to cope with the effects and costs of SAPs, they also came to be engaged in resistance to macroeconomic policy among populations in general. From the 1980s onwards, so-called 'austerity' or 'IMF' protests, both of a violent and non-violent nature, developed throughout the South. Examples include protests by teachers in Liberia against salary cuts, and strikes in Nigeria and Sierra Leone against wage freezes and import curbs. Food riots broke out in the Sudan in the early 1980s when the bread subsidy was revoked, and the removal of subsidies on rice in Madagascar in 1985 resulted in protests motivated by the inability of poor families to feed their children and, as a consequence, sometimes giving them up as bonded labour (Figure 2.1).

Activity 2.3
Consult the website of the campaign group 50 Years Is Enough: US Network for Global Economic Justice (a coalition of US grassroots, solidarity, faith-based, policy, social- and economic-justice and development organisations dedicated to transforming the World Bank and the IMF).

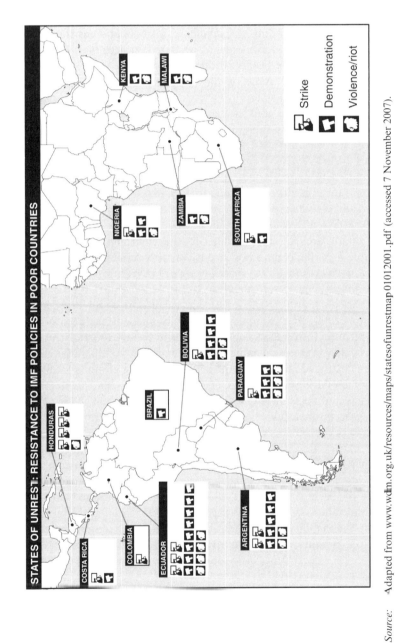

Source: Adapted from www.wdm.org.uk/resources/maps/statesofunrestmap01012001.pdf (accessed 7 November 2007).

Figure 2.1   Map of resistance to IMF policies in countries of the Global South

Read their fact sheet on SAPs (2004) available to download from www.50years.org/factsheets/SAPs-FactSheet_3.9.04.pdf. Think about their views on SAPs and then consider those of the IMF and the World Bank. Are the views of the 50 Years Is Enough campaign valid? Are they over-stated?

ALTERNATIVES TO SAPS: HIPC AND THE EMERGENCE OF PRSPS

In light of widespread criticisms of the impacts of SAPs and subsequent protests, the World Bank, the IMF and other development agencies have since changed their policies to make them more socially aware and orientated towards poverty reduction (see also Chapters 7 and 11, this volume). Initially, palliative measures in the form of social investment funds (also called emergency social funds (ESFs) or social dimensions of adjustment programmes), were created to ameliorate the worst effects of SAPS, such as the Ghanaian Programme of Actions to Mitigate the Social Costs of Adjustment (PAMSCAD) which included 23 anti-poverty interventions, including credit, access to water, health, drugs and nutrition (Brydon and Legge, 1996; Simon, 2008). However, these were often short-term programmes that rarely reached the very poorest, concentrated solely or mainly on infrastructure and did not address the root causes of poverty.

As the 1990s progressed there was recognition among the IFIs that SAPs needed to be rethought and that social investment funds were not necessarily the answer. This gave rise to the replacement of SAPs by Poverty Reduction Strategies (PRSs) as part of the HIPC initiative, first developed in 1996 and then revised in 1999 to form HIPC II. This reflected a wider move to reduce poverty and to address debt in the Global South, as well to include Southern countries in decision-making (Simon, 2008). The HIPC II involved the IMF and the World Bank linking lending policies with concrete poverty reduction plans. In an effort to move away from imposing conditionalities on developing countries (see Chapter 11, this volume), the IFIs instituted a series of procedures to encourage individual countries to come up with their own designs for poverty reduction in return for debt relief. For instance, if a government wants debt relief (linked with previous adjustment loans that they have problems repaying), and their debt is worth more than 150 per cent of its exports, it can apply for HIPC status. In order to secure debt relief, a country must put in place a PRS in the form, first of an interim PRSP, and subsequently a full PRSP. By March 2008, 33 countries had succeeded in gaining HIPC debt relief, with 23 having reached the completion point (Benin, Bolivia, Burkina

---

BOX 2.2   MAIN TYPES OF LENDING ASSOCIATED WITH THE HIPC

World Bank:
i)   *Poverty Reduction Strategy* (based on Poverty Reduction Strategy Papers).

IMF:
i)   *Poverty Reduction and Growth Facility* (PRGF). This was formerly called the Enhanced Structural Adjustment Facility (ESAF) until 1999 (for very poor countries). A PRGF loan requires a PRSP. Once a PRSP is approved a country is eligible for a PRGF and debt relief under HIPC.
ii) *Stand-By Arrangements* (SBA). These are the most common loans granted by the IMF. They are short term to provide support to countries facing short-term balance of payments problems.
iii) *Extended Fund Facility* (EFF): EFFs are longer-term loans than SBA loans, but shorter term than PRGF loans.

SBAs tend to be concentrated in Latin American countries while PRGFs are lent mainly to African countries.

Source: www.imf.org/external/np/exr/facts/howlend.htm (accessed 17 April 2008).

Faso, Cameroon, Ethiopia, The Gambia, Ghana, Guyana, Honduras, Madagascar, Malawi, Mali, Mauritania, Mozambique, Nicaragua, Niger, Rwanda, São Tomé and Príncipe, Senegal, Sierra Leone, Tanzania, Uganda, and Zambia), at which debt relief becomes irrevocable,[1] and 10 more receiving interim assistance (Afghanistan, Burundi, Central African Republic, Chad, the Democratic Republic of the Congo, the Republic of Congo, Guinea, Guinea-Bissau, Haiti and Liberia).[2] The HIPC is linked with various new types of loans from the IMF and the World Bank as detailed in Box 2.2.

Poverty Reduction Strategy Papers are at the core of these current lending initiatives. According to the World Bank, PRSPs are a requirement for countries in order to receive its concessional assistance through the International Development Association (IDA), and from the IMF (through the Poverty Reduction and Growth Facility [PRGF]). In addition, they are the basis for the provision of debt relief under the enhanced HIPC

Initiative.[3] In their attempt to promote pro-poor growth, facilitate empowerment through good governance, enhance security through investing in human capital, as well as providing social safety nets/social protection measures (Craig and Porter, 2003), PRSPs are based on a series of core principles comprising the following criteria: country driven, cognisant of the multidimensional nature of poverty, adopting a long-term perspective for poverty reduction, and being results and partnership orientated. They are expected to be based on participation beyond the governments of given countries, especially involving consultation with NGOs and other members of civil society (known as stakeholders). While claiming not to be prescriptive, the World Bank also stipulates that a PRSP needs to include: 'A description of the participatory process that was used, comprehensive poverty diagnostics, clearly presented and costed priorities for macroeconomic, structural, and social policies, appropriate targets, indicators, and systems for monitoring and evaluating progress.'[4] At April 2008, 58 countries had completed PRSs, with a further eight in negotiation.[5]

Although it is still early days, these new lending arrangements have been the subject of divergent opinion. On the one hand, identified positive aspects of PRSs are that they move away from concentrating only on economic growth and focusing on a broad-based approach to poverty reduction. Consideration has also been given to those most disadvantaged in society arguably through a participatory approach that aims to be open and consultative. Poverty Reduction Strategy Papers have also emphasised the need for good governance (accountability and transparency), as well as a focus on health and education, and encouragement of greater collaboration between governments and civil society (Craig and Porter, 2003). By the same token, several commentators have argued that the shift from SAPs to PRSs has amounted to cosmetic changes only. The fundamental principles of neoliberal lending have not really altered, only a shift in the emphasis of conditionality away from preconditions (Bradshaw and Linneker, 2003). Furthermore, despite a focus on flexibility and the claim that PRSPs have no blueprint, broad neoliberal principles – including privatisation and trade liberalisation – must be followed under the assumption (if not the evidence) that neoliberal macroeconomic reform and faster growth with low inflation are conducive to poverty reduction (Oxfam, 2006; Panos, 2005). The extent to which PRSPs are really country owned is also debatable given that they still require World Bank and IMF approval for the disbursement of funds. Moreover, ultimately, PRSPs do not address the causes of poverty but, rather, the symptoms.

Another very common criticism relates to 'participation' which is often nominal, and a far cry from full, open and transparent consultation. In an example from Nicaragua, Bradshaw and Linneker (2003) show how the interim PRSP was presented to the IMF and the World Bank without consultation with civil society or, indeed, their knowledge. Following pressure, the full PRSP involved some limited discussions with invited people only (those sympathetic to, rather than critical of, the government). As a result, civil society developed a parallel PRSP process entailing widespread consultation throughout the country, even if the government did not use the findings from this exercise. Gender issues have also largely been neglected in PRSPs, or, when they have been included, these have been at early stages in the consultation process (ibid.). Zuckerman (2002) also discusses this with reference to the Ugandan PRSP where gender issues were very strong in the early stages, reflecting a vibrant women's movement in the country, but when these were scaled up nationally to influence the actual report, gender differences and inequalities were obscured or had been deleted. More generally, most PRSPs have been found to make stereotyped references to women, and to neglect children's issues (see Chant, 2007a: 6ff).

Notwithstanding that the effects of PRSPs are dependent on country and context, and despite some improvement in the lending structures of the IFIs and a greater commitment to reducing poverty in line with the MDGs, most people on the ground in the Global South and beyond continue to feel the adverse effects of the imposition of neoliberal strategies. This is a major reason why protest against IMF and World Bank imposed policies continues throughout the world today.

Activity 2.4
Consult the two documents available on the website of the World Development Movement (WDM):

1. *One Size for All*, downloadable from: www.wdm.org.uk/resources/reports/debt/onesizeforall01092005.pdf.
2. *Popular Protest*, downloadable from: www.wdm.org.uk/resources/reports/debt/popularprotest01052005.pdf.

To what extent do you think that these represent an exaggerated view of the negative dimensions of the PRSP process and the current policy prescriptions of the IMF and World Bank? To what extent to do you think that the HIPC initiative can really address debt in the Global South?

POST-DEVELOPMENT

Although the latter half of the twentieth century is widely recognised as the 'era of development', it is important to note that by the 1990s the concept of development had been declared dead in some circles, and given way to a rival movement called 'post-development'. Post-development refers to 'a critique of the standard assumptions about progress, who possesses the keys to it, and how it may be implemented' (Sidaway, 2008: 16–17). Thus, it is linked with an increasing body of work with some roots in the dependency school, which considers development from the perspective of the South itself, and argues against the idea of modernisation as development. Associated with such commentators as the Colombian anthropologist, Arturo Escobar, post-development is highly critical of how standard views of development categorise populations and countries in the South in over-generalised and deprecating ways. In Escobar's own words, a process of 'discursive homogenisation' constructs the 'Third World' as a uniform, oppositional entity to the developed world, whereby: 'a squatter in Mexico City, a Nepalese peasant, and a Tuareg nomad become equivalent to each other as poor and underdeveloped' (Escobar, 1995: 53; see also Esteva, 1992; Illich, 1997). Feminists from the South, such as Gayatri Spivak (1988) and Chandra Mohanty (1991) have also contributed to these debates in their critiques of the so-called 'Third World woman' who is uniformly victimised and lacking agency (see McEwan, 2001; also Chapter 8, this volume).

Post-development is rooted in postmodern theory which involves a rejection of notions of modernisation and modernity in favour of highlighting diversity, context and alternative voices. There is a strong emphasis on bottom-up, non-hierarchical growth strategies which consider each situation on its own context-specific merits (Potter et al., 2008). Post-development also intersects with post-colonial interpretations, especially in their emphasis on the need to highlight alternative, local and excluded perspectives on development (see Simon, 2006, for a discussion). In an attempt to move away from the 'grand narratives' or 'meta theories' (overarching theories characterised by high levels of generalisation and abstraction) integral to modernisation or dependency, some advocates of post-development argue for abandoning the term 'development' altogether.

However, this is not generally thought to be productive in that many similar 'development issues' such as poverty, powerlessness, social disorder, environmental degradation and so on, continue to affect the vast majority of the countries of the South. As such, some argue that we do not have the luxury of talking about diversity and identities, except perhaps in terms of diversity in forms, experiences and strategies for coping with inequality (Schuurman, 2008).

Critics of post-developmentists argue that their views are not really beyond, outside or subsequent to development discourse, but rather represent the repackaging of a set of criticisms and contradictions long evident within development thought (Lehmann, 1997; Sidaway, 2008). A more fundamental criticism of this approach is that it overstates the case for the

BOX 2.3   SUMMARY OF DEVELOPMENT THEORIES

Modernisation
- Evolutionary theoretical origins (Durkheim, Weber, Parsons)
- Diffusionist theoretical origins (Myrdal, Hirschman, Friedmann)
- Linear
- Pits 'traditional' societies against 'modern' societies
- Obstacles to development (especially traditional culture)
- Value systems and attitudes important (need to be changed to modernise)
- Pro-capitalist but allows for state intervention
- 'West is Best'
- Rostow; Hoselitz
- 1940s to 1960s

Dependency
- Marxism/neo-Marxism/imperialism
- Latin American Structuralism/ECLA
- Core–periphery model/satellite–metropolis
- External obstacles to development
- Capitalism as cause of underdevelopment
- Historical context important, especially colonialism
- Anti-capitalist/pro-radical change (revolution or national de-linkage from [ex-]colonial powers)
- Frank; Baran
- 1960s to mid-1970s

World systems
- Core/semi-periphery/periphery model
- External obstacles but room for change
- Anti-capitalist (system will collapse of own accord)
- Wallerstein
- Mid-1970s to mid-1980s

Neoliberalism
- Neoclassical economics (Adam Smith)
- Anti-Keynes and 'Development Economics'
- Overriding importance of free market and free trade
- Failure of development due to state intervention
- Strongly pro-capitalist (foreign investment encouraged)

- Encompassed in structural adjustment programmes and PRSPs 1980s to present
- Von Hayek; Friedman (Milton), IMF and World Bank

Post-development
- Postmodernism
- Rejection of meta-theories and grand narratives such as modernisation and dependency
- Emphasises perspectives from the South rather than the North
- Diversity and difference
- Context-specific
- 1990s to present
- Escobar; Sidaway; Esteva; Illich

pitfalls of development. While it is generally recognised that there are always winners and losers in development, to reject the concept itself is to deny any possibility of progress, or to ignore tangible improvements in life chances, health and material well-being that have been evident in parts of the South, notably East Asia (Sidaway, 2008; see also Gardner and Lewis, 1996, and McEwan, 2003, on the need for a materialist post-colonial perspective on development). Most importantly, therefore, any calls to reject 'development' need to be very clear about what exactly is being rejected. Without such clarity, there is the risk that all cases of development 'failure' will be taken as a failure of the concept itself, rather than the particular context- and policy-specific outcome.

Post-development may, therefore, be a useful theoretical development if it is constructed not as a rejection of the possibility of change, but as a criticism of all change as 'development' and of particular forms of interventionist or intentional 'Development' (Box 2.3; see also Chapter 1). Thus framed, it lends itself to alternative visions of improvement through considering, for example, democracy, popular culture, resourcefulness and environmental impact. While there is no question that there is a need for development in the sense of change for the better, the theoretical question remains as to how this may be best achieved (see also Easterly, 2006).

NEW THINKING ON DEVELOPMENT: GLOBALISATION

Current exploration of both the theory and practice of development can no longer be undertaken without some consideration of the concept and processes of globalisation. Indeed, some feel that 'globalisation studies' may, or should, come to eclipse 'development studies' in the twenty-first century (see Schuurman, 2001). However, while globalisation might be one of the most ubiquitous terms used in the world today or what Rigg (2007: 10) calls 'the defining process of the age', it is also highly contested. Perrons (2004: 3), for example, states that: 'Globalisation is sometimes used to explain contemporary events but it is a summary term for processes that require explanation not an analytical concept.' Perrons goes on to note that most definitions share a focus on globalisation as encompassing the inter-connectedness of the world both in terms of physical distance as well as the flows of goods, people, money, information and ideas. These interconnections have been brought about by technological developments such as the internet, as well as improved communications more broadly and greater ease of transport. This has arguably led to a 'shrinking world', albeit one which remains divided (ibid.; see also Sassen, 2006; Willis, 2005: 173).

In more specific terms, globalisation is usually thought to comprise three main strands. First is economic globalisation, which stresses the increasing integration of economic activities where distance is much less important and where transnational corporations, for example, now subcontract production processes to different places throughout the world (see Chapter 5, this volume). The second is cultural globalisation, associated with the growing convergence of consumption patterns and lifestyles across the world rooted in the dominance of the West and especially North America in such 'global culture', referred to sometimes as 'McDonaldisation' or 'Coca Cola-isation' (see Sklair, 2002). Finally, political globalisation refers to the erosion of rights, functions and activities of nation states as other bodies such as the IFIs take on a more important role (Potter, 2008b).

In relation to development processes, especially from the disciplinary perspective of Geography, there have been suggestions that both a focus on places and place specificity will decrease and that certain types of divisions across the world could potentially diminish. In response to such claims, Rigg (2007) notes that globalisation operates at a range of scales and that the global is not eroding or erasing the local. Instead, globalisation processes can be identified at the local level (see also Perrons, 2004; Sassen, 2006). In addition, globalisation is very uneven in its effects across the world, with some places more open to globalisation processes than others. For example, rural dwellers in Mali are likely to have very different exposure to, and experiences of, globalisation compared with the inhabitants of middle- or upper-income neighbourhoods in a metropolis such as Buenos Aires, Argentina. Thus globalisation is not a singular or undifferentiated process but, rather, intersects with the specific historical, social, cultural and economic contexts and circumstances of different places, sometimes referred to as 'glocalisation'. The upshot of these observations is to emphasise that globalisation is a complex, contradictory and uneven process. Indeed, some sceptics would argue that the process itself is not new, but is a continuation of trading patterns and interchanges which have been occurring for centuries (Gilbert, 2008a; Willis, 2005). Nonetheless, most agree that the scale of contemporary interconnectedness is unprecedented.

In terms of the role of globalisation in development the main debates revolve around whether this will bring greater equality as benefits 'trickle down' to the poorer countries and the poor within them, or whether it will intensify divisions and inequalities throughout the world and within countries. The former, more positive, interpretation reflects some early modernisation theory rooted in the notion that the spread of Western capital, culture, technology and information are inherently benign. This viewpoint is one propagated by the IFIs together with many other development institutions. The UK's Department for International Development, for instance, published a White Paper in 2000, *Eliminating World Poverty: Making Globalisation Work for the Poor* (DFID 2000a), which makes clear that globalisation can bring many benefits to poor nations if 'managed properly' (see Potter et al., 2008; Willis, 2005).[6]

A more negative viewpoint links globalisation with the inexorable and exploitative spread of capitalism around the world. With the critiques rooted in many of the challenges to the neoliberal policies of the IFIs, globalisation is assumed to be a destructive force only interested in spreading the 'wisdom' of the market across the globe with little consideration for the disadvantaged and poor. Just as SAPs and PRSPs are often claimed to benefit the elites of impoverished countries (see above), so broader globalisation processes are claimed to do the same, thereby exacerbating inequality. As Joseph Stiglitz, a former Chief Economist of the World Bank notes (cited in Gilbert, 2008a: 191): 'Globalisation has been hijacked by the special interests in the North, often at the expense of the poor in developing countries.' This has led to a growing divide between 'the haves and have nots' with the latter continuing to live in dire poverty (Stiglitz, 2002: 5). Aspects of these views are encompassed in the various dimensions of the 'anti-globalisation movement' or what is more accurately called the 'counter-globalisation' or 'global justice movement'.[7] While much of the focus of this negative perspective is on economic aspects of globalisation, and on the IFIs and countries of the G8 in particular, the culturally homogenising forces of global (US) retail chains such as McDonald's, Walmart and Starbucks have been deemed detrimental to countries of the Global South. Interestingly, and perhaps not surprisingly, a common pattern for corporate entities such as these has been to ally themselves with 'good causes' in the development arena. For example, despite arguably playing a major role in adding to problems of childhood obesity and Attention-Deficit Hyperactivity Disorder (ADHD) worldwide, McDonalds teams up with UNICEF to support International Children's Day, and supports a variety of other UNICEF causes. Without a hint of irony, some initiatives such as accessing McDonald-sponsored internet concerts or free postcards geared to increasing awareness of children's issues which they themselves can personalise with their own message, entail a trip to a local McDonalds to buy a 'Big Mac' (see Richey and Ponte, 2006).

Other initiatives in this vein have been those aligned with the musician Bono's launch in 2006 of 'Product Red^{TM}'. Marking a discernible encroachment of 'celebrity culture' into the world of development assistance, and a transition eloquently summed up by Richey and Ponte (2006) as 'from "Band Aid" to "Brand Aid"', firms such as American Express, Gap, Converse and Armani pledge a percentage of profits from their red-branded products (sunglasses, T-shirts, credit cards and so on) to the Global Fund to Fight AIDS, Tuberculosis and Malaria, headed by Jeffrey Sachs, a (reformed) economist, and director of the UN Millennium Project (see Sachs, 2005). As summed up by Richey and Ponte (2006: 2): 'Brand Aid brings modernisation theory into postmodern times: consumption becomes the mechanism for compassion.' They further note that sometimes the workers in developing countries who manufacture these goods are employed in less than decent conditions: 'Product RED, in its positive spin, masks the social and environmental relations of trade and production that underpin poverty, inequality and disease', a process also known by the Marxist term 'commodity fetishism', whereby in order to gain legitimacy, capitalism attempts to conceal the exploitative conditions under which commodities are produced (ibid.: 24).

Another critically important dimension of an increasingly globalised world is the extent to which it has become 'borderless'. This can partly be seen through the emergence of a range of different trading blocs around the world where trade tariffs within the designated nations are abolished. This can facilitate greater freedom of trade, information, products and ideas, but it is invariably the most powerful 'partner' in a given bloc who stands to make most gains. For instance, the USA is without doubt the dominant partner in the NAFTA free-trade zone, with Canada and especially Mexico in more junior roles (see Willis, 2005). Another indisputable dimension of globalisation is the increasing movement of people through international migration. Indeed, between the 1970s and 2005, the proportion of international migrants doubled to 190.6 million (Willis, 2008). This has also been partly responsible for increasing levels of transnationalism (where a range of economic, political, social and cultural ties are maintained between source and destination countries). However, these flows are uneven and reflect important dimensions of global inequality. Much movement reflects the desperation of people either fleeing conflict or economic insecurity. While most flows remain within the Global South itself, there is an increasing movement of people from poor countries in the Global South to serve the economic and social needs of the well-off in the Global North, especially in the low-paid service economies of the cities of the North such as London (see May et al., 2007).[8] Furthermore, for poor people from the South, freedom of movement around the world is a myth; unless they are drawn from the national middle classes or elites, many would-be migrants from the South are obstructed by immigration legislation. Many too, who are forced into making illegal and often highly dangerous passages, across land or water, lose their lives along the way, by drowning at sea when their precarious boats capsize or suffocating to death in sealed containers and lorries (see also Chapter 3).

Not only is globalisation inherently diverse as a concept and a process, but it invariably cross-cuts most development issues in some form or another. Given this wide scope and multidimensionality, many aspects of globalisation will be touched upon in other chapters in this volume.

Activity 2.5
Read Ben Fine's chapter on Joseph Stiglitz in David Simon's (ed.) (2006) *Fifty Key Thinkers on Development*. Consider the role played by Stiglitz in challenging the 'Washington Consensus' and in highlighting the idea that neoliberal globalisation is just as likely to bring about negative outcomes for countries and individuals as it is to bring benefits.

NEW THINKING ON DEVELOPMENT: WAR, CONFLICT AND EVERYDAY VIOLENCE

Another area which has received increasing attention in recent years from a development perspective is that of violence and conflict. This has been precipitated by several events and processes. Critically important have been the attacks of '9/11' and '7/7' in 2001 and 2005 respectively, the 'War on Terror' and the recent invasions of Afghanistan and Iraq. Linked with these, as well as other conflicts around the world, it is now acknowledged that war, conflict and violence are important development issues. Indeed, violence interrelates with development processes causally, in terms of outcomes and in relation to finding solutions to reducing violence. This applies to violence occurring at all levels, including so-called 'everyday violence' referring to the crime, delinquency and routine acts of violence that are now commonplace throughout the Global South, especially in cities. Violence in all forms undermines sustainable development (McIlwaine, 2008), recognising that lack of development can also precipitate violence in the first place.

War is extremely difficult to define (Unwin, 2008). One of the most commonly used definitions of armed conflict is that of the Stockholm International Peace Research Institute (SIPRI) which identifies wars as prolonged combat between state armies and/or organised armed groups, involving weapons and battle-related deaths of at least 1000 people. However, many of these definitions are now inadequate because much fighting across the world is among non-state actors, with the objectives of combat as likely to be economic as political, or over sovereignty. Also, rather than fighting battles, unarmed civilians are often targeted (SIPRI, 2007). Categorisations are also difficult, although these are now usually accepted as interstate conflict, internal conflict and state formation conflicts (Unwin, 2008).

In terms of how wars have changed over time, there has been an overall increase since the 1950s globally, with a total of 17 major armed conflicts in 16 locations in 2006 alone, although between 1997 and 2006, there were 34 different conflicts, only three of which were interstate (Ethiopia and Eritrea, India Pakistan, Iraq and USA). Most conflicts during the last decade have occurred in Africa and Asia, mirroring the situation post-1945 in which 93 per cent of all wars have been in the Global South (SIPRI, 2007) (see Figure 2.2). Indeed, the intermeshing of poverty and violence in countries with weak governance and institutional capacity was one reason why in its 2007 stock-taking of progress towards the MDGs, the World Bank chose to focus a substantial part of its *Global Monitoring Report* on 'fragile states' (see World Bank, 2007a).

Partly reflecting the increasing complexity of armed conflicts, civil wars can also be conceptualised as 'Complex Political Emergencies' (CPEs) (Unwin, 2008). Complex Political Emergencies refer to various forms of economic, political and social destabilisation often linked with natural disasters and have occurred, *inter alia*, in Kosovo, the Democratic Republic of the Congo, Afghanistan and Haiti. These conflicts are often prolonged, especially in relation to international wars, with most casualties being civilians. Civil wars or CPEs are also more likely to be ethno-nationalist and fought by different militias, rebel armies or other private military organisations. They also create predatory social forms whereby certain elements of society benefit from war. In Afghanistan, a war economy emerged based on the opium trade, with warlords competing for drug production and markets. These are sometimes called 'conflict entrepreneurs'.

In thinking about why wars occur, the causes and consequences are interrelated, multiple and closely bound with development processes. Focusing

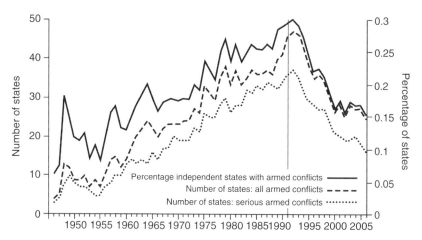

Source: Adapted from http://members.aol.com/CSPmgm/conflict.htm (accessed 10 November 2007).

Figure 2.2   States experiencing warfare, 1946–2006

on civil wars, one study found that between 1960 and 1999, war was most likely to be experienced in poorer countries with low growth rates and a high proportion of primary commodity exports (Collier and Hoeffler, 2000). Although economic deprivation is usually a major element in wars, it is rarely the only catalyst. Furthermore, the very poor are unlikely to agitate for war (as they lack the time and resources to do so), compared with wealthier groups who may feel they have more at stake. While ethnicity may combine with poverty and income inequality to spark war, this is only likely to occur where dominance over power and resources lies with one ethnic group over another (such as in the case of the majority Sinhalese over the minority Tamils in Sri Lanka). Moreover, ethnicity (and religion) are often used to justify war even when it is not the main reason.

One of the undoubted biggest causes of war is unequal access to income, property and natural resources such as land, oil and diamonds, sometimes called 'resource wars' (Le Billon, 2007). When one ethnic or class group has greater access to resources then war is also more likely, such as the case of the Biafran war in Nigeria in the late 1960s. Again, however, these conflicts are usually more complicated than just access to resources. The classic case here is the US war in Iraq which was motivated partly by the concern to control oil supplies, but also by the desire for continued dominance over the global political economy, and to resist Islamisation, particularly of an extremist nature (ibid.). Wars also proliferate in countries where the state is weak and finds it difficult to ensure public security. This is especially important in African states where independence has been relatively recent and the rule of formal law has taken some time to take hold. Geography and terrain are also critical in that the more mountainous or inhospitable the terrain, the more likely conflicts are to emerge.

There are also factors that allow wars to flourish. For instance, rebel groups are business organisations and need financing. This may come from diaspora funding (from migrants), from the drug economy and from extortion. In Colombia, the FARC (Revolutionary Armed Forces of Colombia) – the largest guerrilla group – depends on drugs, illegal taxation and kidnapping to fund itself. Also, rebel armies need young men to fight for them and, so, in countries with high levels of unemployment and low levels of education for male youth in particular, there is greater scope to recruit them. Access to arms is also critical, especially small arms whose availability has increased substantially in the past few decades. This is further facilitated by globalisation processes; global criminal networks provide arms to rebel armies, while neoliberal policies imposed by the IFIs generate unrest (see above).

Economists often link wars and conflicts to greed and/or grievance, some of which is engendered by development processes themselves, and which, in turn, can have major effects on development outcomes (Collier and Hoeffler, 2000). Not only do the human costs of war involve the death of combatants, but also civilians either directly or by starvation and disease. Often referred to collectively as 'war deaths', only 6 per cent of these in the Democratic Republic of Congo resulted from direct military action (ibid.; see also World Bank, 2007a).

Poverty is likely to increase after war due to the loss of life together with the collapse of economies. This is linked with the destruction of infrastructure, crops, the channelling of scarce state resources into military rather than social welfare expenditures, as well as capital flight, with Collier and Hoeffler (2000) estimating that one year of conflict reduces a country's growth rates by 2.2 per cent. Often the social dimensions are even more important. Besides death and injury among male combatants as well as women and children, many also suffer from increased vulnerability to diseases such as HIV/AIDS, malaria and tuberculosis. In some cases, such as Rwanda, rape was used as a tool of war and it has been alleged that some HIV-infected soldiers deliberately infected women civilians (McIlwaine, 2008).

War has also created widespread population displacement and refugees who move across border (refugees) or within countries (Internally Displaced Persons [IDPs]). Countries with large numbers of displaced people include Sudan, Afghanistan, Liberia, Angola and Colombia. Partly linked with this is that war undermines the social fabric of societies (or its 'social capital' – networks of organisation and trust). Psychological distress and trauma are also major effects, ranging from depression to post-traumatic stress disorder. Gender roles and relations can also change. Women may have greater power and control in society during wars than during peacetime because men are more likely to be combatants. In some cases this can lead to lasting changes in gender relations, although this is not always evident.

In short, war, conflict and development are intimately interlinked. Yet it is also sobering that more funding goes into fighting wars than to addressing development concerns. For instance, the cost of reaching the MDGs in 2006 was estimated at approximately US$135 billion, while world military expenditure was a staggering US$1204 billion (SIPRI, 2007).

Everyday Violence, Crime and Conflict

Another crucial element of war and conflict are the relationships with everyday violence at the local level. It has been shown that even when a war or armed conflict ends, other types of violence and crime persist and/or increase.

Violence is defined by the World Health Organisation (WHO, Krug et al., 2002: 5) as, 'The intentional use of physical force or power, threatened or actual, against oneself, another person, or against a group or community, that either results in or has a high likelihood of resulting in injury, death, psychological harm, maldevelopment or deprivation'. Amid a huge range of different and contested categorisations, Moser and McIlwaine (2006) have classified violence as political, social or economic in nature where the primary motive is to exert power. These different classifications are not mutually exclusive however. Although political violence tends to be linked with war, it can also interrelate with social and economic violence on the ground. Everyday violence can also be called 'endemic violence', 'peacetime crime' or 'ubiquitous violence'. As noted above, violence as an umbrella term covers a huge range of different of acts of delinquency, robbery, mugging, attacks, intra-family violence, gang violence, drug- and alcohol-related violence and gender- and age-based violence. Indeed, a core characteristic of everyday violence is its diversity. For example, in Colombia, a recent study found that residents across nine low-income neighbourhoods identified an average of 25 different types, with one community distinguishing as many as 60. In Guatemala, there was a total average of 41 types of violence, with one community identifying as many as 70 (ibid.).

Everyday violence is incredibly hard to measure due to lack of data, partly on account of non- or under-collection and reporting. Yet using homicide rates as a proxy measure, it appears that the scale of everyday violence is high; in 2000, global deaths due to homicide were almost twice as much as those related with war (Krug et al., 2002). Everyday violence has also been increasing in the Global South, especially in the past two to three decades. This is particularly marked in Africa and Latin America, with Africa currently viewed as the most violent continent on the basis of crime victimisation rates. In 2000, the WHO (Krug et al., 2002: 11) estimated homicides in sub-Saharan Africa at 22 per 100 000 and in Latin America at 19 per 100 000. Everyday violence is most common in urban areas, with cities such as Johannesburg in South Africa, Medellín in Colombia and Rio de Janeiro in Brazil, standing out among the most notorious. Violence is also concentrated in particular areas of cities, usually in the poorest sectors where law-enforcement agencies rarely venture. This creates other problems such as 'area stigma' (Moser and McIlwaine, 2006) whereby people from violence-prone neighbourhoods experience widespread discrimination (Rodgers, 2004). Everyday crime and violence is often greater in post-conflict countries, such as South Africa, Guatemala and, currently, Iraq. This often manifests itself in a proliferation of street gangs made up of former guerrilla or military members, a growing drugs industry with networks established during conflict, and an increase in domestic and gender-based violence (McIlwaine, 2008; McIlwaine and Moser, 2001; 2007; Moser and McIlwaine, 2004; 2006).

Just as the causes of war and armed conflict are interrelated, so too are the causes of everyday violence. Moreover, some of the factors that have caused war also generate everyday violence. Again, poverty is critical in that the daily living conditions of the urban poor heighten the potential for the emergence of conflict or crime, especially in situations where inequality is rife. In extreme cases, people may resort to robbery in order to feed themselves. Although it is important to note that criminality and violence extend across the social spectrum (Moser, 2004), low-income male youth seem especially prone to resort to crime in order to vent their feelings of anger and disaffection, especially in areas afflicted by unemployment. Criminal networks and gangs often provide young men with a livelihood as well as respect and status in their lives (Moser and McIlwaine, 2006; Rodgers, 2004). Impunity linked with fragile state law enforcement means that it is easy to commit crime and violence without being caught.

The effects of everyday violence can be direct and indirect. There are direct costs to the health service, police, judicial system, housing and social welfare, and indirect costs, such as higher morbidity and mortality due to homicides and suicides, abuse of alcohol and drugs, and depressive disorders. In addition, 'economic multiplier effects' influence the labour market and inter-generational productivity, and 'social multiplier effects', the quality of life. For example, In Brazil, people feel increasingly afraid because of everyday violence and so invest in private security including insurance, armoured cars and private guards. This amounts to 10 per cent of Brazilian GNP. Such fear also weakens trust and limits participation in social networks (Krug et al., 2002).

In terms of solutions, many seem to have been largely ineffective. Sometimes the answer is seen as using more violence through army and the police, although this often simply generates more fear and resentment. Even more worrying, is that people themselves are increasingly taking the law into their own hands because they do not trust the security forces. For instance, in Guatemala, there is widespread lynching where people accused of crimes end up murdered, often involving being doused in petrol and set alight (Moser and McIlwaine, 2004; 2006). As with war, lack of development and inequality provide fertile grounds for the emergence of criminal culture, thereby urging more imaginative and holistic policy attention than has been apparent to date.

LEARNING OUTCOMES

By the end of this chapter and having completed the essential reading and activities you should be able to:

- Define the modernisation approach to development and identify the main criticisms.
- Outline the nature of the dependency school and identify its main criticisms.
- Outline the tenets of neoliberalism and its main policy partner, SAPs, the HIPC initiative and PRSPs.
- Identify and explain the main problems with SAPs and assess the extent to which PRSPs are an improvement on earlier policies.
- Define post-development and its main criticisms.
- Compare and contrast different development theories.
- Outline the meaning of globalisation and the reasons for its importance in understanding development processes.
- Assess the importance of global war and conflict as well as everyday violence as key development issues.

NOTES

1. As part of the Multilateral Debt Relief Initiative (MDRI) in 2006, provisions were made for the International Development Association (IDA) (the branch of the World Bank which provides interest-free loans) to cancel all debt outstanding and owed by HIPCs to the IDA at the end of 2003 as soon as these countries reached the HIPC completion point. The debt then becomes irrevocable.

2. For more details see www.worldbank.org/debt (accessed 17 April 2008).
3. See www.worldbank.org/prsp (accessed 17 April 2008).
4. See www.worldbank.org/prsp (accessed 17 April 2008).
5. See http://go.worldbank.org/LYE7YNYBH0 (accessed 17 April 2008).
6. See www.dfid.gov.uk/pubs/files/whitepaper 2000.pdf (accessed 17 April 2008).
7. See, for example, the Global Justice Movement: www.globaljusticemovement.org/ (accessed 17 April 2008).
8. See www.geog.qmul.ac.uk/globalcities/ (accessed 17 April 2008).

FURTHER READING

Krug, Etienne, Dahlberg, Linda, Mercy, James, Zwi, Antony and Lozano, Rafael (eds) (2002), *World Report on Violence and Health*, Geneva: World Health Organisation (downloadable from www.who.int/violence_injury_prevention/violence/world_report/en/full_en.pdf).
This report provides an excellent overview of the main patterns, causes, and consequences of war and everyday violence. Although the emphasis is on the health outcomes, the wider development causes and implications are also considered.

Panos (2005), *Who's Richer, Who's Poorer? A Journalist's Guide to the Politics of Poverty Reduction Strategies*, London: Panos (downloadable from www.panos.org.uk/PDF/reports/prsptoolkit1.pdf).
This short book provides an engagingly clear, yet rich, account of how neoliberalism has been enshrined in the policies of the IFIs. It identifies the failures of SAPs and outlines the core components of and problems with PRSPs.

Potter, Robert, Binns, Tony, Elliott, Jennifer A. and Smith, David (2008), *Geographies of Development*, 3rd edn, Harlow: Pearson Education.
Chapter 3 in this volume provides a clear overview of theories and approaches to development, ranging from the classical approaches through to post-development. Chapter 4 outlines the nature of globalisation and engages with the debates about its novelty and outcomes.

Rist, Gilbert (1997), *The History of Development: From Western Origins to Global Faith*, London: Zed.
This text provides a sophisticated discussion of how development has been conceived over time, reflected in ideological shifts and theoretical advances. It also critiques the notion of Western intervention in the so-called development project.

Roberts, J. Timmons and Bellone Hite, Amy (eds) (2007), *The Globalisation and Development Reader: Perspectives on Development Global Change*, Oxford: Blackwell.
This collection brings together a range of classic articles in relation to development theories including those by Rostow, Gunder Frank, Cardoso, Wallerstein, Stiglitz, Sachs and others.

USEFUL WEBSITES

www.brettonwoodsproject.org/ – website of the Bretton Woods Project, an organisation that monitors the World Bank and the IMF. It produces reports and briefings on the policies of these institutions focusing on social and environmental concerns in particular

www.prspsynthesis.org – website of the PRSP Monitoring and Synthesis Project run by the Overseas Development Institute

www.comminit.com/ – website of the Communication Initiative (CI) network which promotes sharing experiences about development strategies and includes various discussions about development theories

www.globalisation.eu/ – website of the Globalisation Institute, a European think tank which considers Europe's role in the global economy as well as issues such as world poverty

3.   Transforming populations

INTRODUCTION

This chapter considers trends in population in developing regions including efforts to regulate growth through population control and family planning programmes, and evolution of these in the wake of the most recent world summit on population in Cairo (1994). The discussion also reviews the phenomenon of demographic ageing which is occurring in the context of rising life expectancies and falling birth rates in many countries. The chapter proceeds to review population mobility, examining predominant patterns of movement within and from the Global South. Particular attention is paid to patterns of rural–urban migration, the characteristics of migrants according to age, gender and socio-economic status (often referred to as 'migrant selectivity'), and the nature of rural–urban linkages.

TRENDS IN POPULATION GROWTH

During the past five decades the world population has more than doubled from 3 billion to nearly 7 billion, yet as little as a century and a half ago, the global population was just 1 billion. However, although the absolute annual increase in global population peaked at 88 million in the late 1980s, the average annual increment now stands at only 78 million (Leone, 2008). If this downward trend continues, then the world population may only reach 9 billion by 2050 (Brown, 2008: 24), and will probably not double its present size until well into the twenty-second century.

The exceptional population growth experienced in the last few decades – reaching its highest mean worldwide rate of 2.04 per cent in the late 1960s – owes primarily to demographic increase in the Global South. Here 95 per cent per cent of all current population growth takes place, not only on account of its geographical extent and because it already has 80 per cent of the global populace, but because of higher rates of population increase. Although, at a global scale, population is presently growing at 1.37 per cent per annum, in developing areas the mean is 1.44 per cent (see Figure 3.1) and in sub-Saharan Africa, the fastest growing region in the world, 2.3 per cent (Leone, 2008).

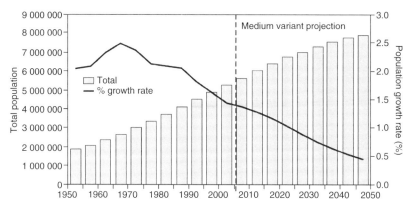

Source: Adapted from Leone (2008: figure 1).

Figure 3.1 Population trends in developing regions, 1950–2050

Reasons for Continued Population Growth

One reason for persistently high rates of demographic growth in many developing countries is the comparative youth of populations. In the South as a whole, nearly one-third of the population is under 15 years of age, whereas this is only one-fifth in advanced economies (Leone, 2008). Populations in the Global South are also growing because births continue to outnumber deaths. While fertility levels have dropped substantially since the 1960s and 1970s (indeed more than halved in many Latin American and Southeast Asian countries), death rates had already fallen to quite low levels by this period and continued to do so thereafter (see Table 3.1). The general decline in death rates in the post-war era (except in post-1980s Africa – see below) is attributed mainly to advances in health care, disease prevention and the containment of epidemics, and improvements in people's standard of living through better nutrition, and greater sanitary infrastructure such as cleaner water and more effective sewerage disposal. Even if infant mortality is seven times higher in developing than developed regions (at 59 per 1000 as against 7.5 per 1000), reductions in the South have been impressive, halving in a number of countries in the period 1970–94, and in some nations, such as Costa Rica and Sri Lanka, dropping by two-thirds.

Demographic Transition Model

Trends in population growth in developing regions over the last few decades broadly correspond with the projections of the so-called 'Demographic

Table 3.1   Crude birth and death rates, and total fertility rates, major world regions

Region	Crude birth rate (per 1000 pop.)		Crude death rate (per 1000 pop.)		Total fertility rate			
	1970	1992	1970	1992	1970	1980	1990	2000
Sub-Saharan Africa	47	44	20	15	6.5	6.6	6.3	5.7
East Asia and Pacific	35	21	9	8	5.7	3.0	2.5	2.0
South Asia	42	31	18	10	6.0	5.3	4.2	3.5
Middle East and North Africa	45	34	16	8	6.8	6.2	5.0	3.7
Latin America and Caribbean	36	26	10	7	5.2	4.1	3.2	2.6
Low- and middle-income economies average*	38	27	13	9	5.6	4.1	3.6	3.0
High-income economies average	18	13	10	9	2.4	2.2	1.8	1.7

Notes:
Crude birth and death rates = no. of live births and deaths respectively per 1000 population in one year.
Total fertility rate = average no. of children that would be born to a woman if she survives her childbearing years (15–49 years).
* Eastern Europe and Central Asia are now included in low- and middle-income average figures.

Sources: World Bank (1994: table 26; 2000: table 7); UNICEF Statistics (www.unicef.org) (accessed 4 March 2008).

Transition Model' (DTM). This is based on the historical experience of Europe and North America and posits an evolution from high mortality and fertility through to low fertility and mortality where population growth is close to zero (see Figure 3.2). In between these extremes, there are two intermediate stages. In the first, or 'early transition', phase, population expands significantly as death rates fall relative to births on account of improvements in living standards, diet and public health. In the second (or 'late transition') phase, a gap remains between birth and death rates, but is of less magnitude due, *inter alia*, to increased education, restrictive legislation on child employment and access to family planning. Most countries in the Global South are now at this point of late transition, and have undergone a much more rapid transformation in population behaviour – over a few decades – than was experienced by their Northern counterparts where comparable

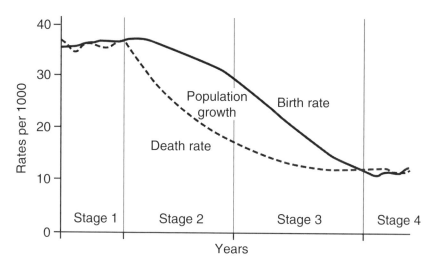

Source: Adapted from www.populationaction.org/Publications/Reports/The_Security_
Demographic/asset_upload_file928_5132.jpg (accessed 12 February 2008).

Figure 3.2   Demographic Transition Model

shifts took more than a century. This said, as with all models based on
totalising assumptions about the unilinear nature of historical change, the
DTM cannot account for the contemporary experience of Africa, where
demographic structures are 'transforming in a unique way – unlike in any
other region of the world' (Kakwani and Subbarao, 2005). Here not only is
the risk of death among infants and the elderly declining slowly, but as a
result of HIV/AIDS, wars and civil conflicts, and environmental disasters,
deaths among 'prime age adults' are disproportionately high.

FERTILITY MANAGEMENT AND FAMILY
PLANNING

While reproductive behaviour is affected by a multiplicity of factors such
as culture, education, income, migration and urbanisation, a significant role
in the general reduction in birth rates in the last few decades has been
played by family planning programmes. The World Bank, for example, estimates that 15–20 per cent of the reduction in birth rates is directly attributable to the adoption of contraception.

Although there are numerous views on population, the neo-Malthusian
notion that unchecked fertility contributes to poverty, underdevelopment
and environmental degradation has been a pervasive principle underpinning

---

BOX 3.1   REPRODUCTIVE RIGHTS

Reproductive rights embrace certain human rights that are already recognised in national laws, international human rights documents and other consensus documents. These rights rest on the recognition of the basic right of all couples and individuals to decide freely and responsibly the number, spacing and timing of their children and to have the information and means to do so, and the right to attain the highest standard of sexual and reproductive health. It also includes their right to make decisions concerning reproduction free of coercion, discrimination and violence.
Cairo Programme of Action, International Conference of Population and Development (ICPD), Paragraph 7.3, 1994

Source: Corrêa (2008).

---

global international population policy (see Furedy, 1997; Johnson, 1987; 1995). During the 1960s and 1970s, when rates of population growth in the Global South were construed as alarming enough to provoke pronouncements of a 'population explosion', the 'international' community (dominated by the most powerful economies) pressed for an urgent and dramatic reduction in fertility. This general campaign, marked *inter alia* by the founding of UN Fund for Population Activities (UNFPA) in the late 1960s, and the first World Conference on Population at Bucharest in 1974, led to major financial disbursements from the North to facilitate the introduction (or extension) of efforts to control population in the South.

In turn, because family planning programmes in developing countries have frequently taken the form of 'population control' rather than 'birth control' interventions, they have often met with criticism. While 'birth control' refers to the ability of couples to freely determine their fertility, 'population control' evokes the regulation of fertility in the interests of national or global objectives, thereby acting to 'influence people towards a particular outcome, rather than to provide free choice' (Furedy, 1997: 65). Particular antipathy to aggressive international anti-natalist population agendas has come from feminist quarters. This is not surprising given that women have been the main objects in family planning programmes, with little regard for their general health and 'reproductive rights' (Box 3.1). The narrow range of techniques and methods promoted have usually been designed by men or in male-dominated scientific establishments, and in many cases have had negative side effects, as in the controversial injectable hormone 'Depo Provera' and high oestrogen pill (see Hardon and Hayes, 1997; Wangari, 2002). Moreover, while repeated pregnancy and childbirth can undoubtedly cause problems for women, little appreciation has been accorded to the importance of motherhood for women's social status and legitimacy in developing societies. The fact that many poor women have had little choice in adopting contraception, or the ability to select from as wide a range of options as their counterparts in North, has led to the challenge that the introduction of family planning programmes has not liberated women in the South, but simply replaced one form of patriarchal control with another (see also below).

Sustained pressure from the feminist lobby to uphold women's reproductive rights appeared finally to bear fruit in 1994, when the third UN International Conference on Population and Development (ICPD) in Cairo formally recognised the reproductive rights and health approach to population growth. This reflected a shift from viewing population regulation as a means to achieve economic development, to placing people and sustainable development at the centre (Furedy, 1997; Johnson, 1995). In an attempt to eliminate the coercive or overly persuasive character of many previous programmes, and building on the 'quality of care' framework developed under Judith Bruce at the Population Council, the Cairo Programme of Action recommended that family planning be guided by imperatives of 'appropriate patient–provider interaction' and 'informed choice' (see Box 3.2).

The Cairo conference marked an undeniable victory for the women's movement, with some suggesting that the prevailing population paradigm shift was possibly 'one of the most significant achievements of contemporary feminism' (Corrêa with Reichmann, 1994: 4; see also Chant with Craske, 2003: 77). However, it should also be recognised that as far back as the 1970s the population establishment had used the position of women in a society as a means to pursue its objective (Furedy, 1997: 126). Thus, although recent years have seen a much fuller adoption of the language of 'rights' and 'choice' for women, this could also be regarded as a tactic to perpetuate anti-natalist (fertility reduction) agendas (ibid.; see also Smyth, 1994; Zhang and Locke, 2004: 43). This would certainly appear to be the case in Peru, where in 1995 President Alberto Fujimori introduced a draconian 'family planning' programme which led to the sterilisation of an estimated total of nearly 280 000, mainly rural and indigenous, women in a space of only four years. Although the programme was couched in the rhetoric of the Cairo consensus, and nominally afforded women the 'right to choose', a number of qualifications suggest otherwise. These include the systematic targeting of poor, rural women (who in the early 1990s, had an average fertility rate of 5.9 versus 2.7 among their urban counterparts), the award of incentives to health personnel to secure four to six sterilisations

---

BOX 3.2   RECOMMENDATIONS FOR FAMILY PLANNING PROGRAMMES, INTERNATIONAL CONFERENCE ON POPULATION AND DEVELOPMENT'S *PROGRAMME OF ACTION* 1994–2015

- Family planning programmes should ensure information and access to the widest possible range of safe and effective family planning methods (appropriate to the individual's age, reproductive history, family size preference and so on) to enable men and women to make free and informed choices.
- Information should be provided about the health risks and benefits of different methods, side effects and their effectiveness in preventing sexually transmitted diseases, including HIV/AIDS.
- Services should be safe, affordable and convenient for users.
- Services should ensure privacy and confidentiality.
- A continuous supply of high-quality contraceptives should be ensured.
- Services should comprise expansion and improvement of formal and informal training in sexual and reproductive health care and family planning, including better training in interpersonal communication and counselling for family planning personnel.
- Family planning services should provide adequate follow-up care, including for the side effects of contraceptive use.

Source: Hardon (1997).

---

per month, the use of rewards to 'family planning acceptors' such as food and clothing (a considerable amount donated by the United States Agency for International Development [USAID]), and widespread allegations of up to 200 000 cases in which sterilisation was forced, and often unbeknown to the women themselves (Boesten, 2007).

While the Peruvian case is by no means an isolated one, there is also evidence that several countries have made concerted efforts to bring their family planning interventions more in line with the spirit of Cairo (see later). This may well have added to rising trends in contraceptive prevalence, which now averages well over 50 per cent across the Global South. By the same

Table 3.2   Contraceptive prevalence in developing regions, 1990 and 2000

	% of women aged 15–49 years using contraception* (excludes traditional methods)		% change 1999–2000
	1990	2000	
Sub-Saharan Africa	16	23	+46
Middle East and North Africa	37	54	+45
South Asia	39	48	+25
East Asia and Pacific	71	84	+20
Latin America and Caribbean	62	73	+19

Note: Although figures may include contraceptive use by women's sexual partners, data at a national level is often only collected for formally married women or women who are in co-resident unions with men.

Source: UNICEF 'Statistics on fertility and contraceptive use', table 3 (www.childinfo-org/eddb/fertility/index.htm) (accessed 4 March 2008).

token, the rate in sub-Saharan Africa stands at only 23 per cent (Table 3.2). Despite some major advances in countries such as Ghana and Uganda in the past decade (Table 3.3), in poor nations such as The Gambia, only 9 per cent of the population use contraception (Chant, 2007a: 131). One reason commonly cited is religion. Around 95 per cent of the Gambian population is Muslim, and although UNFPA is working with Islamic NGOs to promote reproductive health and the rights of the girl child, many imams (religious leaders) use prayer sessions and the mass media to discourage contraceptive use, upholding the widespread belief that this runs counter to the Koran (ibid.: 132; see also Figure 3.3). Similar religious campaigns against family planning have also been observed in countries where the Roman Catholic church maintains a powerful presence in national polity (ibid.: ch. 5 on the Philippines; Chant with Craske, 2003: ch. 4 on Latin America).

Another reason noted for low take-up of family planning among poorer populations in the world is the persistence of high infant and child mortality. In Bangladesh, for example, 56 infants die in every 1000 live births. This rate is 104 per 1000 in Mozambique and as high as 114 in Burundi. Other documented reasons for resistance to family planning include limited knowledge of, or access to, family planning (sometimes referred to as 'unmet needs'), reluctance to resort to artificial birth control given the risky, unappealing, draconian and/or narrow range of techniques available, a preference for traditional methods, the social importance attached to

Table 3.3   Trends in modern contraceptive use, selected countries

Country	Year	% using modern contraception
Cameroon	1991	4.3
	2004	12.5
Ghana	1988	4.2
	2003	18.7
Kenya	1989	17.9
	2003	31.5
Mali	1987	1.3
	2001	5.7
Uganda	1988	2.5
	2001	18.2
Egypt	1988	35.5
	2000	53.9
Morocco	1987	28.9
	2004	54.8
Kazakhstan	1995	46.1
	1999	52.7
Bangladesh	1994	36.6
	2004	47.6
Indonesia	1987	43.9
	2003	56.7
Philippines	1993	24.9
	2003	33.4
Brazil	1986	56.5
	1996	70.3
Colombia	1986	52.4
	2005	68.2

Source: World Bank (2007a: table 3.6).

motherhood among women and virility among men, and belief in the welfare gains of large families (see Boesten, 2007; Patel, 2008).

In order for family planning to become a genuine tool of choice, more needs to be done to translate the spirit of the Cairo Programme of Action into practice, including encouraging men to take greater responsibility for fertility behaviour. This is especially important in sub-Saharan Africa where as many as 24.5 million people are living with HIV, and young women aged 15 to 24 are disproportionately at risk – being three times more likely to be HIV positive than their male counterparts (Gupta, 2006; see also Chapter 10, this volume). Yet although there are encouraging signs of increased condom use within and beyond Africa, a mere 3 per cent of Latin American

Source: Photo by Sylvia Chant.

Figure 3.3 Family planning poster, public health clinic, Sukuta, The Gambia

couples rely on male condoms for family planning, and 1 per cent or less on male sterilisation (Chant with Craske, 2003: 83). The International Planned Parenthood Federation (IPPF), which is the largest international NGO provider of reproductive and sexual health services and is a federation of national, voluntary Family Planning Associations (FPAs) from around 180 countries, argues that it is not surprising that many men do not take responsibility in reproductive matters given the marked targeting of women to date (see Gutmann, 2005; 2007). For this reason the IPPF have been concerned to promote initiatives which include men, such as in Sierra Leone, Trinidad and Tobago, and India. Here national FPAs have established male clinics which provide family planning services as well as information on Sexually Transmitted Infections (STIs), HIV/AIDS and on other issues concerning sexual and reproductive health (Zhang and Locke, 2004: 45). Bringing men into discussions and interventions touching upon fatherhood, family planning and sexual health have also featured in ActionAid's 'Stepping Stones' programme, which has been implemented mainly in Africa and Asia, PRO-PATER in Brazil and 'Fathers Inc.' in Jamaica. In India in 2005 an innovative campaign called 'What Kind of Man are You?' was jointly launched by Breakthrough, an international human rights organisation and the UN Development Fund for Women (UNIFEM), to encourage men to use condoms to protect their wives from HIV/AIDS infection. This uses print, television and internet media to popularise a message which is vital given that an estimated 2 million women in India are HIV positive, most of whom contracted the disease from their husbands.[1] It is also encouraging that from 2003 onwards, ground-breaking research into a swift and nominally fully reversible male vasectomy has been underway in China. The operation takes only 10 minutes and, as opposed to the traditional method of cutting the male reproductive organs, involves instead the simple insertion of a removable tube in the vas deferens to block the passage of sperm. As of 2007, the procedure had already been patented, clinical trials had been conducted on 500 men (around one-quarter of the desired total), and approval was being awaited for wider use (see Gutmann, 2005).

Although there has traditionally been considerable controversy around abortion, it is widely argued by feminists that more attention needs to be given to the provision of legal safe abortion, especially in light of high rates of maternal mortality stemming from illegal and/or self-induced terminations. In Mexico, for example, there has been some, but insufficient, progress on this front. On the one hand, post-abortion care is far better now than 30 years ago, and in April 2007, abortions up to the end of the first trimester were legalised in the capital, Mexico City. On the other hand, however, surgical terminations in public facilities persist in being permitted only on extreme grounds (for example, in cases of incest or threats to mothers' lives), and a non-surgical alternative – the 'abortion pill' Mifespristone (also known as 'RU-486') – is still not officially registered even if it has now been added to the WHO's list of 'essential drugs'. These gaps in provision force an estimated 500 000 women a year to resort to clandestine terminations (Kulczycki, 2007).

Another area requiring attention is the issue of sexuality and sexual rights in relation to reproductive health. An exciting and pioneering body of work has recently broken onto the development scene which critiques the overwhelming tendency for reproductive health interventions to concentrate on the 'dangers' rather than the 'pleasures' of sex and sexuality, to address sexuality only as something to be contained and regulated through strategies for birth control and HIV/AIDS prevention, and to sideline sexual rights as subordinate or even irrelevant to matters of development (see, for example, Armas, 2007; Cornwall and Jolly, 2006; Ilkkaracan and Jolly, 2007; Jolly, 2007; Undie and Benaya, 2006). Such a narrow, not to mention alarmist, approach, has had a range of untoward consequences. One is that it has arguably obstructed advances towards safer sex practices, with Cornwall and Jolly (2006: 7) noting that the conventional manner of promoting condoms as 'tools for disease prevention' is likely to have much less appeal than strategies which might encourage people to regard them as 'erotic accessories' integral to happier and more fulfilling lives and partnerships. A second consequence identified of speaking about the dangers of sex, and working with very limited knowledge of sexuality and sexual rights, is that this seems to have perpetuated the stereotype that men are 'predators' and women 'victims', and to have marginalised lesbian, gay, bisexual and transgender (LGBT) populations (Jolly, 2007: 3; see also Spronk, 2008). Frequently the sexual and reproductive health needs and rights of non-heterosexual populations are completely left out of the picture. A third major consequence of narrow, health-obsessed and danger-ridden conceptualisations of sex is that this has arguably acted to reinforce a stereotypical image of sub-Saharan Africa, the heartland of the HIV/AIDS pandemic, as a 'primal other, Africa as an icon of dangerous desire, Africa as the projection of self never fully tamable' (Comaroff, 2007: 197). As further noted by Bhana (2007: 4), this arguably perpetuates colonialists' constructions of Africans as 'hypersexual', and with particular regard to men a 'rampant African male sexuality exhibiting lust, desire, and danger'. In turn, this has led to a reassertion of 'censure around African sexuality' requiring its 'intensified surveillance and repression' (see also Undie and Benaya, 2006: 6). In light of this and the preceding points, the call of the World Health Organisation (WHO) to respect people's sexual rights as human rights, is not only timely but imperative (see Box 3.3).

BOX 3.3　WORLD HEALTH ORGANISATION WORKING DEFINITION OF SEXUAL RIGHTS

Sexual rights embrace human rights that are already recognised in national laws, international human rights documents and other consensus statements. They include the right of all persons, free of coercion, discrimination and violence, to:

- the highest attainable standard of sexual health, including access to sexual and reproductive health care services
- seek, receive and impart information related to sexuality
- sexuality education
- respect for bodily integrity
- choose their partner
- decide to be sexually active or not
- consensual sexual relations
- consensual marriage
- decide whether or not, and when, to have children
- pursue a satisfying, safe and pleasurable sexual life.

The responsible exercise of human rights requires that all persons respect the rights of others.

Source:　Adapted from Ilkkaracan and Jolly (2007: 10), based on WHO (2004).

DEMOGRAPHIC AGEING

Another critical issue in population is 'demographic ageing', which refers not only to the progressive increase in the average age of a given population, but to the share of the population defined as 'elderly'. This is usually set at those aged more than 60 or 65 years. Although only 8 per cent of the population of the Global South is currently over 60 years (compared with around 25 per cent in the North), in many countries, numbers of people over 60 are growing substantially. By the year 2025, it is estimated that one-eighth of the population in developing regions will be 60 years old or more. In turn, given its share of the global population, the South already contains 50 per cent of over-60-year-olds, and by the year 2025 this is expected to have risen to 70 per cent.

At one level demographic ageing is an extremely healthy sign, indicating, *inter alia*, ongoing decline in mortality and rising life expectancy. Although the HIV/AIDS crisis has led to setbacks in sub-Saharan Africa such that life expectancy in the region is now only 52 years, Aboderin (2006: 25) notes that older Africans who currently reach age 60 can expect a further 16 years of life, which is not much less than in the advanced economies. Moreover, partly due to disproportionate mortality among younger people, the percentage share of people aged 60 or over in sub-Saharan Africa is expected to rise to 10 per cent by 2050. More generally, populations in the developing world gained an average of 25 years on their lives between 1950 and 1990. In Latin America, the Caribbean, East Asia and the Pacific, mean life expectancy presently stands at 68 years, just less than 10 years behind that in advanced economies (77 years).

Accepting that a growing number of elderly can bring increased problems of dependency, declining birth rates are likely to counter this so that there will actually be a net reduction in dependency ratios (proportion of the economically dependent to the economically active population) over the next 50 years. This is sometimes referred to as a 'demographic dividend' or 'demographic bonus' and is often seen as having favoured the development of 'tiger economies' such as Korea, Singapore and Taiwan over countries such as the Philippines where tardy reductions in fertility combined with increasing life expectancy have resulted, instead, in a 'demographic onus' (see Chant, 2007a: 206). Yet although falling fertility may help to offset the growing 'burden' of elderly in developing populations, the Elderly Dependency Ratio is anticipated to increase around threefold between 2000 and 2050 (Leone, 2008). In light of this it has been argued that urgent steps need to be taken to stop population ageing from becoming 'the next social crisis to face the developing world' (Lloyd-Sherlock, 1997: 231; see also Aboderin, 2006; Ahmed Obaid, 2007). At present, most elderly people in developing countries have to rely on their children's support in old age. However, declining birth rates may render this less feasible. In China, for example, McNay (2005) points out that increasingly protracted life expectancies mean that by 2030, a typical 40-year-old urban woman will have to care for her parents for 17 more years (or about twice as long) as she did in 1990. Furthermore, she may well have to support two sets of grandparents. This so-called '1-2-4' pattern is becoming of such concern to the Chinese authorities that in cases where both partners in a couple are only children they are now permitted to have two offspring between them. Yet this may not solve the prospective problems attached to 24 per cent of the Chinese population falling into the 65-plus age group by 2050, hence in some cities, such as Wei Hai, as many as 10 000 homes are already undergoing construction for the 'abandoned elderly' (see Ahmed Obaid, 2007).

Gender Differences in Ageing

One of the major challenges of a growing proportion of elderly people in developing countries is that they do not have access to the same formal economic and health-care support systems as in advanced economies (see Ofstedal et al., 2004). This raises the likelihood that increased numbers of people may live out their latter years with a markedly low level of health and quality of life (Aboderin, 2006; Gorman, 1996). This is especially likely to apply to women, (a) because women live longer than men, and (b) because women are generally less protected by social security and pensions.

In respect of women's longer lives leading to an 'excess' of women in upper age groups, in Mexico, a five- to six-year differential between male and female life expectancy in the 1990s translated into there being 112 women for every 100 men aged 60 years or more (Varley and Blasco, 2000: 48). In Bolivia, there were 121 women per 100 men aged 60 plus, in Chile, 132 and in Argentina, 135. Among people aged 80 or over, gender imbalances were even greater, at 153 women per 100 men in Bolivia, 188 in Chile and 199 in Argentina. With regard to pensions, and accepting that coverage is low in general (even in a relatively wealthy country like Mexico, for instance, this is less than 10 per cent of people aged 60 plus), women are particularly disadvantaged. This situation owes first, to women's limited access to formal and/or full-time employment with contributory pension schemes, second, because of their lower average earnings and, third, because of less continuity in their working lives (Chant with Craske, 2003: 92–3). In Peru, for example, women's periodic unemployment and fluctuating incomes make it hard for them to fulfil the minimum pension requirement of 20 years' contributions. This forces many Peruvian women to rely on their husband's pensions, which drop as much as 55 to 60 per cent of their value when they become widowed (Clark and Laurie, 2000).

Many elderly people resist becoming dependent on their relatives, or at least their dependence is not one-way (Lloyd-Sherlock, 1997; Ofstedal et al., 2004; Vera Sanso, 2006). Indeed, in many HIV/AIDS-stricken communities in sub-Saharan Africa, the elderly are becoming the major breadwinners and/or caregivers to orphaned children (Kakwani and Subbarao, 2005; see also Aboderin, 2006). Nonetheless, elderly dependency of some degree is likely given limited pensions, and because older people have difficulty securing income-generating work, which in some instances forces them into begging (see Figure 3.4). This is exacerbated by a dearth of institutional care in most countries, and minimal support from health and welfare services (Varley and Blasco, 2000: 48). Lack of public provision also carries a set of gender implications in so far as caring for older kin tends to fall within the remit of women's domestic and familial roles.

Source: Photo by Sylvia Chant.

Figure 3.4   Elderly beggars on the steps of El Santuario del Quinche church, El Quinche, Ecuador

79

Although there has been no discussion on ageing comparable with that on fertility in international policy arenas, 1982 saw the launch of the Vienna Plan of Action on Ageing which established specific targets for the inclusion of older people in social and economic development (Beales, 2000: 15). More recently, the Beijing Declaration of 1995 stressed the need for approaches to development that were explicitly inclusive of women of all ages. The Copenhagen Declaration of the same year also called for generations to 'invest in one another and recognise diversity and generational interdependence guided by the twin principles of reciprocity and equity' (ibid.). The year 1999 was designated as the International Year for the Older Person by the United Nations (Clark and Laurie, 2000: 80), which has also established a series of 'Principles for Older Persons' emphasising independence, dignity, self-fulfilment, care and participation. International NGO networks such as HelpAge International (HAI), which has 7000 member and partner organisations, are currently trying to get these principles adopted as a legally binding charter of rights which all governments will have to observe.

Given that much of the rhetoric emphasising the rights of older people has not yet translated into practice, it is no surprise that the elderly have often been forced to act on their own behalf. In Bolivia, for example, male beggars have organised themselves into a Council of Venerable Old Persons (which now includes women), to demand legal documentation (Beales, 2000: 17). This has spawned other groups such as 'New Dawn' which campaigns for pensions and free health care for elderly Bolivians. In Peru, social movements have established 'Clubes de Tercer Edad' (Elderly People's Clubs) which provide an opportunity for older people, many of whom are isolated, to mix with one another and to forge links with other movements in order to gain better access to nutrition (Clark and Laurie, 2000: 85).

Activity 3.1
Think about the different experiences a low-income person in Asia, Africa or Latin America is likely to encounter in old age compared with an individual who is well-off financially. Factors you might consider here include housing, pension entitlements, savings and health status. Then identify what government agencies or other organisations might do to alleviate the economic and other difficulties faced by poor elderly people.

MIGRATORY MOVEMENTS IN AND FROM THE GLOBAL SOUTH

Alongside issues of growth and composition in the analysis of population in the South, another critical element is demographic mobility, with millions of people engaged in a wide variety of movements differentiated by direction and duration (see Chant with Craske, 2003: 228–30).

While a lot of the literature on migration in the Global South focuses on intra-national movements from rural to urban areas, rural-to-rural migration is also common (especially on a seasonal basis), as are movements between cities and across national borders. Indeed, in 2007, numbers of international migrants, in terms of people living in countries outside their place of birth, totalled 192 million, equating to 3 per cent of the world's population (Brown, 2008: 12).

Cross-border movements have long featured in the demographic dynamics of developing regions. In Latin America, for example, around 5 per cent of the populations of Argentina and Venezuela are migrants from poorer countries such as Colombia, Bolivia and Paraguay, and in Costa Rica, between 6 and 8 per cent of the population is of Nicaraguan origin. In many cases, however, international movement is between South and North. Major international flows include those from Mexico and other parts of Meso-America[2] and the Caribbean (especially El Salvador and the Dominican Republic) to the USA, from the Caribbean, South Asia and, increasingly, North Africa and West Asia to Europe, and from South and Southeast Asia to the Middle East. In 2005, for example, the Chinese diaspora was estimated at 35 million, and the Filipino diaspora, 7 million (more or less equivalent to one-tenth of the national population) (IOM, 2005). One of the most positive aspects of international migration for development (from the perspective of nation states and institutions of global governance) is the substantial level of remittances sent from migrants to their home countries. Indeed, these now far exceed the proportion provided by ODA (or foreign aid) (ibid.; see also *Habitat Debate*, 2006: 17). However, the use of remittances as the 'new development finance' is not without criticism. At one level this accords with the individualisation of effort associated with neoliberal economic policy. However, it is also the case that people who move from South to North to make a living and/or to finance the economic sustainability of their home countries often do so at considerable personal cost. Most such migrants work in extremely exploitative working conditions in the lower and unprotected echelons of Northern labour markets, especially in service sectors such as cleaning and care work (Datta et al., 2007; Sassen, 2002b).

In respect of the duration of migratory movements, deficiencies in data preclude exact estimates. This is perhaps particularly marked for international migration which comprises varying levels of undocumented movement. Yet even at an intra-national scale, determining whether migration is 'permanent' or 'temporary' is fraught with difficulties.

The fact that most developing countries have sustained or started to undergo a notable rural–urban transition in the post-war period suggests that the permanent transfer of populations from rural areas to towns and cities has prevailed. Yet it is important to acknowledge that many censuses fail to capture short-term movements over small distances. In Mexico, for instance, the census only documents interstate or international migration. In Costa Rica, moves are registered at the level of the 'canton' (an inter-mediate administrative entity between districts and provinces), but people are only classified as migrants when living in a canton different to their place of birth or where they resided five years prior to the census enumer-ation (Chant with Craske, 2003: 230). This does not, accordingly, pick up on temporary migrations in the intervening period, whether internally or overseas, and is especially pertinent in this context given that between 1984 and 2000 no national census was undertaken in the country. Further com-plications arise from the fact that decisions on the duration of migration are not a 'one-off' process – migrants may well intend to move permanently, but end up returning to their places of origin 20 years later. Alternatively, a migrant who leaves his or her home area or country may only move tem-porarily (for example, to earn enough cash to invest in property or a busi-ness), but ends up finding a good job in their destination, marrying and/or having children, and staying permanently. While longitudinal community-level case studies can clearly reveal more of the complexity of migratory patterns, they are not easily extrapolated (Durand and Massey, 1992).

THEORETICAL APPROACHES TO RURAL–URBAN MIGRATION

The literature on migration and development is threaded with a wide range of theoretical approaches (see Durand and Massey, 1992; Radcliffe, 1991). This partly reflects the plethora of migration patterns discussed above, and in part the fact that while most population movement is underpinned by livelihood considerations, forced displacement occurs due to civil war, famines, ecological disasters and climate change (see Brown, 2008). This said, three main theoretical models of long-term rural–urban migration can be identified.

Neoclassical/Equilibrium Approach

The 'neoclassical' or 'equilibrium' approach draws on neoclassical eco-nomics and Parsonian sociology, and maintains that migration is a rational individual response to wage-rate differentials. People move to cities because of the 'pull' generated by better employment opportunities, wages and living conditions. Also exerting an influence on migrant decision-making are rural 'push' factors such as declining access to land, diminishing agricultural productivity, competition from large farming enterprises and so on. While the neoclassical model goes some way to recognising the structural determinants of migration, however, personal choice remains paramount.

Common critiques of the neoclassical approach revolve around its rather categorical and unproblematised assumptions, namely, that people are motivated by the idea of economic betterment (and/or that it is necessarily 'rational' to respond to market incentives), that people are actually free to make (informed) decisions and that migrants will automatically be able to improve their lot in urban areas. This said, some precepts of the neoclassical model seem to be borne out in practice. As noted by UNFPA (2007: 37), for example: 'When migrants move to urban centres, they are making rational choices. Even if urban working and living conditions present many serious difficulties, they are perceived as preferable to rural alternatives – otherwise migrants would not keep coming.'

Structuralist/Neo-Marxian Model

The 'structuralist' or 'neo-Marxian' model rejects the voluntaristic thrust of the neoclassical paradigm and emphasises that people tend to move not because they want to, but because they have to. While the neo-Marxian approach by no means denies the role played by individual agency, the emphasis is much less on personal choice than on objective material constraints. Neo-Marxian analysis emphasises migration as the outcome of capital's needs for a large and cheap supply of labour in developing world cities. As such, population movements are best understood in relation to the global requirements of capitalism. That the spatial movements of people, both nationally and internationally, tend to follow concentrations of capital at a world scale, clearly demonstrate some plausibility in this proposition.

Structuration

Striking a balance between migration as an outcome of 'individual choice' versus migration as a product of 'structural constraint' is a third approach referred to as 'structuration'. Structuration acknowledges the importance of both macroeconomic and micro-social processes, and has perhaps been best elaborated under the auspices of the 'household strategies approach', which views the organisation of household livelihoods and reproduction as crucial in shaping mobility (see Chant and Radcliffe, 1992; Radcliffe, 1991). In this model, consideration is given to the different functions of households in different socio-economic contexts, including a 'sustenance' function which, in practical terms, conditions who might be released to migration (or not), a 'socialising' function, which has an important ideological effect on who migrates and why, and a 'network' function, which arises once migration is under way and relates to the manner in which migrant members of family groups affect the moves of others. The model also emphasises how differences and divisions between household members not only in respect of tasks and obligations, but also in relation to power and identity, are critical in understanding who migrates, why, where, with whom and for how long. As might be expected, the household strategies approach is particularly enriching for the conceptualisation of women's migration, first, because women's behaviour is usually less autonomous than men's and more contingent on their roles within domestic environments at different stages of the life course[3] and, second, because viewing individuals in the context of their households highlights the ways in which gender is cross-cut by other dimensions of migrant selectivity such as age, marital status, fertility and education (Chant with Craske, 2003: ch. 9; see also below).

Despite the advantages of the household strategies approach over the other two models, operationalising the 'household' part of this theoretical framework is by no means easy, especially when some members of domestic units may make individual decisions that take little account of the wishes of fellow members. Moreover, since households are both diverse and dynamic, consideration must be given to how a heterogeneous household universe influences the mobility of individuals within different units.

The 'strategies' part of this theoretical approach is no less problematic. While household strategies may on the surface imply forethought and collective action, identifying strategies, especially household strategies, is difficult since migration decisions are often short-term individual reactions to ad hoc circumstances, rather than tightly determined plans reached through democratic consensus among household members. Notwithstanding these problems, in adopting a more holistic view of mobility than other models, the household strategies approach has proved of greater use in capturing the multifaceted nature of migration. In turn, it demonstrates that even if employment and economic imperatives are major factors, they are intimately interwoven with social, family and cultural considerations (see Chant with Craske, 2003: 229–30; Tacoli, 2006).

THE SELECTIVITY OF RURAL–URBAN MIGRATION

Recognising that migration needs to be conceived of as a dynamic, developmental process, in which decisions made by migrants at a given moment affect the course and selectivity of migration in later periods (Durand and Massey, 1992), the early stages of migration are often characterised by the movement of lone individuals, in which age, gender, education and socio-economic status have commonly been identified as key dimensions of 'selectivity'.

Age Selectivity

While the findings of migrant selectivity studies are often complex and contradictory and defy generalisation across space or time, most migrants seem to be young, predominantly in the 15–24 age group, and rarely over 30. The main reasons given for this skew towards youth are fourfold. First, young migrants are more mobile and freer to take risks on account of being single and/or unencumbered by dependent children. Second, young people are less likely than their older counterparts to have economic and property stakes in their home community. In sub-Saharan Africa, for example, rural land shortages are making it increasingly difficult for young men and women to engage in farming, which raises the likelihood of their migration (see Tacoli, 2002). Third, young people stand a better chance of getting jobs in towns and cities, especially if they have benefited from the spread of education to rural areas. Fourth, being young (and single) is likely to make it easier to obtain urban lodging, whether in the form of lone migrants 'living-in' with their employers, or becoming an additional member in the homes of relatives already established in urban areas (see Roberts, 1995: ch. 4).

While economic motivations are usually the main reason for young people's migration, sociocultural imperatives linked with becoming an adult and/or widening personal experience are also important. Research in Africa and Southeast Asia has indicated that moving to towns for a few years offers young males the chance of 'proving themselves' as grown men. In northern Thailand, for example, men acquire social esteem by spending time away from the village before they settle down to marry (Singhanetra-Renard and Prabhudhanitisarn, 1992). Migration is also noted as a means of escaping obligations to, and control by, elders. By the same token, some young people move because they are told to do so by parents or senior kin and therefore may have little choice in the matter. In many cultures, particularly in Southeast Asia and sub-Saharan Africa, notions of 'filial piety' and 'parent repayment' exert an especially strong influence on young migrant women who almost invariably comply with the moral obligation of sending money home wherever their destination (see Tacoli, 2002).

Gender Selectivity

Regional differences seem to be particularly important when examining the gender selectivity of migration streams. Although, in general, women are more likely to predominate in rural–urban movement in Latin America and Southeast Asia, they are less likely to do so in Africa and South Asia. While women's access to land in rural areas throughout the Global South tends to be limited in relation to men's – one estimate being that women are only 15 per cent of landowners worldwide (see UNFPA, 2007: 19) – where rates of women's participation in agriculture are high, as they are in many African countries (at over half the rural labour force), levels of female outmigration have traditionally been lower than men's. This is the reverse in Latin America, where the share of women in agriculture is usually less than 20 per cent. Young rural women in particular come to represent 'surplus labour' in their households and/or have few means of attaining a livelihood on an independent basis (see Radcliffe, 1991; 1992). The impetus for moving is strengthened by the fact that urban employment opportunities for women in Latin America, albeit in a relatively narrow range of occupations such as domestic service and factory work, are greater than in Africa. The influence on gender-selective migration of economic opportunities for women is reflected in the composition of sex ratios: in the towns and cities of Africa and South Asia, these tend to be masculine, whereas in Latin America and Southeast Asia they are often strongly feminine (see Table 3.4).

Having identified that labour constraints and opportunities impact upon gender-selective migration, it is critically important to stress that employment is not the only factor stimulating female movement. Women may also migrate for marriage, to gain increased access to reproductive services (such as health and education), and/or to escape gendered inequalities and power relations within households and communities in source areas (see Chant with Craske, 2003: ch. 9; Willis and Yeoh, 2000; also Box 3.4). In addition, it is important to recognise that women's propensity to migrate (or not) may be neither 'autonomous' nor 'voluntary', since women are subject to a range of gender-differentiated social, ideological and practical constraints which tend not to apply to men. In parts of South Asia, North Africa and the Middle East, for example, single women are often not allowed to migrate by parents, and will only do so if it is marriage related. This compounds the tendency for rural–urban migration to be male dominated in these areas. Restrictions on female movement have also been common in sub-Saharan Africa, although in recent years women's participation in

Table 3.4   Urban sex ratios: selected developing countries, 1990s/2000s

Region/country	Men per 100 women total	Men per 100 women in urban areas
AFRICA		
The Gambia (1993)	100	107
Kenya (1999)	98	120
Malawi (1998)	96	107
Mozambique (1997)	92	98
Namibia (1991)	94	99
Swaziland (1997)	90	98
Tunisia (1994)	102	103
Uganda (2001)	95	94
Zambia (2000)	100	100
Zimbabwe (1997)	92	99
LATIN AMERICA AND CARIBBEAN		
Bolivia (2001)	100	94
Brazil (2000)	97	94
Chile (2002)	98	96
Costa Rica (2003)	100	94
Dominican Republic (1993)	95	90
Ecuador (2001)	100	98
El Salvador (1992)	94	90
Mexico (2000)	95	94
Paraguay (2002)	102	94
Saint Lucia (2001)	95	91
Uruguay (2003)	94	91
Venezuela (1998)	101	98
ASIA		
Iran (1997)	104	105
Jordan (2000)	108	109
Syrian Arab Republic (2003)	105	106
Bangladesh (2001)	104	114
India (2003)	107	110
Cambodia (1998)	93	95
Indonesia (2000)	99	100
Malaysia (2000)	101	102
Philippines (1990)	96	92
Thailand (2002)	99	94

Sources: UN (2005: table 1b; 2006a: table 6).

BOX 3.4   WOMEN'S MIGRATION HISTORIES IN MEXICO AND COSTA RICA

Employment, public services and family networks are often cited as key factors influencing rural–urban migration in Latin America, but the finer details of these and their interactions are often neglected in macro-level analyses. Even brief accounts of individual women's migration, however, enhance understanding of the complex underpinnings of gendered mobility.

Case 1: Migration as a means of avoiding family contact
Lupe is a 39-year-old single mother living in the international tourist resort of Puerto Vallarta, Jalisco, Mexico. Her decision to migrate to the town in her teens was spurred by conjugal breakdown. A native of Guadalajara, the capital of Jalisco state, around 140 miles to the west of Puerto Vallarta, Lupe had married at the age of 15 in order to escape the pressures of an unhappy home life dominated by a hostile and authoritarian step-father. She termed this bid for freedom '*Salida número uno*' ('Exit no. 1'). Regrettably, married life proved equally disagreeable and claustrophobic, so, shortly after the birth of her first child, Lupe decided to leave her husband, thereby embarking on '*Salida número dos*' ('Exit no. 2'). Since Lupe's decision was strongly disapproved of by her mother and step-father, she decided it would be best to leave Guadalajara in order to escape family pressure to return to the marital home. The reasons that Lupe chose the tourist town of Puerto Vallarta were material and psychosocial in nature. On a practical front, she recognised that, as a woman, she was more likely to find a job in a town which was dominated by services rather than industry. In personal terms, she felt she would fare better as a lone mother in Puerto Vallarta which, like other coastal resorts in Mexico, had a reputation for being less conservative than inland cities. Another factor influencing Lupe's decision was that, since she knew no one in Puerto Vallarta, her anonymity would provide greater protection from scrutiny and gossip than in a city where people knew her background and might have a vested interest in encouraging her to patch things up with her husband.

Case 2: Migration as a means of conjugal separation
Martilina's migration to Liberia,the capital of Guanacaste province in north-west Costa Rica was stimulated by a similar catalyst –

conjugal breakdown – although in this case, the primary reason for moving to a town where no one knew her was to avoid violent recriminations from her husband, Hernán. As a mother of five children living in the town of Nicoya, about 65 miles south of Liberia, Martilina had suffered for several years from Hernán's economic unreliability, and his unpredictable and violent bouts of temper. She had thought about leaving home on several occasions, but could not bring herself to do so, partly for fear of reprisals, and partly because with few skills and only two years of primary education, she feared she would be unable to find a job to support her children. Beyond this, she had invested considerable effort in building their home in Nicoya and knew she stood to lose everything if she was to leave. Nonetheless, when her eldest children reached an age when they could provide some economic assistance, Martilina grew more confident about making the break. After a few weeks of secret planning, Martilina and her children left home in the middle of the night carrying as many belongings as they could between them. They left no indication of where they had gone for fear that Hernán would track them down, and have had no contact with him since. The decision to move to Liberia was mainly because the family's lack of contacts in the town was greater guarantee that information on their whereabouts would not trickle back to Hernán. By the same token, as the capital of the province, there was more likelihood of finding employment, and schools for the younger children.

Source: Chant with Craske (2003: 235–6, box 9.1).

rural migration has increased. This is attributed partly to economic crisis, which has required more women to seek income-generating work, partly because women's employment opportunities have expanded in towns (especially in international tourist resorts) and partly because of women's growing desires (and capacity) for personal independence (see Tacoli, 2002).

Educational and Socio-economic Selectivity

In respect of educational selectivity many studies have found that migrants have traditionally had higher literacy rates and more years of schooling than non-migrants. This continues today, with the Economic Commission for Latin America and the Caribbean (ECLAC) noting that educated young people are more likely to migrate than people with no or limited schooling. One idea offered for this pattern is that education acts to broaden people's horizons and raise expectations, which, in turn, makes migration more desirable. Another crucial factor, however, is that education undoubtedly facilitates people's access to work in urban environments where a certificate of primary education (if not secondary education) is normally required for formal employment.

Finally, research has shown that the average migrant tends to have higher socio-economic status than non-migrants. One conceivable reason is that higher-income individuals are not only likely to be more educated, but to have greater exposure to information and the media, and, accordingly, be more aware of the benefits that an urban move might bring. What is equally likely, however, is that better-off households can afford to save some kind of cash surplus to help the migrant member get to the city and maintain themselves during the early stages of finding employment and somewhere to live.

THE IMPACTS ON RURAL AREAS OF OUT-MIGRATION AND RURAL–URBAN LINKAGES

While it is often asserted that migration to towns and cities improves the lives of those who migrate, it is also important to consider the effects of migration on areas of origin.

On the negative side, a major consequence for rural areas of permanent out-migration to towns is the depletion of human resources in the countryside. Since it is the young and the better educated who tend to migrate, the old and the infirm are left behind, with serious consequences for the subsistence economy and for rural production in general. Such tendencies seem to be particularly marked where it is mainly men who move and women who are left behind. The resultant 'feminisation of agriculture' weakens productive potential given that for physical or cultural/symbolic reasons women may not be allowed to plant certain types of crop, or handle certain types of machinery, such as ploughs, quite apart from being prevented from taking major decisions when their men are away (see Radcliffe, 1992).

Another consequence for rural areas of outmigration may be increased impoverishment. This may occur not only because of the erosion of the human resource base, but also because remittances from migrant relatives may lapse over time. This is especially so where women are left behind as *de facto* (temporary/circumstantial) heads of household by their husbands (see also Chapter 9, this volume). Alternatively, communities which predominantly rely on the remittances of young single daughters may be better off.

Leading on from this, strong and persistent links are often maintained between migrants and their source communities. Rural people may visit their urban relatives, and vice versa, on a fairly regular basis and, although cash flows tend to be greater from the towns to the villages, all manner of home produce such as fruit, vegetables, corn and so on may flow back in the other direction (Moßrucker, 1997). Several studies have indicated that female migrants in particular bring substantial monies back to the villages, which are then invested in school fees for younger brothers and sisters, house-building, boosting family savings and generally supplementing living expenses. Migration may not only inject major financial resources into home areas, but skills as well, when people return to their home areas with a new range of urban trades. Although it has been asserted that rural–urban ties are weakening in some contexts, Tacoli (2006) argues with reference to Africa that strong links with home areas are not only an essential part of the social identity of migrants, but also a means by which they can spread their assets (and risk) across space. In an age where communications are getting progressively easier, but risk and uncertainty are also on the rise, it is entirely possible that links between rural and urban localities, as well as across international borders, will intensify rather than diminish.

LEARNING OUTCOMES

By the end of this chapter and relevant reading you should be able to:

- Outline and explain the major trends in population growth in developing regions over the last six decades.
- Describe the interests of different stakeholders in fertility management, and identify key reasons why Western family planning methods have not been universally adopted by populations in the South.
- Outline the major patterns of migration in the Global South, and identify and explain the key factors involved in migrant selectivity with reference to the applicability of different theoretical models.
- Identify the benefits and drawbacks to rural areas of outmigration to towns and cities.

NOTES

1. See www.breakthrough.tv/Campaign_detail (accessed 23 March 2008).
2. Meso-America refers to Mexico and Central America (Belize, Costa Rica, El Salvador, Guatemala, Honduras, Nicaragua and Panama).

3. The term 'life course' is preferred to 'lifecycle' because it does not assume that people move through the same paths over their lifetimes. Paths can clearly vary according to such factors as culture, society and sexual preference.

FURTHER READING

Chant, Sylvia with Craske, Nikki (2003), *Gender in Latin America*, London: Latin America Bureau/New Brunswick, NJ: Rutgers University Press.
Chapters 4 and 9 of this book deal with most of the issues included in this chapter, including family planning, demographic ageing and migration. Although the geographical focus is Latin America, the theoretical and thematic discussions are relevant to the Global South more generally.

Furedy, Frank (1997), *Population and Development*, Cambridge: Polity.
One of the most comprehensive sources on the theoretical links between population and development, and how these have played out in respect of international policies for 'population control' and 'birth control'.

Habitat Debate (2006), 'Cities – magnets of hope. A look at global migration problems', Special issue, **12** (3), 1–24, (downloadable from www.unhabitat.org).
A useful collection of short articles, dealing not only with internal but international migration, and covering issues such as gendered migration, migrant remittances, the urban policy implications of migration and migrants' housing rights.

Hardon, Anita and Hayes, Elizabeth (eds) (1997), *Reproductive Rights in Practice: A Feminist Report on the Quality of Care*, London: Zed.
An excellent collection of papers which identify different types of family planning programme in the Global South, and cover the recommendations for family planning issued at the third World Conference on Population at Cairo in 1994. There are also country-specific case studies in the book which trace the evolution of family planning programmes in selected parts of the Global South.

Tacoli, Cecilia (ed.) (2006), *The Earthscan Reader in Rural–Urban Linkages*, London: Earthscan.
A substantial contribution to the literature on rural–urban migration which includes a theoretical overview of linkages between source and destination areas of migrants in the Global South, and which contains several case studies of rural–urban ties in different countries.

USEFUL WEBSITES

www.iom.ch – website of the International Organisation for Migration
www.ippf.org – website of the International Planned Parenthood Federation – contains a comprehensive series of country profiles detailing recent evolution of family planning programmes over time
www.popcouncil.org – website of the Population Council
www.unicef.org – website of the United Nations Children's Fund
www.unfpa.org – website of the United Nations Fund for Population Activities

4. Urbanisation and shelter

INTRODUCTION

This chapter outlines patterns of, and trends in, urbanisation in the Global South from the second half of the twentieth century. It highlights the major processes responsible for urban growth and how governments have responded to phenomena such as 'urban primacy' and 'hyperurbanisation'. The chapter also touches upon the concepts of 'sustainable cities' and 'urban livability', evolving forms of urban management in the wake of rec-ommendations emanating from successive UN-Habitat conferences, and some of the most pressing policy priorities as more than half the world's population come to reside in cities. The discussion also covers access to shelter in urban areas of the South with particular reference to self-help housing and changing policy approaches to shelter delivery for the urban poor.

CHARACTERISTICS AND PROCESSES OF URBANISATION IN THE SOUTH

During the period 1950–2000, the global urban population grew nearly four times over, from 730 million to 2.8 billion, and by 2008, to 3.3 billion. This latter figure is not only equal to the Earth's total population in 1960, but means that for the first time in history half the world's inhabitants now resides in towns and cities. At a current annual growth rate of 2 per cent, average urban population increase across the world is virtually double that of the population in general. If these trends persist, the bulk of demo-graphic growth in coming decades will concentrate in urban areas and by 2030, we could see a total urban population of around 5 billion (see Figure 4.1). Most of this will be accounted for by Africa and Asia alone, where 'the accumulated urban growth of these two regions during the whole span of history will be duplicated in a single generation' (UNFPA, 2007: 1).

Alongside increasing trends to urban residence, is a tendency for growing city size. As many as 400 cities in the world now have populations of 1 million or more (termed 'million cities'), when two centuries ago, only two cities fitted this bill – London and Beijing (then Peking) (Satterthwaite,

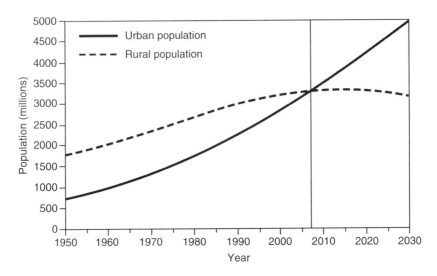

Source: Adapted from Beall and Fox (2007: figure 1).

Figure 4.1   World population and urbanisation trends

2005). The capital of Costa Rica, San José, while small by Latin American standards, and often appearing so in visual terms (see Figure 4.2), actually qualifies as a 'million city' when the boundaries are drawn around the San José Metropolitan Area which encompasses adjacent towns such as Heredia, Alajuela and Cartago.

A large number of centres with the current status of 'million city' (or more) experienced a twentyfold or more growth in population in only 50 years (1950–2000). These include many lesser-known centres such as Campinas, Conakry, Jeddah, Kaduna, Lomé, Niamey, Ougadougou, Santa Cruz and Shenzhen and Yaoundé, as well some of the more 'usual suspects' like Abidjan, Dar es Salaam, Dhaka, Khartoum, Kinshasa, Lagos, Nairobi, Tijuana, and Seoul (Satterthwaite, 2005; see also below). Moreover, by the year 2000 there were 42 cities with 5 million inhabitants, and as many as 18 with populations of 10 million or more.

Cities with 10 million plus inhabitants are termed 'mega-cities', and over three-quarters of these are in the developing world, including São Paulo, Rio de Janeiro, Mexico City, Buenos Aires, Lagos, Mumbai (formerly Bombay), Calcutta, Delhi, Dhaka, Karachi, Jakarta and Metro Manila (see Figure 4.3). Although the number of 'mega-cities' is anticipated to rise to 26 by 2020 (by then Mumbai, Delhi and Mexico City may well have become 'meta-cities', comprising 20 million or more residents), the

Source: Photo by Sylvia Chant.

Figure 4.2 San José, Costa Rica

Source: Photo by Sylvia Chant

Figure 4.3   Metro Manila, Philippines: skyline of the Makati business district

majority of urbanites will continue to live in centres with less than 1 million inhabitants (Satterthwaite, 2005). Often referred to as 'smaller', 'intermediate' or 'secondary cities', these have consistently contained more than half the total urban population in recent decades (see Figure 4.4).

Despite international attempts to standardise urban thresholds, the exact number of inhabitants a settlement must contain to qualify as 'urban' varies widely from country to country, ranging from as little as 1000 to 20000 (Satterthwaite, 2008). Moreover many countries use criteria other than population size to define urban areas, such as a settlement's political or administrative status, or the proportion of the labour force engaged in non-agricultural activities. Bearing in mind that international data sources tend to use countries' own definitions, which in strictly numerical terms lessens comparability, the share of the world population in urban areas in 2000 was purportedly 47 per cent, compared with 37.8 per cent in 1975 and a mere 13 per cent at the start of the twentieth century. Whereas around three-quarters of the population in the Global North have been urban since the mid-1960s, in developing regions this grew from 24 per cent to 40 per cent between 1965 and 2000 (UNCHS Habitat, 2001). As of 2005, when the world urban population was almost 49 per cent, 38 per cent of Africa's population resided in urban areas, 40 per cent in Asia and 77 per cent in Latin America and the Caribbean (UNFPA, 2007: 10–11). During the first three decades of the twenty-first century it is anticipated that an average of 7.1 million new residents a year will be added to urban areas in Latin America and the Caribbean, 15 million in Africa and as many as 43 million in Asia, such that 80 per cent of the world's urban population will be in the Global South by 2030 (see Figure 4.5).

The phenomenal pace of urban growth in the Global South during the past 60 years has led to this 'second wave' of urbanisation' being regarded as an 'historic shift' – the 'first wave' being the earlier, but much slower urbanisation of Europe and North America which took place over more than a century (see UNFPA, 2007). While national population growth rates in developing regions were in the order of 2–3 per cent per annum between the 1940s and 1980s (see Chapter 3), urban population growth rates averaged as much as 4–5 per cent during the same period (Gilbert and Gugler, 1992). Indeed, although rates have generally slowed down or levelled since the 1980s, especially in Latin America, in many countries in the South these still far exceed the developed world average of 0.75 per cent (see Table 4.1). In global terms, this has meant progressively shorter interludes of absolute increase. For example, while by 1960 it had taken 10000 years for the population living in urban areas to reach 1 billion, the next billion was added within 25 years, and for the population to increase from 3 to 4 billion by 2018 it will take only 15 years (see Satterthwaite, 2007: 1).

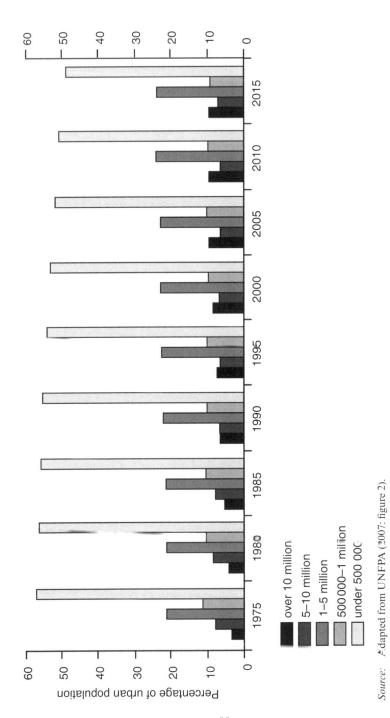

Source: Adapted from UNFPA (2007: figure 2).

Figure 4.4   World urban population by size class of settlement, 1975–2015

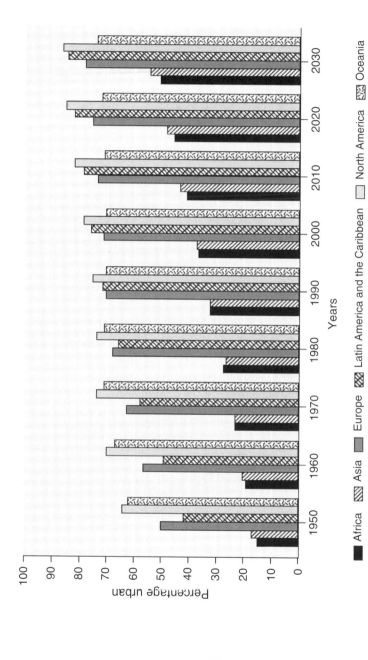

Source: Adapted from UNFPA (2007: figure 3) (www.unfpa.org.swp/2007/presskit/pdf/sowp 2007_eng.pdf).

Figure 4.5 Percentage of population in urban areas by region, 1950–2030

Table 4.1   Characteristics of urbanisation: selected countries of the Global South, 1970–2015

	Average annual population growth (%)			Average annual rate of urban population growth (%)			Population in capital city as % of urban population	
	1970–80	1980–92	2000–15*	1970–80	1980–92	2000–15*	1990	2000
Kenya	3.7	3.6	1.5	8.5	7.7	3.5	26	23.2
Egypt	2.1	2.4	1.5	2.5	2.5	2.3	39	34.1
India	2.3	2.1	1.2	3.9	3.1	2.7	4	4.1
Malaysia	2.4	2.5	1.4	5.0	4.8	2.4	22	10.8
Indonesia	2.3	1.8	1.1	5.1	5.1	3.1	17	12.7
Philippines	2.5	2.4	1.6	3.8	3.8	2.6	32	24.0
Mexico	2.9	2.0	1.2	4.1	2.9	1.6	34	24.7
Brazil	2.4	2.0	1.1	4.1	3.3	1.5	2	1.4
Argentina	1.6	1.3	1.1	2.2	1.7	1.3	41	37.7

Note: * Estimate.

Sources: UNCHS Habitat (2001: tables A1, A2 and B1); World Bank (1994. tables 25 and 31; 1996: tables 4 and 9).

Absolute population increments are clearly critical in determining urban growth, but also important differential *rates* of urban and national population growth. In Botswana, for example, only 4 per cent of the population was urban in 1965. However, thanks to urban population growth averaging 11.5 per cent per annum between 1970 and 1990 (more than three times that of the national mean of 3.2 per cent), by 2000 the proportion of people living in urban areas swelled to 50.3 per cent, notwithstanding that the majority of Botswana's urban centres remain small in size. Indeed, even the capital, Gaborone, had fewer than 200 000 inhabitants in 2001, with the next three towns down the urban hierarchy – Franciatown, Selebe-Phikwe and Lobatse – having under 100 000.

Demographically, two factors account for the massive urban transformation in less-developed countries in the post-war period:

1. Greater levels of natural increase in towns and cities (especially larger cities).
2. Migration.

Natural increase is becoming an increasingly important component of urban growth. Although rural fertility remains higher than in urban areas, mortality rates are also of greater magnitude. In the late 1990s, for example, the urban infant mortality rate in Bolivia was 58 per 1000 live births, whereas the rural rate was 94 per 1000. Other important factors fuelling the rising importance of natural increase in urban growth are the mounting size of urban centres, their frequently youthful age structure, and diminishing pools of potential rural–urban migrants. As summarised by Pelling (2002), as cities grow, so too does the proportion of population increase consti-tuted by *in situ* growth. Although it is difficult to determine with any preci-sion how much urban expansion is accounted for by natural increase, consensus tends to settle on an estimated figure of 60 percent (UNFPA, 2007).

Yet for cities at earlier stages in their development, both past and present, there is no doubt that migration has traditionally been massively significant. In Brazil, for example, an estimated two-thirds of Rio de Janeiro's population increase between 1940 and 1950 was due to in-migra-tion, with a further 45 per cent of the increase between 1950 and 1960. Up to 59 per cent of growth in the Ivory Coast capital of Abidjan between 1970 and 1980 was constituted by migration, and as much as 65 per cent of its Sierra Leonean counterpart Freetown (Gilbert and Gugler, 1992). In Mexico in the early 1970s, it was estimated that over 1000 migrants arrived in the capital every day. In China, where there were strict controls on rural–urban migration up to the late 1970s, that migration predominates in contemporary urban growth – with an estimated 18 million moving annu-ally to the country's rapidly expanding hubs of export industry – is also attributable to low urban fertility, which until recently was the result of an aggressive 'one child' policy (see UNFPA, 2007: 12–13; also Chapter 3, this volume).

Among the factors identified as responsible for migration-driven urban growth in the early post-war period are 'urban bias' in state and private sector investment in economic activity, greater provision of welfare (for example, education and health services) in towns and cities, modernisation and restructuring of the agricultural sector, and the development of trans-port and communications (see Gilbert and Gugler, 1992; Satterthwaite, 2007).

A further factor, particularly pertinent to Africa, is decolonisation, which often led to the lifting of bars on indigenous settlement in urban areas, and frequently favoured capital cities as the nerve centres of inde-pendent nation building (Satterthwaite, 2007: 47–51). Also important in many parts of this region have been wars and civil conflicts, often motivated by a combination of environmental, economic and political factors, with climate change anticipated to be a major force in years to come (Brown, 2008). Although, as discussed in Chapter 2, crime and violence are more pronounced in urban than rural areas, and ethno-political clashes in Kenya during the spring of 2008 were concentrated in the capital, Nairobi, in some instances the civilian victims of internal conflict have flocked to cities in the belief that they will be less vulnerable than in the countryside. Luanda, for example, contains the vast bulk of Angola's Internally Displaced Persons (IDPs).

It is important to bear in mind that different reasons for urban growth may predominate at different points in time. For example, the original impetus for concentrated urban growth in Dhaka stemmed from the Partition of India in 1947, when it became the capital of East Pakistan, and from 1971, the capital of Bangladesh. Yet in the past 20 years, continued growth of the metropolis has been less due to its centralisation of political and administrative functions, as to the massive expansion of export-oriented garments production (Satterthwaite, 2005: 47–8).

Urban Primacy and Hyperurbanisation

Aside from high growth rates of urban populations in the post-war period, another classic feature has been that of 'urban primacy' which refers to the situation whereby one or two cities in a given country are disproportion-ately larger than the rest, giving rise to a 'top-heavy' urban hierarchy. Notwithstanding different methods of measuring urban primacy, a common variant is that primacy obtains where the population of the major city is substantially more than twice that of the second largest city, more than three times that of the third and so on. Generally speaking the largest city is a capital or port, often created and/or consolidated during colonial occupation. On average primate cities are four times larger than the next largest city in developing regions. Indeed, in Middle America, up to 60 per cent of the national population resides in capital cities, with the most strik-ing example being Guatemala City, which is 125 times larger than Guatemala's second urban centre, Quetzaltenango (Pelling, 2002).

Often associated with urban primacy in developing regions is the phe-nomenon of 'hyperurbanisation' (sometimes referred to as 'overurbanisation' or 'urban inflation'). This term conveys the notion of a level of demographic growth out of proportion with the capacity of the urban economy (particu-larly the industrial sector) to support its populace (see Gilbert, 1995; Gilbert and Gugler, 1992). Another aspect emphasised by UNCHS Habitat (2001) is the often heavy concentration of investment and economic activity in one or two cities, which undermines the prospects for balanced economic growth at a national scale. The fact that in 1981 Manila had 60 per cent of all manu-facturing plants in the Philippines is illustrative here.

Yet while it is true in many cases that rapid and dramatic urban growth can cause problems for developing nations, the concepts of hyperurbanisation and primacy have both been contested as highly subjective and ethnocentric (Gilbert, 1998). This is especially pertinent at present when so many 'global cities', most of which are located in the North, are extremely large in size, are characterised by high densities of skills, infrastructure and investment, and are pre-eminent in economic growth (Satterthwaite, 2005). Indeed, although reactions to urban growth in the South have often been negative, berating the 'costs' of unplanned city sprawl such as poverty, unemployment, crime, disease and political volatility, a number of individuals and organisations have sought to dispel the myth of skewed urban growth as a unilaterally 'bad thing'. For example, UNFPA's 2007 *State of the World's Population Report*, subtitled *Unleashing the Potential of Urban Growth*, affirms, on the one hand, that 'The current concentration of poverty, slum growth and social disruption in cities does paint a threatening picture' (UNFPA, 2007: 1), but, on the other, qualifies the statement by noting that 'no country in the industrial age has ever achieved significant economic growth without urbanisation. Cities concentrate poverty, but they also represent the best hope of escaping it' (ibid.; see also Figure 4.6).

As it is, there is mounting evidence that primacy will be a lesser issue in the twenty-first century than in the twentieth. Declining primacy owes partly to the negative effects of size such as congestion, protracted journeys to work and lack of affordable land. Another set of factors is economic, with some of the South's primate giants having been hit very hard either by national economic crises or neoliberal economic restructuring, or both. In Mexico, for example, during the 'lost decade' of the 1980s, up to one-quarter of the capital's manufacturing jobs were lost (Gilbert, 1998). Where traditional firms did not shut down completely in the wake of increased global competition, they often relocated to smaller centres as a means of cutting costs (see Satterthwaite, 2007). Added to this, the shift in national economic policy from import-substitution to export industry favoured a number of other urban locations with pre-existing concentrations of export activity, such as on the US–Mexico border (see Chapter 5, this volume),

Besides economic reasons for movement away from primate cities, considerations revolving around environment and quality of life seem to be playing an increasingly important role, especially among middle-income groups (Izazola, 2004). Accepting the multiplicity of factors involved, beyond Mexico, rates of urban primacy are slowing down in favour of the growth of 'secondary' or 'intermediate' cities in a number of other Latin American countries such as Argentina, Chile and Brazil.

Diversification of migration destinations is also noted in Africa, especially north of the Sahara. In Egypt, for example, major cities such as Cairo and Alexandria have ceased to be centres of rural in-migration, with a

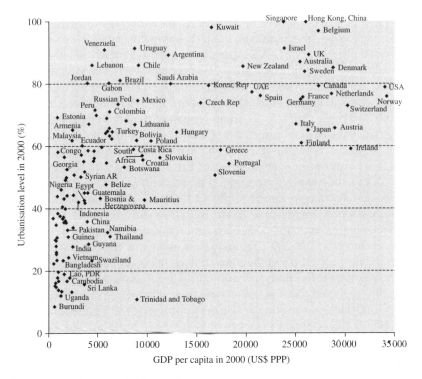

Source: Satterthwaite (2007: figure 14).

Figure 4.6   *The association between levels of urbanisation and average per*
          capita income, 2000

spatial diffusion of urban development through the growth of agro-towns,
urban villages and new industrial centres (see Bayat and Dennis, 2000).

Such tendencies are not so apparent in Southeast Asia, however. Here, a
number of contrasting trends have been noted for countries such as
Malaysia, China, Indonesia, including.

1. Renewed polarisation of metropolitan centres, particularly those
    which are centres of multinational manufacturing.
2. The formation of so-called 'mega-urban regions' which extend far
    beyond their metropolitan cores.
3. The emergence of 'global cities' for the international management and
    control of circuits of capital.
4. A new focus on transborder regions (see UNCHS Habitat, 1996; Van
    Grunsven, 1998).

Table 4.2   The world's largest cities by region, 1800–2000

Region	1800	1900	1950	2000
Number of 'million cities'				
World	2	16	75	380
Africa	0	0	2	37
Asia	1	3	28	192
China	1	1	12	86
India		1	5	32
Europe	1	9	22	53
Latin America and the Caribbean	0	0*	7	51
Northern America	0	4	14	41
USA		4	12	37
Oceania	0	0	2	6
Regional distribution of the world's largest 100 cities				
World	100	100	100	100
Africa	5	2	3	8
Asia	63	22	42	49
China	23	13	18	17
India	18	4	6	8
Europe	28	54	26	10
Latin America and the Caribbean	3	5	8	16
Northern America	0	15	19	15
USA	0	15	17	13
Oceania	0	2	2	2
Average size of the world's 100 largest cities	187 520	728 270	2.0m	6.3m

Notes:
* Some estimates suggest that Rio de Janeiro had reached 1 million inhabitants by 1900 while other sources suggest it had just under 1 million.
Cities that have changed their country-classifications and nations that have changed regions are considered to be in the country or region that they are currently in for this whole period. For instance, Hong Kong is counted as being in China for all the above years while the Russian Federation is considered part of Europe.

Source: Satterthwaite (2008: table 2).

Indeed, Asia, more generally, is a clear leader in terms of both its number of 'million cities', and in respect of being home to nearly half the largest 100 cities in the world (Table 4.2). This said, despite the suggestion that 'global cities' are emerging, it is important not to conflate these with the likes of 'mega-cities' such as Shanghai, Beijing, Tianjin and Jakarta, which are obviously huge in size, but probably do not rank as 'global cities' if these are understood as centres of 'command and control'.

Indeed, it has been asserted that the only truly global cities in this corner of the world are Tokyo and Osaka, with Taipei being the only prospective global city outside the traditional economic core (see Sassen, 2002a; Taylor et al., 2000).

URBAN POLICIES AND MANAGEMENT

Having identified some key features of urbanisation in the Global South, this section reviews policy interventions which have characterised the last few decades, including strategies to stem primacy and hyperurbanisation and to promote sustainable urbanisation, as well as new forms of urban management.

Although many cities in developing nations have grown rapidly and haphazardly in the absence of adequate or proactive planning, various efforts have been made to quell primacy and hyperurbanisation, usually by attempting to stem the tide of rural outmigration, or by diverting the population from the largest cities (see Gilbert and Gugler, 1992). Over and above evictions from urban areas, or the denial of essential services to poor migrants, one strategy has entailed the direction of more investment and/or public expenditure to the rural sector. Even today, India's concern to arrest urban development has led to the establishment of a National Rural Employment Scheme (launched in 2005), which guarantees 1000 days of employment in every financial year for each rural household with an adult member willing to do unskilled manual work (UNFPA, 2007: 12; see also Gupta, 2009). Whether or not this will actually discourage rural–urban migration remains to be seen, with experience suggesting that disparities between rural and urban wages and infrastructure have usually failed to stall people's movement. This is even the case in socialist countries such as Cuba and China, which, prior to economic liberalisation in the 1990s, endeavoured to make migration to urban areas illegal without proof of employment. On top of the assertion that attempts to prevent migration are 'futile', they can also be counter-productive or even damaging. As asserted by UNFPA (2007: 3 and 69), restrictive measures constitute a 'violation of people's rights . . . Opposing migration and refusing to help the urban poor for fear of attracting additional migrants merely increases poverty and environmental degradation'.

Regarding strategies to divert migrants from primate cities, the two most common interventions have been decentralisation and the creation of new towns.

Decentralisation

Efforts at decentralisation have aimed to encourage migration to pre-existing smaller and intermediate urban centres either by creating more in the way of infrastructure, services and employment, and/or restricting the location of new enterprises in large cities and metropolitan areas. This has often involved the stimulation of industrial development in secondary urban centres via the granting of subsidies, tax concessions, loans and grants. For example, in Peru between 1958 and 1990, successive administrations attempted to induce firms to locate outside Lima through granting graduated relief on profit taxes, the greatest reductions being given to companies moving into the most peripheral *selva* (jungle) region, the second greatest to those settling in the intermediately located highlands and the third to those operating on the coast beyond Lima itself (Becker and Morrison, 1997).

Although different versions of this kind of policy have been pursued in a wide number of countries, and with varying degrees of success, the power of macroeconomic processes has usually been more significant than specific government attempts to (re)direct migration. In other words, secondary urbanisation has been driven primarily by market forces, such as diseconomies of scale in metropolitan areas, and/or the development and expansion of new economic activities associated with neoliberal restructuring such as international tourism and export manufacturing. This is certainly the case in Mexico City during the 1980s, which experienced net outmigration to smaller cities within a 200 kilometre radius, such as Querétaro, Toluca and Puebla, as well as to core centres of the *maquiladora* (export manufacturing) industry on the northern border such as Tijuana and Ciudad Juárez. Although post-1990, the situation is more one of 'migratory equilibrium' (Izazola, 2004), there is little doubt that cities in Mexico other than the capital, especially in the northern and central states, now exert powerful comparative attractions for a range of economic, environmental, social, cultural and political reasons (ibid.). In turn, tendencies towards metropolitan de-concentration more broadly in Latin America have been such that Gilbert (1995: 323) has argued that 'The recession achieved in ten years what attempts at regional development had failed to do in thirty.'

Creation of New Towns

Following on from this, the experience of new town creation is also one of rather mixed achievement. Over and above addressing the problems of urban primacy and hyperurbanisation, new towns have been created in order to alleviate urban congestion, to redistribute population, to exploit natural resources, to revive economically depressed areas, to address housing needs and to make new capital cities (see Atash, 2000). Sometimes this has consisted of setting-up 'satellite towns' or 'suburban growth poles' near enough to the capital or largest city so that they benefit from proximity to long-established centres, but sufficiently distant to constitute separate settlements. Examples here include the development of the satellite town of Petaling Java near Kuala Lumpur, Malaysia or Banweol to the south of Seoul in South Korea (Gilbert and Gugler, 1992). New towns have also been created in isolated areas. One classic example is Brasilia which became the political capital of Brazil in 1968 and was intended to open up the interior. Other notable examples of new administrative capitals include Islamabad (Pakistan), Chandigarh (in the Indian Punjab) and Lilongwe (Malawi) (ibid.).

In relation to new town policies in Iran, Atash (2000) identifies four main sets of issues inhibiting success:

1. Delays and incompleteness resulting from the length of time involved in preparing new town master plans, the shortage of public and private capital to develop new towns, lack of co-ordination among different stakeholders (government ministries, agencies, development companies, contractors and so on) and lack of technical, administrative and managerial support.
2. The fact that development companies tend to build housing first, but neglect ancillary infrastructure such as shopping centres, educational facilities and so on, which makes life very hard for new residents.
3. The lack of identity, character and sense of place in new centres, which often become 'soulless dormitory towns'.
4. The high cost of developing barren, raw land into developable sites in new towns, which pushes up the price of land and housing. Together with lack of employment opportunities, this is clearly offputting for prospective settlers.

SUSTAINABLE URBANISATION

'Sustainable urbanisation' has become a major element in the urban development lexicon since the second UN conference on Human Settlements – HABITAT II – held in Istanbul in 1996. However, now, as then, there is no clear consensus on how the term should be defined.

In its most inclusive form the concept embodies several goals and dimensions – economic, environmental, social, political, demographic, institutional and cultural. Yet, not only is it difficult to pursue all objectives simultaneously, but sometimes advances in one dimension may cause regressive tendencies in another (Satterthwaite, 1997). Indeed, in many cases sustainable development initiatives can perpetuate existing social and economic inequalities. Programmes of basic services, sanitation, water supply and so on, so fundamental for more environment- and social-friendly sustainability, for example, are often glossed over in the interest of investments orientated to enhancing the economic competitiveness of large-scale capitalist enterprises. Since this frequently undermines the livelihoods of smaller producers and the poor, it can comprise their present and future well-being. In relation to the intermediate regional city of Ujung Pandang, on Indonesia's eastern island of Sulawesi, Parnwell and Turner (1998) argue that because the local economy is so competitive and unequal the 'urban underclass', whose main preoccupations revolve around 'survivalism', have little chance of setting their sights above basic day-to-day subsistence. This is compounded by the fact that the Indonesian government has given very little support to small-scale enterprises. The only features that look likely to be sustained in Ujung Pandang for the foreseeable future are poverty and inequality (ibid.; see also Fold and Wangel, 1998; Pelling, 2002).

Environmental issues have occupied a particularly prominent, and contested, role within sustainable urbanisation debates. On the one hand, cities are often associated with pollution and greenhouse gases (particularly carbon dioxide emissions), resource degradation and waste generation, and, as such, responsible for leaving a massive 'ecological footprint' extending way beyond their territorial boundaries (You, 2007). On the flip side is that cities are also environmentally vulnerable. In the context of climate change, for example, low-income urban populations occupying flimsy housing on precarious land sites are deemed to be at considerable risk from the hazards associated with sea-level rise and extreme weather events (ibid.; also Brown, 2008; *Environment and Urbanisation*, 2007a; Satterthwaite et al., 2007). By the same token, there is considerable evidence to suggest that urban localities actually offer better chances for long-term sustainability. Although the space occupied by urban settlement at a global scale is currently increasing at around twice the rate of the numbers of urban inhabitants, towns and cities actually concentrate half the earth's population on only 3 per cent of its land area. High average density, in turn, allows for lower unit costs of infrastructure and service provision (with knock-on effects for people's health), as well as greater prospects for recycling, less use of motorised transport and so on (see UNFPA, 2007).

Yet how far urban planning privileges different dimensions of sustainability will depend very much on theoretical and political standpoints (not to mention power and resources) of different stakeholders. As Pelling (2002) has argued, it is often the case that a 'weak sustainability' approach prevails. 'Weak sustainability' has little regard for the intrinsic value of ecological assets because it believes that technology can solve environmental problems, and human capital can act as a substitute for natural assets. This is described by Pelling as being an 'anthropocentric' view. Yet in practice it often boils down to a 'business as usual' attitude which allows cities (and their wealthier inhabitants) to carry on with little regard for their impacts on the increasingly large hinterlands from which they draw their resources or dump their wastes. At the other end of the spectrum, 'strong sustainability' is characterised by a more 'ecocentric' view and seeks to minimise the loss of natural capital in the first place. Accordingly, there is emphasis on prevention rather than cure, such that, instead of manufacturing fuel-efficient cars, consideration is given to how cities might be designed to minimise the need for vehicular transport. The 'strong sustainability' approach is also interested in promoting more equitable consumption patterns (ibid.).

In some cases, it appears to have been possible to serve a number of priorities simultaneously, as discussed by Muller (2008) in South Africa. In the immediate post-apartheid era the new democratic government sought to expand water and sanitation to unserved communities, and in 2001 undertook to supply a basic amount of water free of charge to all citizens. While this innovative policy intervention has not been without problems, Muller (2008: 67) concludes that 'addressing social and environmental dimensions together with economic dimensions can lead to more effective and sustainable policy'.

Yet whether this kind of initiative, and the scope to prioritise social and environmental concerns to the same degree as economic growth elsewhere, is a big question, especially in light of growing competition between cities of the south for footloose foreign investment. As pointed out by Douglass (2002), the number of countries with policies favourable to foreign investment has increased dramatically over the past 20 years. In 1980, only 19 developing countries had 'open door' regimes offering tax holidays, free infrastructure, greenfield sites and other dispensations to foreign investors. By 2000, a staggering 149 countries had jumped on the bandwagon, and with even greater concessions in respect of subsidies, tax relief and freedom from regulation (see also Chapter 5, this volume). Cities are vital to these strategies, and while at one level Douglass notes that competition has the potential to increase economic efficiency, there is so much risk and short-termism that the longer-term viability and resilience of cities and regions is threatened (ibid.). In turn, the chances of social elements of sustainability being given precedence are undermined by neoliberalism, which has placed emphasis on cities (re)asserting their roles as 'engines of growth' and pillars of economic efficiency. The tools to advance these objectives include dereg-ulation and/or the reform of regulatory regimes in land, housing, finance, infrastructure, services and employment, the 'enablement' of markets and privatisation, decentralisation, and institutional and management capacity building. This scenario departs significantly from the notion that states should play a strong role in controlling, directing and rationalising urban growth. Even if this was often difficult in practice, ideally a 'Master Plan' would direct land uses, the location of activities and infrastructure and so on (see Burgess et al., 1997).

Yet somewhat paradoxically, perhaps, it is precisely the 'rolling back' of the (centralised) state, which has opened up space for new, more democ-ratic forms of urban governance. As noted by the compiler of UN-Habitat's 2001 *Global Report on Human Settlements*, Willem van Vliet (2002: 38):

> The new planning is less codified and technical, more innovative and entrepre-neurial. It is also more participatory and concerned with projects rather than whole urban systems . . . It seems to forge agreements through negotiation and mediation among contesting parties . . . As planning becomes more difficult to define as a state-based process of intervention, it finds expression in a greater diversity of forms, including advocacy for and mobilisation of community-based groups that seek to assert their rights to the city.

With planning gradually shifting from being a relatively closed physical and technocratic exercise, to being more open, participatory and inclusive, governments and municipalities arguably come under greater pressure not just to play the role of 'enablers' to facilitate the functioning of markets, but also to act as agents for greater social justice and environmental sus-tainability (van Vliet, 2002). These principles are strongly endorsed by the UN-HABITAT/World Bank 'Cities Alliance', a global coalition of cities and development partners, whose aim is to promote better cities (UN-HABITAT, 2006). Similarly, regional initiatives such as the Urban Management Programme of Latin America and the Caribbean professes a desire not only to strengthen the contribution that cities can make to economic growth, but to work with cities to further social development and the elimination of poverty (see *Environment and Urbanisation*, 2001a).

Indeed, as exemplified in the example of free water in South Africa (Muller, 2008), this can be conducive to economic buoyancy. Without investments in the social sector, markets do not work particularly efficiently. At the very least, therefore, there is a strong instrumental impetus to check the unfettered operation of market forces.

URBAN LIVEABILITY

Another concept which has emerged out of debates on sustainable urbanisation is that of 'urban liveability'. Douglass (2002: 59) asserts that 'urban liveability' has evolved as a reaction to the degradation of cities as living spaces due to the aggressive pursuit of economic growth and intensification of intercity competition. The concept of the 'liveable city' emphasises the importance of investments in the physical and social quality of life, and embraces four main elements:

1. Widening life chances through investments in human capital and well-being (for example, through health and education), making homes and communities safe and nurturing for people, and building social capital (relations of trust and reciprocity) via daily interaction and collective problem-solving.
2. Meaningful work and livelihood opportunities – not just for economic ends but for self-esteem and personal fulfilment, including household work as well as paid work.
3. A safe and clean environment for health, well-being and economic growth – that is, eliminating pollution, rubbish, and ensuring the adequate provision of services and infrastructure.
4. Good governance – a 'liveable city' is one in which governments, community-based and private sector interests work alongside one another.

Common terms in this lexicon include inclusion, participation, partnerships and transparency. Cutting across these four elements, are the goals of social and environmental justice, gender equality, poverty reduction and citizen empowerment.

These principles are also enshrined in the MDGs (see Chapter 1), with particular importance for urban areas being two targets in MDG 7 – namely, access to an improved water source and sanitation (Target 10), and improvements in the lives of 100 million slum dwellers (Target 11) (Box 1.1). Both are critical given the charge that 'Urbanisation is virtually synonymous with slum growth' (UN-Habitat, 2006), as substantiated by figures from UN-Habitat's Global Urban Observatory which reveal that the growth rate of slums is often only marginally behind urban growth rates in general. In sub-Saharan Africa, where this is particularly pertinent, for example, in 2004 slum growth was 4.53 per cent per annum, and urban growth, 4.58 per cent.

The issue of how 'slums' are defined is clearly critical in this diagnosis. Although the term 'slum' originated in Europe in the nineteenth century, it has increasingly come to be the accepted nomenclature for areas of low-income housing in developing countries. This is partly because of an initiative undertaken in 2002 by a team comprising personnel from UN-Habitat, the UN Statistics Division (UNSD) and the UN-Habitat/World Bank 'Cities Alliance' to forge a definition of 'slum' which would allow for more accurate quantification and be of more use for governments and other partners 'on the ground'. The resultant definition involves five criteria revolving around physical, social, economic and political deprivation, with one or more of the following constituting a slum:

1. Lack of access to an 'improved water supply' – meaning adequate amount (notionally 20 litres per person per day), affordable cost (less than 10 per cent of household income), and not involving 'extreme effort' on part of women and children.
2. Lack of access to 'improved sanitation', for example, direct connection to a public sewer or septic tank, in the form of a private toilet, or a communal toilet not shared by 'too many people'.
3. Overcrowding – more than two people per habitable room.
4. Non-durable housing structures – housing built in a hazardous location, or which is vulnerable to rapid destruction, and/or which is composed of poor quality building materials not up to task of providing people with protection from the elements.
5. (In)security of tenure – where people do not have effective protection from forced evictions, that is, do not possess *de jure* occupancy rights (formal title deed or rental contract), or *de facto* rights (*perceived* protection against forced eviction) (see Arimah, 2007; Unger and Riley, 2007; UN-Habitat, 2006).

Several of these aspects are discussed below in relation to access to shelter, but it is important to flag up here that although slums are not new, they presently exist on a massive scale, housing around one billion people. This equates to one in three urban dwellers, among whom 90 per cent are in the developing world (see Figure 4.7). As of 2005, sub-Saharan Africa had the highest share of its urban population residing in slums (72 per cent), South Asia the next highest, at 57 per cent, and Latin America the lowest, at 31 per cent. Although the overall proportion of people living in slums in developing regions declined from 47 per cent in 1990 to 41 per cent in 2000, the numbers involved are huge, and in light of this, Target 11 of the MDGs, to improve the lives of 100 million slum dwellers, is hardly likely to scratch the surface, especially given the projection that poor people will continue to comprise a large proportion of urban inhabitants in future (Arimah, 2007). Indeed, in light of this scenario, and based on experiences of the past, three urgent policy priorities have been identified for the urban transition of the

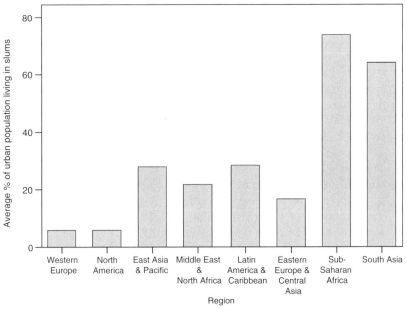

Source: Adapted from Beall and Fox (2007: figure 3).

Figure 4.7   Slum population by world region

twentieth-first century. These are, first, that the rights of the poor to the city
are respected. This includes advances in social development which promote
gender equality and empowerment, such as universal education and facilities for meeting reproductive health needs. These are not only important in
their own right but could also go a long way to reducing natural increase in
urban areas, which is often highest in slum neighbourhoods (Figure 4.8).
The second main priority is the need to plan urban land use in such a way
as to reduce poverty and ensure sustainability. This would nominally
involve ensuring that city authorities anticipate the land and infrastructural
needs of low-income residents, rather than letting settlements develop in a
random, sprawling and unserviced way with all the attendant health and
environmental implications. The third priority, reflecting the principle that
'good governance' is essential to decent, sustainable cities, is to broaden
stakeholder involvement in urban politics and planning. This requires
greater support by governments and international agencies of community
organisations that have frequently played a vital role in protecting the liveli
hoods and rights of low-income groups, as discussed below in relation to
housing.

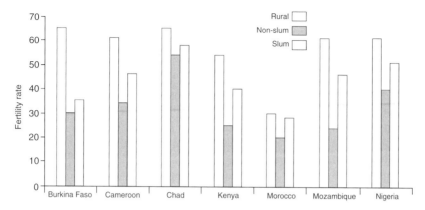

Source: Adapted from UNFPA (2007: figure 4).

Figure 4.8   *Average total fertility rate of residents of rural areas, urban slums and non-slum urban areas, selected African countries, 2003–04*

ACCESS TO SHELTER

Decent shelter for all is a *sine qua non* of sustainable urbanisation, but given the large number of slum dwellers in Asia, Africa and Latin America, it is clear that the prospects of this are somewhat remote. Shortfalls in shelter and urban services are usually attributed not just to poverty, but to the failure of state capacity and political will.

Although conventional private sector housing is usually well beyond the financial possibilities of low-income populations, governments have rarely stepped in to fill the breach. This is because, as Gilbert (2002: 305) describes, housing occupies a rather 'awkward' realm between the economic and the social. According to Gilbert the traditional disinterest of economists in housing is because they do not regard it as contributing to economic growth, even if it is arguably inconceivable that a labour force would not need to have shelter! As far as social planners are concerned, housing has not been a priority due to cost: it is expensive to produce (the per capita cost of housing is higher than the per capita cost of providing primary education, or even medical care), and unlike other social interventions, which tend to be targeted, for example, education to the young, pensions to the old and health care to the sick or pregnant, everyone wants a house (ibid.).

Public expenditure on housing has thus been small, and in Latin America, for instance, has seldom risen above 2 per cent of GDP (Gilbert, 2002). Given the general decline of central government spending on the social sector in the wake of neoliberal restructuring, there are only small chances of raising current levels.

This also applies in the majority of countries outside the region. Except for socialist nations such as Cuba, or the likes of wealthier states like Singapore and Hong Kong, where the pressures of small island development have left little option other than for planned growth (see Drakakis-Smith, 1987), comprehensive public housing programmes are rare. And in cases where public or international agency-sponsored housing is provided, this tends to falls into the hands of state employees, formal sector workers and the better-off among the poor, as in the classic case of the *superbloques* of Venezuela built in the 1950s under the dictatorship of President Marcos Pérez Jiménez. Most of the very poor, whose homes in the squatter settlements had been bulldozed in the name of rehousing, ended up crowding in with other poor families in order to be able to pay the rents and maintenance charges, or were forced to leave altogether (see Potter and Lloyd-Evans, 1998). Since state housing policy here and elsewhere has tended to allocate housing to the 'haves' rather than the 'have-nots', the poor have generally had to find their own solution. Among the main alternatives are the following.

Outright or Semi-outright Homelessness

This is sometimes described as 'rooflessness' and involves people 'sleeping rough' or in very makeshift arrangements. Examples include the rooftop dwellers of Cairo, or the pavement dwellers of Mumbai or Calcutta who pay a nightly rent for the right to a space on the sidewalk. Mosque-dwelling is also noted for some Islamic countries. Yet what is possibly surprising, as noted by Gilbert (2008b), is that except in South Asia, where an estimated 7.8 per cent of the population lives on the streets, levels of homelessness are actually less in Africa (0.8 per cent), East Asia (0.4 per cent) and Latin America (0.6 per cent), than in the advanced economies (0.9 per cent).

'Sharing'

Sharing involves multi-occupancy whereby people lend out part of their home or land plot 'rent free' to relatives – usually before they get their own home (see Beijard,1995; Varley,1993). Since sharing is frequently a temporary, if sometime protracted, phenomenon, and the boundaries are often blurred between what is actually a shared residence and what is an extended household united by shared function (see Chapter 9, this volume), precise figures are difficult to determine.

Renting

This is predominantly in the private sector and falls into two main types:

1. Inner-city tenement buildings, which may be purpose-built, or which may be converted from old houses subdivided into single rooms and small apartments with communal facilities. The latter are known as *vecindades* in Mexico, and *mesones* in El Salvador. In the Greater Banjul Area of The Gambia, rental compounds often take the form of 'line houses', where single-storey rows of four or five units face on to each other over narrow concrete passageways. In this type of rental arrangement the landlord usually lives off-site, and manages the property through formal rental contracts (see Figure 4.9).
2. Renting in peri-urban irregular settlements (see below), where tenants and landlords may live side by side on the premises, and tenancies are based on more informal agreements (Gilbert, 2003; Kumar, 1996; 2001).

The proportion of people in rental accommodation varies from country to country and city to city depending on land availability, price and ease of access to home ownership (see Table 4.3). While it is important to acknowledge that some people choose to rent because they only intend to stay temporarily in towns, or prefer to invest what income they have in a business (see Edwards, 1982; Gilbert and Varley, 1991), it is more usually the case that financial constraints, combined with rising land scarcity, force them into rental tenure. This would appear to be particularly applicable to female-headed households (see Chapter 9, this volume). For example, a study by Miraftab (2001) drawing on a UN Gender and Habitat programme in 16 low-income communities in Ghana, Senegal, Tanzania, Uganda, Zambia, Sri Lanka, Colombia and Costa Rica, found that increasingly high costs of housing relative to people's incomes (owing, *inter alia*, to rising competition for urban land, downward raiding by impoverished middle classes and so on), is making home ownership particularly inaccessible to women. As such, households with female heads often end up in rental accommodation where they may be much more constrained in their use of space (for example, for income-generating ventures), than in owner-occupied shelter (see also Chant, 2007c, and below).

Owner-occupancy (or Quasi Owner-occupancy) in Irregular or Self-help Settlements

Irregular settlements are referred to popularly as 'shanty towns' (see Table 4.4), and have long housed the majority of the urban poor in most parts of

Source: Photo by Sylvia Chant.

Figure 4.9 Rental 'line house', Banjul, The Gambia

Table 4.3 Tenure categories by region, 1998 (percentages)

Region	Formal owner	Formal rental	Squatter (including informal rent-paying)	Other
Africa	25	23	38	15
Asia (without China)	29	19	45	7
China	35	50	9	6
Eastern Europe and Central Asia	65	34	1	3
Latin America and the Caribbean	48	21	25	6
Western Europe and others HICs	40	57	2	1
World	42	34	19	5

Source: Adapted from UN-Habitat (2004: table 5).

the Global South (see Gilbert and Gugler, 1992; UNCHS Habitat, 2001; Vaa, 2000). Irregular settlements originate through the appropriation of land via invasion or informal sale/purchase, and, as a result, are characterised by an absence of legal title in the first instance.

Irregular or self-help settlements may be divided into two main types:

1. *Squatter settlements.* These occur as a result of invasions on private or publicly owned land.
2. *Low-income or clandestine subdivisions.* Here the poor buy cheap land which is sold off illegally, usually without services, by owners or brokers who lack authorisation to sell for low-income housing development. Thus settlements are illegal or clandestine because they offend planning regulations: they lack official permission and/or they fail to comply with minimum norms of servicing and building standards (Gilbert and Gugler, 1992).

In many cases the only land available to the poor is that which is not being used for other purposes. As such, land may be peripherally located (whether physically distant, or beyond the reach of existing transport and service networks), and/or is situated in areas liable to geological or environmental hazard, such as hillsides, ravines, river banks, estuarine or marine fringes, or railway sidings (see Figures 4.10 and 4.11).

As the term implies, self-help housing is generally financed and organised by households themselves, although it is not necessarily self-built

Table 4.4   Terminology for self-help settlements

	Academic/planning term	Vernacular/popular term
Generic	Self-help settlements	Shantytowns
	Irregular settlements	(Peri-urban) slums
	Informal settlements	
	Spontaneous settlements	
	Human settlements	
	Popular settlements	
	Uncontrolled settlements	
	Unauthorised settlements	
Specific (re. mode of occupation)	Squatter settlements/squatments/invasion (illegal/informal possession) Low-income/clandestine/pirate subdivision (illegal/informal purchase)	
Country-specific terms (selective list)	Argentina – *villa de misería* Bangladesh – *bustee* Brazil – *favela* Chile – *campamento* Colombia – *urbanización pirata, barrio pirata/clandestino* Costa Rica – *barrio de tugurios* Dominican Republic – *barrio, barrio marginal, barrio marginado* Ecuador – *suburbio* Egypt – *ashwaiyyat* Ethiopia – *chica* India – *bustee, jhopadpatti* Indonesia – *kampung* Iran – *halabi-abad, zagheh-neshini, hashieh-neshini* Jamaica – *shackyard* Kenya – *kijiji* Korea – *panjachon* Mexico – *colonia popular, asentamiento irregular, zona urbano-marginada* Morocco – *bidonville, mudun safi* Pakistan – *katchi abadi* Peru – *pueblo jóven, barriada* Philippines – *barong-barong* South Africa – *umjondolo* Sri Lanka – *pelli gewal* Tanzania – *maband, uswahilini* Thailand – *salam* Tunisia – *gourbiville, bidonville* Venezuela – *rancho, barrio*	

Table 4.4 (continued)

	Academic/planning term	Vernacular/ popular term
Terms for versions involving planning intervention	Human settlements Squatter upgrading programmes Incremental housing programmes Site-and-service schemes Core-housing projects	

because it often involves the recruitment of paid labour for more complicated aspects of construction. However, in the early stages of settlement development, housing tends to be built by people themselves using makeshift materials that can be dismantled and reassembled elsewhere in the event of eviction. Residents in many of these settlements also have to endure living without domestic piped drinking water, electricity, sewerage, paved roads and rubbish collection. Although this situation may persist for years, over time the likelihood is that services will arrive, and settlers will be able to purchase legal land titles through government agencies. Even if the latter process is often, again, protracted and highly politicised, many authors contend that 'security of tenure' – the main indicator of MDG Target 11 – is a prerequisite for the transition to a more permanent dwelling, as well as a gateway to increased access to credit, expansion of domestic businesses and so on. This is often interpreted as possession of a legal title deed, although some have argued that secure tenure is as much a 'state of mind', and that at least lack of formal title avoids land rate charges (see Gilbert, 2008b; Varley, 1987).

A number of advantages of self-help housing for the poor have been identified. One major benefit is that, unlike government or conventional private sector housing, which offers a completed high-priced product, self-help housing provides a flexible, progressive alternative which allows the poor to spread costs out over time, and to graduate their investments in accordance with their economic situation (Turner, 1982). A second advantage is that until legal titling brings the poor into the land registry and taxation system they are effectively able to avoid some official charges, as well as to save money which might otherwise have been spent on rent (Gilbert, 2008b). Third, self-help allows the poor to design their own dwelling environments, potentially more appropriate to local cultures, climates and resources. Last, but not least, self-help ownership can represent an investment. An important element here is that over time urban land tends to become increasingly scarce, added to which legalisation and service

Source: Photo by Sylvia Chant.

Figure 4.10 Foreshore housing, Metro Cebu, Philippines

Source: Photo by Sylvia Chant.

Figure 4.11   Railway siding settlement, Metro Manila, Philippines

provision are also likely to raise the value of the asset. Second, ownership gives the poor a form of collateral which can potentially facilitate access to credit. Third, unlike rental tenure, ownership and freedom of control over property provides scope for entrepreneurial ventures. For example, poor owner-occupiers in self-help settlements may engage in petty landlordism (see Figure 4.12), or operate small family businesses on the premises (see Gilbert, 2003; Kumar, 2001; also Chapter 6, this volume).

However, as intimated previously, there are also several disadvantages. Occupants may have to live for several years in a shelter of markedly inferior quality. Coupled with an absence of basic urban services such as water and sewerage this can be extremely onerous, especially for women, who are the most direct users of housing as primary providers of domestic labour and childcare (see Figure 4.13). Moreover, services which are paid for on the private market to substitute for lack of public or regulated private provision, such as tanker water or kerosene for lighting, are usually more expensive, not to mention inconvenient (see Chant, 1996; 2007c). For this reason it is no surprise to find that targets for the improvement of basic infrastructure and services feature alongside 'significant improvements for slum dwellers' in MDG 7.

Other criteria for improving the conditions of slum dwellers include better housing quality, more space per capita, secure tenure (for renters as well as owner-occupiers), property-related citizen entitlements such as an official address, police services and so on, and diminished 'exclusion' and/or discrimination against slum-dwelling populations (D'Cruz and Satterthwaite, 2005: 11).

CHANGING POLICY APPROACHES TO SHELTER

From the 1950s to the 1970s, self-help housing fell outside the remit of official housing policy in the bulk of developing countries (Pugh, 1997). Although the appearance of peri-urban slums and squatter settlements was sometimes likened to a 'cancer' or 'fungal growth', a policy of 'laissez-faire' or 'benign neglect' prevailed in the belief that these settlements were only a temporary phenomenon – a short-term outcome of massive rural–urban migration that would disappear in time (Arimah, 2007: 4–5). Such tolerance began to wear thin rather quickly in some countries, however, especially those in Latin America where the incidence and scale of urbanisation were greater. Wealthier urban inhabitants regarded land invasions as a threat to the institution of private property, and the settlements which grew out of them as breeding places of crime, social unrest and political insurrection. With these kinds of attitudes it is hardly surprising that many

Source: Photo by Cathy McIlwaine.

*Figure 4.12   Incremental building in low-income settlements to
accommodate petty landlordism (adding floors to rent out),
Bogotá, Colombia*

municipal and national governments tried to blot out the settlements, attempting to remove the squatters with verbal persuasion and, failing that, by coercion or physical eradication (sometimes with the helping hand of the police or military) (see Gilbert and Gugler, 1992).

Source: Photo by Sylvia Chant.

Figure 4.13   Women carrying washing back from River Cuale, Puerto Vallarta, Mexico

Self-help and John F.C. Turner

Although evictions continue today in many countries (see below), the seeds of an about-turn in neglect and/or negativity towards self-help housing were sown as far back as the 1960s, when, on the basis of fieldwork in self-help settlements in Peru, an American anthropologist, William Mangin, and a British architect-planner, John F.C. Turner, highlighted that 'shanty towns' were inhabited by stable, law-abiding and upwardly mobile aspiring citizens who demonstrated a remarkable capacity to create homes and neighbourhoods. Reflecting on a total of eight years in the *barriadas* of Peru, for example, Turner (1982: 101) claimed that 'Like the people themselves, we saw their settlements not as slums but as building sites. We shared their hopes and found the pity and despair of the occasional visits from professionals and politicians quite comic and wholly absurd.'

Having shown that the inhabitants of these settlements were merely poor, and not idle, parasitic, criminal or revolutionary, Turner pointed out how self-help housing made a very efficient use of abundant labour and scarce capital. Integral to his positive take on self-help housing was the notion of housing as a 'verb', as well as a 'noun', namely that the significance of housing lay not only in its 'exchange value', but in its 'use value'. Although the physical and servicing standards of self-help housing were often sub-optimal, at least they provided the poor with a means of accessing work in urban areas. With jobs secured, investments in improving quality could be made over time at the poor's own pace. As a 'progressive product', self-help shelter made a lot more sense than buying a finished housing unit of too high a quality at too high a price. 'Freedom to build' in self-help settlements also allowed the poor to design their dwelling environments in accordance with their own wishes. Other arguments offered by Turner for favouring self-help over government-built housing included its low cost. It could be constructed for up to half the price of government housing due to the absence of administrative charges (see Turner, 1970; 1972; 1976).

Key policy recommendations which emerged out of Turner's work were that governments should not only tolerate self-help, but even keep out of it unless able to make concessions towards facilitating access to land, and providing essential services and basic building materials. Turner also advocated dropping 'minimum norms' for servicing levels, in that as long as the poor had a home then services could wait.

Criticisms of Turner and Self-help

Despite the persuasive nature of these arguments, many challenged Turner's views on self-help, and deemed his policy prescriptions as naive.

One set of criticisms involved implicit claims of universal validity. For example, unserviced self-help might be tolerable in desert climates such as Lima where Turner had based his fieldwork, but less so in contexts where there was greater liability to heavy rains or flooding (see Edwards, 1982; Gilbert and Gugler, 1992).

There were also attacks on the voluntarism in Turner's analysis, especially from Marxian writers such as Rod Burgess. Burgess argued that while Turner had emphasised that in an ideal world people would choose to build their own homes over time, what Turner interpreted as choice was effectively compulsion in the absence of alternatives (Burgess, 1982).

The notion that self-help offered the poor 'freedom to build' was seen by Burgess as giving governments a cast-iron excuse to do nothing for the poor. Self-help 'individualised' the housing issue and let governments off the hook. In turn, self-help had a politically pacifying and/or conservative effect in that buying into ownership or quasi-ownership gave people a 'stake in the system' and diminished the likelihood of political unrest, which might arguably be the only really effective path to social justice. Indeed, Burgess felt that Turner had focused too much on blaming governments and bureaucracy for inefficiencies in the housing market, rather than turning the spotlight on the root causes of the housing problem, such as capitalism and inequality. Finally, a big question hovered over how governments might actually take up Turner's proposal that they should facilitate access to land for low-income groups, when 'slum clearance' continues to be depressingly common, especially where urban land is purportedly needed for 'city beautification', luxury housing, sports stadia, national security and so on, and/or where destruction of communities is politically-motivated. In Seoul, South Korea, for example, 5 million slum dwellers have been forcibly evicted in the past 30 years in the interests of the city's economic transformation (Satterthwaite, 2005). In Zimbabwe, Operation Mrambatsvina ('Restore the Order'), launched by President Robert Mugabe in May 2005, led to the burning and/or bulldozing of 25 informal settlements in Harare and other cities in the space of only four months. This left an estimated 700 000 people homeless and/or deprived of livelihoods, some of whom had no alternative but to return to rural areas (see Arimah, 2007: 5–6).

Other criticisms of self-help emanating from neo-Marxian scholarship more generally, included the notion that self-help cheapened or 'devalorised' labour power because it exerted downward pressure on wage rates, and involved house owners in a process of 'double exploitation'. Not only were occupants exploited in the workplace, earning low wages, under conditions of little protection and so on, but also in the home. In having to spend their spare time constructing their own shelters, this meant a lengthening of the working day (see Harms, 1982).

Notwithstanding these criticisms, Turner's support of self-help was seminal in provoking the transition from an era of 'autonomous self-help' (1950–71) to 'aided self-help' (1972–85) (Pugh, 1997). From the early 1970s onwards, governments began viewing self-help as a solution (rather than a problem), and started to regularise tenure and to introduce services. This was strongly influenced by the fact that in 1972, the World Bank declared strong support for self-help housing in developing countries, followed in 1976 (after the first Habitat Conference in Vancouver) by the UN, and other international aid and development agencies such as USAID and Save the Children.

The major types of programmes initiated by governments and international agencies during the era of 'aided self-help' were twofold:

1. *Sites and service schemes.* These consist of providing plots with basic services on which the poor build their own homes according to overall guidelines, but with some flexibility in terms of the time they take to construct a home of officially acceptable standards. In some cases serviced land plots come complete with a basic 'wet core' of bathroom and kitchen, and perhaps a living room as well. These are known as *core-housing programmes.* In site-and-service and core-housing programmes, the poor usually pay a deposit and then repay a social interest loan over 10 to 25 years.

2. *Squatter upgrading programmes.* Upgrading consists of initiatives to improve existing settlements via the transfer of legal land title, and the introduction of basic services, amenities and infrastructure. This alternative is more common, and as Gilbert (2008b) notes, has progressively eclipsed site-and-service schemes, partly because it is cheaper, and partly because it can go some way to preserving 'social capital' (that is, the social networks which people have built up in their neighbourhoods over time). Upgrading programmes often require community participation in project development, where, if not in the planning and design of the upgrading programme, residents become involved in the project implementation phase, which might involve co-operative house-building, the community digging of drainage channels and so on. Despite this input, however, charges for installation and services are still imposed upon residents. Indeed, while the World Bank may have showcased their support of self-help using Turner's rhetoric, considerations of 'user pay' rather than 'user control' have usually been uppermost, and in the process self-help was essentially converted into an arm of neoliberal economic policy (Pugh, 1997).

Since the post-1980 scaling-down of state bureaucracies and social programmes the idea that governments should 'help the poor to help

BOX 4.1   WORLD BANK RECOMMENDATIONS
            FOR OPERATIONALISING THE UNCHS
            GLOBAL STRATEGY FOR SHELTER FOR
            THE YEAR 2000

1. The development of housing finance systems.
2. The targeting of subsidies.
3. The development of property rights (regularising tenure, removing rent controls, etc.).
4. Infrastructure improvement.
5. The introduction of regulatory audits to remove regulations inhibiting housing sector development.
6. Improved organisation and competition in the building industry.
7. Institutional reform.

Source: World Bank (1993) cited in Pugh (1997).

themselves' and be 'enablers' rather than providers of housing has taken an ever firmer hold. Heralding the effective demise of 'aided self-help' in the mid-1980s, this new 'enabling' agenda, actively promoted by the World Bank and other multilaterals such as UN-Habitat, refers to states having important overall roles in policy-making, but leaving the provision of shelter (which upholds the idea of private property rights) to the market, NGOs, CBOs and household self-help in various forms of partnership. As Tannerfeldt and Ljung (2006: 146) assert 'The task of the state is to create the legal, institutional and economic framework, but not to provide housing' (see also Berghäll, 1998). An important thrust of enabling is that private entrepreneurs should get more involved in catering for low-income demand, including micro-finance, with support from the state, and using, where possible, 'sweat equity' (that is, people's own labour converted from 'leisure time' to productive use) to bring supply costs down (see Datta and Jones, 1999; *Environment and Urbanisation*, 2007b; 2008). Another key element in the enabling approach is land regularisation, with Gilbert (2002: 313) noting that integrating self-help housing into the formal economy through the offer of title deeds is 'part of a wider effort to transform housing from a state-led sector into one that follows the rules of the market'.

Shortly after the finalisation of the UN-Habitat's Global Strategy for Shelter to the Year 2000, the World Bank produced a seven-point strategy for its operationalisation, which continues to be the major point of reference for contemporary 'enabling' strategies (see Box 4.1).

Efforts to ensure that enabling works to the favour of the poor include the initiative 'Cities Without Slums', launched by the Cities Alliance, which calls for conventional slum upgrading (improved services, tenure security) to be accompanied by other measures to reduce poverty, such as job creation and improved governance. Such approaches are often referred to as 'enablement plus' strategies (see Arimah, 2007). In order to increase finance for slum upgrading, a Slum Upgrading Facility (SUF) was established in 2004 by UN-Habitat, managed conjointly with Cities Alliance, which aims to mobilise domestic resources, mainly through facilitating links between actors and donors, and developing sustainable finance mechanisms (ibid.: 9–10).

These initiatives are important, not only continuing but supporting an incremental approach to housing long undertaken by the urban poor, and in many cases leading to successful outcomes. This is especially so where community-based associations have evolved into city-wide or national federations, and managed to supplement members' savings with donations from governments, NGOs and international agencies. In some cases this has resulted in the attainment of commercial bank creditworthiness for housing finance, neighbourhood improvements and the like (see D'Cruz and Satterthwaite, 2005). For example, in Mumbai and Pune in India, collaboration among two people's movements – the National Slum Dwellers Federation and *Mahila Milan* ('Women Together'), together with their main NGO supporter, SPARC (Society for the Promotion of Area Resource Centres) – have led to the production of hundreds of community-designed and managed toilet blocks (ibid: 23) (see also Box 4.2). In Thailand, the eminently successful '*Baan Mankong*' (Secure Housing) programme, which seeks to reach 300 000 households in 2000 slums with improved housing and living conditions and secure tenure, is based on subsidies for infrastructure and loans to community-based savings groups which come from a government agency – the Community Organisations Development Institute (CODI) – which explicitly supports community-driven slum upgrading and new housing initiatives spearheaded by the poor themselves (ibid.). In some instances, inspiring examples of 'community driven development' (CDD) in individual countries have led to international initiatives such as the network of community-based housing groups represented by Shack/Slum Dwellers International (SDI), founded in 1996, which fosters interchange on processes and practices in places as far apart as India, South Africa and the Philippines, and works to garner the support of major donors (see *Environment and Urbanisation*, 2001a; 2001b). Indeed, D'Cruz and Satterthwaite (2005: 1) go as far as to say that:

BOX 4.2   FUNDS OF URBAN POOR
FEDERATIONS: SELECTED COUNTRIES

Philippines – **Urban Poor Development Fund** has US$700 000 from members' savings and US$1.7 million from the Philippine government and international agencies.
South Africa – **uTshani Fund** – kickstarted by a 4 million rand grant from northern donors, followed by a 10 million rand grant from the state Department of Housing. Currently there are around R48 million in the fund (about US$5.3 million).
Cambodia – **Urban Poor Development Fund** – established with US$103 000 ccontributed by the federation, the Asian Coalition for Housing Rights and MISEREOR, a German charity. Presently it has US$365 000, including money from the Prime Minister's fund.
Zimbabwe – **Gungano Fund** – US$242 000 from member savings, a loan from the South Africa federation, and grants from donors.
Namibia – **Twahangana Fund** – US$300 000 from member savings plus support from government and international donors.

Source: D'Cruz and Satterthwaite (2005: box 2)

'Perhaps the most significant initiative today in urban areas of Africa and Asia in addressing poverty and in contributing to the achievement of the Millennium Development Goals is the work of organisations and federations formed and run by the urban poor or homeless.' This is not just on account of the scale of their achievements in assisting the urban poor and in making government more effective, but also because of their capacity 'to lower unit costs and mobilise local resources – so that external support goes further – and to recover costs for many initiatives, thus greatly reducing and sometimes even eliminating the need for external funding' (ibid.: 2; see also Greene and Rojas, 2008, on Latin America and the Caribbean).

Yet despite the positive outcomes achieved by urban poor organisations, some notes of caution about the enabling approach, as well as about the prospects for improvements in slum dwellers' conditions, are in order. One is that local and national governments, in their role as 'facilitators' of productive partnerships among different stakeholders, may actually find it very difficult to influence private entrepreneurs and mortgage companies to lend to the poor, let alone at subsidised interest rates (Berghäll, 1998). Another qualification is that efforts made by the urban poor can potentially let governments off the hook. Even if there is evidence to suggest that governments and the poor can work creatively together (D'Cruz and Satterthwaite, 2005: 5), and that the supply costs of housing and services may be brought down through popular participation, it is also true that legalisation and upgrading programmes can be vulnerable to patronage and corruption (see Vaa, 2000, on Bamako, Mali). Moreover, rental housing, despite its growing numerical importance, has not been adequately addressed in many contexts.

Gilbert (2003) suggests that part of the neglect of rental housing stems from the 'over-idealisation' of home ownership in donor countries in the Global North in which private property has often been viewed as an integral part of successful capitalist development. Additional factors identified by Mitlin (1997) for the common tendency for governments to sponsor owner-occupancy over rental housing include, first, that subsidies for home ownership tend to be fixed and pertain to single dwelling units. As such, they are easier to manage than subsidies for rental accommodation which conventionally stretch out indefinitely and across a wider range of stakeholders. A second reason is that it is difficult for governments to ensure that the value of the subsidy is actually passed on to tenants. Yet despite these considerations it would be well for international donors and governments in the South to address long-standing calls emanating from UN-Habitat conferences to put their weight behind increasing the supply of affordable rental housing, especially in the light of continued urban growth and declining availability of land for self-help shelter.

Activity 4.1
Write a list of the advantages of self-help owner-occupied housing as a shelter alternative for low-income groups, and the disadvantages from the perspective of:

1. A national or local government housing department.
2. A 'typical' male and/or female self-help dweller.

Now attempt to a draw up a housing project proposal that would be feasible to implement and bring most benefits to its occupants.

LEARNING OUTCOMES

By the end of this chapter and relevant reading you should be able to:

● Outline and explain patterns and trends in urban growth in major regions of the South over the past 60 years, and evaluate the part played in these by policy initiatives.

- Identify the major housing sub-markets available to low-income groups in cities of the South.
- Trace the major shifts in shelter policy in the Global South from the 1960s to the present day.

FURTHER READING

Beall, Jo and Fox, Sean (2007), *Urban Poverty and Development in the 21st Century: Towards an Inclusive and Sustainable World*, Oxford: Oxfam GB Research Report (downloadable gratis, and free print copy available on request from www.oxfam.org).
A clear, concise and up-to-date overview of urbanisation in the Global South, with particular emphasis on the causes and consequences of urban poverty, and suggestions for action for a more equitable future.

Chant, Sylvia (2007c), *Gender, Cities, and the Millennium Development Goals in the Global South*, Gender Institute, New Series Working Paper, Issue 21, London: London School of Economics (downloadable from www.lse.ac.uk/collections/genderInstitute/pdf/CHANTpercent20GIWP.pdf).
Through the lens of the MDGs, this publication focuses on gender inequalities in towns and cities and identifies the importance of 'engendering' the urban development agenda.

D'Cruz, Celine and Satterthwaite, David (2005), 'Building homes, changing official approaches', *Poverty Reduction in Urban Areas Series, Working Paper 16*, London: International Institute for Environment and Development (downloadable from www.iied.org/pubs).
An informed and interesting review of how initiatives undertaken by organisations of the urban poor in countries such as India, Thailand and South Africa can improve housing and services in slum neighbourhoods.

Gilbert, Alan (2003), *Rental Housing: An Essential Option for the Urban Poor in Developing Countries*, Nairobi: United Nations Centre for Human Settlements (downloadable from www.unhabitat.org).
A substantial review of the much neglected rental sector in urban areas of the Global South including analysis of different rental sub-markets and suggestions for policy.

Satterthwaite, David (2007), *The Transition to a Predominantly Urban World and its Underpinnings*, Human Settlements Discussion Paper Series, Theme: Urban Change No. 4, London: International Institute for Environment and Development (downloadable from www.iied.org/pubs/).
A comprehensive and well-substantiated review of trends in urbanisation throughout history, paying particular attention to the 'urban revolution' experienced in the Global South in the twentieth and twenty-first centuries.

United Nations Fund for Population Activities (UNFPA) (2007), *State of the World's Population 2007: Unleashing the Potential of Urban Growth*, New York: UNFPA (downloadable from www.unfpa.org).
Urbanisation was selected as the special theme of UNFPA's 2007 report in light of

half the world's population becoming urban. It is a major source of information on issues such as urban demographics, urban poverty, housing, sustainable urbanisation and urban governance.

USEFUL WEBSITES

www.citiesalliance.org – website of global coalition of cities and development partners to promote international support for better cities/'cities without slums'

www.unhabitat.org – website of the United Nations Centre for Human Settlements

www.lboro.ac.uk/garnet/UrbanKaR/DFID-KAR-URBAN.html – website for *Urbanisation*, a regular newsletter produced by the UK Department for International Development which covers topics relating to shelter, services, poverty and governance in the cities of the South

www.poptel.org.uk/iied/urban/pubs/hifi_news – website for *Hi-Fi* newsletter which reports on innovative solutions for housing and housing finance

www.sdinet.org – website of Slum/Shack Dwellers International, a federation of low-income urban groups working on improving conditions in their communities, exchanging views with other counterparts in developing countries on 'best practice', and influencing national and international agencies

5. Industrialisation and trade for development

INTRODUCTION

This chapter outlines key patterns, trends and models of industrialisation in the South, which reflect the broader theoretical approaches to development covered in Chapter 2, especially in relation to economic globalisation. It begins by distinguishing between Import Substitution Industrialisation (ISI) and Export-oriented Industrialisation (EOI). It considers the origins and nature of the New International Division of Labour (NIDL), and within this discusses the global 'feminisation' of labour with special reference to the role of gender in export manufacturing. The discussion also considers how far industrialisation, trade liberalisation and the transformation of the formal labour market contribute to development. It concludes with an exploration of how labour standards, codes of conduct and free trade initiatives can address some of the inequalities inherent in some aspects of industrialisation and trade.

INDUSTRIALISATION AS A DEVELOPMENT STRATEGY

As discussed in Chapter 2, the post-Second World War economic boom in Western Europe and the USA strengthened the notion that similar models of industrialisation would increase prosperity in predominantly agricultural economies in the South. The roots of these ideas lay in the Bretton Woods conference in 1944. As well as establishing the major multilateral organisations such as the IMF and the World Bank (see also Chapter 11, this volume), Bretton Woods was concerned with establishing a favourable international environment to encourage economic growth, as well as protecting the capitalist system against the growing force at the time of the former USSR. Thinking at the conference was influenced to some degree by the work of the economist, John Maynard Keynes, whose basic premise was that capitalist economies would run more smoothly with some level of state intervention, especially during times of economic depression. This drew on the experience of the 1930s which showed that leaving the market to its own devices would not lead to economic recovery. This represented a departure from previous classical and neoclassical models and thinkers (such as Adam Smith) where the focus is on the free market and individual liberty as important for economic success; if everyone works for their own personal benefit then ultimately this will benefit all in society (see Hewitt, 2000).

Bretton Woods paved the way for new thinking on approaches to development, with the state accorded an important role in the management of capitalist economies. Within post-Second World War economic thinking the main concern was to achieve economic growth. In turn, this was seen as the key not only to economic development but to societal development more generally. The main notion was that wealth generated at the macro-level would 'trickle down' to all and bring 'development' at micro-level (see Chapter 2). However, the link between economic growth and development remains contested. Organisations such as the World Bank still maintain that this relationship is broadly valid, whereas others point to the absence of proven direct links. Yet the promotion of free (or freer) trade has remained central to the reconstruction of the global economy since the end of the Second World War. This was ensured first through the General Agreement on Tariffs and Trade (GATT), established in 1947 as a multilateral forum for free trade negotiations, and then through its successor, the World Trade Organisation (WTO), founded in 1995. Essentially the WTO promotes a neoliberal world order that incorporates free trade, opening markets across the world and encouraging export-led growth (Gwynne, 2008).

Behind the push for freer trade is the notion that industrialisation is the main way to achieve economic growth. A powerful theoretical pillar for this was provided by the Prebisch-Singer thesis, its key idea being that, over time, developing countries would have to export more of their primary commodities just to maintain the level of imports from the developed world. This is because of 'declining terms of trade'. Very simply, this means that prices in Northern or technically advanced countries rise more quickly than in those in the Global South. There are two main reasons for this:

1. As an economy industrialises, capital concentrates. This means competition decreases over time (some firms cannot compete and therefore fold, with only a small number remaining). This allows prices to be pushed up. Producers of primary products, however, tend to operate in competitive markets that keep prices, and thus profits, low.
2. Income elasticities of demand. Demand for finished goods (such as CD players, televisions and so on) rise as incomes rise, yet demand for primary goods (such as bananas) varies less with income. In other words, there are only so many bananas you can or want to eat, whereas there are many varieties of CD players you may want to buy.

Given these economic processes, there is arguably only one way forward. This is to change the structure of the economy and production, with industrialisation viewed as the key to 'development'. However, accepting the importance of industrialisation as a process, different types of industrialisation have been developed and implemented (Chataway and Allen, 2000). Before examining these in greater detail, it is important to point out that globally, the industrial sector represented only 21.3 per cent of total global employment in 2006 (compared with 40 per cent for services and 38.7 per cent for agriculture). This proportion has been static for 10 years with 21.4 per cent employed in industry back in 1996. There are also some important regional variations with sub-Saharan Africa having the smallest industrial sector representing only 8.8 per cent of the total employment in 2006 (a slight decline from 9.0 per cent in 1996). Beyond Eastern and Central Europe, the highest sectoral share for industry is in East Asia where it represents 25.8 per cent (an increase from 25.2 per cent in 1996), followed by 22.9 per cent in the Middle East and North Africa (an increase from 21.7 per cent), 19.8 per cent in Latin America and the Caribbean (a decline from 20.3 per cent), 18.8 per cent in South Asia (an increase from 15.4 per cent), and 17.8 per cent in Southeast Asia and the Pacific (an increase from 16.4 per cent) (see ILO, 2007; also Chapter 6, this volume).

IMPORT SUBSTITUTION INDUSTRIALISATION

Between the 1940s and the 1970s, economic growth was encouraged in many developing countries by means of ISI. Associated theoretically with the dependency school of thought, this is an inward-looking strategy in which domestic industries are developed to supply internal markets previously served through imports. In line with its theoretical antecedents, ISI was most frequently, although not exclusively, implemented by governments of the political Left.

Import Substitution Industrialisation is generally encouraged by the state through the imposition of high import tariffs, restricted import quotas and controlled access to foreign exchange, together with disincentives to exporters. Such domestic industry may either be locally owned by the state or private sector, or foreign owned, where Foreign Direct Investment (FDI) in domestic markets is encouraged through a series of incentives. Major industrial concentrations were created as a result of this model in countries such as Argentina, Brazil, China, India, Mexico and South Africa, which represented a significant transformation in the global organisation of production. Import Substitution Industrialisation focused mainly on basic sectors such as food, drink, tobacco, clothing and textiles production where a home market already existed (Potter et al., 2008).

However, ISI has not, on the whole, led to sustainable economic growth. As Hewitt (2000) notes, a major failing is that savings made by substituting imports in one sector are lost through the associated need for imports in another (for example, the import of machinery to manufacture consumer products), and the frequent and costly use of foreign experts to manage and/or train local personnel in technical operations. Although there have been countries in which this model appeared to provide the means to diversify economically, such as in Taiwan, or develop a relatively self-sufficient national economy, as in the case of India, few nations have been able to progress much beyond it (Potter et al., 2008; Willis, 2002).

In the case of Brazil, for example, between the mid-1950s and early 1960s, the country experienced a 'Golden Period' as the state-directed industrial sector managed to break away from first-stage ISI products such as processed food, beer and garments, to upgrade production to higher-order consumer goods, especially in the car industry, together with machine tools and components. This shift was borne out in the growth of industrial output of around 10 per cent per annum and the decline in the import of consumer goods (light industrial goods) between 1949 and 1964. However, even at its height, Brazil was having to import from overseas in order to diversify into higher technology and heavier production. Thus the extent to which 'dependence' on the North was reduced can be called into question. Indeed, heavy industry required huge external borrowing which was one of the factors behind the debt crisis not only in Brazil, but Mexico and Argentina, in the 1980s. Perhaps ironically, while Brazil remained dedicated to industrial production, it had to export more and more coffee in order to finance its rising external debt.

Indeed, other problems with ISI arose in relation to the fact that many countries had small internal markets, and even when regional trading areas were created, too many countries were producing similar products. Lack of competition also led to inefficiency which spelt high prices for consumers as well as a lack of innovation. Also important is that ISI policies mean that countries do not exploit their national comparative advantage, which can negatively affect economic growth and development. Thus, overall, while ISI was embraced by many countries as a way of forging an independent industrial path, in practice this proved hard to do.

EXPORT-ORIENTED INDUSTRIALISATION

From the 1960s onwards, economic policy throughout the Global South has become focused on trade liberalisation, promoting external investment in export rather than import markets. This was incorporated in a strategy of EOI underpinned by a belief in the potential of a free market to deliver benefits in respect of economic growth and national development in accordance with the precepts of neoliberalism (Chapter 2). Contrary to ISI, EOI involves tariff reductions, the elimination of quotas and the relaxation of import licensing. National variations have been significant in terms of the method and timing of liberalisation, and indeed the extent to which economic growth has been sustained or even initiated (Greenaway and Milner, 2008). The degree to which EOI has been adopted by national governments depends on the political character of the state in a given country, with those on the political Right and Centre Right more likely to be favourable. Foreign Direct Investment is usually more likely to occur in countries viewed as politically 'safe' and/or democratic, as well as those which have (former) colonial ties with investors. Although EOI strategies pre-date the international recession of the 1980s and 1990s, they are strongly associated with Structural Adjustment Programmes. While varying in nature between places, EOI has been widespread in the Global South in recent decades, especially in countries of Asia and Latin America (see below).

Globalisation of Trade

In the second half of the twentieth century, the world trading system became more liberalised. Indeed, world trade growth has been higher than growth in production since 1950 and particularly since 1985 (Gwynne, 2008). An important dimension of this is the increase in the share of the developing world in global manufacturing exports (from 4.4 per cent in 1965 to 30.1 per cent in 2003) (Kiely, 2008). Globalisation of trade and production through EOI within a country involves governments offering financial incentives to multinational corporations or companies (MNCs) (also known as transnational corporations or companies – TNCs). This encourages the latter to transfer labour-intensive aspects of production process to the South, notably the assembly of finished or semi-finished goods, via the establishment of branch plants, or what are sometimes referred to as 'world market factories'. In turn, the products assembled in these factories are exported back to industrialised nations. In practice, this type of production has commonly been situated in geographically concentrated enclaves called 'Export Processing Zones' (EPZs) established by governments in the South who provide infrastructure and services in what are effectively specialised industrial estates (Potter et al., 2008). In EPZs, duties and taxes are minimal or non-existent, and together with financial incentives, there are fewer regulations in terms of national employment and environmental legislation (Gwynne, 2008). Above all, however, it is the lure of cheaper labour which attracts MNCs to the EPZs of the Global South. The kinds of product that are particularly amenable to relocation include textiles, garments and electronics (especially circuit boards for computers and other electrical equipment). Other products include audiocassettes, toys and footwear (see Box 5.1). A typical activity in a garments branch plant, for example, is the sewing of an item of clothing such as a pair of jeans using imported denim, zips, studs and thread. The jeans are then returned to the parent company (usually in the North, or to one of the wealthier countries in the South, such as Korea) for labelling and sale (Chant and McIlwaine, 1995; Gwynne, 2002; see also Figure 5.1). While in the past, EPZs tended to house a range of different industries, there are now specific zones orientated towards one particular activity such as the jewellery zone in Thailand or the leather zone in Turkey, as well as single-commodity zones (tea in Zimbabwe), together with single factories (Export-oriented Units in India) or single-company zones (as in the Dominican Republic).[1]

EXPORT PROCESSING ZONES

Export Processing Zones come in a range of shapes and sizes, including Free Trade Zones (FTZs), special economic zones, bonded warehouses, free ports, and customs zones.[2] Export Processing Zones have been established in a range of locations, but have mainly been concentrated in the Asia-Pacific region, including the NICs of Taiwan, Hong Kong, Singapore and South Korea, as well as the Philippines, Thailand and Malaysia and, more recently, southern China. Most EPZs are located in Asia, with over 900 zones employing 53 million people (40 million are in China alone). The next largest concentrations are in Mexico and Central America with 5 million people being employed in 155 zones. These zones also exist in many other countries in the Latin American and Caribbean region, including Puerto Rico, the Dominican Republic, Honduras, El Salvador and Mexico (Gwynne, 2002) (see also Table 5.1). Especially referred to by their local name are the factories on the US/Mexican border area termed *maquilas* or *maquiladoras* (see Willis, 2002). Globally the ILO estimated that in March 2007 there were 2700 or more EPZs throughout the world, which represents an impressive increase from an overall total of only 79 EPZs in 1975 (Gereffi, 2005).

The trade and production regime described above is ostensibly beneficial for both the host nation and the global firms. The former benefits from a relatively rapid increase in its manufacturing base without having to provide the means for this production, except beyond land and basic infrastructure. Job creation and the potential stimulation of the local and national economy are further advantages. As far as the global firms are

BOX 5.1   EXPORT ORIENTED
           INDUSTRIALISATION AND GENDER IN
           THE MACTAN EXPORT PROCESSING
           ZONE, LAPU-LAPU, THE PHILIPPINES

The Mactan Export Processing Zone (MEPZ 1) is one of several such zones in the Philippines and is situated in the country's second largest city, Metro Cebu. It now boasts 100 companies with overspill having led in 1997 to the establishment of MEPZ II, yet as recently as 1993, MEPZ 1 had only 50 factories. As is the situation today, most companies in the Zone were foreign-owned (mainly Japanese, North American and British), and around three-quarters of the workforce was female. Among the 10 factories surveyed in a field-based research project undertaken by Chant and McIlwaine (1995), for example, 80 per cent of the workforce was female, ranging from 32 per cent in an electric light making factory, to 94 per cent in a factory producing car stereos.

In interviewing personnel and general managers of factories in the zone, a range of entry criteria emerged as important. First, women were more likely to predominate in factories using a lower amount of high-technology methods as it was believed that men were more capable of operating machinery than women. Workers were also generally young (between 18 and 25 years), single migrants with a high school education. However, this profile was more prevalent in electronics factories rather than garments as the latter also valued experience and were thus more likely to employ older women. Marriage was not always viewed as a barrier to entry as many employers felt that married women were more reliable because they had a family to support and thus needed to keep their jobs. A host of gender stereotypes were also used to recruit the mainly female labour force. The most commonly cited one in this case (and elsewhere in the world) was that women had 'nimble fingers' making them better at assembling electronic parts and sewing clothes (see earlier). As one employer in a factory making raincoats noted, 'women have good hands'. Women were also thought to be more diligent and patient, with another employer in a factory producing binoculars stating that their anatomy and biology allows them to sit in one place for longer than men'. In turn, all women workers were required to have a 'pleasing personality', which referred to patience, deference to those in authority, deportment and good looks. Women were also more likely to work in rank and file positions in factories, and although women were employed in administrative jobs, it was men who held all the major decision-making positions. Many of the factories were also run on basic patriarchal principles with managers boasting about their 'family atmosphere', which essentially meant that the managers (most of whom were men) were father figures wielding power and authority over their daughters, the workers.

In respect of the workers themselves, interviews revealed that women were aware of the exploitative nature of their jobs, especially in terms of working conditions. This commonly involved not being able to leave their positions on the factory floor, or even to use the toilet, which often led to discomfort and/or urinary tract infections. In addition, many were exposed to dangerous chemicals, causing skin complaints and respiratory illnesses. However, women recognised benefits as well. One of the main advantages declared by workers was that they were able to earn more in these factories than in any outside the zone and certainly more than most alternative work. In turn, they were able to help out their parents and other family members (often by giving and/or sending home up to 50 per cent of their wages), and to save some money to set up their own businesses. They were also likely to marry later at around 25 years of age (compared with around 20 among the wider population in the locality), and negotiate to have fewer children. Many also reported having greater decision-making control in the home because of their earning capacity.

Source: Chant and McIlwaine (1995); see also Investor's Guide to Mactan EPZ at www.dticebu.net.ph/02_d_08.html (accessed 22 April 2008).

concerned, the main benefit is reduced production costs. The mobility of this type of production also means that it can be shifted to a more profitable (cheaper) area if incentives in one EPZ are cut. However, this clearly inheres disadvantage for the host nations, which come to rely heavily upon export processing, rendering long-term economic sustainability potentially very fragile. Another problem, identified by Rigg (2007: 108) is that such factory work leads ultimately to 'immiserising growth'. Although EPZ expansion may be associated with some increase in national income and employment, it has also been shown to push wages down as countries wishing to attract multinationals compete with one another in a 'race to the bottom' (see also Chapter 6, this volume). Recognising that the promotion and success of EPZs varies according to the particular constellation of the state, MNCs

Source: Photo by Sylvia Chant.

*Figure 5.1   Garment factory assembly line, Mactan Export Processing
Zone, Philippines*

and macroeconomic forces in given times and places (see Gwynne, 2008;
Kiely, 2008), questions hang over the cost-effectiveness of this strategy
when in countries such as Kenya the government has spent US$514 million
creating EPZs, but has seen no more than 2000 jobs (effectively amounting
to a price of $275 000 per job created   see Jauch, 2002).

The shifting of MNC production processes to the Global South has been
a significant contributor to the New International Division of Labour, and
forms a fundamental part of the increasing globalisation of production

Table 5.1   The geographical extent of EPZs globally and the proportion of employment generated, 2007

Geographical area	Employment	Number of zones
Asia	53 089 262	900+
Of which China	40 000 000	
Of which bonded factories in Bangladesh	3 250 000	
Central America and Mexico	4 988 459	155
Middle East	1 070 275	50
North Africa	643 152	65
Sub-Saharan Africa	816 474	90+
United States	330 000	713
South America	456 175	43
Transition Economies	1 131 462	400
Caribbean	542 163	250
Indian Ocean	189 412	1
Europe	45 472	50
Pacific	145 930	
Total (estimated)	63 118 236	2700+

Notes: The Indian Ocean includes Mauritius and Madagascar. The zones in the USA are warehousing facilities for trans-shipment rather than manufacturing.

Source: Adapted from EPZ Employment Statistics downloadable at www.ilo.org/public/english/dialogue/sector/themes/epz/stats.htm (accessed 21 April 2008).

and consumption (Gilbert, 2008a). The NIDL, while difficult to define precisely, refers to a wide range of broad processes linked with globalisation. These include the ways in which most parts of the world now form part of the global market, and the manner in which manufacturing is now spread across the world, as discussed above. The NIDL also incorporates the globalisation of services and especially producer services (such as banking). The investment and portfolio capital moving across the world has also increased, as has the movement of people (see Chapters 2 and 3, this volume). Finally, as shown above, the importance of MNCs in the world economy is central to the NIDL, accounting for around 25 per cent of world production and 70 per cent of world trade (Gilbert, 2008a: 187). The effects of these broader shifts have been widely debated: some perceive that they have marginalised countries of the Global South and led to increased global inequalities and poverty, while others view the changes as positive (ibid.). Although in general terms, as suggested by Kiely (2008), the reality is probably somewhere in between, a number of scholars have emphasised that the terms of trade of the global economy are inherently unequal in gender terms and actively militate against women (see Randriamaro, 2006; also Bell with Brambilla, 2002, for examples).

THE GLOBAL 'FEMINISATION' OF LABOUR

An important dimension of the NIDL is the dominance of women among factory workers who have routinely constituted between 70 and 90 per cent of the numbers employed in export-oriented branch plants. This has contributed to women comprising over one-third of the world's manufacturing workforce in a process commonly referred to as the 'global feminisation of labour' (Standing, 1989; 1999). More specifically, in 2000, almost 35 per cent of the manufacturing workforce in Latin America were women, with 41 per cent in Asia. In export processing in particular, more than 80 per cent of the workforce in Southeast Asia comprised women (Randriamaro, 2006). Standing (1989; 1999) suggests that the term 'feminisation' is appropriate not only because an increasing number of women are engaged in such jobs, but because more and more occupations in the industrial sector bear the characteristics of jobs traditionally performed by women (that is, unskilled, precarious, poorly paid, etc.). The globalisation of flexible labour is, accordingly, noted by Standing (1999) to be an integral aspect of the global feminisation of labour (see Bell with Brambilla, 2002, for a range of examples). This begs the question of why women are thought more suitable for low-skilled industrial work.

Reasons for Employing Women in Export Processing

Women have become the preferred labour force in export manufacturing for a range of reasons, many of which relate to social and economic inequalities arising from cultural, legal and political constructions of gender (see Chapter 8, this volume). First, for example, it is often assumed that women are cheaper to employ than men. Indeed, nowhere in the world are women paid more than men on average even in the same job (Standing, 1999; see also Brown and Domínguez, 2007; Chant and Pedwell, 2008; Chapter 6, this volume). This is usually because women are assumed to be supplementary wage earners in households rather than the main breadwinners. A related factor is the idea that female labour is not worth as much as male labour. In addition to being assumed to be cheaper to employ, women are preferentially recruited on account of numerous dubious stereotypes. The most widely reported is that they are thought to be physiologically better suited to light manufacturing work than are men. Much of the work involved in multinational assembly operations, such as sewing garments, assembling circuit boards and so on, requires what Elson and Pearson (1981) classically termed as 'nimble fingers' (see also Pearson, 1998). This is based on the assumption that women's smaller hands and fingers give them greater manual dexterity, which in turn is reinforced through their childhood socialisation in 'feminine' tasks such as needle-work and embroidery. Women are also thought to have a greater capacity than men for monotonous assembly-line work, albeit due to rather tenuous time and motion studies which reveal that women perform better than men in simple, repetitive tasks, making fewer mistakes and with higher produc-tivity. The higher and more reliable productivity of women is seen as a key part of keeping production costs to a minimum (ibid.; see also Box 5.1).

Women's purportedly docile nature is another important factor. Women are thought to be more likely to take orders from senior personnel than men, and to be less prone to form unions and/or organise to demand higher levels of pay and better working conditions. As well as this so-called 'natural' docility, the demands of women's domestic situations give them less time to engage in industrial struggles. Accordingly, factories are thought to lose less production time through labour disputes and benefit from having a more acquiescent workforce. Women's domestic responsibil-ities also make for a more flexible or 'disposable' workforce in the eyes of employers. Since women tend more often than men to give up work on marriage and/or childbirth, there is frequent voluntary turnover among personnel. This works very much in the interests of multinational branch plants whose production cycles, and therefore labour demand, may fluctuate greatly in response to market circumstances (Elson and Pearson, 1981). Women are also often 'burnt out' after a few years of tough working conditions and may not wish to return to the factory floor. All this helps managers to avoid redundancy payments which might other-wise be entailed in compulsory dismissals (Chant and McIlwaine, 1995; Fernández-Kelly, 1983). This situation of women working in export facto-ries in the South has led Melissa Wright to comment on the creation of the 'myth of the disposable Third World woman' (2006: 1). This reflects how women factory workers are constructed as worthless, human and industrial waste, despite their often massive contributions to industrial growth.

Another significant trend in the industrial sector, with important gender dimensions, is that of increased outworking. Certain forms of manufacturing production are increasingly subcontracted outside factories to small-scale workshops and individuals working in their own homes. In the case of the latter, the bulk of workers are usually female. In Mexico, for example, jobs in the shoe industry such as the hand stitching of uppers and adornments comprise women in their homes who are paid by the batch on a piece-rate basis (Chant, 1991). Other goods include assembling components for plastic flowers, toys, staples, pens, cartons and latches (Benería and Roldán, 1987). In the Philippines, an estimated 500 000 homeworkers were involved in the production of fashion accessories in the early 1990s, among whom 82 per cent were women (Chant and McIlwaine, 1995; see also Figure 5.2). This trend, again, highlights the increasingly blurred divide between formal and informal labour markets (see also Chapter 6, this volume).

As flexible labour strategies have become more pervasive throughout the industrial sector, it has been increasingly likely for women to substitute more widely for men in industrial employment, and for labour force feminisation to have become a much more generalised phenomenon. However, it should also be noted that recent years have witnessed the beginning of a 'de-feminisation' of labour in certain sectors of industrial activity. Shifts towards production of higher value-added goods with greater capital and technological intensity require more specialised skills, which appear to be deemed the preserve of men, thus leading to an increased demand for male over female labour (see Pearson, 1998; Razavi, 1999; Safa, 2002). In the *maquiladora* industry of Mexico, for example, where there is a rising tendency for more skilled work in the export manufacturing sector, women's employment on the factory floor has dropped from 71 per cent in 1990 to a mere 54 per cent (Brown and Domínguez, 2007: 2). In addition, women are often the first to be made redundant when factories shut down or shed workers.

Exploitation or Emancipation?

Yet women's still massive incorporation into export manufacturing in recent decades has led to mixed views about the implications for women's status and socio-economic mobility. This debate falls into two main camps. On the one hand, some commentators note that women are highly exploited as factory workers on the basis of the gender stereotypes noted above, as well as the poor working conditions and low pay that accompany factory employment. On the other hand, it has also been found that significant advantages accrue to women through being involved in this type of work. These include postponing marriage and childbirth, having fewer children, and enjoying improved self-esteem along with increases in decision-making power and autonomy, especially at the household level (Pearson, 1998; see also Rigg, 2007 on Indonesia and Bangladesh).[3] In addition, many women have begun to organise politically around their status as workers and as women (Athreya, 2002; see also Chant and McIlwaine, 1995; Chant and Pedwell, 2008; Pearson, 1998). In reality, the outcomes for women are often context specific and may be both positive and negative (see Randriamaro, 2006; also Box 5.1). A further factor to bear in mind here is that disparities in the spread of industrialisation through the NIDL has led to concerns that

Source: Photo by Sylvia Chant.

Figure 5.2 Woman jewellery outworker with son, Metro Cebu, Philippines

large parts of the world have been marginalised at the expense of others. This begs the question of how far global economic 'integration', and in particular industrial production, is the answer to development.

To some extent these provisos also apply to another aspect of the NIDL, notably the global off-shoring of services (Gilbert, 2008a; see also Chapter 6, this volume). Even if this is less geographically concentrated than industrialisation, and the tertiary or service sector is almost invariably the biggest employer of both male and female workers in cities in the South, some segments are more unevenly distributed than others, including those relating to the so-called 'knowledge economy'.

Potentially forming the 'new frontier' of economic development strategies for Southern countries, this sector focuses mainly on Information and Communication Technology (ICT) jobs especially in the form of call centres. Call centres are usually subcontracted firms which provide telemarketing, technical or customer services for larger TNCs. They employ a largely English-speaking, highly skilled and inexpensive workforce, many of whom are women. Using satellites, telephone calls are routed across the world, usually from North to South. India has been at the forefront of the ICT expansion, reflected in a growth from 60 to 800 call centres receiving outsourced work from foreign companies between 2000 and 2003 alone (Mirchandani, 2004). Among the several hundred companies outsourcing to call centres in India are British Airways, Dell Computers, GE Capital, Swiss Air and American Express. Although India is currently at the apex of this industry, it is developing fast in other countries of the Global South as the benefits of such a transnational service sector are becoming an increasingly important growth stimulus (see also Chapter 6).

Activity 5.1
Imagine that you are a recruitment manager in a garments factory in an export processing zone in Southeast Asia. Write a list of the reasons why your labour force is predominantly female. Then imagine that you are a female worker in the same factory. Compile a list of the reasons why you are working there, and the effects of this employment on your life.

INDUSTRIALISATION AND DEVELOPMENT: FAIR AND ETHICAL TRADE AND PRODUCTION IN THE CONTEXT OF FREE TRADE

Leading on from the above, to what degree is industrialisation, as part of globalisation, a key element in future development? In terms of the distribution of production, capital tends to concentrate in certain areas, and once established, growth tends to be cumulative. Most FDI tends to be located in the Global North. Indeed, the share of global FDI for developing countries in the period between 2003 and 2005 was around 35 per cent. In terms of proportionate shares in investment for particular regions, in Asia and Oceania this was 21 per cent, in South, Southeast and East Asia, 18.4 per cent, in Latin America and the Caribbean, 11.5 per cent and in Africa, 3 per cent (Kiely, 2008: 184). Thus, while most parts of the world now form part of the global market in terms of exposure to consumption, access to this consumption is far from universal and the production of consumer goods remains highly uneven. Overall, therefore, the liberalisation of trade, the shift towards export-oriented strategies and the spread of the NIDL has progressively led to a dislocation between spaces of production and consumption (Gwynne, 2008) with various social inequalities emerging as a result (Kiely, 2008; Randriamaro, 2006).

Given this hierarchy of capital investment and often contradictory outcomes of industrialisation and trade liberalisation, optimism about the capacity of neoliberalism to foster global economic development has been contested. While industrialisation is not a panacea, and may cause as many problems as it solves, it remains an important part of the development process. The fact that many countries and regions in the South are excluded or marginalised from industrialisation, and indeed that much development agency work deals with the repercussions of this exclusion, suggests that more diverse models of industrialisation should be considered. While small-scale 'populist' alternatives to industrialisation are often considered utopian and untenable, the increasing popularity of 'people-centred' development within international, state and non-governmental development agencies has highlighted the importance of finding new channels for addressing development needs (Chataway and Allen, 2000; see also Randriamaro, 2006).

In the industrial sector, efforts have also been made to make production processes more equitable and working conditions less exploitative. This has mainly been through the imposition of labour standards encompassed within the ILO Declaration on Fundamental Principles and Rights at Work adopted in 1998, as well as a range of Codes of Conduct formed by trade unions or MNCs themselves (sometimes known as Voluntary Codes of Conduct [VCCs] or Practice) (see Pearson, 2007). These types of initiatives have roots in earlier declarations including the OECD's Declaration on International Investment and Multinational Enterprises in 1976 and the ILO's Tripartite Declaration of Principles Concerning Multinational Enterprises and Social Policy in 1977. In various ways, these codes and declarations seek to maintain a minimal level of protection for workers, and especially those working in factories in the Global South. Not surprisingly, these have been very controversial. While many Northern governments and NGOs favour these codes and standards, the business sector is often reluctant to enforce them, frequently claiming that they are a restriction of the free market. In turn, some Southern governments and some NGOs fear that these standards can be used for protectionist ends. Reflecting Rigg's (2007) comments on 'immiserising growth' mentioned earlier, there is also fear that such codes will 'equalise down' wages and working conditions. Furthermore, most labour standards are not currently enforced in the production process and tend to concentrate on governments rather than MNCs, as well as neglecting gender issues (Randriamaro, 2006).

Although many trade unions are trying to enforce these standards more strongly, their success has been patchy. For example, in a study of 20 VCCs that commit companies to adhere to basic labour rights along their global production chain, Jenkins and Pearson (2001) found that manufacturers, trade associations, trade unions and NGOs all wanted different things from the VCCs. Therefore, codes created by trade associations were less likely to reflect the concerns of shop floor workers in contrast to those developed by labour unions or NGOs. The VCCs also often failed to meet the ILO Core Labour Standards, as well as focusing mainly on the formal factory sector, thus excluding subcontracted and piece-rate workers. They also concentrated on the female-dominated sectors such as garments, despite public pressure to address child labour. This study also highlighted that women's concerns such as sexual harassment and reproductive health were often absent from codes in cases when they were not directly involved in drafting them. Moreover, there was also found to be little inspection or monitoring of implementation of codes. Yet many of these campaigns have managed to orchestrate very successful lobbying and to actually change the working lives of people in factories in the South. One such high profile initiative is the Clean Clothes Campaign (CCC). The CCC works with consumers, trade unions, advocacy groups and other organisations to take responsibility for workers' rights. National CCC affiliates target companies in their own countries as well as work as part of the international CCC network. In particular, they co-ordinate international initiatives such as the Play Fair 2008 campaign. A similar example is provided by the Ethical Trading Initiative (ETI) which involves companies, trade unions and NGOs in campaigning work to ensure the implementation of labour codes.

Another important dimension of the need to create a fairer deal for workers in the Global South has been the emergence of the concept of fair trade, although this refers mainly to the agricultural rather than the industrial sector. This model was developed in the 1970s by Oxfam and other development organisations focusing mainly on the need to develop fairer terms of trade for small-scale producers who were perceived as being unable to compete with large TNCs and the host of 'middlemen' involved in exporting primary products such as coffee, bananas as well as handicrafts (Gwynne, 2008). Fair or ethical trading has now been recognised by the EU Parliament as an important aspect of development aid. Over time, the fair trade system has become more formalised with the Fairtrade Labelling Organisations International (FLO) established in 1997. By 2006, FLO had become an association of 20 Labelling Initiatives that promote the Fairtrade Certification Mark (ibid.). These standards aim to provide an advocacy function in terms of sensitising people to what free trade means, as well as promoting consumer confidence and demand. They also ensure that producers in the Global South receive fair terms of trade and prices, as well as being linked with initiatives that focus the establishment of cooperatives and a range of social projects (Gwynne, 2008; see Box 5.2). Although the fairtrade consumer market is still small in global terms, it has grown considerably especially since 2000 particularly in Europe. For example, in the UK, sales of fairtrade and ethical produce increased by 90 per cent between 2000 and 2002 alone (Randriamaro, 2006).

Activity 5.2
Access the Fairtrade Organisation website at www.fairtrade.org.uk/. Identify the five guarantees behind the Fairtrade Certification Mark. Assess the extent to which these can really improve the terms of trade on a global level, and whether they can bring about any sustained improvement in the lives of producers in the Global South.

LEARNING OUTCOMES

By the end of this chapter and having completed the essential reading and activities, you should be able to:

- Describe the difference between ISI and EOI, and outline the nature of the NIDL.
- Identify what is meant by the global 'feminisation of labour' and explain why women have traditionally been the preferred labour force in export manufacturing.
- Assess the advantages and disadvantages of EOI and trade liberalisation for addressing development problems in countries of the Global South.
- Outline the ways in which fairtrade and ethical labour standards campaigns can address some of the global inequalities in trade, production and exploitation in the Global South.

BOX 5.2   FAIR TRADE BANANAS IN COSTA RICA
AND FAIR TRADE COCOA IN GHANA

COSTA RICA: In 1980, a banana co-operative called Coopetrabasur was established in Costa Rica by a group of former Chiquita workers who had been left redundant when Chiquita pulled out of the region. Now a major fair trade producer of bananas to Europe, Coopetrabasur does not use paraquat or other pesticides, it has stopped recycling plastic waste, and started planting trees (among other things). The co-operative is well-run along egalitarian lines, providing decent wages for workers who previously felt exploited by the multinational. As one of them noted: 'becoming free commercially, to have access to markets, to have the opportunity to dream of being free, to dream of being looked upon as a human being, not an object'. He went on to note that before he had only one small task of loading banana boxes onto trains. Yet now, he felt like an 'international businessman'.

GHANA: The Kuapa Kokoo cocoa co-operative in Ghana comprises mainly women. It supports independent women smallholders to ensure that they get fair prices for the cocoa, but also that they become involved in community projects. They retailed with the Cocoa Marketing Board who negotiated directly with the Day Chocolate Company in the UK. This cooperative made an additional US\$ 1 million between 1993 and 2001 that was reinvested in social projects. Participation in this co-operative was reported by the women as increasing not only their returns for selling the cocoa but also their psychological health through improved self-esteem, morale and confidence.

Sources: www.fairtrade.org.uk/downloads/doc/unpeeling_the_banana_ trade.doc (accessed 22 April 2008); Randriamaro (2006: 44).

NOTES

1. See www.ilo.org/public/english/dialogue/sector/themes/epz/epzs.htm (accessed 21 April 2008).
2. See the ILO's typology of EPZs at www.ilo.org/public/english/dialogue/sector/themes/epz/typology.htm (accessed 22 April 2008).
3. As noted in Chapters 3, 8 and 9 in this volume, it is important to remember that delaying fertility and/or marriage do not automatically mean that women are more 'empowered' or have greater autonomy over the course of their lives.

FURTHER READING

Chataway, Joanna and Allen, Tim (2000), 'Industrialisation and development: prospects and dilemmas', in Tim Allen and Alan Thomas (eds), *Poverty and Development into the 21st Century*, Oxford: Oxford University Press, pp. 509–32.
This chapter provides a detailed yet clear assessment of the relationship between industrialisation processes and development. It highlights the conceptual issues and illustrates them with case studies.

Gwynne, Robert N. (2008), 'Free trade and fair trade', in Vandana Desai and Robert Potter (eds), *The Companion to Development Studies*, 2nd edn, London: Hodder Arnold, pp. 201–6.
This short article provides an excellent overview of the main issues surrounding the issue of free and ethical trading in relation to wider development processes.

Kiely, Ray (2008), 'Global shift: industrialisation and development', in Vandana Desai and Robert Potter (eds), *The Companion to Development Studies*, 2nd edn, London: Hodder Arnold, pp. 183–6.
This is another short article which outlines how industrialisation contributes to wider development goals from a global perspective. It is concise yet very instructive.

Randriamaro, Zo (2006), *Gender and Trade, Overview Report*, Brighton: Institute of Development Studies (downloadable from www.bridge.ids.ac.uk/reports/CEP-Trade-OR.doc).
This document provides an up-to-date account of the gendered nature of trade and industrialisation in the South. It outlines not only the gendered patterns of industrial employment but also engages with the debate about whether industrial employment is exploitative or empowering for women.

USEFUL WEBSITES

http://en.maquilasolidarity.org/ – website of the Maquila Solidarity Network, a Canadian based labour and women's rights organisation reporting on factory conditions in Latin America, the Caribbean and Asia

www.unctad.org – website of the United Nations Conference on Trade and Development

www.fairtrade.org.uk/ – website of the UK Fairtrade Organisation that explains the categorisation, outlines campaigns and reports on research

www.maketradefair.com/en/index.htm – website of Oxfam's fair trade campaign

www.traidcraft.co.uk/ – website of development NGO, Traidcraft, campaigning and working towards trade justice

www.nosweat.org.uk – website of a campaigning group addressing exploitative conditions in sweatshops

www.cleanclothes.org/ – website of the Clean Clothes Campaign group aiming to improve working conditions in the global garment and sportswear industries

www.ethicaltrade.org/ – website of the Ethical Trading Initiative

6.   Making a living in cities

INTRODUCTION

This chapter examines the concept of 'making a living' in cities of the South with particular reference to the 'informal sector' of employment and to livelihoods among the urban poor. Following a brief overview of urban labour markets, an outline is given of the origins and characteristics of the informal sector, together with debates on its role in urban economies. How different is the informal sector from the formal sector, especially in light of an increased 'informalisation' of urban labour markets during the past three decades of neoliberal economic restructuring? Is the informal economy a sector of subsistence or 'last resort' for people excluded from work in the formal sector, or can it be regarded as a seedbed of indigenous entrepreneurial activity and economic dynamism? What directions have policies towards informal employment taken over time? The final section of the chapter broadens the discussion of employment to consider the livelihood strategies adopted by low-income households, and their gender dimensions, during and after recession and the implementation of structural adjustment programmes in the 1980s and 1990s. It also considers strategic objectives of the International Labour Organisation's 'Decent Work' agenda.

EMPLOYMENT, WORK AND 'MAKING A LIVING' IN CITIES OF THE SOUTH

It has long been difficult to map Western interpretations of employment onto the developing world. In the North, 'employment' generally refers to work carried out in return for a wage or other form of remuneration. However, this only usually covers activities registered in national statistics, thereby excluding forms of employment undertaken in the informal economy or the household. 'Work' on the other hand, is a broader term that includes all productive ventures, including those which are unwaged and not directly remunerated. Thus, household reproduction, community activities and unpaid subsistence production, often carried out by women, are included here (see UNIFEM, 2006). This broad conceptualisation is particularly important in cities of the South where livelihoods and making a living are often ensured through subsistence and small-scale income-generating activities rather than waged employment in a strict sense (McIlwaine et al., 2002; see also Gilbert and Gugler, 1992; Lugo and Sampson, 2008; Wield and Chataway, 2000).

The issue of unemployment is also problematic in that it too is generally associated with the wage economy. Officially, unemployment refers to the situation where someone is without paid work or self-employment, but is looking for work and therefore constitutes part of the 'economically active population' (EAP). Yet what has sometimes been referred to as the 'luxury unemployment thesis' has shown that only the relatively well-off are able to be unemployed in the absence of social security and/or assistance from family. In light of the problems associated with this essentially ethnocentric concept, the notion of 'underemployment', sometimes termed 'disguised unemployment', is often perceived to be more expedient for the Global South. This denotes situations where people work fewer hours than they would like, where work is part-time or occasional, where people's skills are underutilised, or where productivity is low (Potter and Lloyd-Evans, 1998).

In view of the above, it is more appropriate to discuss employment in developing world cities in relation to 'livelihoods' and the notion of 'making a living' (McIlwaine et al., 2002). This frequently involves the self-styled generation of means to make an income, or the development of strategies to ensure survival that perhaps entails larger collectivities such as households or kin networks (Wield and Chataway, 2000). Given the difficulties of obtaining wage employment in the formal sector, it is no surprise that a large proportion of the economically active population work outside the formal economy. Therefore, when exploring the nature of employment, and especially urban employment, it is important to adopt a holistic approach that incorporates notions of 'work', 'underemployment' and 'livelihoods'. Above all, consideration of the 'informal sector' and the growing informalisation of labour markets are crucial in understanding evolving urban economies in the Global South.

URBAN LABOUR MARKETS AND ECONOMIC DUALISM

Urban labour markets in developing regions have grown massively in the past four or five decades for two interrelated reasons: first, the exodus of migrants from rural areas to towns and cities (Chapters 3 and 4, this volume) and, second, the expansion of industry and services at the expense of agriculture (Chapter 5). In sub-Saharan Africa, for example, employment in agriculture declined from 79 per cent to 63 per cent of the labour force between 1965 and 2005, and in Southeast Asia and the Pacific the proportion fell from 70 per cent to 43 per cent over the same period.

In respect of economic activity in the South, the tertiary or service sector is almost invariably the biggest employer of both male and female urban workers. The service sector encompasses a diverse group of activities, ranging from commerce to transport to personal, public, financial and business services. Even in a highly industrialised country like Chile, services employ 52 per cent of the male labour force at a national level and as many as 82 per cent of women. These levels are higher still in less industrialised nations such as Peru, where 66 per cent of male workers and 86 per cent of female workers are engaged in tertiary occupations. As for industry, this employs only 27 per cent of male workers and 14 per cent of female workers in Latin America and the Caribbean as a whole. Moreover, in some countries in the region, notably Colombia, Brazil, Uruguay and Argentina, the share of the labour force in industry actually dropped between the 1960s and 1990s.

The reasons why services occupy a larger (and growing) share of the labour force in most cities of the South is in part accounted for by the fact that although export-oriented industrialisation in developing nations is usually labour intensive, import substitution industrialisation has conventionally been capital intensive (see Chapter 5). Another important factor is that service employment has often been stimulated by the expansion of public employment, at least until the 'downsizing' of many state bureaucracies in the wake of neoliberal restructuring from the 1980s onwards. Counteracting the latter to some degree is the revolution in ICT, which in the past decade has created a new tier of service employment in many countries (see Lugo and Sampson, 2008; UNDP, 2001; also Figure 6.1). A further factor accounting for the increase of tertiary activities is that these have been an integral part of 'informal sector' expansion, notwithstanding that much 'informal' employment does not actually enter into national accounting systems.

While 'informal employment' is primarily found in commerce and services, it also occurs in manufacturing production, with the result that urban labour markets as a whole have often been seen as cross-cut by a division between 'formal' and 'informal sectors'. The 'informal sector' is frequently equated with precarious, low-productivity, poorly remunerated employment, although in reality the sector is highly heterogeneous both in terms of remuneration and activity. Many people in the informal sector, for example, work on their own account in street-vending, the running of 'front-room' eateries, stalls or shops, the operation of domestic-based

Source: Photo by Sylvia Chant.

Figure 6.1   Small-scale computer enterprise, Bakau New Town, The Gambia

industrial units, and the transport of passengers and goods. Other informal workers, however, are engaged as unpaid labour in family firms, are employed by micro-entrepreneurs or are subcontracted by large formal sector firms, especially in labour-intensive industries such as toys, footwear and clothing. Many informal workers combine one or more activity in their daily struggles for livelihood, with recycling, pawning and barter being common in situations of resource scarcity (see Chant, 2008b; McIlwaine et al., 2002; also Figures 6.2–6.6). For these reasons, although the terms 'informal sector' and 'informal economy' are often used interchangeably, some prefer the latter since it 'challenges the ideas that informality is confined to a single sector of economic activity, or that the informal and informal sectors of the economy are independent of each other' (Neto et al., 2007: 4). Indeed, as will become more apparent below, informal employment is increasingly found in the formal as well as in the informal sector (Chen, 2009).

The term 'informal sector' first appeared in the academic and policy literature in the 1970s. It is usually associated with the Ghana-based fieldwork of anthropologist Keith Hart and the subsequent 'Kenya Mission' of the International Labour Organisation (see Hart, 1973; ILO, 1972). Hart classified informal employment as that which fell outside the boundaries of formal sector enterprise (factories, public services, registered commercial establishments, for example), and subdivided the sector into 'legitimate' and 'illegitimate' activities. The former comprised work which made a contribution to economic growth, albeit in small ways, such as petty commerce, personal services and home-based production. 'Illegitimate' informal activities, alternatively, described occupations which, if not necessarily 'criminal' in nature, were arguably of questionable worth to national development, including prostitution, begging, pickpocketing and scavenging. In general terms, however, Hart viewed the informal sector as making a positive contribution to life in Southern cities. Although much work in the informal sector might be described as 'underemployment' or even 'disguised unemployment', Hart asserted that this provided a valuable, and frequently viable, alternative to formal sector work. Moreover, in a situation where there were few safety nets for the poor and unemployed, the informal sector acted as a buffer against outright destitution.

While other terms have been used to describe the informal sector, and numerous criteria have been used to categorise formal versus informal activity (see Table 6.1), the single most important factor in contemporary definitions is regulation (Roberts, 1994. 6). As delineated by Tokman (1991: 143), informal enterprises tend to characterised by an absence of one or more of three criteria:

Source: Photo by Sylvia Chant.

Figure 6.2   Home-based commerce, Puerto Vallarta, Mexico

Source: Photo by Sylvia Chant.

Figure 5.3   Ambulant manicurist, Metro Cebu, Philippines

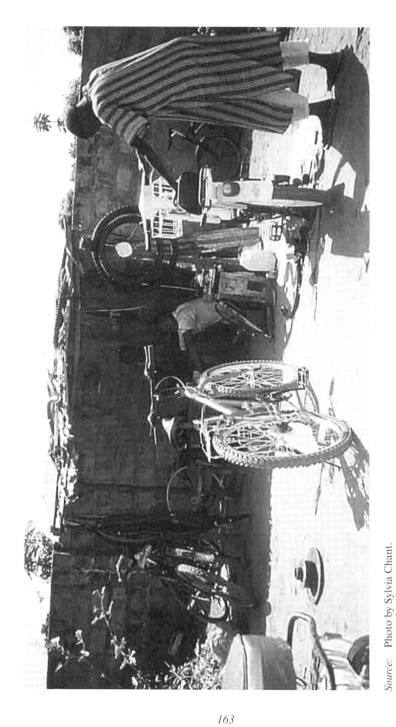

Source: Photo by Sylvia Chant.

Figure 6.4   *'Bicycle doctor', Kanifing, The Gambia*

Source: Photo by Sylvia Chant

Figure 6.5 Pedicab driver, Metro Manila, Philippines

Source: Photo by Sylvia Chant.

Figure 6.6 *'Barbing salon' and home-based shop, with a line in second-hand shoes, Kanifing, The Gambia*

1. Legal recognition as a business activity.
2. Legality concerning payment of taxes.
3. Legality vis-à-vis labour matters.

The latter comprises official norms regarding working hours, social security contribution, fringe benefits and other aspects of labour protection. Since this is often the most expensive element for employers it is also the most commonly bypassed (ibid.; see also Ghosh, 2009). Indeed, because the term 'informal economy' is broader than 'informal sector', referring to

Table 6.1   Common characteristics used to define formal and informal employment

Formal sector	Informal sector
Large scale	Small scale
Modern	Traditional
Corporate ownership	Family/individual ownership
Capital intensive	Labour intensive
Profit orientated	Subsistence orientated
Imported technology/inputs	Indigenous technology/inputs
Protected markets (e.g. tariffs, quotas)	Unregulated/competitive markets
Difficult entry	Ease of entry
Formally-acquired skills (e.g. school/college education)	Informally acquired skills (e.g. in home or craft apprenticeship)
Majority of workers protected by labour legislation and covered by social security	Minority of workers protected by labour legislation and covered by social security

Sources: Chant (2008b: table 2); Drakakis-Smith (1987: table 5.5); Gilbert and Gugler (1992: 96).

labour relations as opposed to scale of enterprise, this is another reason why the term is increasingly preferred, even if paucity of data makes evaluation of size and growth even more difficult (see Tsikata, 2009).

Leading on from this, data on informal activities based on any criteria should be treated with extreme caution, not only on account of their irregular and/or clandestine nature, but because of their huge diversity (Schneider, 2007; Thomas, 1995). Bearing in mind the difficulties of enumeration, informal employment is estimated to account for 51 per cent of non-agricultural employment in Latin America, 65 per cent in Asia and as much as 72 per cent of sub-Saharan Africa (or 78 per cent if South Africa is excluded) (Neto et al., 2007). Notwithstanding the additional complications of diverse classificatory schema across space and through time, levels have also been rising in the last few decades. In Latin America, for example, seven out of 10 new jobs during the 1990s were in the informal sector (Chant, 2008b), and in Nigeria, where the informal sector has more than doubled its share of the urban labour force since the mid-1960s, to a current level of 57.9 per cent, as much as 90 per cent of new job creation is informal (Okunlola, 2007). Informal sector activities have also come to represent a major share of non-agricultural GDP, ranging from 29 per cent in Latin America to 41 per cent in sub-Saharan Africa, even if the urban informal sector's GDP share is lower than its employment share due to the prevalence of low-productivity ventures.

GROWTH OF THE INFORMAL SECTOR AND INFORMALISATION

Expansion of the informal sector in the period 1950 to 1970 was attributed to the creation of labour surpluses in cities that resulted from the combination of rural–urban migration with limited labour demand in emergent industries. According to Chen et al. (2004) this emphasis on the differential between economic and demographic growth was linked par excellence with the 'dualist school' of thought which conceptualised the formal and informal sectors of the economy as effectively separate entities, the latter often equated with the vestiges of traditional production. From the 1980s onwards, however, growth in informal employment has been linked primarily with recession and neoliberal economic restructuring. On top of the pressures exerted by the growth of the population of working age (a legacy of high fertility and declining mortality rates during the 1960s and 1970s), many households have had to send more of their members out to work, most commonly adult women, to combat the declining purchasing power of wages and rising prices (see González de la Rocha, 2001; McIlwaine et al., 2002; Roberts, 1994; 1995). Thus economic necessity has contributed to rising tendencies in female labour force participation in the post-war period, fuelled *inter alia* by increased education, access to contraception and rising age at marriage. In turn, the saturation of the informal sector is often argued to have hit women the hardest because, aside from their heavy representation in the sector (Figure 6.7), their limited skills and resources confine them to the lowest tiers of informal activity (see Chant, 2008b; Chant and Pedwell, 2008; Kabeer, 2008; Klasen, 2007; McIlwaine et al., 2002; also Figures 6.8–6.10).

Job losses in the formal sector add to the numbers entering informal work 'from below'. One such group of job losses has come from the downsizing and/or privatisation of public sector bureaucracies. In Argentina, for example, five major firms under government control up to 1989 (Argentine Airlines, ENTEL [the telephone company] and three other utility companies [gas, electricity and sanitation]), employed 100 000 workers before privatisation, but a mere 51 000 subsequently (Geldstein, 1994). Formal jobs have also been lost (or downgraded) in the private sector due to firm closure in the wake of increased global competition, or because of the introduction or intensified use of casual and/or subcontracting arrangements as a means of cutting costs. Testifying to Chen's (2009) assertion that much recent growth in informal employment has been *within* the formal sector, this has often been done with the direct or indirect support of the state, with Roever (2007: 15) noting for Latin America that 'making labour standards more flexible in the region has created a new class of urban informal workers:

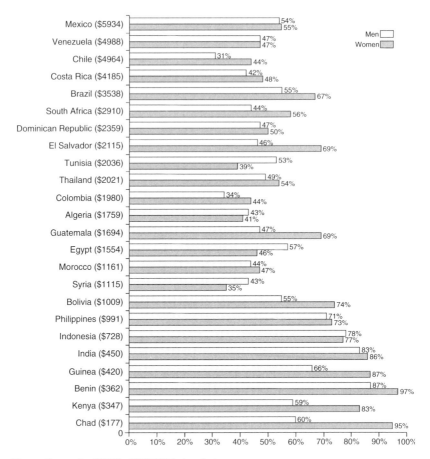

Note: Per capita GDP in US$2000 in brackets.

Source: Adapted from Heintz (2006: figure 5).

Figure 6.7 *Estimated percentage of total non-agricultural employment in informal sector by sex, 1994–2000*

those who are informally employed by formally registered enterprises'. While there is little doubt that formal sector firms have always evaded some labour regulations, the tendency to bypass these more systematically is a new phenomenon, on top of which many companies have also run down the wages, benefits and security conventionally attaching to formal sector jobs by introducing easier hiring-and-firing policies and employing larger proportions of plant-based workers on a casual basis (see Chant, 2008b; Roberts, 1991; Standing, 1991; 1999). In Southern Africa, for example, a

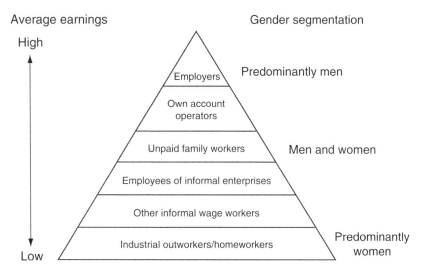

Average earnings   Gender segmentation

High

Employers   Predominantly men

Own account
operators

Unpaid family workers   Men and women

Employees of informal enterprises

Other informal wage workers

Industrial outworkers/homeworkers   Predominantly
women

Low

Source: Adapted from Chen et al. (2004).

Figure 6.8   Gender segmentation of informal employment

range of countries have introduced legislation in the last decade or so to lower labour standards and restrict union rights in order to attract multinational firms. This 'race to the bottom' has been so intense that in the mid-1990s both Zimbabwe and Namibia actually suspended national labour laws as a means of inducing footloose foreign investment (Jauch, 2002).

Another significant process in the informalisation of urban labour markets has been the need for smaller firms (or 'microenterprises') to move wholesale into informality as a result of declining ability to pay registration, tax and labour overheads. Reluctance to formalise is exacerbated by the often long drawn-out and complicated procedures required. For example, in Latin America and the Caribbean, it can take 70 days to undergo 11 procedures associated with starting a legal business, at a cost of 60.4 per cent of GNI per capita. In sub-Saharan Africa, the same number of procedures takes slightly less time (averaging 63 days), but costs as much as 225.2 per cent of GNI per capita (Neto et al., 2007: 5). As for a more specific, and especially protracted, example, in Egypt it takes more than 500 days and costs the equivalent of two-and-a-quarter years of minimum monthly salaries to open a bakery (Camaiora, 2007: 8). In light of this, it is no surprise that as Thomas (1996: 99) summarises, the 'top-down' informalisation promoted by governments and employers has been matched by a 'bottom-up' informalisation stemming from the need for retrenched formal sector workers and newcomers to the labour market to create their

Source: Photo by Cathy McIlwaine.

Figure 6.9   Women shoe traders in Gaborone, Botswana

own sources of earnings and/or to avoid the punitive costs attached to legal status.

The informal sector has become increasingly competitive during the last three decades, with more entrants to the sector, people working longer and harder days, and attempting where possible to diversify their income-generating activities. All this has tended to squeeze profits, with ILO figures for Latin America and the Caribbean revealing that there was a 42 per cent drop in income in the informal sector between 1980 and 1989. In turn, although the informal sector has continued to expand during the years of crisis and restructuring, it has not been able to absorb all the job losses in the formal sector. In Argentina, for instance, urban unemployment in 1991 was 20.2 per cent, compared with 5.6 per cent in 1986 (Bulmer-Thomas,

Source: Photo by Sylvia Chant.

Figure 6.10   Informal roadside recycling business, Fajara, The Gambia –
beaten and smelten tin cans are converted to cooking pots
(around 100 cans for each pot)

1996a: 326). The capacity of the informal sector to mop up unemployment is thus by no means infinite, and serves to underline how symbiosis rather than separateness is a more accurate term to characterise the configuration of urban labour markets in the Global South (see Fernández-Kelly and Shefner, 2006). This in many ways has undermined the argument that the informal economy is an 'adjustment mechanism' and grows in a counter-cyclical fashion, that is, expands during economic slumps and contracts during periods of economic growth. Instead, the health of certain types of informal activity, especially independent self-employment and subcontracting, may well be more pro-cyclical and require a buoyant formal sector in order to keep afloat (see Chen et al., 2004; Gilbert, 1998).

LINKS AND CONVERGENCE BETWEEN THE FORMAL AND INFORMAL SECTORS

Leading on from the above, recent decades of crisis and neoliberal restructuring have made the interconnectedness between the formal and informal sectors more visible, particularly in relation to the dependence of the latter on the former for contracts, supplies and economic viability. Detailed empirical studies have revealed that the informal sector is linked to the formal sector in numerous ways (see Box 6.1), thereby challenging previous notions of labour market dualism. This challenge has gained further currency through the aforementioned tendency for large-scale firms to make recourse to informal labour arrangements.

Yet although linkages have become increasingly visible, their recognition is not new. An early attempt to resist the construction of the formal and informal sectors as discrete and autonomous entities was Moser's seminal neo-Marxian exposition on 'petty commodity production'. This theorised urban labour markets as a continuum of productive activities in which large formal sector firms benefited from the existence of micro-entrepreneurs (Moser, 1978). More recently these ideas have been worked into the thesis of 'structuralist articulation' which views urban labour markets as 'unified systems encompassing a dense network of relationships between formal and informal enterprises' (Portés and Schauffler, 1993: 48). Chen et al. (2004) include this perspective under the heading of 'structuralist approaches', wherein although it is recognised that links between large- and small-scale firms are often exploitative, it is also acknowledged that some opportunities may be opened up for informal enterprises by globalisation and neoliberal strategies of export promotion. In many respects, this has encouraged recommendations for a more active and sympathetic policy stance towards the informal sector.

CHANGING POLICY APPROACHES TO THE INFORMAL SECTOR

Until relatively recently there was no explicit policy towards the informal sector in most developing countries. This was mainly due to anticipation

---

BOX 6.1　ECONOMIC LINKAGES BETWEEN THE FORMAL AND INFORMAL SECTORS OF THE URBAN ECONOMY

UFS = Urban formal sector
UIS = Urban informal sector

Backward linkages

a) Informal vendors sell products (for example, soft drinks, cigarettes) obtained from manufacturers, wholesalers and retailers in the UFS.

b) Informally produced goods such as cooked foodstuffs, home-made clothing and embroidered items are likely to comprise raw materials supplied by the UFS.

Forward linkages

a) The UIS may produce intermediate goods destined for final elaboration and distribution through the UFS. This may occur through subcontracting or purchase on the part of the UFS.

Benefits for UFS of subcontracting to UIS

i) Formal employers may avoid paying legal minimum (or above-minimum) wage.

ii) Formal employers avoid obligations to provide social security contributions and fringe benefits to workers in informal enterprises.

iii) Formal employers can respond more flexibly (and at lower cost) to fluctuations in product demand.

b) The (cheap) goods and services produced in the UIS, when consumed by UFS workers, arguably subsidise the wages of the UFS.

Source:　Thomas (1996).

---

that labour surpluses would eventually be absorbed by formal industry and services. Another factor was the reluctance of economists and civil servants to acknowledge informal activities as anything other than a 'parasitic', 'unproductive' form of 'disguised unemployment' (see Bromley, 1997; Portés and Schauffler, 1993).

In effect, the informal sector was (and in many circles still is) viewed as an employer of 'last resort' or a fragile means of basic subsistence in situations where social welfare provision for those outside the formal labour force is minimal or non-existent (Gilbert, 1998: 67). As stated by Mitullah (2007: 10):

informal sector policies. One outcome of advocating de-control of economic enterprise is that a precedent is set for greater deregulation in the
formal sector. This in turn contributes to broader processes promoted by
multilaterals such as the IMF and the World Bank to liberalise production
and markets in developing regions, which have often been harmful to low-
income groups (see Hart, 2007: 17 on the informality's instrumentalism to
neoliberalism during the 1980s and 1990s). Although it is often argued that
deregulation encourages investment and therefore creates more employment, Portés and Schauffler (1993: 55), among others, stress that the repeal
of protective legislation on wages, work conditions, health and accident
insurance, and unemployment compensation threatens a greater incidence
of worker abuse, minimal wages and disincentives for employers to provide
training and/or engage in technological innovation. In this sense, support
of the informal sector can potentially have very anti-redistributionist consequences (see also Fernández-Kelly and Shefner, 2006).

Indeed, alarmed by the widely observed deterioration of employment in
the last two decades, and the fact that around 3000 people die every day
from work-related accidents or disease, in 2001 the ILO launched an initiative called 'Reducing the Decent Work Deficit'. The 'Decent Work'
agenda has the goal of obtaining productive work for all in conditions of
freedom, equity, security and human dignity. It is a goal both for individuals and for nations, and is built around four strategic objectives, all of which
are cross-cut by gender (see Box 6.2). While recognising that pressures in
the global economy make enterprises less willing to countenance workers'
rights, or to pay for social protection, the ILO's argument is that there are
major economic dividends from decent work. For example, better-paid
workers tend to have higher levels of job satisfaction and productivity, and
respond positively when they are entitled to good quality jobs, profit-
sharing and a decision-making voice in the workplace (ILO, 2001; see also
Chant and Pedwell, 2008).

The ILO is concerned that 'Decent Work' principles should extend as far
as possible to the informal sector, with another important element in policy
discussions on the informal sector per se being to increase its efficiency.
Prominent obstacles at present include lack of working capital through
limited access to mainstream financial institutions and business support
services, concentration in highly competitive low-income markets, disad-
vantageous locations, obsolete technology, poor supply of public services,
the social atomisation of informal entrepreneurs due to the irregular and/or
chaotic nature of supplies, and the existence of a 'craftsman ethic' which
prevents some informal entrepreneurs from changing their traditional
methods of production (Ishengoma, 2007; Portés and Itzigsohn, 1997;
Portés and Landolt, 2000). Many of these constraints apply more to female

---

BOX 6.2 STRATEGIC OBJECTIVES OF THE ILO'S 'DECENT WORK' AGENDA

1) *Employment*
This refers to job creation through sound and sustainable investment and growth, access to the benefits of the global economy, supportive public policies and an enabling environment for entrepreneurship.

2) *Standards and fundamental principles and rights at work*
Following on from the ILO Declaration on Fundamental Principles and Rights at Work of 1998, this objective calls for the creation of work that does not involve forced labour, exploitation, discrimination and denial of association (for example, prohibition on the formation of trade unions).

3) *Social protection*
This principle is concerned with ensuring that workers have formal protection for old age, invalidity, sickness and health care, and with creating safe and dignified working conditions.

4) *Social dialogue*
This advocates the opening of channels of communication between different stakeholders in the economy, and particularly about giving workers in the informal economy more of a voice and representation.

Source: ILO (2001).

---

than male workers in the informal economy, as portrayed by Chakravarty et al. (2006) for Surat, in southern Gujerat, India (see also Kabeer, 2008).

A strongly favoured intervention for the informal sector on the institutional/macroeconomic side of the labour market is the relaxation or repeal of regulations and policies which obstruct entrepreneurship but do not serve any obvious or legitimate public regulatory purpose (Portés and Schauffler, 1993; Tokman, 1991). There has also been advocacy for governments to consider simpler and diminished requirements for regulation. For example, these may include a 'single window' or 'one-stop-shop' for registration (as introduced, for example, by the Shanghai Municipal Government), tolerance of progressive implementation, graduated fees according to firm output, size and location, and/or subsidies for informal enterprises to pay labour costs as part of poverty reduction strategies and social protection policies (Chen, 2009; Ishengoma, 2007; Neto et al., 2007: 5). One case where various strategies have been combined is that of Chile, which in 2002 introduced the Law of Family Micro-enterprises. This relaxed restrictions on domestic enterprise such that any legitimate economic activity could be carried out from home provided it was non-contaminating. Although the law has not created as many registrations as hoped for, by 2005 around 2000 Chilean micro-enterprises had been formalised (Chant and Pedwell, 2008). Indeed, that it is now considerably easier to bring a small business into the formal sector in Chile is evidenced by the fact that whereas there are only nine steps to formalisation, lasting an average of 27 days and costing 10 per cent of income per capita, in Latin America as a whole the respective figures are 11 steps and 70 days at a cost of 60.4 per cent of per capita income. A further programme, 'Chile Emprende', launched in 2005 has also helped to enable microenterprises to access financial support and credit (ibid.).

On the supply side of the labour market, there has been interest in policies geared to education and training to promote the diversification of the informal sector, to enhance access to credit, to provide assistance in management, marketing and packaging, and to introduce measures to promote greater health and safety. These initiatives are particularly relevant for groups such as ambulant traders and food vendors, among whom women feature prominently. There have also been calls for decentralised policies to accord with needs and skills in different localities (Portés and Schauffler, 1993: 56), and the orientation of policies away from individual firms or workers as a means of utilising the social networks and social capital (reciprocity, trust, social obligations among kin, friends, neighbours and so on) which so frequently fuel the operation of the informal sector (McIlwaine et al., 2002; Portés and Landolt, 2000).

HOUSEHOLD LIVELIHOOD STRATEGIES

As mentioned earlier in this chapter, employment is clearly vital to people's survival and well-being, and is usually the major element. However, it is not the only one, with many of the urban poor in developing countries drawing on multiple activities and resources in order to get by. The ways in which people's diverse activities, capabilities and assets (stores, resources, claims and access) are mobilised and pursued are referred to as 'livelihood strategies' (Chambers, 1995). While there are slight variations in theoretical and policy approaches to livelihoods, ranging from the 'sustainable livelihoods' framework used by the UK Department for International Development (Carney, 1998), the 'asset vulnerability' framework (Moser, 1998; Moser, 2007b), and the 'capital assets' framework (Rakodi, 1999), all reflect an

---

BOX 6.3   CAPITAL ASSETS OF THE POOR

Human capital
– vocational skills, knowledge, labour (access to/command over), health.
Social capital
– relationships of trust, reciprocity and exchanges that facilitate co-operation, and may provide for informal safety nets among the poor (NB. there can also be 'negative' social capital in the form of violence, mistrust and so on).
Natural capital
– natural resource stocks, for example, trees, land, biodiversity.
Physical capital
– basic infrastructure and producer goods such as transport, shelter, water supply and sanitation, energy and communications.
Financial capital
– savings (whether in cash, livestock, jewellery), and inflows of money, including earned income, pensions, remittances and state transfers.

Source: Rakodi (1999).

---

attempt to codify the multiple resources on which household livelihoods depend (also Bebbington, 1999). Since a livelihoods approach concentrates on what the poor have rather than what they do not have (Moser, 1998), scope is opened up to appreciate in a more holistic way how the poor actively negotiate survival (see also Chapter 7, this volume).

Carole Rakodi's (1999) exposition of the 'capital assets' approach to livelihoods concentrates on assets, which constitute stocks of capital of varying types (human, social, natural, physical and financial) which can be stored, accumulated, exchanged or depleted and put to work to generate a flow of income or other benefits (see Box 6.3). Depending on the local environment, social and cultural context, power relations within households and so on, people may manage assets differently, although on the whole 'households aim at a livelihood which has high resilience and low sensitivity to shocks and stresses' (Rakodi, 1999: 318).

Accepting that poverty has always called upon the poor to be resourceful, in the past three decades it has been argued that urban household livelihoods have come under unprecedented strain due to recession and neoliberal economic restructuring. Interest in this took off in the 1980s with the outbreak of debt crisis and the implementation of SAPs across a wide range of countries, especially in Latin America and sub-Saharan Africa (see Chapter 2). According to Elson (1989), the four main phenomena which affected households during this period – and which continue to have resonance today – were as follows:

1. *Changes in income*:
    (a) For employees, wage reductions and reduced availability of jobs.
    (b) For the self-employed, changes in product prices and product demand – products become more expensive to make due to increased prices of components, and harder still to sell given lower demand for goods resulting from reduced purchasing power of the population.
2. *Changes in the prices of basic commodities*. Escalation of food prices due to removal and/or reduction of subsidies, and the switch in farming from subsistence production to the cultivation of cash crops for export markets.
3. *Changes in public expenditure*. Especially pertinent to the social sector, in which services such as health and education have been cut back, and/or been subject to the introduction or increase of user charges.
4. *Changes in working conditions*. Changes in hours at work, increased intensity of activity in working hours, a decline in job security, the reduction of fringe benefits and so on.

Exploring how these changes have affected low-income people is inevitably complicated by variations in contextual factors such as local labour market conditions, pre-existing levels of national poverty, and the specific measures adopted by different countries to restructure their economies. Nonetheless, the findings of case studies from different parts of the world indicate broadly similar patterns in terms of the effects on households of recession and restructuring, and their responses to these processes.

Rakodi (1999) posits four common strategies through the lens of the capital assets framework for livelihoods:

1. *Strategies to increase resources, by intensifying the use of natural, physical or human capital.* This includes diversification of economic activities, starting businesses, migrating, renting out rooms, increasing subsistence production, and increasing 'occupational density'. The latter involves adopting multiple earning patterns by sending more members into the workforce, rather than relying on a single breadwinner. Many of these new workers are women who may have hitherto been economically inactive.

2. *Strategies to change the quantity of human capital.* This can be brought about in two main ways. First, household size might be increased through the retention or incorporation of members, who may work in remunerated activities themselves, or who may take on domestic chores and childcare in order to release wives and mothers into the labour force. Alternatively, households might opt for cutting consumption costs by lowering fertility, by engaging in migration, or by shedding members who are failing to make an adequate contribution to household well-being. The latter is sometimes the case when men do not pull their weight in the household forcing women and children to set up on their own (see Chapter 9, this volume).
3. *Strategies involving drawing on stocks of social capital.* These include borrowing, seeking charity, begging and, perhaps most importantly, strengthening people's extra-domestic links with kin and friends beyond the household unit for the purposes of securing and/or exchanging money, food, labour and so on.
4. *Strategies to mitigate or limit a decline in consumption.* These encompass the avoidance of 'luxury' purchases or expenditure, the withdrawal of children from school, the scaling down of social engagements, the buying of cheaper or second-hand clothes, and reduced spending on food and drink. Although people normally try to protect food consumption above all else, studies from countries as diverse as Mexico, Ecuador, the Philippines, Zambia and Cuba indicate that recession and restructuring have led to the poor eating fewer meals per day and also cutting down substantially on expensive items such as meat, milk and fresh fruit juice.

While Rakodi's classification of strategies is fourfold, they are underpinned by two main imperatives: to minimise consumption ('expenditure-conserving' or 'negative' strategies), or to maximise income ('income generating' or 'positive' measures) (see also Benería and Roldán, 1987; González de la Rocha, 1994). To a large degree it is conceded that these tactics enabled the poor to cushion themselves from the worst ravages of post-1980 recession and restructuring. For example, in Guadalajara, Mexico the increase in multiple-earning strategies and household extension in one low-income settlement between 1982 and 1985 resulted in a fall of real per capita income of only 11 per cent despite a fall of *circa* 30 per cent in the wages of household heads (González de la Rocha, 1988).

Yet even if most households have managed to fend off destitution in the crisis years, many have only done so at the cost of unprecedented self-exploitation and self-denial. Moreover, there is considerable doubt that these efforts can withstand further deterioration in national economic performance and polarisation. Mercedes González de la Rocha (2001), for example, warns that persistent poverty in Mexico for over two decades has effectively brought the poor to their knees. While the mobilisation of house-hold, family and community solidarity served as vital resources in the past, there is a limit to how many favours people can call on from one another and how effective these exchanges are in the face of huge structural impedi-ments to well-being. Indeed, disturbing evidence of weakened social capital and solidarity is also noted for South Africa by Bähre (2007) and for Nicaragua by Rodgers (2007). Another major worry is that the dispropor-tionate burdens which have fallen on women have stretched their personal reserves to full capacity such that there is no further 'slack' to be taken up (see also Elson, 1992; González de la Rocha, 2007; Moser, 1992).

GENDER-DIFFERENTIATED IMPACTS OF STRUCTURAL ADJUSTMENT

Ingrid Palmer (1992) posits that structural adjustment worsened women's position by intensifying two gender-based misallocations in the market, notably:

1. Unequal terms of male and female participation in employment.
2. Women's subjection to a 'reproduction tax' which derives from their responsibility for a disproportionate share of unpaid labour in the home.

The effects of restructuring on these misallocations among the urban poor fall into three main categories:

1. The informal sector becomes more crowded, therefore women suffer a greater fall in income given their disproportionate concentration in this sector.
2. Reductions in social service expenditure mainly affect reproductive labour and *ipso facto* women who are primarily responsible for domes-tic labour and childcare.
3. The introduction or raising of user charges for health and education means that women are more likely to be discriminated against in terms of access to schooling and medical care, which has numerous knock-on effects on human capital accumulation and well being.

These trends have four critically important implications for gender roles and relations among the urban poor. First, women are increasingly 'burnt out' by their arduous multiple roles and responsibilities such that, although increased labour force participation can enhance women's power and autonomy, in many cases it also adds another layer of oppression, espe- cially given the concentration of women in the lowest tiers of the occupa- tional hierarchy, both in formal and informal employment. Second, many authors have documented increased conflict between men and women, especially since men have shown few signs of moving into the domestic sphere to help their overburdened wives. Third, and related to this, some studies have noted a growing 'crisis of masculine identity' whereby men are suffering on account not only of their reduced access to jobs but the fact that their wives are earning and sometimes bringing in a bigger wage. These tendencies appear, in turn, to be linked with increases in violence, drug addiction and alcoholism. Fourth, the movement of adult women into the labour force can impact negatively on daughters who may have to neglect their education or be pulled out of school altogether in order to take care of younger siblings and/or to perform household chores. This obviously threatens the prospects for socio-economic mobility of younger women, and may exacerbate gaps between male and female education, training and employment.

Overall, therefore, it is possible to see two tiers of exploitation arising with neoliberal economic restructuring, one which affects the poor as a whole, and one which affects women in particular (Afshar and Dennis, 1992; Chant with Craske, 2003). Although poverty and gender oppression are not invariably linked, the pressures of maintaining household liveli- hoods on a daily basis arguably detract from broader gender struggles through which women might appreciably improve their situation (see Chapter 8, this volume). On top of this, as argued by Lind (2002: 229) in the context of Ecuador and Bolivia, where women have not only played a vital role in keeping their households and communities afloat through grassroots efforts, but where they have also been targeted by the state as 'volunteer or undervalued labour' in development initiatives: 'poor women increasingly have been viewed as the "answer" to a weak welfare state as well as a source of cheap labour' (see also Bradshaw, 2008; Chant, 2008a; Molyneux, 2006 in relation to conditional cash transfer [CCT] and/or micro-credit programmes in other contexts such as Nicaragua, Mexico, The Gambia and the Philippines).

Activity 6.1
Write a list of the main strategies that informal business operators might adopt to maintain household well-being in the context of increased economic competition, falling profits and rising prices. Classify these strategies according to whether they constitute 'income-generating' or

'expenditure-conserving' measures, and identify the types of 'capital assets' which may be mobilised in the process.

LEARNING OUTCOMES

By the end of this chapter and relevant reading you should be able to:

- Critically review the criteria which have been used to delineate the 'informal' and 'formal' sectors of urban labour markets in developing countries, and provide examples of informal and formal occupations.
- Outline the reasons for, and consequences of, the increased tendency to informalisation in urban economies.
- Identify the major impacts of neoliberal economic restructuring at the grassroots, and the coping mechanisms adopted by low-income households.

FURTHER READING

Chant, Sylvia and Pedwell, Carolyn (2008), *Women, Gender and the Informal Economy: An Assessment of ILO Research and Suggested Ways Forward*, Geneva: ILO (downloadable from www.ilo.org/wcmsp5/groups/public/---dgreports/---dcomm/documents/publication/wcms_091228.pdf).
An overview of ILO's work on women, gender and the informal economy, drawing out the implications for gender inequality and decent work across developing and transitional economies.

Chen, Martha Alter, Vanek, Joan and Carr, Marilyn (2004), *Mainstreaming Informal Employment and Gender in Poverty Reduction: A Handbook for Policymakers and Other Stakeholders*, London: Commonwealth Secretariat.
This book is downloadable chapter by chapter from www.idrc.ca/en. It is, *in toto*, one of the most comprehensive sources on analysis of, and policy approaches to, informal economic activity, with a gender perspective mainstreamed throughout.

Habitat Debate (2007a) 'A look at the urban informal economy', **13**(2), 1–24, Nairobi: UN-Habitat (downloadable from www.unhabitat.org).
Includes several short articles cited in the present chapter, which between them cover issues such as the growth and dynamism of the informal economy in different countries of the Global South, and the implications of different policy interventions.

Rakodi, Carole (1999), 'A capital assets framework for analysing household livelihood strategies: implications for policy', *Development Policy Review*, **17**, 315–42.
A thorough review of the 'assets' beyond waged work on which low-income households may draw, and the common strategies used during periods of particular

economic hardship. Synthesises the findings of many case studies and offers a livelihoods framework based on different groups of 'capital assets' such as financial, human and social capital.

Thomas, J.J. (1995), *Surviving in the City: The Urban Informal Sector in Latin America*, London: Pluto.
A very detailed and historically grounded analysis of the origins and evolving character of the urban informal sector over time, with particular reference to Latin American cities.

USEFUL WEBSITES

www.ilo.org – website of International Labour Organisation
www.livelihoods.org – website called Livelihoods Connect created by the UK Department for International Development on the livelihoods approach to reducing poverty

7. Poverty, vulnerability and exclusion

INTRODUCTION

Poverty has already been acknowledged in earlier chapters as being crucial in understanding development processes, with poverty reduction now the core issue driving international development policy. This is mainly through the centrality of poverty in both the MDGs and the PRSPs. In light of the widespread importance of poverty, this chapter is dedicated to reviewing definitions, measurements and conceptualisations of poverty. It interrogates the meaning of the term 'poverty', examining both early and more recent alternatives to explaining the multidimensionality of poverty such as vulnerability, livelihoods and chronic poverty. It also outlines the nature of poverty in the South in respect of its geographical distribution and the populations most likely to live in poverty.

WHAT IS POVERTY? DEFINITIONS AND MEASUREMENTS

It has long been recognised that poverty is an extremely complex entity. In basic terms, poverty refers to a shortage of income (White, 2008). However, in the development context, the multidimensional nature of poverty has been increasingly emphasised. Definitions frequently depend on the disciplinary viewpoint adopted, as well as who is deciding what poverty means – the poverty 'expert' or the poor themselves. Who is defined as poor in different societies is likely to vary, depending on value systems as well as economic variables (Thomas, 2000b: 11). As a quotation from a young boy from Guatemala cited in McIlwaine (2002: 82) illustrates: 'For me, being poor is having to wear trousers that are too big for me.' The World Bank reveals further competing claims on the term:

> Poverty is hunger. Poverty is lack of shelter. Poverty is being sick and not being able to see a doctor. Poverty is not having access to school and not knowing how to read. Poverty is not having a job, is fear for the future, living one day at a time. Poverty is losing a child to illness brought about by unclean water. Poverty is powerlessness, lack of representation and freedom.[1] (See also Chant, 2007a.)

Maxwell (1999) identifies a series of useful 'fault lines' in debates on defining poverty (see Box 7.1). Although nine are specified, at base they reflect two broadly different ways of conceptualising poverty. The first focuses on poverty as income and consumption, drawing heavily on the use of poverty lines measured by statistics. The second highlights subjective interpretations of poverty relying on participatory methods to identify what people themselves regard as poverty.

INCOME AND CONSUMPTION MEASURES: POVERTY LINES

The most common way of measuring poverty is through identifying access to material goods such as income or consumption (see Box 7.1; also Coudouel et al., 2002). This is calculated in a quantitative manner using poverty lines. A poverty line refers to a threshold below which people are considered poor. While there are wide variations in how this is calculated, the two main methods are, first, according to estimates of income in terms of what is earned or, second, as a level of consumption defined as what is needed to be consumed or expended in order to survive (Morduch, 2006a).

Drawing on household survey data, poverty lines estimate a level of income or expenditure necessary for buying sufficient food to satisfy the average nutritional needs of household members. This is called the 'food poverty line' and is used to identify the extremely poor. More commonly, this 'basic basket' of food items is added to an allowance for basic clothing, fuel and rent, to calculate a figure below which a household is said to be living in poverty. Consumption lines are more commonly used than income because people are usually more able to identify expenditures than income (Morduch, 2006b; White, 2008).

Poverty lines reflect absolute measures of poverty. For instance, the World Bank developed two international poverty lines in an effort to provide cross-country comparisons in their 1990 *World Development Report*. The first identified those with an income per capita of below US$370 per year (using 1985 adjusted prices), as 'poor', while those with less than US$275 were 'extremely poor'. The 2000/2001 *World Development Report* updated these poverty lines using the standard as US$1.08 a day (sometimes referred to as the 'Copenhagen Measure'), and US$2 per day based on 1993 adjusted international prices (World Bank, 2000; see also Coudouel et al., 2002).

BOX 7.1   FAULT LINES IN THE POVERTY DEBATE

- **Individual or household measures**

Following early measurements of poverty, much work still uses the household as the unit of poverty analysis. Other analyses disaggregate to the individual level to capture differences within households in terms of the factors affecting deprivation among women, men, children, the elderly and so on.

- **Private consumption only or private consumption plus publicly provided goods**

Poverty may be defined in terms of private income or consumption, or as including the value of goods and services provided publicly.

- **Monetary vs non-monetary components of poverty**

Monetary measures are often considered sufficient proxy for poverty, yet there is a clear fault line between these definitions of poverty and those which incorporate such factors as self-esteem or participation.

- **Snapshot or timeline**

Many surveys assess poverty at a specific point in time. However, there is also a long history of thinking about poverty in terms of life cycle experience, seasonal stress, and shocks. There has been increasing attention to understanding movement in and out of poverty, especially in light of SAPs.

- **Actual or potential poverty**

Some analysts include as poor those who are highly sensitive to livelihood shocks, or who are considered especially vulnerable.

- **Stock or flow measures of poverty**

The definition of poverty as income focuses on the flow of material goods and services. An alternative is to examine the stock of resources a household controls, notably its assets or capabilities.

- **Input or output measures**

It has been argued that a focus on income assumes an automatic link between income and participation, or functioning, in the life of a community. Income in this sense measures an input to the capabilities of an individual, rather than their well-being.

- **Absolute or relative poverty**

Poverty may be measured in absolute terms, such as the '$1 a day' used by the World Bank, or relative to different societies using, for example, measures of half of mean income, or exclusion from participation in a given context.

● **Objective or subjective perceptions of poverty**

The use of participatory methods has greatly encouraged an epistemology of poverty which relies on local understanding and perceptions.

Sources: Maxwell (1999); Thomas (2000b).

Variations in Poverty Lines

In an effort to measure relative poverty, a series of technical methods have been developed. The most common are the 'headcount index' and the 'poverty gap'. The headcount index measures the incidence of poverty through calculating the percentage of the population living below a poverty line – in other words, the proportion of the population that cannot afford to buy a basic basket of goods (Coudouel et al., 2002). Yet, this fails to account for how far people live below the poverty line. Thus, the poverty gap measures the depth of poverty and provides information on how far off households are from the poverty line through measuring the average distance below the poverty line expressed as a percentage of the poverty line. This measures the severity of poverty and the amount of resources needed to bring those below the poverty lines to a reasonable living standard (ibid.). Finally, a poverty severity index is similar to the poverty gap, but puts more weight on those furthest below the poverty line. These three measures are sometimes referred to collectively as the Foster-Greer-Thorbecke poverty measures (White, 2008; also Morduch, 2006b). A poverty severity (squared poverty gap) measure can also be made that takes into account the distance separating the poor from the poverty line (the poverty gap), as well as inequality among the poor. This is done through placing a higher weight on those households further away from the poverty line (Coudouel et al., 2002).

The above types of measure are important in complementing analysis of the incidence of poverty. For example, although poverty may be widespread, there may only be a small poverty gap (for example, when lots of people are just below the poverty line). In other cases there may be a low incidence of poverty but a high poverty gap (when few people are below the poverty line but those who are have very low levels of consumption or income). These differences are important for thinking through policy interventions as well. For instance, one programme may be effective at reducing the number of poor but might only help those close to the poverty line. Other policies might have little effect on the overall incidence of poverty, but might be very important in addressing the needs of the very poor or 'indigent' (Coudouel et al., 2002).

Criticisms of Poverty Lines

While poverty lines are useful for making cross-country comparisons, they have been widely criticised. One of the most pertinent criticisms is that income or consumption patterns only allow identification of who lacks resources at a given moment in time, but not those who have insufficient capacity to achieve access to resources on a more sustained basis. This is sometimes referred to as analysis of both the 'ends' and the 'means' of poverty, with 'means' being especially influenced by gender, ethnicity and class (see Kabeer, 2003). A second set of criticisms pertains to comparability among countries. Although exchange rate fluctuations can to some extent be ironed out by 'purchasing power parity' (PPP) which converts local prices and costs into internationally comparable prices (see McIlwaine, 2002, for a summary), what constitutes poverty is clearly mediated by social and cultural norms and practices which vary across time and space. A third group of criticisms of particular relevance to gender is that data for poverty lines are usually collected and calculated at the household level. This ignores intra-household inequalities in resource allocation which appear to systematically disadvantage women and children (see Chant, 2003; 2007a). Related to this is that poverty lines do not account for household size, thereby failing to consider economies of scale from living in larger households, such as utilities (ibid.). In turn, much income earned by the poor is not included in national accounts since it is generated in the informal sector (see Chapter 6, this volume). Similarly, own production is also overlooked even though it is often an important part of total consumption. This may include 'wild foods' (collected in the locality) and subsistence agriculture (White, 2008). In short, the choice of poverty line is arbitrary, but ideally needs to be chosen and calculated for a given country according to prevailing social norms of what is an acceptable minimum. This might be a legislated minimum wage in some countries but not in others. Furthermore, it is also possible to use some qualitative data as well, especially in deciding what goes into the basic basket, although these are harder to measure accurately (Coudouel et al., 2002).

SUBJECTIVE AND PARTICIPATORY APPROACHES

Given the problems inherent in defining and measuring poverty according to quantitative, static methods, qualitative approaches that emphasise the multidimensionality of poverty have become more popular over time (Chambers, 1995; see also Box 7.1). In essence, qualitative assessments attempt to incorporate subjective components of poverty, and/or the perceptions of the poor themselves. These may include factors such as spiritual and political freedom, self-respect and powerlessness, as well as environmental quality, health status, freedom from violence and so on (ibid.). In addition, they can identify other processes such as household participation in networks, the reasons for variations in patterns in household income and consumption, as well as the strategies developed by households to reduce vulnerability to hardship. Importantly, these techniques can often provide insights as to why a situation occurs, for instance, why certain groups in society may be poorer than others because they are discriminated against on grounds of gender or ethnicity (Coudouel et al., 2002; McIlwaine, 1997).

The identification of subjective elements has primarily been through the use of qualitative, participatory methodologies which are conducted with poor people, and geared to eliciting how they themselves define poverty. These methods have revealed that the relationship between income and poverty is not straightforward. In a widely cited example from India, Jodha (1988, cited in Chambers, 1995: 185–6) notes that people often perceived they were better-off when they were able to buy shoes, or to reside in separate living quarters from livestock, even at times when incomes had fallen. Another example from urban Jamaica highlighted how 'very, very poor people' were defined as 'blind ladies, beggars, the elderly and those living in shacks' (see McIlwaine, 2002: 86; see also Figure 7.1).

Some challenges to these participatory approaches have emerged, first, because they are difficult to measure and, second, because they often fail to adequately problematise and/or incorporate dimensions of power, especially in relation to gender. This is because participatory studies use focus group discussions to gather information, which, in turn, are nominally based on a consensus of views. Recognising that silences can be as meaningful as verbal articulation, those who find it difficult to express themselves in public may not speak up and their opinions are accordingly excluded (see Cornwall, 2003). Another difficulty is how the data from participatory assessments can actually be used. For example, although emphasis may be placed by grassroots respondents on more abstract phenomena than income such as self-esteem or spiritual well-being, it is probably harder to develop policies which address these kinds of issues over material ones (White, 2008). Despite this, participatory approaches are now widely accepted as important and useful ways of examining poverty in the South. A strengthening of this new-found legitimacy has undoubtedly come about as a result of the World Bank's 'Voices of the Poor' project conducted for the 2000/2001 *World Development Report* (World Bank, 2000). This was a huge and important project based on Participatory Poverty Assessments (PPAs) conducted in 60 countries, and with over 60 000 poor women and

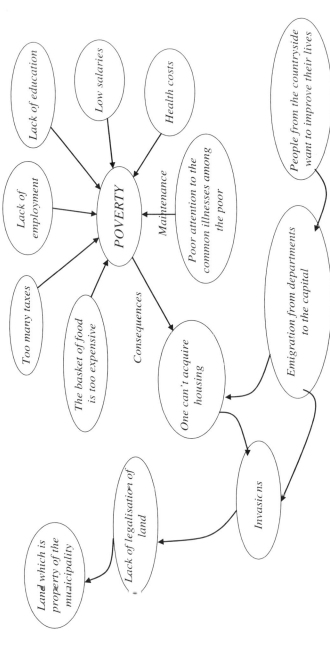

Source: Adapted from McIlwaine (2002: 93).

Figure 7.1 Causal impact diagram of poverty in Guatemala City (drawn by a group of six adult men in a local community hall)

192

men.[2] The importance of participatory approaches is also now enshrined in the *PRSP Sourcebook* which guides countries in creating poverty profiles as part of the PRSP process (Coudouel et al., 2002; see also Rigg, 2007: 76–7; see also Brock and McGee, 2002).

In addition to participatory approaches, other qualitative research tools include ethnographic and sociological case studies, as well as institutional political investigations. More specifically, these might involve participant observation, and in-depth semi-structured interviews from an ethnographic or longitudinal perspective. As noted above, such tools can provide information that is not possible to collect from household surveys, especially in relation to perceptions, and social cleavages. Moreover, they may assist in designing household survey questionnaires or in assessing the validity of survey results at the local level.

ALTERNATIVE CONCEPTUALISATIONS OF POVERTY

In line with the shift towards participatory approaches to poverty assessment, the constitution of poverty itself has also come in for greater scrutiny and (re)elaboration. This has involved notions of 'entitlements' and 'capabilities', drawing on the seminal work of Amartya Sen (1981; 1985) on food security and famines in rural areas. Entitlements refer to the resources that the poor use in order to withstand short- and longer-term shocks. As well as income from wage labour, 'entitlements' may refer to public goods such as health care and basic services, or to private income from the sale of assets, and resources from own production such as food, social security claims, and so on. In turn, Sen highlights that people may also be deprived because of lack of choice or capability rather than their material circumstances per se (see Kabeer, 2003, and Thomas, 2000b, for useful summaries; also Bebbington, 1999).

Also important in relation to entitlements and capabilities is the concept of vulnerability. Again, analysing vulnerability allows for a more dynamic interpretation of disadvantage than reliance on income data. The key to vulnerability is the extent to which the poor can develop coping strategies which allow them to withstand shocks. As with entitlements, this can be done through mobilising 'assets', as discussed in Chapter 6 in the context of the 'capital assets' approach. As a further example here, Moser's (1998) 'asset vulnerability framework', highlights how, in addition to wage labour, assets may include human capital (health and education), productive assets such as housing and land, household relations (referring to how different household structures may mediate the extent to which income is pooled, consumption shared and so on) and social capital (networks of trust and reciprocity). Since people experience vulnerability when they have few assets upon which to draw, it is possible to be relatively well-off in income terms, yet be vulnerable, due, for example, to lack of savings, lack of land and property ownership, and limited access to publicly subsidised services such as education and health care. An increasingly significant source of vulnerability in many developing countries is posed by conflict, crime and violence. As crime rates soar, people feel insecure and vulnerable (McIlwaine and Moser, 2003). Gender and ethnic dimensions of vulnerability are also important in that women and ethnic minority groups may be discriminated against making them vulnerable, yet not necessarily poor in terms of income (see McIlwaine, 1997, on Costa Rica). As Maxwell (1999) notes, planning for these groups means understanding both short-term coping strategies, as well as long-term adaptations to livelihood stress (see also Rigg, 2007).

Another increasingly popular concept related with the multidimensionality of poverty is social exclusion. This can be defined as: 'The process through which individuals or groups are wholly or partially excluded from full participation in the society in which they live' (Thomas, 2000b: 14). The term originated in France in the 1970s as a means of conceptualising disadvantage among people who had 'slipped through the net' of state social security schemes. As with vulnerability and entitlements, social exclusion is multidimensional in that it highlights social and political circumstances such as power relations, and social identities as well as economic status. Also similar is that it is dynamic, focusing on the processes or mechanisms by which people are excluded. As such, social exclusion recognises the role of institutions and actors within processes of privation. Finally, social exclusion highlights the importance of being integrated into society rather than lacking access to resources. Although social exclusion has been criticised as a European concept applied to Southern countries, it has gradually been incorporated into poverty discussions in the South, especially within policy debates at organisations such as the International Labour Organisation (see McIlwaine, 2002, for a summary in relation to Central America).

Although there remains considerable debate over what poverty means, it is now well established that poverty is not only about income, but encompasses a much wider range of criteria. Indeed, discussions of poverty now usually refer to 'livelihoods' as a way of highlighting that survival in the developing world is not just about making money, but having access to a range of other resources (Rigg, 2007). Without undue repetition of the details of a 'livelihoods' perspective itemised in Chapter 6, this volume, people clearly mobilise a range of resources to mitigate poverty. The strengths of a 'livelihoods' approach in poverty analysis include its interdisciplinarity and dynamism as well as its holistic take on the various social, cultural and political, as well as material, dimensions of human survival. It also links links intra-household and and extra-household relations, as well as bridging various boundaries such as rural/urban and formal/informal (de Haan and Zoomers, 2005).[3]

Yet livelihoods approaches have also been criticised in relation, *inter alia*, to their lack of attention to power, politics and governance both within communities as well as at national and regional levels. Such approaches can also assume that the enhancement of livelihoods of one group or stratum or class will undermine livelihoods of another group or stratum or class. Whatever the case, livelihoods approaches have often proved difficult to translate into practice by agencies. Indeed, the UK's DFID dropped its Sustainable Livelihoods Framework (SLF) in the early 2000s on grounds that it was difficult to make micro–macro-level linkages, even if it is conceded that it remains a valuable way of examining the muiltidimensionality of poverty at an analytical level (de Haan and Zoomers, 2005).

The final concept to be developed in recent years is that of 'chronic poverty'. This draws on many threads of aforementioned debates on (re)conceptualising poverty but focuses explicitly on severe deprivation. The approach emphasises how chronic poverty is deep-rooted, often passed down generations, and, as a result, is hard to reverse. It is also frequently linked with discrimination (ethnicity, caste and gender) and, as such, how poverty is disproportionately experienced by children, women, the elderly and those facing challenges such as HIV/AIDS. Chronic poverty is also heralded as being experienced in particular environments and conditions (especially remote rural areas, urban slums and conflict zones), and as owing to minimal asset ownership which translates into an inability to create sustainable livelihoods (see Moser, 2007b. In different countries and contexts it can mean different things. For example, in Ghana it is defined by people as 'a beggar with two bags' (someone who has to beg during the season of plenty, as well as the season of hunger) (CPRC, 2005). It is nominally possible, therefore, to distinguish between the 'chronically poor' who are 'always poor' and 'usually poor', the 'transitory poor' whose poverty fluctuates, and the 'non-poor' (ibid.). The important issue about the chronically poor, however, is that they are often overlooked by policy-makers despite comprising an estimated 900 million people worldwide who have little chance of moving out of poverty (ibid.).

Activity 7.1

1. Consider the country where you live, regardless of whether it is in the North or the South. Identify the main characteristics of poverty in your area. Is poverty mainly linked with lack of income, or is it related with other less tangible factors, such as limited access to land and housing or exclusion from certain activities?

2. Go to the website of OneWorld TV at http://tv.oneworld.net/. Listen to the voices of people from various parts of the Global South (especially Bulelwa Benya, Abrahim Mamani, Ana-Maria De Souza, Sunita Dharavath, Nassa Sylvain, David Batista Felix, Emmanuel Kalunga, and Adisu Demissie). After listening to the clips, try and identify whether these people are chronically poor, transitorily poor or non-poor.

THE SCALE OF POVERTY IN THE GLOBAL SOUTH

Bearing in mind the range of conceptual issues just discussed and the problems associated with measuring poverty in quantitative ways, it is useful to present a general picture of the geographical distribution of income poverty in the South. Broadly speaking, and in absolute terms, the majority of the world's poor live in Asia. However, this is reduced if the focus is on social welfare as well as income in light of the relatively high levels of education and life expectancy in China. In terms of the proportions of people living on less than US$1 per day, in 2003, sub-Saharan Africa fared worst with a level of 44 per cent of the total population, followed by 31 per cent in South Asia. In East Asia and the Pacific only 12 per cent lived in poverty, and a mere 2 per cent in the Middle East and North Africa.[4]

However, there are also important distinctions and differences at the sub-regional level. For example, in Latin America 9 per cent of the population was said to be living on less than US$1 per day in 2003, but in Brazil this was only 8.2 per cent, and in Honduras as much as 23.8 per cent (Table 7.1). There are also variations when comparing national poverty lines with international ones. For example, in China, official national poverty lines for 1996 suggested that only 4.6 per cent of the population lived below the line (and only 2 per cent in cities). Yet an international comparison estimated that 16.6 per cent were living on less than US$1 per day (Table 7.1). There are also large variations according to the US$1 and US$2 measures in different regions and countries. In Africa, for example, just under one-half of the population lives on less than US$1 while over three-quarters (76.1 per cent) live on less than US$2 (Table 7.1).

POVERTY TRENDS IN THE GLOBAL SOUTH

Major differences in poverty incidence among different regions of the Global South must be interpreted in light of recent trends. In general terms, there was a fall in the global proportion of the population living in poverty between 1981 and 2004, from 67 to 48 per cent, and in extreme poverty,

Table 7.1   National and international poverty lines in selected countries of the Global South

Country	Proportion of population living below the poverty line						
	National poverty lines				International poverty lines		
	Survey Year	Rural	Urban	National	Survey Year	Percentage population below $1 per day	Percentage population below $2 per day
Latin America							
Brazil	1990	32.6	13.1	17.4	2001	8.2	22.4
Colombia	1999	79	59	64	1999	8.2	22.6
Guatemala	2000	74.5	27.1	56.2	2000	16.0	37.4
Honduras	1993	51.0	57.0	53.0	1998	23.8	44.4
Asia							
China	1996	4.6	2.0	4.6	2001	16.6	46.7
India	1999/2000	30.2	24.7	28.6	1999/2000	34.7	79.9
Indonesia	1999	—	—	27.1	2002	7.5	52.4
Sri Lanka	1995–96	27.0	15.0	25.0	1995–96	6.6	45.4
Africa							
Chad	1995–96	67.0	63.0	64.0	—	—	—
Malawi	1997–98	66.5	54.9	65.3	1997–98	41.7	76.1
Mali	1998	75.9	30.1	63.8	1994	72.8	90.6
Rwanda	1993	—	—	51.2	1983–85	35.7	84.6

Source: World Bank (2005) (downloadable from http://siteresources.worldbank.org/INTWDR2005/Resources/wdr2005_selected_indicators.pdf) (accessed 24 April 2008).

from 40 to 18 per cent (Reddy, 2008). East and South Asia have shown dramatic improvements in poverty reduction over the last three decades, linked with rapid economic growth, especially in the NICs of the region. Since these are mainly concentrated in East Asia it is no surprise that in this sub-region poverty fell from 30 per cent in 1990 to 12 per cent in 2003, while in South Asia, decline was more modest from 41 per cent to 31 per cent.[5] In contrast, the situation in most of Africa has remained largely static as economic growth has been low, and conflict, corruption and environmental disasters have been widespread. In addition, and perhaps most significant, is the rapid spread of HIV/AIDS throughout the continent (see Chapters 3 and 10, this volume). Together with the other factors identified, this has contributed to a minimal decline in poverty of only 1 per cent in more than a decade, from 45 per cent in 1990 to 44 per cent in 2003. Furthermore, the rate of population growth, while also increasing in many Asian countries, has been even greater in most African nations, meaning that the absolute numbers of people living in poverty has risen massively. In Latin America, the decline in poverty incidence was also small, even if the overall proportions have historically been smaller. For example, the World Bank estimates a decline from 11 per cent to 9 per cent living on less than a US$1 per day between 1990 and 2003 (see also Reddy, 2008).[6] This low level of improvement is partly explained by overall rises in poverty in some countries.

WHO ARE THE POOR IN THE GLOBAL SOUTH?

Not only are there variations within regions of the South, but also within countries and communities. A major distinction within most countries is between rural and urban areas, with the incidence of poverty being generally higher in the countryside. Indeed, in all the countries shown in Table 7.1, in only one, Honduras, is urban poverty more prevalent than rural. However, Chambers (1995) notes that in comparing 1990 with 1970, while the poor remain concentrated in rural parts of Asia, urban poverty has increased. This is partly linked with the imposition of SAPs in the 1980s and 1990s, which affected cities more than the countryside due to public sector job losses, rising costs of utilities, less food self-sufficiency and so on (see McIlwaine, 2002; Tsikata, 2009; also Chapters 2 and 6, this volume). Indeed, just as various studies have drawn attention to diminishing quantitative differences in the incidence of rural and urban poverty as urbanisation has proceeded towards the 'tipping point' (Chapter 4), so too have they pinpointed a range of qualitative differences in rural and urban privation. For example, Beall and Fox (2007) draw attention to the fact that the poor in urban areas are more likely to have to rely on the monetised economy and on informal sector work, and are more exposed to crime and violence. Infectious disease may also be a particular hazard in densely settled slum communities, thereby compounding the problems of inadequate housing, services and infrastructure (see Chapters 4 and 11, this volume).

Particular people within countries are also more likely to experience poverty than others. Chambers (1995) notes that these include children, urban women and the elderly, together with refugees or displaced and landless people. Gender in particular is an important source of variation in experiences of poverty, but also one that has been subject to much debate and misinterpretation (see Chant, 2003; 2008d). As noted above, women are generally thought to be poorer than men on grounds that they lack access to resources and the ability to convert their labour into income due to reproductive constraints. Yet, it is extremely difficult to assess gender differences in poverty due to the lack of sex-disaggregated data. This has resulted in the problematic use of female household headship as a proxy for gendered well-being as discussed in detail in Chapter 9. Nonetheless, this association, coupled with women's concentration in low-status, informal-sector occupations, has led many to argue that there has been a 'feminisation of poverty' throughout the South. This is dangerous, first, because there is little empirical evidence to support such a trend; second, because it cannot be assumed that by investing in women, poverty will be reduced; and third, there is no guarantee that poverty reduction will eradicate gender inequalities (Chant, 2008a).

Other important factors influencing experiences of poverty are ethnicity and 'race'. As mentioned earlier, ethnic inequalities may extend beyond income inequalities and reside primarily in vulnerability and social exclusion. In Latin America, for instance, indigenous peoples have suffered from centuries of social exclusion rooted in colonialism and capitalist development. This has often involved their active exclusion through force. In Guatemala, for instance, there was widespread massacre of thousands of indigenous people during the worst years of the civil war in the 1980s. While the situation has improved since the signing of Peace Accords in 1996, and income poverty remains a main concern among indigenous groups, many other privations are experienced (McIlwaine, 2002; McIlwaine and Moser, 2003).

These broad patterns also identify the chronically poor. More specifically, these tend to be people who are discriminated against as ethnic groups and minorities, bonded labourers, poor and/or trafficked women and children, Internally Displaced Persons (IDPs), those who are disabled and stigmatised (especially by HIV/AIDS) and those living in certain types of households (usually large, with high dependency ratios, and sometimes female-headed) (CPRC, 2005). Such groups find it extremely difficult to escape poverty, and in Ghana are often referred to as 'God's Poor' since there is no obvious remedy for their poverty (ibid.).

CAUSES OF POVERTY

Perhaps not surprisingly, the causes of poverty are multidimensional and relate to structural, political, social, cultural and individual factors. At a global level, and as we have seen at various points in the book, world development, trade, power and production tend to militate against countries of the Global South, and especially the most vulnerable within these countries. Arguably, the terms of trade are stacked against developing countries, debt has unfairly accumulated in the South, and the SAPs of the IFIs have further exacerbated poverty and inequality. Despite attempts by governments and IFIs to reorientate their work around poverty reduction, most agree there is still a long way to go (as the discussion on the MDGs in Chapter 1 testifies). Linked with this, many have identified globalisation as a major cause of poverty. Therefore, roots of poverty at this scale remain very controversial. For instance, the Make Poverty History Campaign identifies the unjust global trade system, debt and ineffective aid as the reason why poverty levels remain high throughout the world. In turn, they target the G8, the IFIs and other countries of the Global North as those responsible for maintaining poverty.[7]

At national and local levels, a host of interrelated factors underlie poverty including corrupt government, ineffective management of the economy leading to low levels of economic growth, the fragility and/or breakdown of law and order, and failure to invest in the health and education needs of the population (see also Figure 7.1). Thus, poverty interrelates strongly with other social welfare indicators. In particular, the poor are more likely to have lower life expectancy, higher levels of infant mortality, lower literacy rates and higher levels of morbidity (see Chapter 10, this volume). All these factors combine to reduce the well-being of many populations in the developing world. In relation to chronic poverty in particular, the Chronic Poverty Research Centre (CPRC, 2005) identify a series of 'maintainers of poverty' that keep people poor. These include low levels of economic growth, social exclusion, the disadvantaged position of specific geographical and agro-ecological regions, pronounced capability deprivation, weak, failing or failed states and tenuous international co-operation. In turn, they discuss the 'drivers of chronic poverty' which push the vulnerable non-poor and transitory poor into poverty. These include ill health and injury, environmental shocks, natural disasters, violence, impunity and market and economic collapse (ibid.)

POVERTY REDUCTION

Since poverty processes are at the heart of all development concerns, from individual to global levels, it is not surprising that poverty has taken centre stage within debates in development policy arenas (Thomas, 2000b; also Easterly, 2006; Sachs, 2005). As noted earlier, poverty reduction is the focus of the vast majority of multilateral, bilateral and non-governmental organisations throughout the world today (see Chapter 11, this volume). Furthermore, it is recognised that causes of poverty are complex and diverse, which, in turn, requires holistic solutions to reduce it. It is no coincidence that the MDGs pinpoint core issues of the economy, education, health, gender equality, environmental sustainability and international co-operation in order to dovetail thinking on poverty reduction. In addition, lending by IFIs is now linked with poverty reduction through the HIPC II and PRSP initiatives that have replaced SAPs (Chapter 2, this volume). Somewhat ironically in light of the flurry of policy concern over poverty, at a global level it is still the poor themselves who are making the most effort to address their own situations of poverty (Easterly, 2006; Moser, 2007b).

While macro-level initiatives are important in reducing poverty, specific initiatives on the ground are crucial. These can be grouped together under the term 'social protection'. This refers to a range of social safety net measures that aim to reduce vulnerability of the poor, help to protect them against shocks (such as recession, natural disasters and so on), and which build or protect their rights (Devereux and Sabates-Wheeler, 2004; Kabeer, 2008; Moser, 2007a). These may include the provision of basic services such as health and education as well as broader efforts to change legislation to protect vulnerable groups. Actual projects might incorporate the provision of family allowances or child benefit, school feeding programmes or cash for work schemes. One increasingly important type of social protection measure among donors and NGOs are cash transfers. These are non-contributory transfers provided in cash to poor households or individuals. In a study by Save the Children UK, HelpAge International and Institute of Development Studies (2005) in 15 East and Southern African countries, it was found that despite variations, these were more effective than providing food because it increased choice and also led to a more diverse range of ways that the poor were able to deal with poverty and vulnerability. Children and those vulnerable to HIV/AIDs were shown to particularly benefit from such transfers. However, cash transfer programmes may also lack sustainability in the longer term. This has led to the realisation that these type of social protection measures also need to be combined with projects and policies that allow the poor to deal with risk over time and to accumulate their assets (Moser, 2007b, for a range of examples).[8]

Despite numerous efforts to reduce poverty at all scales from the grassroots to the institutions of global governance, it is sobering that poverty persists throughout the world, especially in sub-Saharan African (see Easterly, 2006). Although many still believe in the benefits of large-scale interventions to reduce poverty (Sachs, 2005), it is also worrying that the aim to eradicate poverty by 2015, as enshrined in the MDGs, is now acknowledged to be unattainable. Thus, as suggested by many NGOs across the world, whose objectives are often shaped by concerns of rights and justice, it is perhaps time to think about challenging the world order in much more powerful and radical ways than has hitherto been the case.

Activity 7.2
1. Access and read DFID's 2006 White Paper on poverty reduction and global governance at www.dfid.gov.uk/wp2006/. Summarise the key elements of poverty reduction in terms of specific strategies as outlined in these papers.
2. Consult the website of 'worldmapper' at www.worldmapper.org/. Search the maps on poverty and assess how these maps reflect both the geographical incidence of poverty throughout the world, but also broader global inequalities.

LEARNING OUTCOMES

By the end of this chapter and having completed the essential reading and activities you should be able to:

- Describe and explain changes in conceptualisations of poverty over time, and outline alternative concepts that have been developed to portray deprivation.
- Describe the nature of poverty in the South, the populations most likely to suffer from poverty, and the main causes.
- Identify how the international development community is attempting to reduce poverty.

NOTES

1. See http://web.worldbank.org/WBSITE/EXTERNAL/TOPICS/EXTPOVERTY/EXTPA /0,,contentMDK:20153855~menyPK:435040~pagePK:148956~piPK:216618~theSitePK :430367,00.html#measuring (accessed 29 April 2008).
2. See www1.worldbank.org/prem/poverty/voices/reports.htm (accessed 23 April 2008).
3. See also www.chronicpoverty.org/CPToolbox/Livelihoods.htm (accessed 23 April 2008).
4. See map and data on devdata.worldbank.org/atlas-mdg/ (accessed 26 April 2008).
5. See devdata.worldbank.org/atlas-mdg/ (accessed 26 April 2008).
6. See devdata.worldbank.org/atlas-mdg/ (accessed 26 April 2008).
7. See www.makepovertyhistory.org/whatwewant/index.shtml (accessed 23 April 2008).
8. See www.undp-povertycentre.org/oct.htm for an evaluation of a range of cash transfer programmes undertaken by the International Poverty Programme (accessed 27 April 2008).

FURTHER READING

Beall, Jo and Fox, Sean (2007), *Urban Poverty and Development in the 21st Century: Towards an Inclusive and Sustainable World*, Oxford: Oxfam GB Research Report (pdf version downloadable gratis, and free print copy available on request from www.oxfam.org).
This report provides an up-to-date overview of the nature, incidence and patterns of urban poverty across the Global South.

De Haan, Leo and Zoomers, Annelies (2005), 'Exploring the frontiers of livelihoods research', *Development and Change*, **36** (1), 27–47.
This journal article provides a succinct state-of-the-art assessment of research into livelihoods over the last two decades. It identifies the most important findings from a range of different studies as well as identifying the ways forward for future research.

McIlwaine, Cathy (2002), 'Perspectives on poverty, vulnerability and exclusion', in Cathy McIlwaine and Katie Willis (eds), *Challenges and Change in Middle America*, Harlow: Prentice Hall/Pearson, pp. 82–109.
This chapter presents an overview of changing conceptualisations of poverty over time, as well as an outline of the pattern and incidence of poverty with a particular focus on Central America and the Caribbean.

Moser, Caroline (ed.) (2007b), *Reducing Global Poverty: The Case for Asset Accumulation*, Washington, DC: Brookings Institute.
Moser's edited collection brings together a range of interesting chapters that focus on how to reduce poverty from the perspective of asset-accumulation that can be used in conjunction with social protection to reduce poverty in the long term.

USEFUL WEBSITES

www.undp-povertycentre.org/ – website of the International Poverty Centre which is a joint project between the United Nations Development Programme and the Brazilian Government. It aims to encourage South–South co-operation on poverty research and training from a policy perspective

www.odi.org.uk/publications/poverty.html – website of the Overseas Development Institute. This offers a series of 'Poverty briefings' on up-to-date issues relating to poverty and development

www.oxfam.org/advocacy/papers/htm – website of Oxfam, UK. This offers access papers on poverty and debt issues

www.worldbank.org/poverty – website of the World Bank with information on poverty including trends over time

www.bridge.ids.ac.uk/ – website of the Institute of Development Studies which has Bridge Reports dealing with gender and poverty issues

www.ids.ac.uk/ids/pvty/index.html – website of the Institute of Development Studies Vulnerability and Poverty Research Team

http://unstats.un.org/unsd/methods/poverty/edocuments.htm – website of the UN Statistics Division focusing on their Handbook on Poverty Statistics: Concepts, Methods and Policy Use

www.makepovertyhistory.org/ – website of the Make Poverty History Campaign
www1.worldbank.org/prem/poverty/voices/ – website of the World Bank Voices of
the Poor Project. Reports from the project can be downloaded from here
www.chronicpoverty.org/index.html – website of the Chronic Poverty Research
Centre

8.   Gender and development

INTRODUCTION

In the past four decades, gender and development has become a major sub-field of development studies and policy. In the discussion which follows, we begin with a basic introduction to the meaning of 'gender', and proceed to consider major gender inequalities in developing regions, together with how these are measured and expressed in gender indicators. Thereafter we examine why and how gender has increasingly been taken on board in international development agendas, and the major policy approaches dominating the field since the UN Decade for Women (1975–85) and, more recently, the Beijing Platform for Action (BPFA) and the MDGs. Issues at the forefront of discussions of gender in the twenty-first century, such as 'women's empowerment' and the incorporation of men in gender and development planning and policy are also covered.

DEFINING GENDER

There are many definitions of gender in the literature on developing and advanced economies, but most share an emphasis on gender as a social construct that shapes the roles and identities of women and men, and the relations between them. A useful working definition of gender issued at the Fourth World Conference on Women (FWCW) in Beijing in 1995 is as follows:

> 'Gender' refers to socially constructed roles of women and men ascribed to them on the basis of their sex, whereas the term 'sex' refers to biological and physical characteristics. Gender roles depend on a particular socio-economic, political and cultural context, and are affected by other factors, including age, 'race', class and ethnicity. Gender roles are learned and vary widely within and between cultures . . . [and] can change. Gender roles help to determine women's access to rights, resources and opportunities. (Cited in Pietilä, 2007: 88)

Gender inequalities occur in 'public' arenas such as the labour market and formal politics, as well as in the nominally 'private' sphere of home and household. Gender inequalities in these different domains are not only

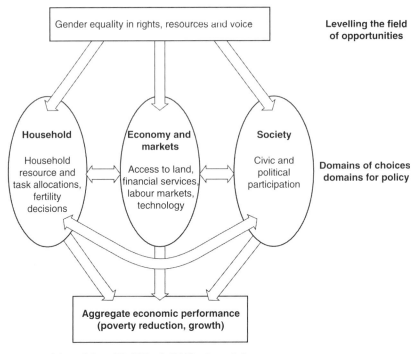

Source: Adapted from World Bank (2007a: figure 3.1).

Figure 8.1   *Gender equality, domains of choice and economic performance:*
              a framework

interrelated with one another, but have major synergies with development. As such, advances towards greater gender equality which straddle economic, political and social dimensions are commonly construed as integral to reducing poverty and improving economic growth (see Figure 8.1). As argued by the UNDP (1995: 1) in its landmark *Human Development Report* on gender: 'Human development, if not engendered, is endangered.'

The extent and manner of changes in gender inequalities over time is hotly debated, and contingent on the specific historical and contemporary circumstances of different countries, and of different groups of women and men, as well as on the particular gender issues in question. For some precolonial societies, for example, it has been argued there was greater gender equality and complementarity in respect of work, parenting and power This said, in most parts of the world, both North and South, greater prestige has traditionally been accorded to men (and masculinity) than women. This bias persists to the present day, as evidenced by often notable 'gender gaps' in well-being, capabilities, resources and power. The importance of gender analysis lies in its quest to interrogate the different bases, manifestations and outcomes of persistent (and sometimes new) inequalities, and its potential to challenge gender injustice. For example, the theorisation of gender as a social construct, which has long been a hallmark of gender and development (GAD) thinking, takes us beyond the idea that gender roles and relations are 'natural' or 'preordained', and to imagine other forms of 'personhood' (see Chant and Gutmann, 2000; Reeves and Baden, 2000). Gender scholarship has also played a major role in documenting women's often invisible histories, in expanding our knowledge of disparities between women and men, and, *inter alia*, in contributing to statistical and other measures through which it is possible to assess how gender gaps are evolving in the context of recent and contemporary development.

GENDER INEQUALITIES AND THEIR MEASUREMENT

Although some gender gaps seem to have narrowed in the past three decades, particularly in education and health (see UNDP, 2000; WEDO, 2005), the general picture of gender at a global scale remains one of glaring difference. For example, women still hold only 10 per cent of seats in national assemblies worldwide and 6 per cent of government positions. In numerous countries, male use of contraceptives is a mere fraction of that of women's (below 5 per cent in most cases) (see Chapter 3, this volume). Women's average non-agricultural earnings are still only 75 per cent of their male counterparts, and in many countries of the South, considerably less. For example, women's average wages in manufacturing are as low as 56 per cent of men's in South Korea, and only 54 per cent in Brazil (UN, 2000: 132). Bearing in mind the relative crudity of quantitative aggregate measures of gender disparities (see below), in no country in the world is there evidence of full equality between men and women in economic, political or social spheres. Indeed, even in the arena of basic demographics, life expectancy, which is generally 5–7 per cent higher for women as a result of their in-built biological advantage, averages only 2–3 per cent higher in developing regions. Here it has been argued that women's genetic 'head-start' is undermined by discriminatory treatment towards girls and women, and by the risks associated with childbearing (Smyke, 1994; see also Chapters 3 and 10, this volume). Disparities such as these constitute a persuasive case for acknowledging the importance of gender as a key axis of social differentiation, and for doing something to redress existing inequalities. Along with nearly four decades of dedicated feminist organising and

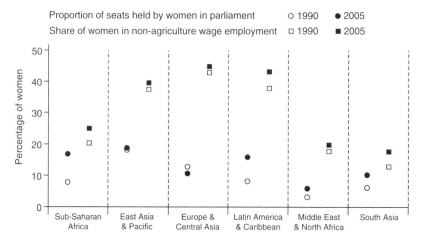

Source: Adapted from World Bank (2007a: figure 3.7).

Figure 8.2   *Progress in share of women in non-agricultural wage employment and proportion of seats in parliament held by women, by region*

campaigning across the globe (see below), it is no surprise that gender nominally features prominently in the MDGs, both as a goal in its own right and as a 'cross-cutting' issue.

The strong emphasis placed on MDG monitoring is particularly positive not only because it highlights changes in some gender inequalities over time, but because it indicates how countries are making progress (or not) towards determined targets, especially those such as employment and political representation which have to date lagged behind educational advances (Figure 8.2). That the MDG process is actually able to track changes in gender is the fruit, in large part, of early feminist campaigning for more and better sex-disaggregated panel data. While acknowledging the difficulty of quantifying the complexities of gender inequalities, as far back as 1979, the Convention on the Elimination of All Forms of Discrimination Against Women (CEDAW), stressed the need not only for sex-disaggregated statistics but for indicators which measured change over time (see Box 8.1). These, in turn, have been deemed an essential part of the struggle to promote and achieve gender equality, especially in policy terms. As summarised by Annalise Moser (2007: 7): 'what gets measured is more likely to get addressed' (see also Dijkstra and Hanmer, 2000).

BOX 8.1   DEFINITION OF A GENDER-SENSITIVE INDICATOR

An indicator is an item of data that summarises a large amount of information in a single figure in such a way as to give an indication of change over time, and in comparison to a norm. Indicators differ from statistics in that, rather than merely presenting facts, they involve comparison to a norm in their interpretation.

A gender-sensitive indicator can be defined as an indicator that captures gender-related changes in society over time. Thus whereas a gender statistic provides factual information about the status of women, a gender-sensitive indicator provides direct evidence of the status of women, relative to some agreed normative standard or explicit reference group.

An example of a gender statistic would be: *'60% of women in country x are literate as opposed to 30% five years ago'.*

An example of a gender-sensitive indicator would be: *'60% of women in country x are literate, as compared to 82% of men, and compared to 30% and 52% five years ago'.*

The norm or reference group in this example is men in the same country, but in other cases might be other groups of women.

Source: Beck (1999: 35).

THE UNDP GENDER INDICES

The most famous published indicators of gender inequality at an international level are the UNDP's Gender-related Development Index (GDI) and Gender Empowerment Measure (GEM). The GDI measures gender disparities in the three main variables making up the Human Development Index, namely, life expectancy, educational attainment (schooling and literacy) and income. While the GDI focuses on the impact of gender inequality on human development, the GEM measures equity in agency – in other words, the extent to which women are potentially able to achieve equality with men (see Bardhan and Klasen, 1999). This is assessed in the GEM through four main variables:

1.   The share of parliamentary seats occupied by women.
2.   The proportion of the total number of legislators, senior officials and managers who are women.

Table 8.1   Gender-related Development Index (GDI): selected countries

	Life expectancy at birth (years) 2001		Adult literacy rate (%) (15 years +) 2001		Combined primary, secondary and tertiary gross enrolment ratio (%) 2000–2001		Estimated earned income (PPP US$) 2001		GDI value
	Female	Male	Female	Male	Female	Male	Female	Male	
High Human Development									
Singapore	80.0	75.7	88.7	96.4	75	76	14 992	30 262	0.880
Korea (Rep)	79.0	71.4	96.6	99.2	84	97	9 529	20 578	0.873
Uruguay	78.6	71.3	98.1	97.2	89	79	5 774	11 190	0.830
Costa Rica	80.3	75.6	95.8	95.6	66	65	5 189	13 409	0.824
Medium Human Development									
Philippines	71.6	67.6	95.0	95.3	81	70	2 838	4 829	0.748
Ecuador	73.2	68.0	90.3	93.4	71	73	1 504	5 040	0.716
Sri Lanka	75.5	69.6	89.3	94.5	64	63	2 095	4 189	0.726
Bolivia	65.4	61.3	79.9	92.3	80	88	1 427	3 181	0.663
Bangladesh	60.9	60.1	30.8	49.9	54	54	1 153	2 044	0.495
Low Human Development									
Cameroon	49.4	46.6	65.1	79.9	43	52	1 032	2 338	0.488
Pakistan	60.3	60.6	28.8	58.2	27	45	909	2 824	0.469
Gambia	55.2	52.2	28.5	43.1	43	51	1 339	2 396	0.457
Zambia	33.4	33.3	30.9	45.0	43	47	554	1 009	0.376
Niger	45.9	45.3	8.9	24.4	14	21	646	1 129	0.279

Notes: Countries listed in descending order of GDI rank in 2003 UNDP *Human Development Report.*

Source: UNDP (2003: table 22).

3.   The female share of professional and technical jobs.
4.   The ratio of estimated female to male earned income (see Tables 8.1 and 8.2).

Both these UNDP gender indices can be regarded as important complementary tools in the analysis of 'gender gaps', as well as indicating the greater prominence given to gender in national accounting and mainstream

Table 8.2 Gender Empowerment Measure (GEM): selected countries

	Seats in parliament held by women (%)	Female % of senior officials and managers	Female professional and technical workers (%)	Ratio of estimated female to male earned income	GEM value
High Human Development					
Singapore	11.8	24	43	0.50	0.594
Korea (Rep)	5.9	5	34	0.46	0.363
Uruguay	11.5	37	52	0.52	0.516
Costa Rica	35.1	53	28	0.38	0.670
Medium Human Development					
Philippines	17.2	58	62	0.59	0.539
Ecuador	16.0	25	44	0.30	0.489
Sri Lanka	4.4	4	49	0.50	0.272
Bolivia	17.8	36	40	0.45	0.522
Bangladesh	2.0	8	25	0.56	0.218
Low Human Development					
Cameroon	8.9	—	—	—	—
Pakistan	20.6	9	26	0.32	0.414
Gambia	13.2	—	—	—	—
Zambia	12.0	—	—	—	—
Niger	1.2	—	—	—	—

Notes: Countries listed in descending order of GDI rank in 2003 UNDP *Human Development Report.*
— = no data.

Source: UNDP (2003: table 23).

global evaluations of economic development. By the same token, a range of problems have been identified. One of the problems with the GDI, for example, is that it is heavily affected by a country's HDI, with wealthier countries tending to have higher GDI scores simply because more of the population have usually benefited from increased life expectancy, educational provision and so on. Thus while the GDI has traditionally been deemed the 'flagship indicator' of gender-related development, Klasen (2006) conjectures that by the second decade of the twenty-first century, this may well have been replaced by a composite indicator of gender inequality that simply averages the female–male ratio of achievement in different components of the index. Another problem with the GDI (as well as the GEM), is that it can gloss over disparities in different aspects of gender within countries. For example, as indicated in Table 8.1, in 2001 Costa Rica had a high level of human development and was one of the richest countries in the South, yet women enjoyed an average of only 46 per cent of male income. By contrast, women's earned income is over 50 per cent of men's in Zambia, which is very poor, and has low human development, or indeed Niger where less than 20 per cent of women receive formal education, and high levels of female illiteracy persist.

As for the GEM the component variables are (like those of the GDI), not only rather narrow in range, but are not relevant to all women. For example, women's earned income is based only on formal sector employment which excludes the vast majority of poor women who are engaged in the informal sector (Kabeer, 2003; see also Chapter 6, this volume). Similarly, women's representation in parliament may have very little to do with political activity or rights among low-income women. As Cueva Beteta (2006: 221) summarises: 'the GEM is an incomplete and biased index on women's empowerment, which measures inequality among the most educated and economically advantaged and fails to include important non-economic dimensions of decision-making power both at the household level and over women's own bodies and sexuality'.

Part of the problem with the UNDP gender indices is that in many cases the data do not exist to make them more refined and/or elaborate. Despite some progress over the past few decades, there continue to be many lacunae in respect of statistics which are either sex-disaggregated or which are especially pertinent to gender (see Moser, A., 2007; UN, 2006b). In several respects, this has also circumscribed the reach of gender targets and indicators within the MDGs. As summarised by the World Bank (2007a: 119–20):

> the official indicators are far better at measuring gender equality than empowerment – the former referring to the 'rights, resources and voice' enjoyed by women relative to men, the latter pertaining to whether women are empowered in an absolute sense – that is, whether they have the ability to exercise options, choice, control and power.

Although the UN Millennium Project Taskforce recommended a vastly expanded range of strategic priorities and indicators for MDG 3 (the dedicated goal for gender equality and empowerment of women), to bring these more in line with the BFPA agreed at the Fourth World Women's Conference in 1995 (see Box 8.2; also Boxes 8.3 and 8.4), the continued dearth of statistical information has been partly responsible for preventing the measures suggested from being incorporated to date.

BOX 8.2   CRITICAL AREAS OF CONCERN IN THE BEIJING PLATFORM FOR ACTION (BPFA)

– The persistent and increasing burden of poverty on women
– Inequalities and inadequacies in and unequal access to education and training
– Inequalities and inadequacies in and unequal access to health care and related services
– Violence against women
– The effects of armed or other kinds of conflict on women, including those living under foreign occupation
– Inequality in economic structures and policies, in all forms of productive activities and in access to resources
– Inequality between men and women in the sharing of power and decision-making at all levels
– Insufficient mechanisms at all levels to promote the advancement of women
– Lack of respect for and inadequate promotion and protection of the human rights of women
– Stereotyping of women and inequality in women's access to and participation in all communication systems, especially in the media
– Gender inequalities in the management of natural resources and in the safeguarding of the environment
– Persistent discrimination against and violation of the rights of the girl child

Source: Pietilä (2007: 73–4).

ALTERNATIVE GENDER INDICATORS AND GENERAL PROBLEMS WITH DATA

Beyond the GDI and GEM, one alternative is the Standardised Indicator of Gender Equality (SIGE). The SIGE omits income, but measures another five variables included in the GDI and GEM, namely, life expectancy, access to education, female labour force participation, female share of higher-level occupations and female participation in parliament, measured either in terms of female:male ratios or female proportion of the total. While the SIGE attempts to measure inequality between women and men without the bias introduced by national levels of human development

---

BOX 8.3   STRATEGIC PRIORITIES FOR GENDER EQUALITY: SUGGESTED AMENDMENTS TO MDG 3

- Strengthen opportunities for post-primary education for girls while simultaneously meeting commitments to universal primary education
- Guarantee sexual and reproductive health and rights
- Invest in infrastructure to reduce women's and girls' time burden
- Guarantee women's and girls' property and inheritance rights
- Eliminate gender inequality in employment by decreasing women's reliance on informal employment, closing gender gaps in earnings and reducing occupational segregation
- Increase women's share of seats in national parliaments and local government bodies
- Combat violence against girls and women

Source: UNMP/TFEGE (2005).

(as in the GDI), one problem is that improvements for women relative to men over time may not represent an actual advance in the context either of declining situations for men, or an overall deterioration in societal well-being (Dijkstra and Hanmer, 2000; UNIFEM, 2002).

A further and more elaborate indicator is the World Economic Forum (WEF) measure of women's empowerment. Based on published national statistics and data from international organisations, together with qualitative survey data from the annual WEF Executive Opinion Survey, the WEF measure includes economic participation, economic opportunity, political empowerment, educational attainment, and health and well-being. Each of these dimensions, in turn, encompasses far more than the conventional stock of criteria. For example, economic participation measures not only the gap between women and men in respect of levels of economic activity, but unemployment levels and remuneration for equal work. Economic opportunity takes into account the quality, terms and conditions of women's employment, including maternity leave benefits, the impact of maternity laws on the hiring of women, the availability of state-provided childcare, and equality between women and men in private sector employment (see Lopez-Claros and Zahidi, 2005). While the WEF measure is

---

BOX 8.4   MENU OF INDICATORS FOR MDG 3
PROPOSED BY THE TASKFORCE ON
EDUCATION AND GENDER EQUALITY

Education
- Ratio of female to male gross enrolment in primary, secondary and tertiary education
- Ratio of female to male completion rate in primary, secondary and tertiary education

Sexual and reproductive health and rights
- Proportion of contraceptive demand satisfied
- Adolescent fertility rate

Infrastructure
- Hours per day (or year) spent by women and men in fetching water and collecting fuel

Property rights
- Land ownership by women, men or jointly held
- Housing title, disaggregated by women, men or jointly held

Employment
- Share of women in employment (wage and self-employment), by type
- Gender gaps in earnings in wage and self-employment

Participation in national parliaments and local government bodies
- Percentage of seats held by women in national parliament
- Percentage of seats held by women in local government bodies

Violence against women
- Prevalence of domestic violence

Source: UNMP/TFEGE (2005: box 1).

---

clearly a positive step towards improvement in the range of variables used to measure gender (in)equality, limited availability of the quality data required means it has only been possible to calculate for 58 countries of the world, thereby excluding most of the Global South.

A further recent development is the Gender, Institutions and Development (GID) database which not only attempts to measure the socio-economic status of women, but also includes 'institutional' variables ranging from intra-household behaviour to social norms, which impact on

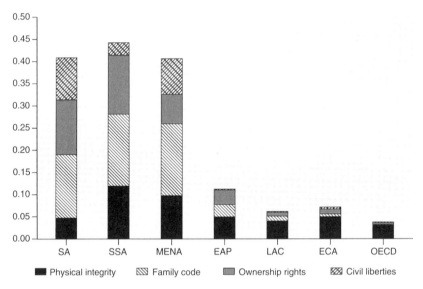

Note: 0 = no discrimination; 1 = maximum level of discrimination.
SA = South Africa; SSA = sub-Saharan Africa; MENA = Middle East and North Africa;
EAP = East Asia and Pacific; LAC = Latin America and the Caribbean; ECA = Europe
and Central Asia; OECD = Organisation for Economic Co-operation and Development.

Source: Adapted from Jütting et al. (2006: figure 2).

Figure 8.3   Regional indices of discrimination against women

gender inequality (see Jütting et al., 2006). More specifically, GID aims to quantify such issues such as Female Genital Mutilation (FGM), Violence Against Women (VAW), provisions of national Family Codes with regard to polygamy, inheritance, land ownership, loans and finance, civil liberties such as freedom of movement and female dress codes, access to social services, and economic roles (ibid.: 18–19). The results of GID analysis indicates that discrimination against women is particularly marked in South Asia, sub-Saharan Africa and the Middle East and North Africa, especially in respect of Family Codes, ownership rights and civil freedoms (see Figure 8.3).

Yet on a more general note, it should be borne in mind that no matter how broad the range of criteria included in gender indicators, their very selection can be problematic, not least because 'progress' is a highly subjective, contested and context-dependent concept. While accepting that standardising data for different nations and regions is helpful in some ways, the meanings of the criteria chosen to encapsulate improvements in women's lives may not travel easily across diverse cultural, social and economic settings.

As one example here, women's rising participation in the labour force is routinely construed as an important indicator of 'progress' given its conjectured links with increased autonomy, power and well-being. Yet this might not be the case where women's wages remain low, or they have to surrender their earnings to fathers or husbands. For example, the Zambian Demographic and Health Survey of 2002 indicated that 60 per cent of married women could not decide on the use of their own earnings (Mboup and Amunyunzu-Nyamongo, 2005). Leading on from this, while Dijkstra and Hanmer (2000) point out that higher female income shares are commonly equated with more gender-sensitive development, we also have to consider what this implies in respect of women's 'double' and/or 'triple burden' (that is, the juxtaposition of income-generating work with other [unpaid] responsibilities in their homes and communities) (see Chant, 2006; Moser, 1993). Given that women can rarely count on much alleviation of their reproductive labour of housework and childcare to offset the additional time they spend in paid work, employment may represent a double-edged sword. In turn, the ability of women to find income-generating activities which allow them to accommodate childcare and domestic duties may be deemed more important by women themselves within the context of prevailing gender norms than the amount of remuneration derived from their business ventures.

In a similar vein, the ability to reduce fertility, as measured by the prevalence of 'modern' contraception, is often stressed as positive for women. Yet this may not be the case in cultures where motherhood (and having big families or many sons) are women's primary source of social status. Moreover, bias towards 'modern' (Western) contraceptive techniques ignores the use and/or efficacy of traditional methods which may have fewer side effects and/or pose less danger to women's health (see Chapter 3, this volume). Simple figures for contraceptive prevalence also tell us little about the extent to which women may have been pressurised or even coerced into controlling their fertility.

In order to avoid some of these value-related problems, one positive step might be to encourage wider participation in the determination of indicators. To date most indicator choice has lain in the hands of small groups of 'international experts', rather than a broad cross-section of different stakeholders such as national governments in the South, NGOs, and/or women and men themselves (see Moser, A., 2007).

Beyond questions of which criteria are chosen to map progress in gender equality, it is also clear that improvements need to be made in the accuracy of data. Most contemporary indicator systems are developed from national censuses, which in themselves may not be reliable given sporadic collection, poor enumeration and imprecise definition of key terms, not to mention gender bias (Beck, 1999; UN, 2006b). Indeed, even for very basic data on population, births and deaths, the United Nations Statistics Division (2005: 6) asserts that: 'there has been very little progress in the official reporting of sex-disaggregated data in the past 3 decades, with 14 countries having failed to report to the UN at all'. This is partly due to the challenges of cost and time involved in conducting censuses on a regular basis. Although 85 per cent of the world's population resides in a country in which at least one census has been undertaken between the 1980s and 2000s, only three-quarters of the world's 204 countries were able to provide sex-disaggregated vital statistics in the period 1995–2003 (ibid.).

On top of this general caveat, one of the most problematic areas in respect of data is that of women's work. As highlighted earlier, since much of this is unpaid and/or carried out in the informal sector of the economy it is extremely difficult to measure. There are also whole areas relevant to gender equality where information may be absent because of its contentious nature, such as rape, sexuality and domestic violence. Even if reporting on the latter has improved in recent years, with a major international study on intimate partner violence conducted in 2002 by the World Health Organisation, self-censorship may preclude the production of accurate or verifiable figures (McIlwaine, 2008). As pointed out by Annalise Moser (2007: 28), women may fear that 'by speaking out they will increase their vulnerability to violence'.

Given the difficulties of collecting as well as quantifying more abstract phenomena pertinent to gender inequality such as power, independence and rights, we need to be careful in how we draw inferences about these issues from the data that do actually exist. For example, low levels of female labour force participation might be construed as indicating lack of personal power, or early marriage and/or high fertility may suggest lack of sexual freedom, but these explanations do not necessarily work for all situations. As pointed out by Beck (1999) and Saith and Harriss-White (1999), among others, gender indicators disclose little about social meanings, or the processes which give rise to gender difference. In turn, a major problem with simple reliance on, and categorical inference from, quantitative measures is the formulation of policies which address the symptoms rather than the causes or underlying determinants of given gender disparities. One way out of this trap is to combine quantitative with qualitative research and analysis. As summarised by Annalise Moser (2007: 1): 'The "hard figures" produced by quantitative methods are crucial in building the case for addressing disparities, whereas qualitative methods enable a more in-depth examination of gender relations and other issues not easily counted'.

Another vital advance concerning data could come from rectifying the situation where we have little information about differentiation between women (or men) on account of their stage in the life course, household circumstances, marital and fertility status and so on. The fact is that particular groups of women such as elderly women, or adolescent girls may be more disadvantaged and/or vulnerable than others, but as with all aggregate measures, such differences are masked (Chant, 2006).

POLICY APPROACHES TO GENDER AND DEVELOPMENT

In general terms, policy approaches to gender and development can be viewed as falling under the auspices of two overarching frameworks: a Women in Development (WID) approach, and a Gender and Development (GAD) approach.

WOMEN IN DEVELOPMENT

The formulation of the term 'WID' dates to the early 1970s. Commonly attributed to the Women's Committee of the Washington DC Chapter of the Society for International Development, concern with women's 'predicament' in developing regions was fuelled by a mounting body of academic research revealing that 'gender-blindness' in the design and execution of development projects resulted in women being 'overlooked', sidelined, and even harmed, by planned interventions (Moser, 1993: 2). The term crossed into the policy arena through its incorporation into the 'WID approach' by USAID (ibid.). Based on the notion that women represented an 'untapped' force in economic growth, and vitalised by calls around the world for a fairer deal for women in development, WID entered its heyday during the United Nations Decade for Women (1975–85).

The UN Decade for Women is widely heralded as a 'milestone' in the advancement of gender equality. Not only was it the most successful of the UN's 'themed decades' in the second half of the twentieth century, enduring through a long series of review and monitoring processes, but it drew on, as well as galvanised, forces for change across a broad cross-section of stakeholders at the grassroots (see Pietilä, 2007; also Box 8.5) . Indeed, the Fourth World Women's Conference in Beijing in 1995 stands out as the most attended UN conference ever, with as many as 189 government delegates, and an overall total of nearly 18 000 participants (Pietilä, 2007: 70; also Box 8.6).

The exhortation to 'integrate' women in development during the UN Decade led to the formation of 'national machineries' to fulfil this objective in around 140 countries. This was complemented by broader initiatives

---

BOX 8.5   MILESTONES ON THE ROAD TO
'EQUALITY – DEVELOPMENT – PEACE'
1970–2005

1970	Resolution of Concerted International Action for the Advancement of Women
1975	International Women's Year – World Conference, Mexico City, World Plan of Action
1975–85	UN Decade for Women (UNDW): Equality, Development, Peace
1979	Convention on the Elimination of All Forms of Discrimination Against Women (CEDAW)
1980	World Conference of the UNDW, Copenhagen
1985	World Conference to Review and Appraise the Achievements of the UNDW, Nairobi Forward-looking Strategies for Advancement of Women (NFLS), 1985–2000
1993	World Conference on Human Rights, Vienna Vienna Declaration and Programme of Action
1994	International Conference on Population and Development (ICPD), Cairo
1995	World Summit for Social Development, Copenhagen
1995	Fourth World Conference on Women, Beijing Platform for Action
2000	General Assembly, 23rd Special Session: 'Women 2000: Gender Equality, Development and Peace in the Twenty-first Century' or Beijing+5, New York
2000	Millennium Summit, New York
2005	Session of the Commission on the Status of Women on Beijing+10, New York
2005	World Summit, New York – World Summit Outcome (WSO)

Source: Pietilä (2007: 115).

---

such as the establishment of women's representatives, bureaux/units and programmes in regional and international organisations, including the Canadian International Development Agency (CIDA), the European Union, the World Bank, the UN and the ILO. These developments were – and continue to be – parallelled in numerous NGOs at national and

---

BOX 8.6 THE UNITED NATIONS WORLD CONFERENCES ON WOMEN

1975 Mexico City,* 19 June–2 July
World Conference of the International Women's Year (IWY)
Outcome: Declaration of Mexico and the World Plan of Action for the Implementation of the Objectives of IWY
Attendance: Conference, 133 states, *c*. 1200 delegates; NGO Tribune, 6000 Participants

1981 Copenhagen, 24–30 July
World Conference of the United Nations Decade for Women
Outcome: Programme of Action for the second Half of the UN decade for Women
Attendance: Conference, 145 states; *c*. 2000 delegates; NGO Forum, 6000–7000 participants

1985 Nairobi, 15–26 July
World Conference to Review and Appraise the Achievements of the UN Decade for Women: Equality, Development and Peace
Outcome: The Nairobi Forward-looking Strategies for the Advancement of Women 1986–2000
Attendance: Conference, 157 states; NGO Forum, 16 000 participants and attendants

1995 Bejing, 4–15 September
Fourth World Conference on Women
Outcome: Beijing Platform for Action for Equality, Development and Peace; Beijing Declaration
Attendance: Conference, 189 states, *c*. 17 000 delegates and observers; NGO Forum, 35 000–40 000 participants

Note: * More information on conferences can be accessed on WomenWatch website – www.un.org/womenwatch/asp/user/list.asp?ParentID=40 (accessed 22 March 2008).

Source: Pietilä (2007: 53).

---

international levels such as Oxfam, Christian Aid, Voluntary Service Overseas (VSO), the International Women's Tribune Centre (IWTC), the Association for Women's Rights in Development (AWID), Development Alternatives with Women for a New Era (DAWN), Women Living Under

---

BOX 8.7   MAIN WID POLICY APPROACHES

Approach	Target group	Time period	Brief characterisation
Equity approach	Women	1975–85	First WID approach. Main goal is to accomplish women's equality with men in development, through changing legal and institutional frameworks which subordinate women
Anti-poverty approach	Low-income women/ female heads of household	1970s onwards	Second WID approach. Premised on the idea that women's disadvantage stems from poverty, rather than gender subordination, the main aim is to raise women's economic status through income-generating programmes
Efficiency approach	Low-income women	1980s onwards	Third WID approach. Main goal is to harness women's efforts to make development more efficient and to alleviate poverty in the wake of neoliberal economic restructuring

Source: Chant and Gutmann (2000: table 2.1).

Muslim Laws (WLUML) and Women's Environment and Development Organisation (WEDO) (see Pietilä, 2007: 84–7; UNDP, 1995).

While different types of WID policy emerged during the 1970s and 1980s (see Box 8.7), three threads in common were:

1. A focus on women as the subject of analysis and operations.
2. The setting-up of separate organisational structures for dealing with women.
3. The development of women-specific policies and projects.

At one level these contributions signalled a major breakthrough. Never before had resources been apportioned to women's development in this way, nor had so many women found their way into the ranks of the international development system. The potential to inculcate awareness of gender in development planning was an historical first. At another level, however, the tendency of WID approaches to concentrate exclusively on women gave rise to widespread doubts about their efficacy and desirability. In conceptual terms, for example, the essentialist notion that women constituted a group whose condition was primarily determined by their sex, sat uneasily with rising theoretical emphasis on the need to understand how women's positions evolved dynamically through their socially constructed relationships with men in different social, economic and political arenas. Leading out of this, concerns emerged around WID's seemingly unquestioned assumption that women would benefit by being 'slotted in' to existing (male-biased) development structures (Parpart, 1995: 227). This presupposed that women's development was a 'logistical problem, rather than something requiring a fundamental reassessment of gender relations and ideology' (Parpart and Marchand, 1995: 13). Another major problem was WID's failure to broach the social differentiation of women on account of age, class, ethnicity and so on (Moser, 1993: 3). The definition of 'women-in-general' as a single identifiable interest group could obviously obscure the effects of other 'cross-cutting differences', which might be equally, if not more, important than gender per se in respect of understanding and addressing inequality.

Leading on from this, the concentration of WID on 'practical gender needs' only answered some of women's problems, and failed to address more fundamental strategic interests such as changing the balance of power between the sexes (see Box 8.8). In effect, WID-influenced interventions tackled the symptoms rather than the sources of gender inequalities, which is undoubtedly one reason why, in many contexts, there has been little progress in various aspects of women's lives in recent decades. While WID made women much more visible in the development process, its tendency to generate 'ad hoc' or 'add-on' solutions has resulted in tokenism and marginalisation of women's long-term interests, at all levels of the planning process as well as 'on the ground'.

In addition, questions also emerged, particularly from women in the South, around the wisdom of drawing women further into a process of

BOX 8.8 PRACTICAL AND STRATEGIC GENDER NEEDS

Now in widespread use in the gender and development lexicon, the conceptual origins of practical and strategic gender needs lie in the classic work of Maxine Molyneux (1984) who distinguished between the ways in which policies of the Sandinista government in Nicaragua in the early 1970s often addressed only the practical gender interests of women, rather than their strategic gender interests (see also Molyneux, 2001: ch. 3). Although Caroline Moser adopted this distinction and adapted it for gender planning in the context of her Triple Roles' framework, by redefining 'interests' as 'needs' (see Moser, 1993), Molyneux is careful to point out that 'needs' and 'interests' are not theoretical equivalents. Whereas 'needs' belong to planning discourses and tend to reflect bureaucratic imperatives, 'interests' emerge out of power relations and are advanced by women themselves 'from below'.

Practical gender needs revolve around the immediate, material needs of women in their existing gender roles (mainly as mothers and housewives). Programmes designed to meet practical gender needs are usually oriented to the domestic and community arena, and to the fulfilment of basic necessities such as food, water, shelter, urban services and so on which enable women to perform their reproductive tasks more efficiently. Since women's 'traditional' gender-assigned roles generally revolve around the care and nurture of husbands and children, the satisfaction of women's practical gender needs is likely not only to benefit women, but all members of their households.

Strategic gender needs aim to go much further than providing women with the practical means of fulfilling their reproductive roles, revolving as they do around issues of status and challenging gender-inequality. As Moser (1993: 39) describes: 'Strategic gender needs are the needs women identify because of their subordinate position to men in their society . . . They relate to gender divisions of labour, power and control and may include such issues as legal rights, domestic violence, equal wages and women's control over their bodies. Meeting strategic gender needs helps women to achieve greater equality. It also changes existing roles and therefore challenges women's subordinate position (see also Molyneux, 2001).

The distinction between practical and strategic gender needs has been increasingly adopted by agencies, such as the Commonwealth Secretariat which in its *Commonwealth Plan of Action on Gender and Development*, identifies the following measures as integral to the fulfilment of strategic gender needs:

1. Equal opportunities in employment.
2. Improved land and property rights for women.
3. Better access by women to education.
4. Non-sexist education.
5. Greater female participation in decision-making.

Sources: Chant and Gutmann (2000: 14, box 2.1), Commonwealth Secretariat (1995), Molyneux (1984; 2001: ch. 2), Moser (1993).

planned change which was heavily influenced by the advanced economies. This led to calls to break with neo-colonial development strategies and to recast development on the basis of the self-determined interests of Southern women (encapsulated broadly in what has come to be known as the 'empowerment approach'). At a more general level, criticisms of WID began to give way to the formulation of a new 'GAD' paradigm.

GENDER AND DEVELOPMENT

Although GAD is by no means a singular approach and appears open to a complex variety of interpretations by different stakeholders, its basic theoretical premise is that gender is a dynamic social construct (see Box 8.9). Not only is gender shaped by a multiplicity of intersecting time- and place-contingent influences (culture, economy, legal and political institutions, for example), but it is further mediated by men's and women's insertion into other socially generated categories such as class, age and 'race' (Moser, 1993: 3). In this light, an undifferentiated and unilateral focus on women is not only conceptually inappropriate, but deprives gender interventions of their transformative potential. Only by accepting that gender is a 'constructed' rather than 'natural part of life' does radical change in gender roles and relations become possible (Parpart and Marchand, 1995: 14). In turn, planning for change in women's lives clearly entails changes for men, with structural shifts in male–female power relations being 'a necessary precondition for any development process with long-term sustainability' (Rathgeber, 1995: 212; see also McIlwaine and Datta, 2003).

BOX 8.9   MAIN POST-WID AND GAD POLICY APPROACHES

Approach	Target group	Time period	Brief characterisation
Empowerment	Women	1980s onwards	First post-WID approach, sometimes referred to as 'WAD' ('Women and Development'). Aims to empower women and to strengthen their self-reliance by means of supporting bottom-up/grassroots mobilisation
Integration	Women and men	1980s onwards	First GAD approach. Concern is to counteract the marginalisation of WID by integrating gender as a cross-cutting issue in development organisations and interventions (often referred to as 'mainstreaming')
Equality	Women and men	1990s	Second GAD approach, emerging in the aftermath of the Fourth World Conference for Women in Beijing, 1995. Goal is to achieve equality and power-sharing between men and women as means, and end, of wider exercise of human

	rights, and people-centred sustainable development

Sources: Chant and Gutmann (2000: 7, table 2.1); Levy (1999); Moser et al. (1999).

Following on from this, while the short-term goals of GAD are often decidedly similar to those of WID (for example, improved education, access to credit, and legal rights for women), these are conceived as stepping stones towards longer-term goals which encompass 'ways to empower women through collective action, to encourage women to challenge gender ideologies and institutions that subordinate women' (Parpart, 1995: 235–6; see also Box 8.10). After the Nairobi conference at the end of the Decade for Women, gender became official UN language. As summarised by Pietilä (2007: 78), in the conceptual reorientation from WID to GAD: 'the politics of gender relations and restructuring of institutions, rather than simply equality in access to resources and options, have become the focus of development programmes, and "gender mainstreaming" has emerged as the common strategy for action behind these initiatives'.

GENDER MAINSTREAMING

Related to the adoption of 'gender relations' (rather than women) as its primary analytical focus, GAD approaches call for the integration of a gender perspective in all development activities and at all levels of the planning process. The term 'gender perspective' is crucially important in so far as it connotes a form of seeing, thinking about and doing development, thereby moving away from the frequently tokenistic or piecemeal efforts implied by epithets such as 'gender component' or 'gender dimension'. In line with the prescriptions of the BPFA, the call to mainstream gender has led to widespread adoption of the terminology of gender equality and mainstreaming – often along the lines of that proposed by the UN Economic and Social Council in 1997 (Moser and Moser, 2005: see also Box 8.11).

As further noted by Moser and Moser (2005: 12) in a review conducted of gender mainstreaming among 14 international development organisations, two other aspects of mainstreaming which are sometimes included in

BOX 8.10   WOMEN'S EMPOWERMENT

'Women's empowerment' is one of the most frequently found terms in the contemporary gender and development literature. It has been especially prevalent since the Fourth World Conference for Women in Beijing in 1995, where the Platform for Action was billed as an 'agenda for women's empowerment', whereby 'the principle of shared power and responsibility should be established between women and men at home, in the workplace and in the wider national and international community' (see DFID, 2000).

An 'empowerment approach' to women in development is argued to be attractive for two main reasons. First, since 'empowerment' has ostensibly emerged from the South, this is appealing to Northern development institutions which conceivably wish to avoid charges of cultural imperialism, especially in relation to gender; second, the bottom-up character of the empowerment approach has much in common with the growing fashion for participatory development (Oxaal with Baden, 1997). This said, 'empowerment' is one of many words which has entered the development lexicon in a rather 'loose' form ('sustainability' and 'civil society' being other examples – see Chapters 4 and 11, this volume, respectively). Care must accordingly be taken not to overuse the term such that it becomes degraded and valueless.

One of the reasons for considerable misunderstanding about 'empowerment' is because its root-concept 'power' is also misunderstood (see Rowlands, 1996). Using an approach based on the work of Michel Foucault, Rowlands identifies that working towards empowerment (and empowerment is a *process* rather than an *end-state*) should not only consist of opening up access to decision making, but also be about changing the way in which people *perceive* themselves. Within her analytical framework, Rowlands proposes three main dimensions: the 'personal', 'close relationships' and the 'collective'.

In the domain of the *personal*, empowerment is about developing a sense of self and individual confidence, capacity and self-esteem, whereby the effects of internalised oppression are shaken off. In the sphere of *close relationships*, empowerment is about increasing one's ability to negotiate relationships and decision-making processes. In the *collective* domain, empowerment is about bringing people together to give them more power than they would have as individuals, whether in their communities, or in national and international institutions.

While empowerment is commonly thought of as growth in capacity to make choices, it is important to remember that 'choice' itself needs to be qualified (Kabeer, 1999). The kinds of choices people make are conditioned by the existence of alternatives, which are usually limited among the developing world poor. Moreover, choices are dependent upon the consequences they entail, which can come at high cost (ibid.).

How to go about putting empowerment projects into practice is also fraught with difficulties. 'Outsiders' or 'change agents' such as NGO personnel staff can be useful in the empowerment process. However, they need to avoid being too prescriptive or heavy-handed in their approaches otherwise the very essence of empowerment, that is, 'to enhance women's capacity for self-determination', is violated (Kabeer, 1999: 462). Considerable patience is also necessary since lasting change in gender roles and relations can only be effected by changes in the psycho-social and political spheres as well as the materialities of life.

Although 'empowerment' is often regarded as a grassroots phenomenon, some have argued that empowerment can only become an effective instrument for challenging and transforming gender inequality when it grows bigger than the local. For example, global competition affects national development strategies, and in turn, job opportunities in local communities, which in themselves both help and hinder local and national development. For any meaningful discussion of and action for empowerment to take place, it is accordingly crucial to take into account the interrelations among these different levels (Parpart, 2008).

Sources: DFID (2000b), Kabeer (1999), Oxaal with Baden (1997), Parpart (1995; 2008), Rowlands (1996).

agency definitions are (1) gender empowerment, and (2) the institutionalisation of gender concerns within the organisation itself. The latter entails recognising institutions as an 'ethnographic object' and redressing gender bias in structures of decision-making and institutional culture, for example, in such matters as staffing, finance, parental leave and support, administrative and other organisational procedures.

In terms of how gender mainstreaming policies are actually put into practice, it has sometimes been felt that with appropriate training in 'gender

---

BOX 8.11   UN DEFINITION OF GENDER MAINSTREAMING

Mainstreaming a gender perspective is the process of assessing the implications for women and men or any planned action, including legislation, policies or programmes, in all areas and at all levels. It is a strategy for making women's as well as men's concerns and experiences an integral dimension of the design, implementation, monitoring and evaluation of policies and programmes in all political, economic and societal spheres so that women and men benefit equally and inequality is not perpetuated, The ultimate goal is to achieve gender equality.

Source: UN (1997: 28), cited in Moser and Moser (2005: 12).

---

competence', accountability measures for good gender practices, building gender networks in organisations and so on, this could ideally help to reduce the 'ghettoisation' of gender concerns from small specialised units. As summed up by Reeves and Baden (2000: 12):

> With a mainstreaming strategy, gender concerns are seen as important to all aspects of development; for all sectors and areas of activity, and a fundamental part of the planning process. Responsibility for the implementation of gender policy is diffused across the organisational structure, rather than concentrated in a small central unit.

However, when gender equality nominally becomes the responsibility of everyone, in practice it can also become the responsibility of no one (Mukhopadhyay, 2007: 140). As such many feminists feel that it is inadvisable to eliminate GAD-specific machinery until there is more convincing evidence for fundamental changes in gender attitudes and relations in organisations (see Standing, 2007; Subrahmanian, 2007). Indeed, as argued by the OECD (2007: 20) sometimes a well-placed lone gender advisor is better than a poorly-placed gender unit. In turn, it is no surprise that a 'twin-track approach' has tended to be regarded as the most appropriate option for the meantime. As discovered in Moser and Moser's research, all international organisations in their survey shared this strategy along with five other components in their policies for gender-mainstreaming (Moser and Moser, 2005: 12; see also Box 8.12).

BOX 8.12   COMPONENTS OF GENDER MAINSTREAMING POLICY

- Dual strategy of gender mainstreaming coupled with targeted actions for gender equality.
- Combined approach to responsibility where all staff share responsibility but are supported by gender specialists.
- Gender analysis.
- Gender training.
- Support to women's decision-making and empowerment.
- Monitoring and evaluation.

Source: Moser and Moser (2005: 12).

MEN IN GAD

As part of ongoing struggles to mainstream gender, another of the most pressing issues for GAD in the twenty-first century is that of the place and participation of men in gender and development policy and planning. The historical emphasis on women's needs and interests in gender planning has been justified by the fact that gender relations almost universally favour men and disadvantage women. Yet it is also the case not only that some men are prejudiced by gendered norms, but that responsibility for change lies with men and women at all levels of the development process. The need for shared responsibility in pursuing gender equality is illustrated by an evaluation of a gender training programme for male community organisers in the Indian state of Tamil Nadu, facilitated by Canadian and Nicaraguan men:

> If women hold up half the sky, then they cannot hold up more than their half of the responsibilities towards gender change. Organisers and participants alike agreed that men of conscience should play more than just a supportive role in this search for justice. Given the critical leadership positions of many men in social movements, to expect anything less would be self-defeating. (Goodwin, 1997: 6, cited in Chant and Gutmann, 2000: 9)

Yet although the conceptual basis of GAD renders men's involvement central to the success of GAD strategies, pragmatically there are few guidelines. On the one hand, this is not surprising given limited experience of involving men in 'gender' programmes at any level, the primary concern of GAD with women's disadvantage, and the problems of navigating a path likely to be strewn with numerous obstacles and conflicts. Not only are there questions of power and politics to be negotiated at every turn, but it could also be levelled that gender relations which, by definition, are complex and dynamic, are a 'slippery' entity in development planning, and extremely difficult to deal with pragmatically. Difficult though the challenge of working with gender relations may be, however, failure to broach substantive tactical issues in respect of male involvement has potentially far-reaching implications. First, it may render reference to men no more than an act of 'window-dressing'. Second, when the practicalities of including men are ill-defined, it is understandable how development agency personnel may be unwilling to take risks and thus fall back on the old WID-centred approach instead (or attempt to devise models which simply see the reassertion of men's complementarity as 'responsible providers' in the context of patriarchal families, as discussed in relation to World Bank gender policy by Bedford [2007]). If including men persists as a misguided, or uncharted territory, however, it could prove impossible ever to identify the extent to which a gender relations approach is actually the most appropriate method for achieving equality between men and women in the context of development assistance (Chant and Gutmann, 2000; 2002; Cornwall, 2000; Cornwall and White, 2000).

PROVISOS ABOUT THE 'EN-GENDERING' OF THE DEVELOPMENT AGENDA

While there is little doubt that significant gains have been made for women in the years since the UN Decade for Women, there are also concerns about progress having been made at a slower rate than desired, and in particular on various of the priorities identified in the BPFA (see Cornwall et al., 2007; Longwe, 1995; Molyneux, 2007; UNRISD, 2005; WEDO, 2005; Woodford-Berger, 2007). One issue of considerable concern is that the 'business case' for mainstreaming gender, espoused most prominently by the World Bank, has tended to eclipse the more fundamental need to extend and guarantee women's rights. 'Efficiency' motives which emphasise the role of women working for others and for development in general (rather than development working for women) (see Figure 8.4) could potentially be as, if not more, detrimental to further advances towards gender equality in the present century. These are undoubtedly reasons why the World Bank's latest (and strongest) gender initiative – notably the Gender Action Plan (GAP) 2007–2010 – has met with fierce critique in academic and civil society circles. Prefaced by the nakedly instrumentalist title 'Gender Equality as Smart Economics', the plan declares its overall aim as 'to advance women's economic empowerment by enhancing women's ability to participate in land, labour, financial and product markets, thus promoting

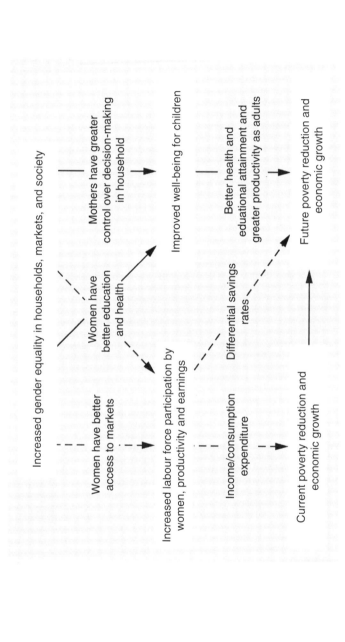

Source: Adapted from World Bank (2007a: figure 3.2).

Figure 8.4 Women's earnings, children's well-being, and aggregate poverty reduction and economic growth – the pathways

shared growth and accelerating the implementation of MDG3 (World
Bank, 2006: 9). In its first year progress report the aim of 'making markets
work for women' is reiterated, although it is only thinly disguised in the rest
of the document that the importance of gender justice and women's
empowerment are of a rather lesser magnitude than investing in women to
reduce poverty, to promote growth, and to benefit others, particularly children (see World Bank, 2008). As Elaine Zuckerman (2007: 1) at the
Washington, DC, based NGO GenderAction claims, the World Bank's
'business case ignores the moral imperative of empowering women to
achieve women's human rights and full equal rights with men'. She goes on
to assert that MDG3 has little chance of fulfilment in light of the World
Bank's 'endless policy conditionalities' at the macroeconomic level, and
argues that, aside from being bereft of a human rights approach that befits
a development organisation whose mission is to reduce poverty: 'Adhering
faithfully to the Bank's decades-old business model, GAP aims to increase
women's participation in land, labour, products and financial markets –
while privatising them as much as possible – which benefits corporations
the most' (ibid.: 2).

   If major multilaterals cannot be trusted with gender, then this may also
be the case with a range of nation states, which look set to enjoy more 'ownership' of development strategies under the new aid modalities enshrined
in the Paris Declaration (PD) of 2005 (see Chapter 11). As argued by
AWID (2007), the shift to budget support rather than individual projects
proposed by the PD, and increased developing country 'ownership' may
not favour women. Added to this, sector-wide approaches may be at odds
with gender as a 'cross-cutting' issue, and there has been little apparent
effort to consult women's rights organisations in the PD implementation
process (see also OECD, 2007). With 'gender-focused' aid often traditionally directed to sectors that reinforce women's roles as mothers and housewives, such as health, food and population (OECD-DAC, 2007), there are
clearly grounds for concern that gender mainstreaming may not occur in
the universal manner advocated by the BPFA. By the same token, some
writers, such as Goetz and Sandler (2007: 172) feel that the 'good governance' agenda promoted by the PD offers an opening through which states
can be made 'answerable *to* women, and answerable *for* promoting their
rights' (emphasis in original).

   Leading on from the above, the question of a rights-based approach
(RBA) to gender and development is one around which there has been considerable debate (see for example, Cornwall and Molyneux, 2008). First, as
argued by Tsikata (2007) there is not one RBA, but many, making for
confusion and contestation; second, the principal international advocate of
development and women's rights has long been the UN, but its current

political weakness makes it 'an unreliable ally in the fight for gender equality and development' (ibid.: 223); third, the issue of how far women's rights can be upheld in a world increasingly preoccupied by matters of security, the ascendancy of conservatism and the religious right renders the optimism of gender activists about RBAs somewhat overplayed (ibid.: 222–3). In light of potential institutional shortcomings at the macro-level, it may well be the case that women themselves will have to continue to wage their battles for gender justice even more ardently than in the past, and do their best through grassroots movements to enjoin men in the struggle.

Activity 8.1
Think about how you would try to assess gains in gender equality made in a particular 'developing' country in the last three decades. Make a list of the sources you would use and the indicators that might be most appropriate to measure progress. Then critically evaluate the limitations you are likely to encounter when comparing advances in gender equality between one country and another.

LEARNING OUTCOMES

By the end of this chapter and relevant reading you should be able to:

- Define gender and make a case for the importance of 'engendering' the study of development.
- Describe the principal indicators used to measure gender, such as the GDI and GEM, and critically evaluate their utility in measuring gender inequality within and across countries.
- Outline the major policy approaches to gender and development and assess their strengths and weaknesses.

FURTHER READING

Chant, Sylvia and Gutmann, Matthew (2000), *Mainstreaming Men into Gender and Development: Debates, Reflections and Policy Experiences*, Oxford: Oxfam.
A report originally commissioned by the World Bank, but published by Oxfam, which, on the basis of consultations with around 40 development organisations in the UK and USA, reviews the case for incorporating men into development policy, programmes and projects.

Cornwall, Andrea, Harrison, Elizabeth and Whitehead, Ann (eds) (2007), *Feminisms in Development: Contradictions, Contestations and Challenges*, London: Zed.

A lively and readable collection of numerous cutting-edge papers arising out of a major conference held at the Institute of Development Studies, University of Sussex in 2003 to assess the outcomes of the institutionalisation of gender into the field of development policy, and concentrating specifically on the construction and implications of 'gender orthodoxies'.

Journal of Human Development (2006), 'Revisiting the Gender-related Development Index (GDI) and Gender Empowerment Measure (GEM)', Special issue, **7**(2), 145–290.
This special issue of the JHD comprises papers prepared (and subsequently revised) in connection with a workshop held in New York which had the aim of evaluating the utility of existing UNDP gender indicators and suggesting ways forward.

Moser, Caroline (1993), *Gender Planning and Development: Theory, Practice, Training*, London: Routledge.
One of the first books to outline different approaches to gender planning, to identify their underlying assumptions, and to evaluate their relevance to improving the lives of women at the grassroots.

Pietilä, Hilkka (2007), *The Unfinished Story of Women and the United Nations*, NGLS Development Dossier 14, New York: UN Non-Governmental Liaison Service (downloadable from www.un.org or via www.siyanda.org).
A detailed history of the adoption of gender equality as a goal of the UN, assessing achievements and outstanding challenges.

United Nations Millennium Project (UNMP), Task Force on Education and Gender Equality (TFEGE) (2005), *Taking Action: Achieving Gender Equality and Empowering Women*, London: Earthscan (online version downloadable from www.unmillenniumproject.org/documents/gender).
The main publication of the Task Force convened by former UN Secretary General, Kofi Annan, to address the shortcomings regarding gender in the MDGs, and to suggest improved targets and indicators.

USEFUL WEBSITES

www.siyanda.org – website maintained by the IDS, University of Sussex. Online database for scholars, practitioners and donors of up-to-date/cutting edge publications and discussion forums on gender and development, with a monthly newsletter featuring the latest gender mainstreaming resources
www.undp/org/unifem.org – official UNIFEM website
www.un.org/womenwatch – website for Womenwatch, the UN gateway for the advancement and empowerment of women, which *inter alia*, allows people to engage on-line with the inter-governmental system
www.icrw.org – website of the International Centre for Research on Women
www.worldbank.org/gender – website on gender at the World Bank
www.thecommonwealth.org/gender – website on gender at the Commonwealth Secretariat
www.awid.org – website of the Association for Women's Rights in Development
http://mdgs.un.org/unsd/mdg – official UN website on MDG indicators

9. Families and households in transition

INTRODUCTION

Following a brief introduction to the concept of 'household' and its relationship with 'family', this chapter outlines the main types of households in developing regions, and examines the relationship between urbanisation and changing household structures, both theoretically and empirically. The second half of the chapter considers the growth of women-headed households and the reasons for their formation. Attention is paid here to the commonly drawn links between the 'feminisation of household headship' and the 'feminisation of poverty' which have led to the stereotyping of women-headed households as the 'poorest of the poor'.

CONCEPTUALISING HOUSEHOLDS AND FAMILIES

Finding a definition of household which has universal applications is difficult. Households vary widely between different societies, and among some linguistic/cultural groups there is no identifiable word for 'household', as is the case with the inhabitants of Mafia Island, Tanzania and the Zinacantecos of southern Mexico (Collier et al., 1997). This said, most censuses and international data sources define households on the basis of two criteria: *space* and *function*, or as the UN (2006b: 12) terms this: 'house-dwelling' and 'house-keeping'. The 'house-dwelling' concept refers to households as units which occupy common residential space, whereas the 'house-keeping' concept pertains to collaboration of household members in basic productive and reproductive activities and consumption, particularly cooking and eating (see also UN, 2006a). In most cases, reproductive responsibilities encompass the raising and socialisation of children. For a number of reasons, therefore, households are extremely important in the analysis of human survival, well-being, and gender-differentiated status and behaviour.

The majority of households comprise members related by family ties of blood or marriage. Yet overlap between 'households' and 'families' does not imply they are synonymous or interchangeable. There are many instances, for example, in which people do not live with kin, but reside alone, or with friends and workmates. As Kabeer (2007: 54) describes: 'the boundaries of the household are not coterminous with the boundaries of the family'. In turn, 'families' are generally bigger than households in so far as they extend beyond the confines of shared living space and may be scattered over wide distances, including across national borders (see Chapter 3, this volume). Another distinction is that 'family' is a more formally identifiable institution than 'household', subject to legislated norms regarding marriage, property, inheritance, the care and guardianship of minors and so on. While most countries, for example, have a 'Family Code' or a 'family section' in the Civil Code, there is no equivalent for 'households'. Having said this, the frequent cross-over between households and families means that the former are often heavily influenced by familial norms and ideologies, and may well depend on ties with wider kin groups for part of their survival (Kabeer, 2007). In this way, neither 'households' or 'families' are bounded entities.

The complications of conceptualising 'households' and 'families' in any general sense stem not only from competing interpretations and cultural-linguistic specificities, but from their seemingly infinite variations on the ground. As stated by Moore (1994: 2) 'there is no such thing as *the* family, only families' (emphasis in original), which vary within and between regions, and over time, due to structural factors such as local economic conditions, patterns of landholding, culture and so on, as well as features intrinsic to family units such as the ageing of members. In turn, there has been long-standing debate as to the universalism of 'the family' as an essentially 'natural' institution for the nurturance of young children, vis-à-vis the idea of family as an ideological construct associated with the modern state (Collier et al., 1997).

HOUSEHOLD STRUCTURES IN THE GLOBAL SOUTH

The particular form which households take is summed up in the term 'household structure', which comprises two features:

1. Sex of the household head
2. Household composition or membership.

In respect of family-based households, composition generally falls into one of two categories:

1. 'Simple' composition, which refers to households which are two-generational, and which consist either of one or two parents and their immediate offspring.
2. 'Complex' or 'extended' composition, which refers to those households which in addition to containing a parent/parents and children, include one or more other relatives such as in-laws, grandparents, cousins and so on.

Complex composition can also describe households where members are not related by blood or marriage, as in 'non-family' or 'semi-family' households (see Box 9.1).

Despite the inherent dynamism of household units, composition is relatively straightforward to identify at any one point in time but this is arguably less so with household headship.

The concept of 'household head' is seen as having its roots in Judaeo-Christian societies where states historically devolved power to men at the household level. 'Household headship' encompasses the notion that one member is responsible for others and occupies a position of authority at the apex of the household unit. This idea was spread to several parts of the world during the colonisation process via religious and 'moral' teachings, and through bureaucratic procedures such as population surveys (Folbre, 1991; Harris, 1981).

Yet this Eurocentric construction of household headship has come under attack on two main grounds: first, it makes no allowance for alternative ideologies and practices of household management; second, it undervalues and renders invisible the role of women. In relation to the latter, for example, disquiet has been expressed at the fact that few censuses make explicit what they mean by household headship. Although some specify instrumental criteria such as primary financial provision or decision-making power, most rely on self- or proxy-reporting which, given male bias in most societies, means that adult men are usually accorded the status of head. Indeed, patriarchal norms are often so pervasive that even where women are not living with partners or husbands, they may name their eldest sons as heads. In most statistical classifications, however, households tend only to be described as female-headed where the adult woman has no partner in residence (Chant, 1997a; see also Box 9.1).

BOX 9.1   TYPOLOGY OF HOUSEHOLD
                STRUCTURES IN THE GLOBAL SOUTH

Household structure	Brief description
Nuclear household	Couple and their biological children.
Female-headed household	Generic term for a household where the senior woman or household head lacks a co-resident male partner. Often, although not always, household head is a lone mother.
Extended household	Household which in addition to one or both parents and children, comprises other blood relatives or in-laws. May be male- or female-headed, laterally or vertically extended, and/or multi-generational.
Nuclear-compound household	Arrangement where two or more related households share the same living space (for example, dwelling or land plot), but operate separate household budgets and daily reproductive functions such as cooking and eating.
Single-sex household	Consists of household in which the senior members are of one sex only (for example, as is common among Ga and Asante in Ghana, where women live with female kin, daughters and infant sons).
Non-family/non-kin household	Consists of household in which members are un-related by blood or marriage, for example, where workmates share accommodation.
Semi-family household	Households which comprise related members and non-related members, as in situations where households have live-in domestic servants or apprentices.

Couple household	Households comprising a married or co-resident couple.
Lone/single person household	Woman or man living alone.
Grandmother-headed household	Grandmother and her grandchildren, but without intermediate generation.
Blended/step-family household*	Household in which one or both partners in a couple is not the biological parent of one or more co-resident children.
Child-headed household	Households in which minors occupy positions of headship usually due to being orphaned by parents who have died of AIDS or as a result of civil or military conflict.

Note: * Also referred to in some sources as 'reconstituted household'.

Source: Based on Chant (2002c: box 2.1).

THE RELATIONSHIP BETWEEN URBANISATION AND HOUSEHOLD CHANGE

Although household structures in developing societies are diverse, in the 1960s and 1970s, during the heyday of modernisation and dependency theories (see Chapter 2, this volume), a commonly held notion was that urbanisation and industrialisation would lead to the progressive replacement of extended arrangements by small nuclear units. A key role in this trajectory was accorded to the changing nature of production. In 'traditional' pre-industrial and/or rural areas (both historically and in the contemporary Global South) where peasant/subsistence production predominated, living as part of a large extended kin group could provide advantages in land and labour power. In modern urban contexts, by contrast, the rationale for living with kin is purportedly diminished. With the ascendance of an industrially based exchange economy most people cease producing for themselves and instead rely on selling their labour power to capitalist entrepreneurs (that is, they work outside the home for factory owners and the like). Since the basis of wage labour is an individualised contract between a worker and an employer, co-resident kin are more likely to become a burden than a benefit.

An additional impetus for household nuclearisation is the shift of functions historically provided by family and kinship groups to 'modern' specialised institutions such as schools, hospitals, the army, government welfare departments and so on. This leaves families responsible for few functions over and above procreation, the raising of children and emotional support (see Hulme and Turner, 1990).

While shifts in the nature or production and societal organisation have been regarded as central to household nuclearisation by scholars from a variety of theoretical standpoints, neo-Marxian theorists linked the process to the increasing vulnerability and exploitability of labour. The functionality of nuclear family units to capitalist economic development rested, first, on their greater scope to migrate to where capital needed workers and, second, because lacking the means of independent production, small nuclear households guaranteed both a supply of labour and a market for capitalist goods.

For theorists working within a liberal/modernisation framework, the nuclear household provided a means of upward socio-economic mobility, thereby conforming with the individualistic capitalist ethos of accumulating wealth. Household extension became not only afunctional but even *dys*-functional, especially if households were supporting dependent, aged or infirm members as well as young children. Indeed, from this perspective extended households became, at best, construed as 'traditional' and, at worst, 'deviant' or 'obsolete' relics from a 'backward' rural past.

Notwithstanding the criticisms levelled against the cultural imperialism of Modernisation views of family evolution, or the narrow economic determinism of neo-Marxian perspectives, the idea that households undergo a transition from an extended to a nuclear form with urbanisation and economic development has found little systematic support in empirical evidence.

One important challenge to the extended-to-nuclear trajectory lies in the fact that extended households have not necessarily been the norm in pre-industrial or rural settings anywhere in the world, past or present. Instead, there are huge variations in the prevalence of extended or nuclear rural households within as well as between nations, depending on class, ethnicity, culture, population pressure, access to land, patterns of land tenure and inheritance systems.

Leading on from this, a second qualification is that nuclear households do not necessarily predominate in cities. In Taiwan, for example, only 45 per cent of urban households fit the nuclear model, and in Bo, one of Sierra Leone's largest towns, up to 75 per cent of households are extended (see Brydon and Chant, 1993: 143–4). Fewer than 30 per cent of households in The Gambia are nuclear, and recent data produced by ECLAC reveal that only 36 per cent of households in the Latin America and the Caribbean region as a whole now conform to the model of male-headed nuclearity (see Chant, 2007a; Chant with Craske, 2003: ch. 7) There is also considerable evidence to suggest that among low-income urban populations, extended households have actually increased in proportion over the past three decades as people have struggled to cope with pressures brought about by recession and neoliberal economic restructuring. Adepoju and Mbugua (1997), for example, stress that one of the reasons why extended family households have persisted in African cities is scarcity of employment. Household extension not only provides 'social insurance' for those without work, but can also be a means of allocating labour more efficiently between adults, of preventing the situation where children might need to be withdrawn from school and of reducing people's vulnerability to destitution. The formation of extended households can also be an adjustment to housing shortages, or permit members to better cope with the daily domestic burdens attached to residence in unserviced peri-urban settlements (see Chapters 4 and 6, this volume). In this way, extended household structures can represent a positive strategy for survival.

A third qualification of the extended-to-nuclear trajectory is that, despite the long-term evolutionist thrust of mainstream theories, little attention has been given to shorter-term household dynamics and historical specificities. The apparent prevalence of nuclear households in many contemporary cities of the South is perhaps only a transitional phenomenon. Households may be nuclear simply because many consist of migrants who are young and just starting their own families and/or have yet to take in relatives intending to move from rural areas (see Chapter 3, this volume).

A fourth challenge to the purported extended-to-nuclear transition resides not only in the questionable assumption that the South should automatically follow in the historical footprints of the North, but that conditions in contemporary developing regions are actually very different from what they were when Europe industrialised in the eighteenth and nineteenth centuries. Developing countries face a situation of dependent capitalism, and often have huge debt burdens and greater poverty. As noted in Chapter 6, many of the urban poor in the Global South are also self-employed rather than salaried workers. Moreover, governments here have rarely divested families of as many functions as in the North even prior to the Washington Consensus-driven 'rolling back of the state'.

*Table 9.1   Percentage of households headed by women in developing
regions, 1995–2003*

	Percentage (weighted)	No. of countries for which data are available
Africa	*23.8*	*37*
Northern Africa	12.9	2
Southern Africa	42.2	3
Rest of sub-Saharan Africa	23.5	32
Asia and Oceania	*13.4*	*27*
Eastern Asia	20.0	5
Southeastern Asia	15.4	5
Southern Asia	9.6	5
Central Asia	27.6	5
Western Asia	10.8	2
Oceania	54.1	2
Latin America and the Caribbean	*23.9*	*21*
Caribbean	33.5	7
Central America	21.2	6
South America	24.2	8

Source: Varley (2008: table 1).

THE FORMATION OF WOMEN-HEADED HOUSEHOLDS

If it is hard to accept a generalised developmentally driven shift from
extended to nuclear household forms in Asia, Africa and Latin America, a
somewhat less contested and seemingly ubiquitous trend dating from the
mid to late twentieth century is a rise in women-headed households. On the
basis of a weighted average of the overall total of 85 countries for which
data are currently available, just over one-fifth of households worldwide are
now headed by women (Varley, 2008; see also Table 9.1). Increases appear
to be particularly marked in urban areas, as indicated by data from Latin
America (Table 9.2).

Notwithstanding variations in levels and rates of increase in female-
headed households in different countries in the South, it is also important
to acknowledge that they differ in type, and in respect of their routes into
this status (see Box 9.2). The incidence of female headship is often highest
where there is a weak tradition or weakening societal emphasis on legal
marriage, together with growing tolerance of marital dissolution. Such patterns have long applied in the Caribbean, and more recently have occurred

Table 9.2   Female-headed households as a proportion of all households in urban areas: selected Latin American countries, 1987–99

Country	Years	% of households headed by women	Percentage point change
Argentina	1990	21	
	1999	27	+6
Bolivia	1989	17	
	1999	21	+4
Chile	1990	21	
	1998	24	+3
Colombia	1991	24	
	1999	29	+5
Costa Rica	1990	23	
	1999	28	+5
Ecuador	1990	17	
	1999	20	+3
El Salvador	1995	31	
	1997	31	0
Guatemala	1987	20	
	1998	24	+4
Honduras	1990	27	
	1999	30	+3
Mexico	1989	16	
	1998	19	+3
Nicaragua	1993	35	
	1998	35	0
Panama	1991	26	
	1999	27	+1
Paraguay (Asunción)	1990	20	
	1999	27	+7
Uruguay	1990	25	
	1999	31	+6
Venezuela	1990	22	
	1999	27	+5

Source: Chant (2002c: table 1), based on data from the Economic Commission for Latin America and the Caribbean.

in parts of Latin America. Where formal marriage continues to be a dominant practice, alternatively, as in many parts of South Asia, the Middle East and North Africa, levels of female headship remain low. Here the majority of female heads are widows, although rising proportions of abandoned women are noted in places such as southern India and Bangladesh

BOX 9.2   TYPOLOGY OF FEMALE-HEADED HOUSEHOLDS

Lone mother households
Mother and co-resident children. Largest group of women-headed households in most parts of the world.

Female-headed extended households
Households headed by lone mother containing co-resident children *and* other relatives. Case studies of many countries, especially in Latin America, the Caribbean and sub-Saharan Africa indicate that extension of household units is more common under female than male headship.

Lone female households
Less common in South than North, but in countries such as India and Mexico, most likely to consist of an elderly widow living alone.

Single-sex/female-only households
In Southeast Asian countries these usually consist of households comprising young women who work in the same factory or enterprise. In West Africa they are common among certain ethnic groups such as the Ga and the Asante, where women may follow the custom of maintaining separate residences from husbands. Single-sex households are also known in areas in which polygamy[1] or polygyny[2] is practised.

'Female-dominant/predominant' households
Households headed by women, where although males may be present, they are only junior males with less power and authority than adult females.

Grandmother-headed households
Consist of grandmothers and grandchildren, but without the intermediate generation. Most frequent in areas where child-fostering is common and where adult women need to migrate to find work, as in Sub-Saharan Africa and the Caribbean.

'Embedded' female-headed units
Units generally comprising a mother and child(ren) *within* other households; hence sometimes known as 'female-headed sub-families'.

Differentiating factors among female household heads
Marital status
Age/life course
Class
'Race'
Sexuality/sexual orientation
De facto/de jure status[3]
Child support
Route into female headship, for example, widowhood/separation/
non-marriage; 'forced'/'voluntary'.

Notes:
1. This is where a man has more than one wife. In Islamic communities, the
    notional maximum is 4.
2. This refers to men engaging in more than sexual relationship with a woman.
3. *De jure* normally refers to situations where women are heads of household by
    law or by virtue of their single status as widows or divorcées, whereas *de facto*
    female heads describe those who may have partners who are absent (for
    example, through labour migration), or who are present but do not provide for the
    household because of disability, sickness, long-term unemployment and so on.

Source: Chant (1997a: ch. 1).

where men have increasingly engaged in international labour migration (see
Chapter 3, this volume). Migration is also a key factor in sub-Saharan
Africa, along with war, civil conflict and environmental disasters, which
have led to the fragmentation of households through population displacement and death (see Adepoju, 1997).

Although numerous factors affect the emergence of female household
headship (see Box 9.3), those with most widespread significance for recent
increases are as follows. First, it is generally agreed that women's mounting
propensity to head households owes to the undermining of traditional economic and kinship structures by capitalist development and 'modernisation' (see Folbre, 1991). Most rural-based developing societies were
patriarchal in nature and allowed women only limited command over
resources such as land, income and labour. Urbanisation, industrialisation
and globalisation, by contrast, have often expanded women's opportunities
for waged work. This has reduced women's dependency on men and accordingly their own capacity to head households. This trend has been exacerbated by declining male employment, especially at the lower end of the
occupational hierarchy. Inability to fulfil social expectations to be family
breadwinners appears to be making men in some countries less likely to
marry, and is also associated with rising rates of conjugal breakdown (see
Chant, 2002b; Moore, 1994). Other economic factors attributed a role in

BOX 9.3   FACTORS AFFECTING THE FORMATION OF WOMEN-HEADED HOUSEHOLDS

I Demographic factors
1)   Uneven sex ratios
    a)   *Gender-selective migration*
    b)   *Gender differentiated life expectancy*
    c)   *War and disease*
2)   Urbanisation
3)   Age at marriage
    a)   *Women's age at marriage*
    b)   *Gender differentials in age at marriage*
4)   Fertility and birth control

II Economic factors
1)   Access to land and property
2)   Production systems
3)   Female labour force participation
4)   Economic restructuring and poverty

III Legal-institutional factors
1)   State attitudes and interventions
2)   Family and divorce legislation
    a)   *Divorce*
    b)   *Child custody*
    c)   *Enforcement of legal provisions*
3)   Welfare and benefit schemes
4)   Women's movements

IV Sociocultural factors
1)   Culture
2)   Religion
3)   Gender roles, relations and ideologies
4)   Kinship and residence
5)   Marriage practices, childbirth and social identity
    a)   *Polygamy*
    b)   *Arranged marriages*
    c)   *Consensual unions*
    d)   *Wifehood, motherhood and social status*
6)   Morality and sexuality

Source: Chant (1997a: chs 3 and 4).

the 'feminisation of household headship' include poverty, with particular emphasis being placed on post-1980 neoliberal economic restructuring (see Chant with Craske, 2003). Cutbacks in public services, the reduction or removal of government subsidies on basic foodstuffs, wage freezes and so on have increased strains and separations within families, as well as diminishing the prospects for women's (re)incorporation in the households of parents and male relatives following widowhood, divorce or abandonment (see also Chapter 6, this volume).

Linked with changes in the labour market, development and globalisation, female household headship has also resulted from increases in internal and international migration. Since most migration streams have been gender differentiated this has led to localised imbalances in proportions of women and men, and where 'sex ratios' are strongly feminine, the greater the likelihood that female household headship will be found (see Chant, 1997a). As discussed in Chapter 3, for example, men in sub-Saharan Africa have traditionally predominated in rural–urban migration leaving women heading households in the countryside. In Latin America and Southeast Asia, by contrast, where female-selective urban movement has prevailed, women-headed households occur more frequently in urban than in rural areas (Chant with Craske, 2003). In Costa Rica, for example, female-headed households have long been more common in urban than in rural areas. In 1987, 20.9 per cent of urban households were headed by women versus 13.4 per cent in rural areas, and in 1995, this urban–rural differential was of a similar magnitude, at 30.9 per cent versus 20.5 per cent (Chant, 2008c: 44). In turn, there has been a progressively greater concentration of female-headed households in towns and cities over time, which partly reflects on-going processes of urbanisation, but also suggests that female headship is more viable in urban environments, undoubtedly because these offer greater economic opportunities for women. While 57 per cent of all female heads were living in urban areas in 1987, this was 69 per cent by 2003 (as against 36 per cent and 54 per cent of households in general), and while only 1 in 3.7 urban households were headed by women in 1987, by 2003 this was 1 in 2.9 (ibid.; see also Chant, 2007a: ch. 6).

Declining fertility is another demographic phenomenon with implications for rising rates of female headship. On the one hand, it reduces the childcare burdens of women, which can increase their scope to enter the labour market, to support themselves financially and to depend less on male incomes. On the other hand, reduced numbers of children mean less likelihood that lone women will be taken into the households of their offspring in later life. This is likely to become a more serious issue in light of the long-term decline in birth rates (see Chapter 3).

Last but not least, increases in women's rights in the spheres of sexual and reproductive freedom, access to divorce, and custody of children, have also led to rises in female headship. Marriage in many societies is not the prerequisite for childbirth that it once was, and marital breakdown has increased as the grounds for divorce have widened, as women have become freer to petition for divorce in their own right, and as their entitlements to conjugal property, maintenance payments and child support have risen. In Thailand, for example, a 50 per cent rise in divorce during the 1980s meant that by the early 1990s, nearly 25 per cent of marriages ended up formally dissolved. In Costa Rica, only 1 in 11 marriages terminated through divorce in 1984, but by 2001 the proportion was 4 in 10 (Chant, 2007a: 294).

WOMEN-HEADED HOUSEHOLDS AND THE 'FEMINISATION OF POVERTY'

The rise in female household headship has frequently met with concern, if not alarm, in public and policy circles. Growing numbers of female heads, especially those who are unmarried, divorced or separated, are widely construed as symbolising a 'breakdown' in the family, especially where the patriarchal (male-headed) unit remains a normative ideal (Budowski, 2002; Chant, 2002b; 2007b; Davids and Van Driel, 2001; 2005; Moore, 1994; Safa, 1998). Part of this anxiety stems from links drawn between rising levels of female headship and a putative 'feminisation of poverty'. Even if the 'feminisation of poverty' should technically imply a trend for women (not just female household heads) to become poorer over time, and is frequently confused with 'feminised poverty', which is merely a state in which women are poorer than men (see Medeiros and Costa, 2006), female-headed households are frequently typecast as the 'poorest of the poor', whether on grounds of their allegedly greater likelihood of being poor or of experiencing more pronounced degrees of indigence than male-headed units. These notions rest upon the fact that women's earnings are less than those of men, that female heads are time- and resource-constrained by their triple burdens of employment, housework and childcare, and because, in most countries in the South, female heads receive little transfer income through state welfare or child maintenance payments from absent fathers (see Chant, 2003; Morrison et al., 2008). Poverty also figures prominently in another conventional wisdom which seems to be perniciously attached to female-household headship, and particularly lone motherhood, namely, an 'inter-generational transmission of disadvantage', whereby children are regarded as suffering as a result of being raised only by women. Alongside poverty, psychological problems emanating from 'father absence', lack of maternal attention, limited parental discipline and so on are deemed to fuel a cumulatively downward spiral of insecurity, poverty and family instability (Chant, 2003; 2007b).

Yet while it cannot be denied that women suffer disproportionately from social and economic inequalities, whether these disadvantages translate wholesale to women-headed households is less certain. Indeed, this would be to assume that households are 'passive' in the face of wider societal influences. In fact they represent an important institution in their own right, and are seemingly capable not only of exerting agency, but of performing a catalytic role in social change.

A mounting body of research has contested unilaterally negative portrayals of female household headship. One critical challenge is posed by evidence from countries as diverse as Vietnam, Indonesia, Colombia, Panama, Zimbabwe, Guinea and Morocco which reveals that in income terms, women-headed units are no more likely to be poor than male-headed households (Chant, 2007a, 2007b; see also Medeiros and Costa, 2008; Sen, 2008). Female-headed households are a diverse group in respect of age and relative dependency of (or indeed, financial contributions from) offspring, household composition, socio-economic status, and access to resources from beyond the household unit (from absent fathers, kinship networks, state assistance and the like). A common finding from a range of countries, for example, is that female-headed households are more likely to be extended than male-headed units. In instances where extension involves the incorporation of other adults this may ease the labour burdens, and/or boost the economic situation of female heads such that they may actually enjoy lower dependency ratios (proportions of non-earning to economically active members) and higher per capita incomes than their male counterparts. Detailed empirical studies at the micro-level have also found a tendency for expenditure within female-headed households to be dedicated to the basic needs of children and less skewed towards personal consumption by adult earners. While in male-headed units, men may spend significant amounts of income on 'non-merit' items such as tobacco and alcohol, in female-headed households, more resources are usually allocated to food, health and education, particularly that of daughters (see Bradshaw, 2002; Chant, 2003; 2008a; Kabeer, 2007). Contrary to prevailing conventional wisdoms, levels of nutrition and educational attainment may thus be higher among children in female-headed units, and less gender differentiated (Chant, 2007b; also Varley, 2008). Aside from the importance of these issues in deconstructing blanket stereotypes, it is also acknowledged that if the 'feminisation of poverty' is broadened to include other dimensions of privation and inequality beyond incomes – such as inputs of labour, imbalances of power and privilege and so on – then greater bias against women and girls may actually occur in male-headed households (see Chant, 2007a; 2007b). In situations where families are affected by male violence or financial neglect, for example, female headship can be an important survival strategy in its own right, as well as enhancing women's personal power and autonomy. As summarised by Sen (2008:6):

> It is clear now that, not only is the empirical generalisation inaccurate, but that a single-minded focus on female-headed households narrows which households we focus on and how we understand what goes on within them . . . Viewing poverty as a gendered experience allows us to broaden the scope of analysis to include all poor households however headed. It also directs us to a wider range of issues beyond simply asking whether women or men are poorer in income terms. These include the ways in which poverty is made a gendered experience by norms and values, divisions of assets, work and responsibility, and relations of power and control.

Even if negative generalisations about female-headed households are unjustified, and caution must be exercised to stop concerns about gender disadvantage falling further into a 'poverty trap' (Jackson, 1996), it is clear that female headship still places women and children at risk in societies where two-parent households are a normative ideal and where social and economic gender inequalities prevail. This is one important reason for long-standing calls to direct public assistance to female-headed households.

Yet although initiatives for female-headed households are now under way in a number of countries, these are often limited in scope. One major fear is that targeting may produce 'perverse incentives' and encourage further 'family breakdown' (Buvinic and Gupta, 1997; Chant, 2002b). However, if protecting the rights, well-being and security of children is the ultimate objective of social policy (UNICEF, 2007), it is important to recognise and support household diversity, as recommended in the BPFA (Chapter 8, this volume). This undoubtedly implies abandoning adherence to an arbitrary Eurocentric norm of family life and adapting social programmes in the South to cater for the multiplicity of domestic contexts in which children are raised in the twenty-first century.

Activity 9.1
On the basis of your reading, consider whether female-headed households in developing societies are likely to face greater social and economic difficulties than male-headed households. Do you think there is a need for targeted programmes of assistance for female-headed households, and if so, what might these programmes entail?

LEARNING OUTCOMES

By the end of this chapter and relevant reading you should be able to:

- Explain the obstacles to defining the terms 'household', 'family', and 'household headship' in any standardised manner.
- Outline the main ideas about household evolution under urban-economic development, and qualify their applicability in light of case study evidence from different regions of the Global South.
- Identify different types of women-headed household and the factors influencing increases in female household headship in different parts of the developing world.

FURTHER READING

Chant, Sylvia with Craske, Nikki (2003), *Gender in Latin America*, London: Latin America Bureau/New Brunswick, NJ: Rutgers University Press.
Chapter 7 of this book traces the intersections between changes in gender roles and relations and household and family life in Latin America, with a theoretical introduction pertinent to gender and household evolution across the Global South.

Chant, Sylvia (1997), *Women-headed Households: Diversity and Dynamics in the Developing World*, Basingstoke: Macmillan.
A comprehensive review of the factors giving rise to a globally ubiquitous increase in female household headship, drawing from, and elaborating in-depth case studies of poor urban households in Mexico, Costa Rica and the Philippines.

Chant, Sylvia (2007a), *Gender, Generation and Poverty: Exploring the 'Feminisation of Poverty' in Africa, Asia and Latin America*, Cheltenham: Edward Elgar.
An in-depth interrogation into the 'feminisation of poverty', drawing from primary fieldwork with women and men in different age cohorts in The Gambia, Philippines and Costa Rica. Includes detailed reviews of marriage, family and household dynamics in these three countries with particular reference to low-income groups. Concludes that the 'feminisation of poverty' should be conceived in a multidimensional manner and that a 'feminisation of responsibility and/or obligation' is not only a global trend, but is often most marked not in female- but in male-headed households.

Kabeer, Naila (1994), *Reversed Realities: Gender Hierarchies in Development Thought*, London: Verso.
Chapter 5 of this volume provides an excellent résumé of theoretical models of household decision-making, with particular reference to the differences between household 'co-operative' and 'collective' models.

Moore, Henrietta (1994), *Is There a Crisis in the Family?*, Geneva: United Nations Research Institute for Social Development, World Summit for Social Development, Occasional Research Paper 3 (downloadable from www.unrisd.org).

An important contribution to the literature on household diversity, pointing up that 'deviations' from the 'standard' patriarchal male-headed household are not anomalous in the context of several societies.

USEFUL WEBSITES

www.un.org/esa/socdev/family/UN&families – UN website on families
www.unicef.org – website of UN Children's Fund
www.unrisd.org – website of UN Research Institute for Social Development

10. Health inequalities and health care

INTRODUCTION

This chapter commences with basic definitions of 'health', and considers the interrelationships between health and development with particular reference to the concept of the 'epidemiological transition'. The discussion proceeds to examine disparities in health and morbidity among populations of the South. Attention is paid to the roles played by gender and socio-economic status in explaining differences in disease patterns, including the incidence of mental health conditions and HIV/AIDS. The remainder of the chapter reviews health-care provision in the South, and policy initiatives aimed at improving the health of disadvantaged groups including the Primary Health Care (PHC) approach.

DEFINING HEALTH

Health is an immensely difficult term to define in a way which is meaningful across countries and across different sets of stakeholders (medical personnel, development professionals, donors, clients and so on). While Western biomedical discourse has traditionally viewed health as the 'absence of disease', human-ecological and public health approaches have emphasised the importance of acknowledging health as a broader social construct, shaped not only by formal health service provision, but by a wide spectrum of economic, environmental and sociocultural influences. This latter perspective is reflected in the constitutional definition of health by the World Health Organisation as: 'a state of complete physical, mental and social well-being and not merely the absence of disease or infirmity' (see Connor, 2008). Yet while this is now the most widely-accepted definition, Lloyd-Sherlock (2002: 173) points out that 'the WHO approach to health is not easily translated into obvious policies or clear strategies, and quantitative indicators are unable to capture the complexity of such a concept'. As such a more limited approach to measuring and understanding health prevails (ibid.). Since mortality is a much less ambiguous phenomenon than morbidity, for example, the health status of populations is conventionally evaluated by the prevalence of diseases that result in death, rather than conditions which are non-fatal, even when the latter may be prolonged and/or severely undermine the quality of life. In turn, health-care provision is often narrowly focused on medical services at the expense of broader interventions pertaining to food security and nutrition, shelter, infrastructure and environmental improvement, all of which can play a vital role in disease prevention, especially among poorer groups in society (see below).

THE RELATIONSHIP BETWEEN HEALTH AND DEVELOPMENT, AND THE 'EPIDEMIOLOGICAL TRANSITION'

Bearing in mind the difficulties of working with contested definitions of health, not to mention 'development' (see Chapter 1, this volume), several important interrelationships between the two have been noted, and for this reason it is no surprise that health features prominently in the MDGs, both directly and indirectly. As summarised by the World Bank (2007b: 11): 'Health, nutrition and population policies play a pivotal role in economic and human development and in poverty alleviation.'

That poor health can hamper development is evident on a number of counts. In economic terms, for example, perpetual vulnerability to illness reduces work capacity and productivity in individuals, as well as provoking absences from work. In combination with malnutrition and under-nutrition, this is also clearly 'bad for business' (see Shetty, 2008). Where concentrations of people in given areas contract particular types of disabling disease such as river blindness (onchocerciasis), for example, this can inhibit the productive use of whole localities (Szirmai, 1997). In countries such as Rwanda, Uganda, Zambia, Zimbabwe, Botswana, Burundi and Namibia, where large percentages of working adults are afflicted by HIV/AIDS, the national labour supply is massively reduced. On top of this, the absence of available, affordable and effective vaccines and treatment, at least until recently (UNAIDS, 2006), has led to a situation where, as Barnett (2002: 393–4) contends, AIDS is effectively wiping out half a century of development gains as measured by life expectancy at birth (see also UNAIDS, 2007). In Botswana, for instance, life expectancy should theoretically be 71 years but as a result of AIDS has dropped to only 36 years (see below).

As for the impacts of development on health, rises in life expectancy and reductions in infant and child mortality have generally been attributed to a mixture of biomedical and socio-economic aspects of developmental change. These include improvements in medical technology, the reduction of major infectious diseases through immunisation programmes and

Table 10.1   Selected health characteristics: global comparisons

| | One-year olds fully immunised against: | | | | People living with HIV/AIDS (% of 15–49 year olds) | |
| | Measles (%) | | Tuberculosis (%) | | | |
	1995–98	2003	1995–98	2003	1997	2003
Sub-Saharan Africa	48	62	63	75	7.58	7.3
Arab States	84	84	88	86	0.16	0.3
South Asia	66	68	79	83	0.62	0.7
East Asia and the Pacific	73	82	88	91	0.58	0.2
Latin America and the Caribbean	89	93	92	96	0.61	0.7
Developing regions average	72	75	82	85	1.18	1.3
OECD countries average	97	91	—	—	0.32	0.3
World average	75	77	83	85	0.99	1.1

Source: UNDP (2000: table 10; 2005: tables 6 and 9).

control of disease vectors, increased provision of health care, improvements in water supply, hygiene and sanitary facilities, increased nutrition, and advances in literacy and education (which have raised people's awareness and knowledge of basic health matters) (see Szirmai, 1997; also Table 10.1). In many cases, these trends have been accompanied by a shift in communicable to non-communicable disease as the principal cause of sickness and death. This corresponds with the tenets of the so-called 'epidemiological transition' model. Accepting that the term 'health transition' is sometimes preferred for its implied concern with health and survival (as opposed to mortality), and because of its emphasis on the importance of social factors on morbidity (Phillips and Verhasselt, 1994b: 13ff.), the epidemiological transition has traditionally been regarded as a unidirectional three stage process. In stage 1, societies are vulnerable to epidemics of infections and famine. In stage 2, these recede, although communicable disease remains significant. In stage 3, degenerative and/or 'human-made' illnesses come to the fore as causes of death. A prospective fourth stage of chronic but non-fatal morbidity (including mental disorders) is now evolving in advanced economies as people's average life expectancy approaches 80 years (ibid.).

The epidemiological transition model is based on the historical experience of Europe and North America where, as long ago as the nineteenth century, the knowledge and resources to control communicable diseases were already in place. Whether or not it is appropriate to apply this model to the South in the twenty-first century, a range of countries do seem to have passed from a situation in which infectious diseases such as cholera, pneumonia and tuberculosis (Box 10.1), though still a threat, are no longer the leading causes of death. This is particularly the case in wealthier regions such as Latin America, where non-communicable conditions such as cardiovascular illness, neoplasms (cancers), degenerative disorders such as Parkinson's Disease, and road accidents are now primary killers (see Chant with Craske, 2003: ch. 5).

Prevailing trends in morbidity not only reflect the greater combatting of communicable disease through immunisation programmes and substantial rises in life expectancy, but people's increasingly sedentary occupations, together with changes in consumption and lifestyle. For example, contemporary diets, especially among urban dwellers, comprise a greater intake of processed foods which contain high levels of salt, saturated fat and sugars, demonstrably proven to be linked with heart disease and/or cancer. Additional risks come from the fact that factory-farmed fruit, vegetables and grains may have been sprayed with harmful chemical pesticides and fertilisers, providing further fuel for the contention that malnutrition is potentially as much a scourge of 'modern' as 'traditional' societies (see Larkin, 1998; Shetty, 2008). Threats to health also come from tobacco smoking and drug-taking, with the World Bank (2007b: 35) drawing particular attention to tobacco addiction along with 'obesity pandemics' in causing premature deaths from pulmonary disease, hypertension, diabetes and the like. Indeed, although one prediction is that non-communicable disease will be the leading cause of death in all low-income countries by 2015 (ibid.: 21), that these deaths may occur before people reach old age is a major worry (see below). On top of this, the emergence and/or expansion of regional epidemics of HIV/AIDS, malaria, drug-resistant TB, SARS (Severe Acute Respiratory Syndrome), avian flu and so on (ibid.: 35) means that, all things being equal, the idea of a straightforward, unilinear evolution of health is difficult to sustain. In turn, this serves to underline the argument advanced by Phillips and Verhasselt (1994a: 12), that developing countries are characterised by 'epidemiological profiles that reflect all types of medical and social needs: infectious and parasitic conditions; chronic and degenerative diseases; psychological and psychiatric morbidity; and the social care needs of very young and very old people'.

BOX 10.1 COMMON COMMUNICABLE/ INFECTIOUS DISEASES IN THE GLOBAL SOUTH ACCORDING TO ROUTE OF TRANSMISSION

1) Diseases transmitted through contaminated water or food
e.g. diarrhoea, cholera.

2) Airborne diseases
e.g. pneumonia, tuberculosis, diphtheria, smallpox, meningitis, whooping cough, measles.

3) Diseases transmitted through direct physical contact
e.g. leprosy, HIV/AIDS.

4) Parasitic diseases
e.g. amoebiasis, ascariasis (caused by roundworms), and ancyclostomiasis (hookworm).

5) Diseases transmitted by animal vectors
a) Malaria – transmitted by *Anopheles* mosquito. Although DDT reduced their numbers for a while, nature is proving resistant. At present there are about 100 million cases a year, mainly in sub-Saharan Africa.

b) Bilharzia (schistosomiasis) – an infectious disease of the intestine and urinary tract caused by worms. It is usually found in humid/wet areas and is carried by snails.

c) Trypanosomiasis (sleeping sickness) – a disease common in sub-Saharan Africa, mainly transmitted by the tsetse fly.

d) Filiariasis – transmitted by mosquitoes, flies or worms, this takes various forms, such as lymphatic filiariasis (elephantiasis), or onchocerciasis (river blindness), and is particularly common in sub-Saharan Africa.

e) Trachoma – a widespread inflammation of the eye membrane passed on by flies which can result in blindness.

f) Dengue – transmitted by *Aedes aegypti* – a day-biting insect which breeds in contaminated pools of standing water. Often referred to as 'break bone' disease due to pain caused in joints. Especially prevalent in South America and East Africa. When contracted on third or fourth occasion can convert to haemmorhagic dengue and cause death.

Source: Szirmai (1997: ch. 5).

HEALTH INEQUALITIES IN THE SOUTH

Part of the reason for epidemiological diversity in the South is that pre-ventive and curative medical interventions are uneven across populations. For example, although almost everywhere in the world the death rate from communicable diseases has diminished due to infant immunisation against major diseases such as diptheria, measles, tetanus and tuberculosis, this applies less to low-income than wealthier groups. On top of this, lack of prompt, accessible, affordable and/or adequate medical attention among the poor means that diseases may progress to a stage where they are untreat-able, cause lasting damage to people's constitutions and/or give rise to lowered immunity to other infections.

Compounding the risks to poor people's health are inequalities in diet and living conditions, with strong historical and contemporary evidence indicating the critical importance to reducing mortality of a wide range of preventative health-care interventions such as clean water, sanitation, improved nutrition and shelter (see Larkin, 1998: 92; Unger and Riley, 2007; Van Naerssen and Barten, 1999: 230; World Bank, 2007b). In Latin America, for example, persistent inequalities in nutrition, education, infra-structure and so on have given rise to major disparities in patterns of disease and death both between and within countries (Abel and Lloyd-Sherlock, 2000: 3). In richer nations such as Argentina the epidemiological profile is very similar to advanced economies, with 'diseases of wealth and modernity', such as cardiovascular disease, tumours and trauma, being the major causes of mortality. This is also true in Mexico, where between 1950 and 1997, heart disease moved from fifth to first place in the rank of killer diseases, the next most important being tumours, diabetes, accidents and cerebrovascular diseases. In poorer countries such as Guatemala, on the other hand, the three leading causes of death are so-called 'diseases of poverty': measles, influenza and pneumonia. It is no coincidence that one-quarter of the population in Central America does not have access to sew-erage, and 29 per cent lack running water, with levels reaching 70 per cent or more in some rural areas. As for intra-national disparities, the under-5 mortality rate is three times higher among the poorest 20 per cent of the population in Southeast and Northeast Brazil, than among the wealthiest quintile. This is serious considering that poverty not only increases people's vulnerability to disease but is usually exacerbated by it (see Chant with Craske, 2003: ch. 5).

Other infectious but eminently preventable and curable diseases such as gastro-enteritic illness and diarrhoea are also skewed towards low-income groups in Latin America, and continue killing enough people to rank among the 10 leading causes of death in the continent. These conditions find fertile terrain not only in rural areas, but in the peri-urban slums of cities in Latin America and other regions of the Global South, where housing is often overcrowded and there is limited or no provision of clean, piped domestic water, sewerage systems and rubbish collection (see Bazoglu and Mboup, 2007; Chant, 2007c; Stephens and Harpham, 1992; Unger and Riley, 2007; also Chapter 4, this volume). Contaminated water supplies and lack of sanitation are associated with gastro-intestinal infections such as cholera, typhoid and hepatitis, while overcrowded housing is linked with respiratory infections such as tuberculosis, as well as meningitis and rheumatic heart disease. The deadly cocktail of overcrowding, inadequate facilities for bathing, unsanitary waste disposal and proximity to putrefy-ing rubbish can also lead to scabies and other dermatological conditions. In this light it is no surprise that in the Philippine capital, Manila, children residing in squatter settlements are nine times more at risk of tuberculosis than other children (Unger and Riley, 2007: 1562), or that in Buenos Aires, Argentina, the post neonatal mortality rate is 80 per cent higher on the periphery of the metropolis, where there are the worst housing conditions (and lowest levels of health insurance), than in the centrally located, and far wealthier, Federal District (Blue, 1996). Echoing these patterns, in urban Ethiopia, the under-5 mortality rate is approximately double in slum settlements than in non-slum areas, at 180 per 1000 as against 95 per 1000 respectively (Bazoglu and Mboup, 2007).

Yet while these examples go some way to endorsing the notion that there may well be an 'urban penalty' in health for slum-dwelling popula-tions in towns and cities of the Global South, poverty afflicts the health of rural residents to an equal if not greater extent (Montgomery et al., 2004). Although Argentina has the highest ratio of doctors to per capita GDP of anywhere in the world, for example, readily preventable diseases such as Chagas (which is spread through skin lesions by blood-sucking insects and can cause death if it invades the heart muscles and central nervous system) remain endemic in poor rural communities. By the same token, the combination of urbanisation and poverty poses complicated and severe problems for residents in urban slums, which again underline the need to exercise caution that the 'epidemiological transition' is neces-sarily a unidirectional, or indeed, positive process. Although, on the one hand, there may be greater likelihood of dying from a non-communicable disease, fatalities of this nature in poor neighbourhoods may result pre-maturely from accidents or injuries caused not only by hazardous terrain, flooding, substandard buildings and proximity to sources of pollution, but by criminal violence, which is often at its most marked in poor urban neighbourhoods (see Chapter 2). On the other hand, high population density in a context of infrastructural deficiency makes risk of death from infectious disease a similarly serious prospect. The example of HIV/AIDS, which in sub-Saharan Africa shows its greatest concentration in urban slums (Ambert et al., 2007: 2–3) is particularly pertinent here.

HIV/AIDS

Explanations for the higher prevalence of HIV in urban areas have often centred on people's greater availability of, and accessibility to, casual sexual partners, greater relaxation in sexual mores and a predominantly youthful age structure. However, as stressed by Ambert et al. (2007: i), while significant, these factors 'over-emphasise the behavioural dimensions of HIV transmission', and point to the need to acknowledge 'systemic linkages' between HIV/AIDs, urban development and poverty. Among the more salient of these links is the limited access of the urban poor to decent water and sanitation. Where these deficiencies give rise, as they so often do, to conditions such as worms, malaria, bilharzia and tuberculosis, common outcomes are malnutrition, compromised immunity, and increased 'viral loads'. These factors, in turn, render people more susceptible to HIV infection and/or to accelerated progression from HIV to AIDS. Women infected by bilharzia, for example, often end up with lesions in the urogenital tract which can lead to a threefold increase in their vulnerability to HIV. In mothers, the risk of passing HIV to babies is up to seven times greater when they are infected by worms (ibid.: 29). On top of this, HIV-positive individuals co-infected with malaria can be as much as seven times more contagious than those without (ibid.: ii).

Other important factors in HIV prevalence associated with urbanisation and poverty include increased dependence on cash incomes, which may force women, in particular, into unsafe 'transactional sex', or 'early sexual debut' and/or assault arising from the lack of privacy and security in the home or in the context of shared sanitary facilities (Ambert et al., 2007: 4; see also Esplen, 2007; Kiwala, 2005; Larkin, 1998: 97–8, McIlwaine and Datta, 2004; UNFPA, 2007: 24; Van Donk, 2006). In addition, lack of health facilities, and competition over increasingly scarce resources of land and services, can decrease social cohesion and the prospects for effective community mobilisation and responses to HIV and AIDS (Ambert et al., 2007: i). Indeed, despite public health campaigns in a wide number of countries to emphasise how HIV/AIDS can be contracted by people from all walks of life, and from circumstances beyond their personal control, and/or is not necessarily a condition which should hamper their full involvement in society (see Figures 10.1 and 10.2), in practical terms, there remains considerable social stigma and, in many

Source: Photo by Sylvia Chant.

Figure 10.1   HIV/AIDS posters, public STI clinic, Metro Cebu, Philippines – how you don't contract HIV/AIDS – and how anyone can catch it

263

Source: Photo by Sylvia Chant.

Figure 10.2 *Abstinence message in HIV/AIDS poster, public health clinic, Sukuta, The Gambia*

cases, alienation, sometimes projected onto a whole continent, as in the case of Africa (see Comaroff, 2007).

Mental Health

Mental health problems also seem to be found most frequently among low-income populations. While mental conditions can clearly occur as a result of individual heredity, genetic malfunction, ageing and so on, the contexts in which people live and work play a critical role (Larkin, 1998: 98). This is especially so in the context of 'common mental disorders' (CMDs), which describe non-psychotic mental or neurotic disorders such as depression, anxiety, fatigue, irritability, poor memory and weak concentration. Aside from the fact that physical ill-health undermines people's mental well-being, the uncertainties attached to inadequate or insecure jobs and housing constitute serious stressors, especially where people have migrated to cities and lack the support networks that may have been provided by kin in their areas of origin.

Indications of the importance of poverty in mental health are evident in a variety of studies. One survey carried out in São Paulo, for example, revealed that the incidence of mental disorders was highest in the poorest socio-economic sub-district (at 21 per cent) and lowest (12 per cent) in the highest income area (Blue, 1996). Research also suggests that mental infirmity is on the increase, with Latin America's rate of neuropsychiatric disorders now being 10.2 per 100 000 persons, which is 56 per cent higher than the world average of 6.5 per 100 000 (Londoño and Frenk, 2000: 24). At one level this is arguably due to the increased registering of psychological and psychiatric illnesses in health statistics. At another level, contemporary social, demographic and economic factors undoubtedly contribute, among the most important being temporary and permanent migration (national and international), employment insecurity and unemployment, the erosion of family and community support systems, and high levels of violence, crime and civil unrest (Larkin, 1998: 98). While mental health has rarely been shown the same concern as physical well-being, the WHO has underlined the urgency of so doing by dedicating its seventh World Health Report to the topic (WHO, 2001).

Gender Inequalities in Health

Aside from the role of socio-economic disparities in helping to explain the uneven distribution of physical and mental health problems, another important axis of inequality is gender, with women and men often suffering different levels and types of morbidity and mortality. Although

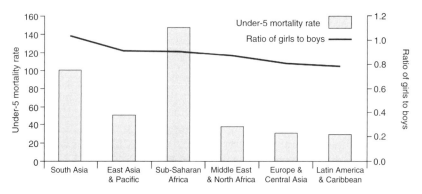

Source: Adapted from World Bank (2007a: figure 3.9).

Figure 10.3 *Female under-5 mortality rate and female–male ratio, 2004,*
selected world regions

physiological differences between women and men are partly responsible, these processes seldom operate in a gender-neutral environment. Accordingly, it is often the case that the low social valuation of women leads to a disproportionate share of ill-health and premature death. In many developing countries, particularly in Asia and Africa, for example, there are higher female than male rates of infant and child mortality as a result of gender bias in nutrition and medical care. This affects weighted regionally aggregated sex ratios for under-5 mortality as shown in Figure 10.3. On top of this, pre- or peri-natal sex selection (female-selective abortion or infanticide) in various parts of South and Southeast Asia have led to a situation in which sex ratios at birth have long been well above the universally accepted 'normal' level of 104–106 males per 100 females. In China, where this is particularly marked, for example, the ratio was as much as 120 male births per 100 female in 2005 (World Bank, 2007a: 124). Coupled with the disproportionate neglect of girls, this has often resulted in a disturbing 'masculinisation' of sex ratios in early childhood (Figure 10.4). For national populations as a whole, this clearly tends to cancel out the female bias in sex ratios which normally accrues from women's biological disposition to longer life expectancy. Indeed, the gravity of the tendency to further masculinisation of sex ratios in some Indian states led to the national government introducing radical new legislation in March 2008 to rectify the situation (see Box 10.2).

Even where women do not face an above-average risk of poor health as children, in later life they may be more vulnerable than men to particular conditions. Aside from the risks to women's health from pregnancy and

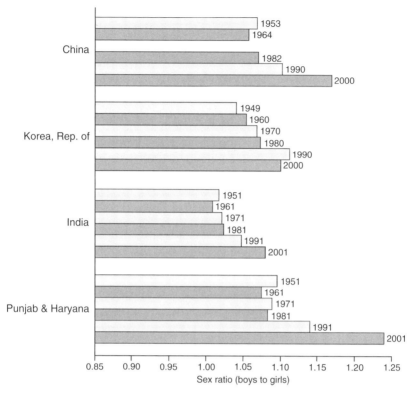

Note: The data for India are for the age group 0–6 years, and for China and Korea, 0–4 years.

Source: Adapted from World Bank (2007a: box 3.2).

Figure 10.4 *Child sex ratios in China, India (Punjab and Haryana), and Korea (1950–2000)*

childbearing, women's primary social roles as mothers and carers expose them to greater threat of contracting communicable disease from others, through tending to sick children and relatives, the handling of body wastes and so on. Women are also at above-average risk of environmental contamination, stress and exhaustion where they have to provide for their families' daily needs in the absence of basic services, infrastructure and adequate shelter (see earlier, and Chapter 4, this volume). Research conducted in India, for example, shows that exposure to cancer particles arising from cooking indoors on open fires is equivalent to smoking 20 packets of cigarettes a day (Østergaard, 1992). While not denying that men are also

---

BOX 10.2   INDIA: A NEW MEASURE TO ADDRESS
            THE MASCULINISATION OF SEX
            RATIOS

In early March 2008 the Indian government pledged to pay poor families to give birth to and bring up girl children in an effort to prevent around 500 000 abortions of female foetuses ('foeticides') per annum, and to redress the situation to further masculinisation of sex ratios at birth from 945 female to 1000 male babies in 1992, to 927:1000 in 2001. In seven of India's states, a cash payment of 15 500 rupees (*c.* US$386) will be given to poor families to keep their girl children. If the girl child reaches 18 years of age, has completed her school education and is still unmarried, parents will be rewarded with a further cash sum of 96 360 rupees (*c.* US$2400). The government is also considering giving life sentences to doctors who undertake sex-selective abortion.

Source: www.guardian.co.uk/world/2008/mar/04/india.gender (accessed 4 March 2008).

---

prone to health hazards, particularly in respect of deaths from behavioural-related factors such as car accidents, violence, alcoholism or drug abuse, the fact is that women's health status among the developing world poor suffers disproportionately from unequal power relations and patriarchal social formations. For example, despite the outlawing of female genital cutting (often referred to as Female Genital Mutilation [FGM]), in many parts of Africa in recent years, in countries such as The Gambia, an estimated 60 per cent or more of the female population undergo cliterodectomy and excision, often as adolescents, and even as babies. Young women have little recourse to resist the procedure, despite the valiant efforts of NGOs such as GAMCOTRAP (Gambia Committee on Traditional Practices) to encourage circumcisers to 'lay down their knives' (see Figure 10.5), and as a result, often end up experiencing painful sex, uro-genitary problems, anaemia and prolonged labour, not to mention emotional and psychological trauma (see Touray, 2006). While there is as yet no proven link between FGM and HIV/AIDS, women's anatomical vulnerability to infection by the virus here and in many other contexts is compounded by the fact that they may not be able to negotiate safe sex. This is especially serious in societies where men routinely seek sexual relations with younger (adolescent) woman who are much more prone to contract HIV/AIDS, and/or engage

Source: Pho o by Sylvia Chant.

Figure 10.5 Signboard of Gambian NGO campaigning against FGM and other harmful traditional practices

*Table 10.2   Sources of death and disability with largest gender differentials
in disease burden among 15–29-year-olds, low- and middle-
income countries*

Disease/condition	Burden of disease (% of total) Females	Burden of disease (% of total) Males	Gender ratio (female/male)
Females			
Fires	2.13	0.90	2.34
Migraine	1.46	0.68	2.12
Panic disorders	2.49	1.24	2.00
HIV/AIDS	12.76	9.03	1.40
Unipolar depressive disorders	8.05	5.82	1.37
Males			
Other unintentional injuries	4.29	8.09	0.53
Road traffic accidents	2.24	7.73	0.29
Violence	1.24	7.58	0.16
Alcohol use disorders	0.68	4.12	0.16
War	0.13	2.68	0.05

Note: The burden of disease has been calculated as the percentage of DALYs lost due to a
specific cause over the total DALYs lost (for men and women separately). For the purposes
of identifying priority diseases for gender equity, all diseases that primarily affect males (for
example, prostrate cancer) or females (for example, maternity conditions) were omitted. The
burden of disease for men and women was multiplied by the sex ratio. The diseases with the
greatest gender differentials are those with a weighted differential above the statistical
threshold of its distribution, that is, mean plus one standard deviation.

Source: World Bank (2007a: table 3.5).

in multiple (and often unprotected) casual sex within and beyond marriage
and regular partnerships (see Chant, 2007c; UNAIDS, 2007). Women and
children are also the main victims of domestic violence, with all its attendant physical and psychological health risks.

The biggest single attempt to quantify gendered vulnerabilities to ill-
health at an international scale has come about with the Global Burden of
Disease project, co-funded by the WHO and the World Bank, and involving the collaboration of 100 researchers across the world. On the basis of
health information from a wide range of countries, the study estimates the
potential years of life lost as a result of premature death, poor health and
disability expressed in a measure known as 'DALYs' (disability-adjusted
life years). The latest figures from this project pertain to 2002, and for the
15–29 year age group reveal significant differences in sources of death and

disability between women and men (see Table 10.2). In many instances it is also the case that inadequate provision of treatment for women's health conditions, particularly beyond maternity, compounds their vulnerabilities (see Chant with Craske, 2003: ch. 5). Indeed, gender inequalities in health and access to health care are especially marked among the poor, and in Latin America, for example, translate into disproportionately high chances of premature death (Figure 10.6).

HEALTHCARE PROVISION AND POLICIES

Healthcare provision plays a vital role in health in developing regions, with public spending identified as more important than per capita income in determining life expectancy (Bhatia and Mossialos, 2004). The level of resources dedicated by governments is especially important for low-income groups, not only on account of their disproportionate share of disease and ill-health, but because they are less able to afford private treatment. Since the late 1990s, for example, average per capita public expenditure on health in low-income countries was only US$5 per annum (compared with US$40 in middle-income countries, and over US$1100 in high-income economies). Given that an AIDS test in some of the poorest countries in sub-Saharan Africa amounted to the annual per capita health budget at that time gives some indication of the magnitude of these discrepancies as well as helping to explain why HIV/AIDS in this region, despite some decline in the last few years (for example, in Uganda, Kenya and Zimbabwe), remains at epidemic proportions (see UNAIDS, 2006; 2007). Coupled with the fact that the scant resources available for health expenditure by poor and heavily indebted countries have often been eroded by debt crisis, neoliberal restructuring and military or civil conflict, that the amount of money available for private expenditure is also limited perpetuates inequality. According to recent World Bank Health and Nutrition Statistics, for example, as of 2004, mean annual combined public and private expenditure on health per capita was just under US$36 in sub-Saharan Africa, and as little as US$23.8 in South Asia, compared with an average of US$3449 in high-income economies.

   In general terms, comprehensive national health-care systems are a rarity in the Global South. Even in Latin America and the Caribbean which is wealthy by developing world standards, and boasts higher levels of public expenditure than most other parts of the South, up to 25 per cent of the population is estimated to lack access to health services and the number of doctors per 100 000 people is only just half that of the average for high income economies (Table 10.3). Only two countries (Cuba and Costa Rica)

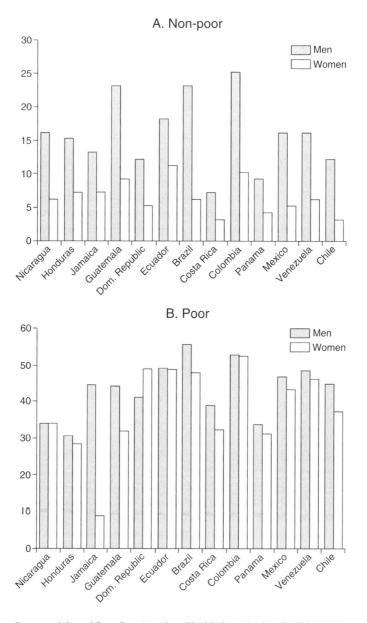

Source: Adapted from Pan-American Health Organisation (PAHO) (2003).

*Figure 10.6   Gender differences in risks of premature death in Latin
America, by poor and non-poor status*

Table 10.3   Doctors per 100 000 people, 1990–2003

Sub-Saharan Africa	14.8
Asia (excl. Middle East)	107.1
Middle East and N. Africa	120.4
Central America and Caribbean	181.3
South America	190.3
Developing countries (mean)	98.4
Developed countries (mean)	361.1

Source: World Health Organisation statistics: www.who.org (accessed 5 February 2008).

have what Londoño and Frenk (2000) describe as a 'unified public model', where everyone is guaranteed access to public health care which is financed and provided directly by the state at all levels. Most other countries in the region, as elsewhere in the South, have a 'segmented model' whereby different social groups are catered for by different health systems – the poor by the public sector, formal sector workers by social security, and middle- and upper-income groups by the private sector, paid for out of pocket or through private insurance funds. According to Londoño and Frenk, the segmented model suffers from a duplication and waste of resources, especially in high-technology services, and major quality differentials among the various segments. Indeed, the service offered by the public sector is often so deficient that poor people end up paying for private treatment that makes huge inroads into their household budgets. In the early 1990s, for example, the poorest 10 per cent of Mexican urban households spent 5.2 per cent of their income on health care, compared with 2.8 per cent among the richest decile, and in Ecuador the poorest decile spent as much as 17 per cent (ibid.). In the Gambia, the non-poor spend more private income on health in absolute terms, with the poor, as in other countries in sub-Saharan Africa and beyond, often resorting to cheaper providers such as 'marabouts' (traditional healers who use a combination of Islamic prayer and 'jujus' [amulets]), and/or doctors who offer alternative therapies, such as Chinese medicine, for a wide range of health problems (see Figures 10.7 and 10.8). Nonetheless, given that nearly two-thirds of the Gambian population fall below the poverty line, health being the second biggest single item of household expenditure at a national level, consuming 18.7 per cent of household income after food (39.1 per cent), presents a significant challenge to the majority of citizens (see Chant, 2007a: ch. 4).

If tendencies to privatisation of health care at a world scale continue, the consequences are likely to be serious, not only in respect of equity, but because in the past 25 years there have been slowdowns or even reversals in

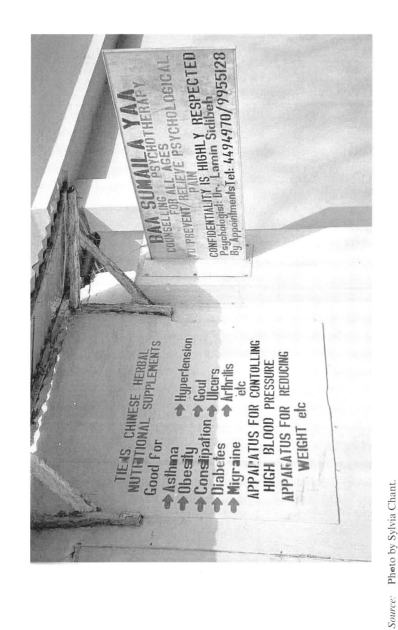

Source: Photo by Sylvia Chant.

Figure 10.7 'Alternative' therapies for health, The Gambia

Source: Photo by Cathy McIlwaine.

Figure 10.8   A traditional healer ('sangoma'), Khayelitsha, Cape Town, South Africa

long-standing improvements in infant and childhood mortality, as well as in the control of major communicable diseases (see Asthana, 1994). Not only have new communicable diseases, such as avian flu and SARS, appeared, but old ones which were supposed to have been contained or eradicated, have resurfaced (see World Bank, 2007a). Haemorrhagic dengue, for example, is presently endemic in 15 countries in Latin America, compared with only seven in 1970 (Ugalde et al., 2002).

Despite the fact that many better-off people pay (and can afford to pay) for private health care, a major criticism of public sector spending in developing countries is that the lion's share (sometimes as much as 70–80 per cent) has been devoted to curative services, including large and costly hospitals, sophisticated high-technology medical equipment, imported pharmaceuticals and the high salaries of specialist physicians (see Bhatia and Mossialos, 2004; Lloyd-Sherlock, 2002). Such biases disadvantage the poor whose needs are predominantly for basic preventative medical care in the form of local health posts, immunisation schemes and elementary training in hygiene, nutrition and first aid.

PRIMARY HEALTH CARE

Recognition of the need to redirect national health efforts came as far back as the 1970s when the World Health Organisation launched a major campaign entitled 'Health For All By The Year 2000', and at the 1978 world conference on health in Alma Ata, USSR (now Almaty in Kazakhstan), advocated 'Primary Health Care' (PHC) as a means of achieving this stated goal.

The cornerstones of the Primary Health Care approach are equity, inter-sectoral co-operation, prevention and community involvement. In respect of equity, the PHC approach calls for the diversion of funds from high-technology, centralised, urban-based facilities, to decentralised, smaller, simpler and more cost-effective units. One country which has adopted this model with some success is Costa Rica. Following its formal adoption of the PHC approach in the early 1980s, Costa Rica established Basic Comprehensive Health Teams (EBAIS) in 800 'health zones' across the country orientated to the most vulnerable in the population. Each team is responsible for first-level health care and referrals to higher-order services, and is supported by a local community-based committee. Subscribing to the principle of community involvement in decisions on health and basic medical provision, the latter has the twin benefit of drawing on local expertise and resources, and in increasing accountability (see Chant, 2007a: ch. 6). Aside from enhancing the skills of indi-

---

BOX 10.3 WOMEN'S PARTICIPATION IN A HEALTH PROJECT IN BOLIVIA

In the late 1980s, the 'Warmi Project' was set up in the remote rural province of Inquisivi, Bolivia. It was funded by the United States Agency for International Development (USAID) and implemented by the Save the Children/USA Bolivia field office. 'Warmi' means 'woman' in Aymara which is spoken in this part of Bolivia, and reflects the fact that the project was not only oriented to women, but was also about involving them in its execution.

The Warmi project used a community-based approach to improve maternal and neonatal health in an area traditionally lacking access to formal heath services. In three areas of the province, the project worked with various groups of women, sometimes based on existing ones, in other cases representing new formations, in a wide range of aspects of maternal and neonatal health. The methodology was highly participatory, and based to a very large degree on women determining the most pressing needs within their communities. Other activities included training and demonstration sessions, literacy programmes, the establishment of emergency funds and the selection of women within the community to learn midwifery locally and in the largest city, La Paz. Within a short space of time (1998–90 to 1991–93), perinatal and neonatal mortality decreased by almost two-thirds, and there was a substantial improvement in health practices, including hygienic births, immediate breastfeeding and care of the newborn, and tetanus toxoid vaccination.

Source: Howard-Grabman (1996).

---

genous practitioners such as 'barefoot doctors', traditional midwives, birth attendants and so on, emphasis is also given to training community residents, which here, as elsewhere, has been shown to have positive results (see Box 10.3). More generally, schemes to enable people to live healthier lives and thus prevent disease include training in food preparation, hygiene and fuel conservation. The idea that preventive health care should be viewed within its wider environmental context also requires that health projects should be backed up by improvements in housing and basic community infrastructure such as water and sanitation (see Unger and Riley, 2007).

Yet despite impassioned calls on the part of the WHO over three decades, PHC has not enjoyed the wholesale adoption that was originally intended. This is partly because traditional health-care systems do not so much coexist with the modern, as lie in their shadow, and are only weakly supported (Phillips and Verhasselt, 1994b). Moreover, in the context of neoliberalism PHC has come to be seen by many donors and governments as 'too ambitious, too expensive and too uncertain in outcome' (Larkin, 1998: 105). In turn, the move towards Selective Primary Health Care (SPHC) has been part of a process since the late 1980s for a discernible marketisation of health care, pushed in large measure by the World Bank's agenda to privatise health services, albeit under co-ordination by national authorities as advocated by the 'New Public Management' (NPM) model (see Bhatia and Mossialos, 2004).

SPHC has been described as a 'profoundly pragmatic' approach which selects health interventions on the basis of cost effectiveness. SPHC packages favour low-cost interventions such as immunisation for a fairly restricted range of childhood diseases such as measles and whooping cough, and pays little more than lip-service to participation in decisions (Asthana, 1994). Although SPHC may well use unpaid community labour in implementation, it ignores the fact that participation also requires people's involvement in the political process and improvements in their institutional capacity to participate. Moreover, while a key objective of Primary Health Care has been to enlist the poor in community decisions, there has been very little emphasis on 'enlisting the rich' and their role as responsible citizens (Abel and Lloyd-Sherlock, 2000: 15).

The World Bank (2007b: 10) professes that the 'ultimate objective' of its new Strategy for Health, Nutrition and Population (HNP) Results (2007–2015) is to 'improve the health conditions of people in client countries, particularly the poor and the vulnerable, in the context of its overall strategy for poverty alleviation'. Although it remains to be seen how this will pan out in practice, the principle is important. On top of this, more finance for health is being made available by a broader range of organisations such as the Bill and Melinda Gates Foundation, and the Global Fund to Fight AIDS, TB and Malaria. Indeed, the latter currently provides around one-fifth of international HIV resources. This is significant given that funding for HIV has risen by nearly US$2 million per annum since 2001 when 189 member states of the UN pledged their commitment to halting or reversing the spread of HIV/AIDS by 2015, as enshrined in MDG 6 (see UNAIDS, 2006; also Box 1.1). This said, although there has been increasing access to Anti-Retroviral Therapy (ART), only one in five people in need worldwide are receiving treatment, and in some sub-Saharan African countries, this is less than one in 10 (ibid.). This typifies a seemingly general persistence in inequality in people's health and access to health care. Unless similar commitments are made to address other factors responsible for a disproportionate burden of disease and early death among the poor, 'Health for All' will remain as elusive in the twenty-first century as it did at the end of the twentieth. In this regard, the theme of the 2008 report of the WHO which calls for the reinvigoration of PHC 30 years after Alma Ata is more than timely.

Activity 10.1
Go to the WHO website and consult the interview with Dr Margaret Chan as she reflected on taking up her position as WHO's Director General in 2007 at www.who.int/dg/chan/interviews/taking_office/en/index.html. What issues do you think influenced Dr Chan's stated priorities for her term in office (for example, the health of women, the health of people in Africa), and to what extent do you think these priorities correspond with the most pressing health needs of the poor in the Global South?

LEARNING OUTCOMES

By the end of this chapter and relevant reading you should be able to:

- Define 'health' and identify its varied interrelationships with developmental change.
- Identify different types of communicable and non-communicable disease, and reasons why particular types of disease are associated with poverty in developing regions.
- Outline the major systems of health care in developing societies, and evaluate the utility of adopting a Primary Health Care approach.

FURTHER READING

Bhatia, Mrigesh and Mossialos, Elias (2004), 'Health systems in developing countries', in Anthony Hall and James Midgely (eds), *Social Policy for Development*, London: Sage, pp. 168–204.
A comprehensive overview of health and health systems in the Global South. Among the key issues covered are the factors explaining differences in health status of populations in different developing countries, the historical background and role of international agencies, changing patterns of health-care finance and delivery, and pharmaceutical policies.

Chant, Sylvia with Craske, Nikki (2003), *Gender in Latin America*, London: Latin America Bureau/New Brunswick, NJ: Rutgers University Press.
Chapter 5 of this book provides a general review of gender differentials in health and healthcare, discussion of intra-regional differences in morbidity and

mortality in Latin America, and gendered aspects of health in the region. This includes gender-differentiated susceptibility to ill-health, gender differences in preventive health care, gender differences in health-care provision (at the level of households, as well as in health systems), and gender differences in access to healthcare.

Szirmai, Adam (1997), *Economic and Social Development*, New York: Prentice Hall.
Chapter 5 of this book outlines the complex nature of the disease burden faced by developing societies, with considerable attention paid to 'diseases of poverty' which disproportionately affect the rural and urban poor. Also covered in the chapter are different theoretical approaches to analysing health with particular emphasis on the interrelationships between health and development.

UNAIDS (2006), *2006 Report on the Global AIDS Epidemic: Executive Summary*, Geneva:UNAIDS (downloadable from www.data.unaids.org/pub/ GlobalReport/2006/2006_GR-ExecutiveSummary_en.pdf).
An excellent state-of-the-art review of global trends in HIV/AIDS prevalence and changing health interventions. Particular attention is paid to the impacts of the UN General Assembly Special Session on HIV/AIDS in 2001, and to the launch of the Global Fund to Fight AIDS, TB and Malaria in 2002.

Unger, Alon and Riley, Lee W. (2007), 'Slum health: from understanding to action', *PLoS Medicine*, **4**(10), 1561–66 (e295) (downloadable from www.plosmedicine.org).
A concise, but eminently wide-ranging, summary of the main impacts of poverty and slum residence on health in urban areas of the Global South. The paper also identifies a number of ways to address the challenge of health in poor urban communities.

USEFUL WEBSITES

www.who.org – website of WHO, from which annual WHO reports since 1995 can be downloaded
www.unaids.org – UN website on HIV/AIDS

11. The development community: from multilateral agencies to community-based organisations

INTRODUCTION

Our final chapter focuses exclusively on the policy arena. It examines the principal actors at the global level, beginning with a brief outline of the role of the state as an agent of development and continuing with a discussion of multilateral development agencies together with bilateral agencies and their role in providing development aid. In focusing on issues of global governance, the first main section highlights the role of politics in North–South power relations and how this influences development policy. The second part of the chapter focuses on civil society, concentrating on the role of NGOs in the development process. In particular, it addresses the issue of how far NGOs have changed in recent years and the implications of their growing importance for development policy.

THE STATE AS AN AGENT OF DEVELOPMENT

Throughout much of the history of international development, the state has been viewed as the principal agent through which development within national boundaries has taken place. In addition, states also provide the main political context within which development organisations function. Yet despite the importance of the state in directing development since colonial times, with the 1960s seeing many developing countries actively establishing large state enterprises ranging from public utilities to mining, agricultural and industrial ventures, this is not necessarily due to an innate ability to foster positive and sustainable development. Indeed, as early as the 1970s, a questioning of the role of the state as agent of development began. Despite abundant international finance available at this time, the economic performance of many developing countries remained poor, and state spending greatly exceeded GDP. By the 1980s, state capacity to contribute to national development was severely impaired by rising oil prices,

mounting debt problems and global economic recession. As such, the state
was progressively seen as part of the problem rather than the solution (see
Thomas and Allen, 2000; Potter et al., 2008 for further discussions).
Similarly, while the principle of aid itself was being criticised by dependency thinkers as an extension of Northern domination and exploitation,
it was also being condemned by neoliberals for contributing to excessive
state interference in markets. With the advent of SAPs, the role of the state
was significantly pared down and its control reduced. In the 1990s, however,
the debate of state versus market became increasingly redundant as a
balance was sought between the two. Reform of the state was viewed as
crucial in ensuring democratic and sustainable development for the future.
Promoted by the World Bank in particular, this agenda was based on the
need to improve the functioning of countries in the South, entailing adherence to principles of openness, democracy, respect for human rights, participation, accountability and effectiveness in public sector management
(Potter et al., 2008). The promotion of this 'good governance' agenda (see
below) also highlights the way in which nation states in the South are often
closely held to account by international agencies and especially the IFIs
through conditionality (see Chapter 2, this volume). In addition, other
types of actors such as civil society (especially NGOs) have increasingly
been considered as important in meeting development goals (see below). As
the following discussion will show, the provision of foreign aid to countries
of the South is not straightforward and has been the subject of much debate
and criticism (see Easterly, 2006; Sachs, 2005 for contrasting views).

THE RISE OF MULTILATERAL DEVELOPMENT AGENCIES

Multilateral development agencies refer to inter-governmental organisations funded by more than one member nation. The main multilateral agencies are the Bretton Woods Institutions of the UN, the World Bank, and
the IMF.[1] The World Bank and the IMF are part of the UN 'family', but
not part of the UN 'system'. In reality this means that they operate separately and independently (Whitman, 2008). Yet together these institutions
form the bedrock of global governance, which refers broadly to the rules,
norms and institutions that operate at a world scale (Boas, 2008). In contrast to global government which would have similar powers to national
governments, global public organisations are funded and governed by
states. There is a lot of pressure on states to join global organisations in
order to demonstrate their international legitimacy. For developing countries, it also allows them to attract investment by demonstrating that they

abide by international rules (ODI, 2002). Institutions of global governance are very controversial in terms of their power, transparency and remit, as discussed below.

The United Nations

As outlined in Chapter 2, the aftermath of the Second World War saw the need to reconstruct Europe, ensure peace throughout the world and to address wider development issues in the Global South. The UN was set up in 1945 with the aim of promoting such economic and social development, and was a clear break from its predecessor, the League of Nations, which aimed solely to maintain stable international relations. Membership of the UN grew from 51 nations in 1945 to a current total of 192 with most countries of the world now members with the notable exceptions of Switzerland and Taiwan (Potter et al., 2008).[2] Initially, its role was limited to providing advice to the governments of member states. It recommended a more expanded role for governments in promoting development beyond the provision of infrastructure, social services and administration. This approach was related to the purportedly peaceful global environment at that time, and by the dominance of major powers within the UN. This meant there was little recognition of the need to transform the structure of international economic relations. In 1962, however, the 'First Development Decade' was declared by the UN, which was to change the organisation's ethos. Increasingly, independent former colonies joined the General Assembly (where every member nation is represented) and brought about pressure on the UN to fully recognise inequitable relations between North and South. Ever since, the UN has invariably taken a more pro-South approach than many governments and other agencies in the North (although this also depends on the specific institution). Most visibly, the annual *Human Development Report* launched in 1990 by the UNDP played a key role in criticising the effects of neoliberalism, as well as highlighting issues of poverty and deprivation, and ensuring that measures of development were broadened beyond GNP. More recently, the responsibility for monitoring and assisting governments in achieving the MDGs has also fallen to the UNDP (see Chapter 1, this volume).

The UN system today comprises a wide range of institutions. The organisation itself consists of six main organs including the General Assembly, Security Council and Economic and Social Council, added to which there are various special commissions and programmes, such as the UNDP and the United Nations Children's Fund. The UN also includes seven functional commissions, a number of standing committees and a range of specialised agencies, such as the ILO and the World Bank (see below). Some other autonomous bodies, such as the WTO, also work closely with the UN (Potter et al., 2008).

Limitations of the UN

There are several constraints on the operation of the UN which reduce its effectiveness as a multilateral organisation, and which have led to repeated calls for reform in the new millennium. The first relates to North–South relations within the UN. While member countries make different financial contributions according to their means, all have the same power to vote in the General Assembly. Southern countries are thus in the majority, but since the resolutions of the General Assembly are not binding, recommendations made can often be ignored by major powers in the North. This said, the Assembly's decisions are powerful in influencing world opinion (Potter et al., 2008), and have often been incorporated into international treaties such as the Climate Change Convention of 1994.

Also extremely significant in reducing effectiveness is lack of funding. The UN relies on a regular budget derived from contributions from member states (not including ODA – see below), based largely on GNP and per capita income. These can be mandatory or voluntary; the assessed mandatory contributions cover the regular budget and peacekeeping operations while the voluntary contributions are used for UN funds and programmes such as the UNDP and UNICEF. In 2006, the UN system had a budget of around US$20 billion per annum. However, the regular budget was only US$1.8 billion in 2006, representing only a small increase from 1996 (US$1.5 billion). A further US$5 billion was allocated for peacekeeping (Lehmann and McClellan, 2006). The non-payment and/or late payment of dues has been a consistent problem for the UN, with the largest contributor, the USA, being the worst offender, owing more than US$1 billion to the regular, peacekeeping and international tribunals budgets. In 2006, only 40 member states paid their dues entirely and on time (ibid.) and at July 2007, seven member states were in arrears under the terms of Article 19 of the UN Charter. These included the Central African Republic, Comoros, Guinea-Bissau, Liberia, São Tomé and Príncipe, Somalia and Tajikistan.[3] In trying to avert financial crises, the UN has to cross-subsidise from its peacekeeping fund to offset its deficit leading to the delay in transferring funds to countries providing troops (see also Potter et al., 2008).

Countries can also use voluntary payments in order to promote their own goals and agendas. Because UN programmes are funded by voluntary contributions, countries can identify those on which they feel they can exert most political influence (Lehmann and McClellan, 2006). In turn, increased competition between agencies for the same monies has led to inter-agency rivalry. Criticisms have also been levelled in terms of duplication of activities and a lack of coherence among progressively downsized UN programmes. In addition, the work of some agencies runs counter to, or undermines, that of others (Whitman, 2008).

In terms of 'peacekeeping', which is perhaps the best-known responsibility of the UN, the use of reactive rather than preventative measures has been increasingly questioned. Linked with this has been criticism of the supposed independence of the UN from national strategic interests. This is because responsibility for peace and security lies with the Security Council made up of five permanent members (the USA, the UK, China, France and Russia) (Potter et al., 2008). As the experience of the US invasion of Iraq showed, the political clout of the UN can be severely compromised. This situation is further exacerbated by the fact that these permanent members also control the world's arms market. Indeed, ultimately, the UN is a political organisation whose developmental roles are shaped by the priorities of its more powerful member states. Yet, somewhat paradoxically, it is the political connotations of the UN which have led to the USA, and many other Northern countries, to renege on paying their contributions on time or in full. At the same time, the Bush administration continues to make demands on the UN in terms of providing funds for peacekeeping such as the current mission to Darfur.[4]

Despite such criticisms, the UN has tried to institute reform especially since the Millennium Summit in 2000. The most recent effort was by Kofi Annan in 2005 as part of the Millennium+5 initiative in his report *In Larger Freedom* (Annan, 2005). However, reform has been widely criticised as being inadequate and unsubstantial, even among bilateral agencies such as DFID (2006). Nonetheless, the UN remains an important source of international development activity and research even though the world in which it was conceived has changed almost beyond recognition. On the positive side, through data-gathering, norm-setting and monitoring, the UN and its agencies have made significant advances in improving agriculture, literacy and infant survival rates, and in raising awareness of vulnerable groups throughout the world, often through its summits on human rights, gender issues, environmental concerns and so on (Whitman, 2008).

The World Bank Group and the IMF

Part of the umbrella UN system, and even more controversial, is the other key multilateral agency, the World Bank Group. This comprises four international development institutions: the International Bank for Reconstruction and Development (IBRD), established in 1944; the

International Finance Corporation (IFC), established in 1956; the International Development Association (IDA), established in 1960, and the Multilateral Investment Guarantee Agency (MIGA), established in 1988. Both the IFC and the MIGA are involved in private sector investment, while the IBRD and the IDA are concerned with government spending and broader development. When talking about the World Bank, it is generally the IBRD which is referred to. The latter will be discussed here in greater detail along with the IMF which was also established in 1944, and is closely associated with the World Bank.

The Bretton Woods institutions were set up to regulate the global economy in the aftermath of the Second World War, concentrating initially on bolstering economic relations between Western Europe and the USA, but progressively becoming involved in economic development in the South (see Hardstaff and Jones, 2006, for a critical review). To become a member of the World Bank, it is first necessary to belong to the IMF. The main distinction between the two institutions is that the IMF is concerned with international economic stability and overall policing of the global economy, and may make short-term loans in order to overcome severe economic crisis. The World Bank, on the other hand, has traditionally been more concerned with the longer-term development of countries in the South, even if these roles have become increasingly blurred over time (Potter et al., 2008).

In 2007, there were 185 members of the IBRD, 179 members of the IFC, 166 of IDA and 171 of MIGA. The most notable difference between the UN and the World Bank is that while the UN operates a 'one country, one vote' policy, the World Bank is run on a 'one dollar, one vote' basis. This means that voting power fluctuates according to national financial contributions. With effect from July 2007, the US vote counted for 16.4 per cent within the IBRD, followed by Japan at 7.9 per cent, whereas India had 3.4 per cent and China only 2.8 per cent.[5] Thus, the G8 countries have over 45 per cent of voting rights in the IBRD, with the remaining share divided among the rest of the world. In turn, high-income countries collectively hold 60 per cent of votes, leaving only 40 per cent for low- and middle-income nations (two African chairs hold 5.31 per cent).[6] With control of these institutions firmly in the hands of the wealthiest industrialised countries, efforts to challenge this inequity have met with stiff resistance. For example, some oil-producing states in the South tried to increase their voting power during the 1970s by raising their contributions, but were prevented from so doing by Northern countries (Potter et al., 2008). Of particular importance is the USA's clout in the governance and power of the World Bank, as noted by Wade (2002: 217): 'The Bank is a source of funds to be offered to US friends or denied to US enemies, and a source of

Anglo-American ideas about effective ways to organise an economy – and increasingly, a polity too.' Having said this, reform of both leadership selection and the voting weight of countries have gained momentum in the last two years under the guise of addressing issues of 'voice and representation'. A similar reform process has been in motion within the IMF.

It is important to emphasise, however, that the IBRD was originally set up to promote the international flow of capital for productive purposes, rather than as an aid agency. The vast majority of its lending is funded by borrowing, with a small proportion paid to the organisation by member states. It is able to offer borrowers more favourable (although still high) interest rates on loans than can commercial banks. In 2006, the IBRD had commitments amounting to US$23.6 billion (6 per cent higher than 2005). Most of this lending was for investment operations (US$16.3 billion) with US$7.3 billion for policy-based operations. Lending commitments to Africa stood at 20 per cent (US$4.8 billion), with Europe and Central Asia at 17 per cent (US$4 billion), South Asia at 16 per cent (US$3.8 billion), East Asia and the Pacific at 14 per cent (US$3.4 billion), and the Middle East and North Africa region 7 per cent (US$1.7 billion).[7] Lending also takes place through the IDA, which provides interest-free loans to the poorest countries (those which in 2000 had per capita incomes of less than US$885). International Development Association loans are mainly funded through ODA, as well as general profits from the World Bank. These loans form around 25 per cent of all World Bank lending (Potter et al., 2008). It should also be noted that the establishment of the IDA has been seen as a way for the US government to sidestep the UN in their involvement in the South, and thus have greater power over the allocation of funds (see Wade, 2002; also below).

The World Bank as a whole remains the largest source of finance and aid for development in the South (Potter et al., 2008). It has also succeeded in becoming a leading source of research and knowledge on poverty and development issues, albeit from a largely neoliberal standpoint. Indeed, it should be reiterated that the World Bank was not established as a development agency, but rather as a bank (and indeed is often just referred to as 'the Bank').

Changing Role and Growing Criticisms of the World Bank

The World Bank has been subject to widespread and increasing criticism over time as its influence has grown, even as early as the 1960s and 1970s, when its role was mainly limited to lending for specific schemes, and especially infrastructure projects such as dams. Environmentalists, for instance, became increasingly concerned about the impact of World Bank interventions, such as the Carajas iron ore project in Eastern Amazonia. This involved the clearance of tropical forest the size of England and France combined. Another controversial case was presented by a Bank highway project in Northwest Brazil which led to major deforestation, as well as the forced resettlement of 30 000 families. The injurious social and environmental impacts of such schemes forced the World Bank itself to recognise that this could severely limit its projects on economic development (Potter et al., 2008; Stiglitz, 1999).

Analysts also pointed out that project failure might have been due to the fact that a project could not be separated from its political and economic context, something which was often ignored (and arguably still is). Therefore, during the 1970s and into the 1980s, the Bank moved more towards programme lending, which involved larger loans aimed at promoting fundamental transformations in recipient countries. The debt crisis of the early 1980s compounded this emphasis on broad-based economic policies (see Corbridge, 2008). It became evident that macroeconomic imbalances responsible for the crisis needed to be addressed. This was attempted through loans for SAPs (Chapter 2). The shift to programme lending was accompanied by increased emphasis on loan conditionality (giving loans subject to specific conditions). Significantly, this implied that economic problems were the result of the fiscal mismanagement by governments in the South, rather than external economic circumstances over which they had no control.

The 1980s and beyond saw a huge increase in the influence of the World Bank on development policy and the most extensive criticisms ever to be levelled against it. As demonstrated in Chapter 2, macroeconomic changes have often been made at the cost of social development. For example, there is increasing evidence that SAPs compound, rather than alleviate, socio-economic and gender inequalities and that the reduced investment levels often associated with SAPs can threaten long-term economic progress. Although the World Bank and IMF have revamped the SAPs through the HIPC Initiative and PRSPs, they have still been heavily criticised. Besides these specific issues, they have also been accused of a lack of accountability to the UN. Indeed, the use of the World Bank and IMF for channelling of ODA, especially by the USA, have been viewed as a means by which powerful economies can secure their national interests in an ostensibly 'legitimate' fashion (Thomas and Allen, 2000). Thus, although multilateral aid is theoretically more politically neutral than bilateral aid, this is not always the case (see Wade, 2002, on the role of the USA).

Other important criticisms of the World Bank lie in accusations that it has overridden the needs of many developing countries in order to impose its own neoliberal agenda. In turn, the Bank has been accused of controlling the economies of developing countries in an imperialist manner (Easterly, 2006). Indeed, criticisms have been so widespread that the World Bank has become a major target for anti-globalisation protests in recent years. Many large NGOs such as Oxfam and Christian Aid in the UK have organised campaigns and consciousness-raising activities over what they argue is the deleterious influence of the World Bank on the countries of the developing world. In addition, several specific coalitions and campaigns have been established to lobby the World Bank (and the IMF). One of the most well known is the '50 Years is Enough' coalition established in 2000 and comprising over 200 organisations committed to the transformation of both institutions. More specifically, they call for the suspension of policies and practices that have caused widespread poverty, inequality and suffering among the world's population and its environment (see Chapter 2, this volume).[8] Another campaign, entitled 'Women's Eyes on the World Bank', comprises five organisations from every region of the world which collectively lobby for greater gender-responsiveness in World Bank policies (see Chapter 8, this volume).[9]

Reform of all the main multilateral organisations is now being called for and has partly been put into motion (Stiglitz, 1999). Reform has the support of all the development community from small NGOs, to larger bilaterals such as DFID (2006). However, it remains to be seen how swiftly this reform will take place and how enduring it will be (see Easterly's [2006] critique of foreign aid that focuses, *inter alia*, on the policies of the World Bank and the IMF).

Activity 11.1
Access the websites of both the World Bank (www.worldbank.org/) and the 'Whirled Bank' (www.whirledbank.org/). On reading some of the articles which outline the key objectives of each organisation, first, write a defence of the World Bank from the perspective of one of its economists, and second, write a critique from the viewpoint of an anti-globalisation protestor.

BILATERAL AGENCIES AND AID

Bilateral development agencies are those established within individual donor countries with all funds coming from their governments. They function as a state department or ministry and as such may change policies as different political parties come to power. The DFID is the UK's bilateral organisation, while USAID is the US equivalent.

Development assistance provided directly by a donor country to a recipient country is known as bilateral aid. Bilateral agencies fund their own programmes as well as channelling monies through multilateral organisations. For example, DFID (2006) noted that 40 per cent of their lending was transferred in this way. Much bilateral aid is channelled through the Development Assistance Committee (DAC) of the OECD, which is made up of 22 countries. DAC transfers bilateral aid to 150 recipient countries and territories in the form of ODA, which refers to resources transferred on concessional terms (at favourable rates) with the aim of promoting the economic development and welfare of developing countries. This can take various forms including grants (the main type), commodities, debt relief and technical co-operation. A distinction can also be made between long-term development aid and short-term humanitarian and disaster relief. Non-DAC members have also been significant donors, notably Saudi Arabia and small Gulf states following the 1973–74 rise in oil prices. A varying proportion of each country's ODA has increasingly been channelled through multilateral agencies and NGOs, but the majority is still managed bilaterally (Burnell, 2008). Indeed, bilateral aid is incredibly important globally, accounting for 63 per cent of all aid to developing countries, compared with 26 per cent from multilateral aid (DFID, 2006: 107).

Variations in, and Criticisms of, Bilateral Aid

One significant variation between donors is the amount of ODA they provide. Although the UN General Assembly recommended an ODA target of 0.7 per cent of GNP in 1970, the average currently stands at between 0.2 per cent and 0.4 per cent. A renewed pledge, 45 years later, puts the timeframe for reaching the target as 2015 in line with, and integral to, meeting the MDGs. The USA and, more recently, the UK are the largest donors in terms of actual volume of ODA, but this contribution represents a much lower percentage of their GNP than others, particularly Scandinavian countries (see Table 11.1). Indeed, it is Sweden, Luxembourg, Norway, the Netherlands and Denmark who have consistently contributed the most over the years, and the USA the least. Notably, the US contribution (0.17 per cent) falls short of the 2–3 per cent used to fund the Marshall Plan to ensure European political and economic stability following the Second World War. In terms of trends, there has been an increase since 2001, but a lot of this was due to geopolitical issues such as fighting terrorism. Indeed, increases in 2005 were linked partly with debt relief for Iraq and Nigeria. Nevertheless, nations able to contribute large volumes of aid (without needing to commit much of their actual GNP) have a great deal of influence on the nature of international aid flows.

Leading on from the above, national and international politics usually play an extremely important role in the allocation of funds. Although the

Table 11.1   Leading donors of Official Development Assistance, by volume and percentage of GNP, 2006

Top 5 by volume			Top 5 by GNP		
	Volume (US$ millions)	Percentage of GNP		Volume (US$ billion)	Percentage of GNP
USA	22 739	0.17	Sweden	3967	1.03
UK	12 607	0.52	Luxembourg	291	0.89
Japan	11 608	0.25	Norway	2946	0.89
France	10 448	0.47	Netherlands	5452	0.81
Germany	10 351	0.36	Denmark	2234	0.80

Source: www.oecd.org/dataoecd/50/17/5037721.htm (accessed 15 April 2008).

Scandinavian countries use foreign aid to fund humanitarian and development efforts, most countries use aid allocation in a much more politically strategic way. Those with former colonies, especially France, give aid regardless of issues such as poverty levels, while the USA prioritises the Middle East (Alesina and Dollar, 2000). Having said this, there are also variations among countries. For instance, it has been found that bilateral aid to former colonies can be as low as 2.6 per cent in the case of Germany and 4.8 per cent for Spain, to a high of 99.6 per cent for the Portuguese (ibid.: 37). However, this relationship is declining over time as other factors such as channelling aid to trading partners, the nature of democratisation of a given country, as well as a range of economic factors have come into play (Berthélemy and Tichit, 2004). Yet, there remains a continuing tendency among donors to subsidise governments that serve their own interests. While the monetary precedent set by the funding of the Marshall Plan has never since been matched in terms of development efforts, what has remained is the tendency for development aid, most overt in the case of that from the USA, to be politically determined. For example, between one-quarter and one-third of US ODA has traditionally gone to Israel and Egypt, which have been long-standing allies (Thomas and Allen, 2000: 208). In turn, the USA has rarely funded countries with communist regimes, such as Cuba since 1959 and Nicaragua between 1979 and 1989, or any nations that serve them little strategic geopolitical or economic interest. Indeed, because ODA is seldom politically neutral it has often been charged with being a tool of exploitation and domination (Burnell, 2008; Fritz and Menocal, 2007).

Some countries may also require that a proportion of their aid be spent on their own goods and services, usually under the auspices of technical co-operation, where a large percentage of the disbursement is used for the salaries of expatriate 'experts' (called 'tied aid'). In addition, there are variations as to where in the world ODA flows. For example, in 2004–05, the region receiving most ODA was sub-Saharan Africa (US$21 754 million), yet this was followed by the Middle East and North Africa (US$17 447 million) despite the latter certainly not being among the poorest regions in the world (see Chapter 7, this volume). This is reflected in the fact that Iraq was the largest recipient of ODA (US$12 924 million).[10]

Overall, the total amount of ODA allocated by the major donors is very low, and relatively little of it is actually used for direct poverty alleviation. Over the past three decades, the political and economic concerns of donors have been underlined by an increasing emphasis on conditionality, which was previously only associated with multilateral donors (see earlier). As such, many donors now require recipients to adhere to certain policies that aim to lead to 'good governance' and 'sound' economic practices (Thomas and Allen, 2000: 209). As noted above, there has been a shift in the 1990s and 2000s towards poverty reduction as the overarching aim of bilateral aid, coupled with the promotion of democratisation and strengthening civil society through creating partnerships (see Potter et al., 2008). This has also been reflected in the recent call for greater aid effectiveness (see below).

'GOOD GOVERNANCE'

Before continuing with a discussion of civil society and NGOs, it is important to briefly outline the nature of this new governance agenda. Accepting that governance is extremely difficult to define, Jenkins (2008) refers to it as the ways in which public power is exercised in a particular context or situation. Usually associated with the market-led development approach promulgated by donor agencies, in practice it involves a host of reforms of state bureaucracies, legal systems, decentralisation and generating transparent civil society, purportedly linked with promoting democracy, participation and accountability (McIlwaine, 2007).

However, there are several problems with this governance agenda when imposed on developing countries. First, it strengthens the hold of development agencies over recipient nations, rather than allowing them to regain lost sovereignty. In turn, the democracy promoted by aid agencies does not include genuine reforms to increase Southern nations' equal participation in development institutions (see earlier), nor does it increase the accountability of Northern or global agencies involved in the South. This reflects a certain 'fear of success' of governance among donors, in that genuine reform would greatly reduce their own power. Similarly, democratic elections central to political reforms are not uniformly encouraged. Where the outcomes of a democratic election are the result of fraudulent vote-counting and/or may be harmful to world security, the international community exhibits a strong desire to control what should be a local process. For example, donor governments and many associated development experts permitted the government of Algeria to ignore the results of the 1992 elections, since the avowedly Islamist party widely thought to have won did not conform with the good governance agenda (Jenkins, 2008; Fritz and Menocal, 2007). Nevertheless, this new aid agenda marked the beginning of a now established trend towards participatory development, and the increasing involvement of various civil society actors in the development process (see Chapter 4 and Chapter 10, this volume).

THE DELIVERY OF AID AND EVOLUTION OF CONTEMPORARY AID MODALITIES

A core element of this new trend has been incorporated into the recent evolution of aid modalities since 2000. These refer to the various ways in which aid is provided by donors to recipient countries and involve an array of different financial aid instruments or tools. They are not a development strategy as such, but rather the 'nuts and bolts' of how aid is channelled from donors to countries (AWID, 2007). The recognition that aid needed to be distributed more effectively and efficiently was made in the 1990s. This was partly in response to the widespread criticisms of SAPs, as well as the problematic nature of much multilateral and bilateral aid, and the lack of success in reducing poverty in countries of the South. Very simply, this new approach involved a shift away from funding individual projects towards a programmatic approach to distributing aid. It also reflected an emphasis on country ownership of development processes with developing countries being viewed as 'partners' rather than 'recipients' (OECD, 2007).

New approaches to foreign aid or the 'new aid architecture' have their roots in some key international agreements. The first of these was the Millennium Declaration of 2000 that set out the MDGs (Chapter 1). This was followed by the Monterrey US Conference on Financing Development in 2002, the Rome High-Level Forum on Harmonisation (HLF-Rome), and the Marrakech Roundtable on Managing for Development Results in 2004, all of which provided the foundation for the Paris HLF in 2005. Attended by development officials and ministers from 91 countries and 26 donor organisations and partner countries as well as members of NGOs, the ensuing Paris Declaration on Aid Effectiveness, subtitled 'Ownership, Harmonisation, Alignment, Results and Mutual Accountability', laid out the ways in which effective aid would be 'founded on a discourse of country-led partnership and co-responsibility' (Fritz and Menocal, 2007: 543; see also AWID, 2007). Ultimately, 61 multilateral and bilateral donors and 56 aid-recipient countries committed to making the practical distribution of aid more streamlined and hence more effective in an attempt to overcome fragmentation, duplication and failure in delivering aid to date (ibid.; also AWID, 2007).

The new aid modalities that have been identified in order to achieve this shift in aid distribution have focused on four core tools (some of which have been around for some time). These include Sector-Wide Approaches known as SWAps that fund whole sectors such as education or health; General Budget Support (GBS) that involves financial assistance to the overall budget of a country (and which has recently been aligned with the MDGs known as MDG contracting); PRSPs linked with the World Bank and IMF and focusing on poverty reduction (see Chapter 2), and Basket Funding where several donors join together to fund a programme, a sector or the public budget (see AWID, 2007).

While it is perhaps too early to tell how effective the Paris Declaration has been, there have already been both positive and negative evaluations. In a study conducted in 2006, it emerged that some significant changes had occurred in terms of a shift away from project-based aid towards more greater programme-based efforts based on a strong awareness of the importance of country ownership and generation of development strategies (OECD, 2007). However, not surprisingly, progress has not been straightforward. Although donor agencies emphasise the importance of programme-based approaches, only a small proportion actually spend more than half of their aid on these (ibid.: 15). There have also been broader criticisms relating to the conceptualisation of development inherent in the new aid modalities in that it presents a very technocratic interpretation (Fritz and Menocal, 2007). This relates to the emphasis on the tools of aid and a neglect of the broader issues of injustice, poverty and gender inequalities (AWID, 2007; see also Chapter 8, this volume). The roles of civil society and other stakeholders in the development process have also been largely neglected in terms of inclusion in decision-making, monitoring and evaluation (AWID, 2007). Indeed, this latter point goes against the current trend towards including civil society much more centrally in development policy and planning.

Activity 11.2
Imagine you work in the government of a country of the Global South which is in receipt of bilateral aid from your former colonial power. Write a list of the advantages and disadvantages of receiving this aid and think about the alternatives that might be open to you (or other Southern countries).

CIVIL SOCIETY AND NGOS

What is Civil Society?

While political scientists and philosophers have long used the concept of civil society (Edwards, 2004), a certain interpretation of it has been co-opted by the development community in recent years. It is beyond the scope of this chapter to discuss the theoretical aspects of civil society in any depth beyond the fact that theoretically, the concept has been attractive to both ends of the political spectrum in recent times. On the one hand, civil society has appealed to neoliberals who see civil society as useful in providing services that the state cannot, while on the other hand, civil society can provide an arena where protest and dissent can challenge existing hegemonies (see McIlwaine, 1998a; 2007). Descriptively, civil society can be understood as the space between the state and the individual, and the associations formed by non-state actors within this sphere. Usually associated with the voluntary sector, NGOs are the main, but not the only, constituent of civil society. Also included are churches and religious organisations, social movements and workers' associations. Some also identify private sector organisations as civil society, but this is less common. Indeed, organisations found in the marketplace, alongside political parties, are usually excluded. A key aspect of civil society is that it is increasingly thought to contribute to democratisation, since civil society organisations (CSOs) may be able to engage with the state and influence decision-making. Indeed, civil society is thought to act as a potential challenge to the state, especially authoritarian regimes (McIlwaine, 2007; Van Rooy, 2008). Civil society not only operates at national, but at international levels. Global civil society relates primarily to international activism and transnational organising, such as the anti-globalisation protest groups mentioned earlier with reference to the World Bank, as well as a host of other types of groups that now operate at this level facilitated by processes of globalisation (McIlwaine, 2007). In respect of development policy, NGOs are the most significant group within civil society, and will thus be discussed here at greatest length.

What are NGOs?

Non-governmental organisations may be defined as non-state, non-market organisations that are autonomous, non-profit-making and focused on different levels of development assistance (Desai, 2008; Edwards and Hulme, 1995). They can be broadly divided into those which provide services (sometimes referred to as ONGOs – operational NGOs), and those that are involved in policy advocacy around such issues as the environment or human rights (sometimes referred to as ANGOs – advocacy NGOs), although the two groups are not mutually exclusive. Within this, there is a wide range of further variations, especially in terms of the scale at which NGOs operate. Small grassroots organisations (GROs) or community-based organisations (CBOs) are the most numerous, and function at the community level. These are usually membership and issue based, for example, water committees, local action groups, women's organisations and so on (see Figure 11.1). GROs and CBOs are often short-lived, especially if their main goals are met. Many consider GROs and CBOs as separate from NGOs, because of their ephemeral nature. Many NGOs, on the other hand, are permanent, staffed by professionals or local elites, and often act as intermediaries (or 'brokers') between people at the grassroots and state institutions.

Local NGOs usually work in one locality (albeit often in more than one community) and are commonly orientated towards a particular issue, for example, health, education, or community development. National NGOs (NNGOs), alternatively, may undertake a range of functions, such as pro-viding services, conducting co-ordinated advocacy work, or acting to facil-itate the grouping together of local NGO units in the form of networks or umbrella organisations. In The Gambia, for example, the NNGO 'TANGO' has more than 30 NGO affiliates drawn not only from local organisations but the international sector (Chant, 2007a: ch. 4). National NGOs such as TANGO are often involved in seeking funding or offering support for communities throughout a given country, although other NNGOs may well focus on single-issue concerns such as gender, health or education. Donors may also own certain NGOs (DONGOs – donor NGOs) in that their funds are used to establish and run them. Also at the national level are NGOs referred to as MONGOs (my own NGO) that are owned and run by individuals whose egos dominate how they function. An example of this would be the Open Society Institute and Soros Foundation Network established by the Hungarian financier, George Soros.[11] Most of these national organisations are not accountable to members.

International NGOs operate on the largest scale, and may be either Northern- or Southern-based. International NGOs (known as INGOs) may also be referred to as BINGOs (big international NGOs) (Bradshaw et al., 2002: 247–8). Well-known INGOs that provide services include Save the Children, Oxfam, Christian Aid and World Vision, while others such as Greenpeace are primarily advocacy based in that they are trying to raise awareness about issues. A final distinction can be made between NGOs that are mutual benefit membership organisations, and those that are public benefit organisations involved in service delivery to others and advocacy or research not necessarily on behalf of a defined client group (Thomas and

Source: Photo by Cathy McIlwaine.

Figure 11.1 Grassroots Women's Association (Asociación de Mujeres), Guatemala City: 'Overcoming the Odds Together' ('Superándonos Juntas')

BOX 11.1   TYPOLOGY OF NGOS

ONGOs – Operational NGOs that provide services.
ANGOs – Advocacy NGOs that are involved in policy advocacy.
GROs – Grassroots Organisations that function at the community level and are usually membership and issue based.
CBOs – Community Based Organisations (CBOs) that are synonymous with GROs.
NNGOs – National NGOs that may provide services, advocacy or research. They may also group together local NGO units in the form of networks or umbrella organisations.
DONGOs – Donor NGOs that are owned and run by donor agencies and operate at the national level.
MONGOs – My NGO that are owned and run by one individual whose ego dominates how it functions and which operates at the national level.
INGOs – International NGOs operating at the global level with headquarters in the North or the South.
BINGOs – Big international NGOs.

Source: Bradshaw et al. (2002: 247–8).

Allen, 2000; see also Box 11.1). It is also important to acknowledge that NGOs are incredibly diverse, representing a wide range of views, influence and capabilities, something that many development practitioners have overlooked (Lewis and Opoku-Mensah, 2006).

The Growth and Importance of NGOs

The number of NGOs has dramatically increased in recent years. Globally, Thomas and Allen (2000: 212) note that their number increased from just over 1000 in the late 1950s to 29 000 in the early 1990s. During the 1990s, international NGOs were reported to increase from 6000 in 1990 to 26 000 in 1999, with the number of foundations nearly tripling from 22 088 in 1980 to 56 582 in 2000. In 2007, the UN had 3052 NGOs formally linked with them (compared with only 41 in 1946). At the national level, countries such as India are said to have more than a million NGOs operating within its borders (World Bank, 2005: 18; also McIlwaine, 2007). Individual NGOs have also grown in size, one example being the Self-Employed Women's Association (SEWA) in India which had almost 1 million members in 2006 (see Box 11.2).

BOX 11.2 CASE STUDY OF AN NGO: THE SELF-EMPLOYED WOMEN'S ASSOCIATION (SEWA), INDIA

Over 90 per cent of working women in India work in the informal sector, or more precisely are 'self-employed' (see Chapter 6, this volume). Until the creation of SEWA, however, these women's needs for fair credit, maternity protection, fair wages, skills training, continual work and legal help were largely unmet. SEWA was recognised as a union in 1972 through the lobbying and perseverance of a young female lawyer, Elaben Bhatt, who established it as part of the larger Textile Labour Union (TLU). With *sewa* meaning 'to serve' in most Indian languages, SEWA has since grown substantially, absorbing more and more trades, and rooting itself in the reality of poor self-employed women. In 2006, SEWA had a membership in India of nearly 1 million spread over nine states. The main goals of the organisation are to organise women workers to gain access to work security, income security, food security and social security. SEWA aims for self-reliance, in that women should be autonomous and self-reliant, individually and collectively, both economically and in terms of their decision-making ability. SEWA's ideals are rooted in Gandhian thinking of non-violence, truth and joining people of all faiths. It does this through establishing other unions and co-operatives. The vast bulk of its 26-member Executive Committee consists of the women it aims to represent including agricultural labourers, '*bidi*' workers (makers of hand-rolled Indian cigarettes), paper pickers, and embroiderers. SEWA currently runs the following programmes:

- SEWA Bank: extends credit to its members and offers women the opportunity improve their economic situation by supplying them with services that they would not find at a traditional bank, as well as more traditional services such as insurance, pensions etc. In 2005–06, the bank had 44 909 members and 291 535 accounts.
- Health care. run by members. The approach emphasises health education as well as curative care. It also involves co-ordination and collaboration with government health services. SEWA has established several midwives and healthcare co-operatives.

- Childcare: via co-operatives and local organisations, in 1999 SEWA was providing a total of 117 childcare centres catering for nearly 6000 children.
- Insurance: this scheme has demonstrated that insurance for the poor can be run in a self-reliant and financially viable way. Members are protected against the various crises that threaten their lives and work (widowhood, fire, and natural hazards).
- Legal help: SEWA provides legal education and support to its members, fighting such issues as harassment, unfair dismissal and the non-payment of wages.
- SEWA Academy: Centre for workers' education and capacity-building. The Academy stresses the self-development of the worker. It is also the means by which SEWA unites its members through common ideology, thus building the broader movement. It works through training, literacy, research and policy action, and communication through print and electronic media.
- Gujarat Mahila Housing SEWA Trust (MHT): set up in 1994, this focuses on housing and infrastructure upgrading and finance, as well as earthquake reconstruction and developing women's homes as their workplaces.

Members are also involved in mass mobilisation through campaigns around issues affecting them, which strengthens the SEWA movement and also highlights their own issues. In addition, through the creation of national level federations, self-employed women are linked, through their primary organisations, to the larger economic structures. SEWA has helped to form unions both nationally and internationally such as the National Association of Street Vendors of India (NASVI), Homenet (an international union of home-based workers), and Women in Informal Employment: Globalising and Organising (WIEGO) (an international research and advocacy agency). Major recognition of SEWA occurred in 2006 when the International Confederation of Free Trade Unions (ICFTU) granted the organisation full membership.

Sources: www.sewa.org/ and www.sewabank.com/ and www.sewahousing.org/ (accessed 20 April 2008).

Linked with this growth is the increasing amount of resources handled by NGOs and the amount channelled through them. In the past, NGOs were traditionally funded through privately raised resources, yet since the late 1980s, they have provided increasingly large amounts for relief and development work. These increases have come from multilateral and bilateral aid which has also been progressively directed through NGOs. For example, OECD figures for 2003 estimate that the private component of NGO grants totals US$10 billion annually (double that of 1990), representing around 15 per cent of the value of current ODA. In total, the OECD has estimated that NGOs are responsible for at least US$12 billion annually (World Bank, 2005: 18). This in itself has led to a proliferation of NGOs, many of which were set up for the sole purpose of competing for ODA funds and, more cynically, as a form of job and wealth creation for the middle classes. In the case of El Salvador, these types of NGOs have been called 'life-boats' (*botes salvavidas*) and comprise mainly professionals who had lost their livelihoods during the civil war of the 1980s (McIlwaine, 1998b). In terms of the World Bank, the involvement of CSOs in Bank-funded projects has grown from 21 per cent of the total number of projects in 1990 to an estimated 72 per cent in 2006 (McIlwaine, 2007).

In line with their huge expansion, NGOs are now generally considered to be extremely important actors in the development policy arena. The reasons for this are manifold. First, from a practical perspective, and as noted earlier, neoliberal policies in the form of SAPs and PRSs have involved widespread privatisation in their effort to 'roll back' the state. This has left a gap in the provision of public services which NGOs have often stepped in to fill. By the same token, there are clearly concerns about the long-term impact of NGO service provision on the sustainability of national health and education systems, and overall quality of services (Desai, 2008). Second, NGOs are seen to be good vehicles for democratisation, and for promoting a healthy civil society through participation and active citizenship. Again, however, the assumed positive political role and impact of NGOs has been questioned (Lewis, 2002; McIlwaine, 2007). Third, NGOs are thought to have a greater capacity to reach the poor, to promote local participation, to operate at low costs and to innovate and adapt. In turn, they are thought to have a greater understanding of local culture and context (Potter et al., 2008).

Linked with their increasing importance, NGOs as a group have also changed roles. Traditionally, NGOs have delivered services in order to alleviate the symptoms of poverty. This may be in the fields of education, micro-enterprises, health, housing and so on. Over time, however, NGOs have been increasingly involved in capacity-building in an effort to address the causes of poverty and generate self-reliance. Some have also evolved to

---

BOX 11.3   GENERATIONS OF NGO STRATEGIES

First generation: Involves the direct delivery of relief or welfare services, particularly relevant to emergency humanitarian situations.

Second generation: Involves the development of the capacities of people to better meet their own needs, and increase self-reliance.

Third generation: Involves the establishment of sustainable development systems, in terms of involvement in the policy formulation of governments and multilateral organisations.

Fourth generation: Involves political advocacy and campaigning to support people's movements and promote a broader social vision.

Source: Bradshaw et al. (2002: 249).

---

inform policy-making as well as get involved in advocacy and campaigning work. Box 11.3 outlines how NGOs, whether individually, or as a sector as a whole, can move through four different generations. This can refer to the development of a single NGO or to the NGO sector as a whole. As part of this transformation, information flows and knowledge sharing are becoming more significant. One important manifestation of this is the rising incidence of partnership between Northern and Southern NGOs (Desai, 2008; McIlwaine, 2007).

Limitations of NGOs

The impact of NGOs is limited in a number of ways although this is obviously contingent upon the type of NGO and at what scale it is operating. Furthermore, evaluating the effectiveness of NGOs and their projects is an inherently difficult task (Lewis, 2002). Generally speaking, NGO projects have limited replicability, in that most are too small to have a significant regional or national impact, and they are usually not part of an integrated strategy. In addition, the majority of NGOs have only limited technical capacity, and are not self-sustainable (Bradshaw et al., 2002). More broadly, there have been ethical concerns about the extent to which international NGOs in particular are able to determine and address the needs of local populations. Since the survival of NGOs is dependent on private donations and ODA, rather than the success of their projects, in practice they are more accountable to their donors than their beneficiaries (Gideon,

1998; Miraftab, 1997). This is more pronounced among organisations with the heaviest reliance on ODA, since this is more likely to come with certain implicit or explicit conditions (Lewis, 2002). This dynamic may also apply to the relationships between Northern and Southern NGOs where the latter effectively become vehicles for the implementation of Northern directives (although it is also the case that Northern NGOs can have such close ties with their Southern partners that they are not essentially truly 'Northern' (see Mitlin et al., 2007). Similar critiques have also been made about the increasing influence of corporate NGOs who wield substantial economic power (Lewis and Opoku-Mensah, 2006).

Also significant is that although NGOs promote notions of participation and empowerment at the community level, this may again be in the interests of donors and the NGOs rather than communities. For instance, people in communities are often encouraged to participate in projects on a voluntary basis, thus providing their labour and expertise for free. In contrast, for Northern governments, donations to NGOs may be cheaper financially than providing conventional bilateral aid through ODA. Ideologically, donors are then seen to be funding organisations working on the ground in ways that are only assumed to be most beneficial to people at the grassroots.

In general, NGOs tend to promote a rhetoric of poverty reduction and empowerment, though in reality this is often not the case (Bradshaw et al., 2002; Desai, 2008). At the same time, monitoring the performance of NGOs involves reporting how money is spent and whether the appropriate activities have been undertaken. Rarely does it involve in-depth investigation of whether NGOs actually make a difference, especially in more intangible realms such as 'empowerment' (see Chapter 8, this volume). Overall, despite the initial enthusiasm for civil society building through NGOs and a continuing close relationship between donors and civil society, their engagement has become more circumspect in recent years (Mitlin et al., 2007). As Tvedt (2006) says, donors are 'becoming disillusioned' with civil society, as they realise that their 'magic bullet' has not materialised (Lewis and Opoku-Mensah, 2006).

Global and Transnational Civil Society

Important debates about NGOs and civil society have recently extended to the global arena. Not only are NGOs functioning over a range of scales from community to international, but civil society itself is being constituted at the global level. Often referred to as 'global civil society', this refers to the range of NGOs which not only extend beyond national borders, but which also lobby against the exercise of global power, especially multilateral organisations and TNCs. A classic early example of global civil society was the anti-globalisation protests during the 'Battle for Seattle' in 1999, although some trace it back to the '50 Years is Enough' campaign against the World Bank and the IMF (see earlier). The emergence of global civil society has been closely linked with the growing influence of international institutions (especially the World Bank, the IMF and the WTO), as well as the increasing numbers of international NGOs. In turn, global civil society is linked with the growing participation of NGOs in global decision-making through major international conferences, especially the UN conferences, such as the Rio Earth Summit, the Cairo Population conference and the Beijing Women's conference. Also important has been the role of communication technologies as well as the global nature of issues such as the environment, debt, HIV/AIDS and the drugs trade.

Yet, the notion of global civil society has also been criticised. Reflecting the diversity within it, the accountability of global civil society has been called into question. In particular, although global civil society critiques the lack of democratic decision-making within IFIs, there is seldom much evidence of democracy or power-sharing within its own circle (Munck, 2007). Global civil society is often dominated by Northern groups and networks which may have little direct contact with the people they claim to represent in the Global South. In addition, global civil society is often popularly understood only to include 'progressive' groups or new social movements that promote environmentalism, feminism, human rights and so on; rarely are groups associated with the political Right included, let alone international terrorist and criminal groups (see Edwards, 2004). In light of these issues, global civil society has increasingly been referred to as 'transnational civil society' in an effort to overcome the problems with reifying 'the global' as uniform. One important dimension of transnational civil society is 'diasporic civil society' referring to the range of migrant organisations in both North and South. These are likely to become increasingly important actors in years to come as migration continues and international remittance flows are captured in order to provide essential development finance (McIlwaine, 2007).

All things considered, the limitations of NGOs operating both within a national and global context should not detract from the impact they have had, and continue to have, on the shape of development in the South. Indeed, as Desai (2008) notes, NGOs are important actors in transformatory development in the developing world. They clearly have a key political role in terms of mobilising people to demand and/or defend their rights, even if the sector does not command sufficient funds to transform the livelihoods of the poor on a large scale. Overall poverty reduction will require, as Thomas and Allen (2000) suggest, an institutionalisation of altruism, such that services provided out of goodwill become a right. The call to build democratic institutions, and to embrace human rights approaches, needs to move beyond empty rhetoric and onto a more substantive and sustained footing. For development goals to be met in any developing country, there is an urgency for all the actors outlined in this chapter, from local to global levels, to be included, and to work together in mutually beneficial ways.

Activity 11.3
Imagine that you are the director of a national NGO in a developing country that is trying to access donor funding in order to develop a poverty reduction programme. Prepare a short justification to present to the donor agency in order to convince them to fund you. Which kinds of benefits could the donor agency derive by providing funding? How could your programme be more effective than one provided by the state or the private sector? What sorts of limitations do you think you would encounter?

LEARNING OUTCOMES

By the end of this chapter and relevant reading, you should be able to:

- Describe the main actors involved in the development policy arena, such as multilateral and bilateral organisations and NGOs.
- Explain the limitations of multilateral organisations and of bilateral aid.
- Demonstrate the importance of NGOs within development processes, outline their recent growth and changing roles, and pinpoint their key advantages and shortcomings.

NOTES

1. The BWIs include the UN, the World Bank, the IMF and GATT (now the WTO). They are named after Bretton Woods in New Hampshire, USA where, in 1944, a series of agreements were put in place in a bid to regulate and monitor financial, political and economic functioning at an international level.
2. See www.un.org/members/list.shtml (accessed 27 April 2008).
3. See www.un.org/ga/art19.shtml (accessed 27 April 2008).
4. See www.betterworldcampaign.org/issues/funding/growing-us-debt-to-the-un.html (accessed 27 April 2008).
5. See web.worldbank.org/WBSITE/EXTERNAL/EXTABOUTUS/ORGANISATION/BODEXT/0,,contentMDK:20124819~menuPK:64020035~pagePK:64020054~piPK:64020408~theSitePK:278036,00.html (accessed 27 April 2008).
6. See www.brettonwoodsproject.org/art-557597 (accessed 28 April 2008).

7. See worldbank.org (accessed 28 April 2008).
8. See www.50years.org/ (accessed 28 April 2008).
9. See www.laneta.apc.org/bmmm/bcomun2.htm (accessed 28 April 2008).
10. See www.oecd.org/dac (accessed 28 April 2008).
11. See www.soros.org/ (accessed 28 April 2008).

FURTHER READING

Easterly, William R. (2006), *The White Man's Burden: Why the West's Efforts to Aid the Rest have Done so Much Ill and so Little Good*, Oxford: Oxford University Press.
Written by a former World Bank economist, this book provides an entertaining and polemical account of problems with foreign aid. Written in an accessible style, it outlines a critique of current aid-giving (with particular reference to the ideas of Jeffrey Sachs, a co-founder of the Global Fund) and makes some suggestions about how future funding should be structured.

McIlwaine, Cathy (2007), 'From local to global to transnational civil society: re-framing development perspectives on the non-state sector', *Geography Compass*, **1**(6), 1252–81.
This provides an up-to-date overview of the meanings of civil society and the role of NGOs in particular in development discourses and practice. It outlines the main tenets of the theoretical approaches to understanding the NGO sector and argues for the need to deconstruct civil society at a range of different scales.

Organisation for Economic Cooperation and Development (OECD) (2007), *Gender Equality and Aid Delivery: What Has Changed in Development Co-operation Agencies Since 1999?*, Paris: OECD (downloadable from www.oecd.org).
This document provides an excellent account of how the foreign aid architecture has changed over time with a particular focus on gender dimensions.

Wade, Robert Hunter (2002), 'US hegemony and the World Bank: the fight over people and ideas', *Review of International Political Economy*, **9**(2), 215–43.
This is an interesting paper on the nature of US involvement with the World Bank from a critical standpoint. It considers the cases of Joseph Stiglitz and Ravi Kanbur in highlighting the power of the USA in the functioning of this institution.

USEFUL WEBSITES

www.oxfam.org/ – website of Oxfam International, major international NGO
www.dfid.gov.uk/ – website for Department for International Development, the UK bilateral development agency
www.worldbank.org/ – website for the World Bank
www.whirledbank.org/ – website criticising the World Bank and its policies
www.un.org/ – website of the United Nations
www.undp.org/ – website for the United Nations Development Programme
www.oecd.org/ – website for the Organisation for Economic Co-operation and Development

www.brettonwoodsproject.org/ – website for the Bretton Woods Project

www.usaid.gov/ – website of the United States Agency for International Development, the US bilateral development agency

www.wdm.org.uk/ – website of the World Development Movement, a UK-based advocacy and campaigning NGO

www.betterworldcampaign.org/ – website of the campaign to improve relations between the USA and the UN. It is funded by the Better World Fund, created by entrepreneur and philanthropist Ted Turner

www.reformtheun.org/ – website of a project to reform the UN run by the World Federalist Movement – Institute for Global Policy (WFM-IGP)

Appendix: useful journals and internet sources

In addition to the annotated reading at the end of each chapter, and the bibliography, useful sources for keeping up-to-date with events in the Global South include journals and internet sources. Many of these are already included in the book in relation to specific issues and data, but it is helpful to have a checklist for further research:

JOURNAL RECOMMENDATIONS

Environment and Urbanisation
Habitat Debate
Habitat International
IDS Bulletin
International Development Planning Review
Journal of Development Studies
Journal of Developing Societies
Journal of International Development
Progress in Development Studies
Third World Quarterly
World Development
Development Policy Review

Regional journals are also important such as:

Journal of Latin American Studies
Bulletin of Latin American Research
Review of African Political Economy
Journal of Modern African Studies
Pacific Asia

You may also wish to consult annual development reports, especially the World Bank's *World Development Report* (Oxford and New York: Oxford University Press) and *World Bank Indicators* (Oxford and New York: Oxford University Press) and the United Nations Development

Programme's *Human Development Report* (Oxford and New York: Oxford University Press).

INTERNET SOURCES

The internet is an invaluable source of information. However, as far as possible you should consult reputable sites such as those mentioned below. Always be aware that the quality of the sites may not be very high. Do not use internet sources as a substitute for books and journals; you should use them only as a complement.

www.actionaid.org/ – website of Action Aid.

www.brettonwoodsproject.org/ – website of the Bretton Woods Project.

www.cafod.org.uk/ – website of the Catholic Agency for Overseas Development.

www.progessio.org.uk/ – website of Progressio (formerly the Catholic Institute of International Relations).

www.dfid.gov.uk/ – website of the UK's DFID.

www.iadb.org/ – website of the Inter-American Development Bank.

www.ids.ac.uk/ids/ – website of the Institute of Development Studies, University of Sussex.

www.odi.org.uk/ – website of the Overseas Development Institute.

www.oecd.org/home/ – website of the OECD.

http://uk.oneworld.net/ – website of One World which links to a wide range of sites related to development and development agencies and NGOs.

www.oxan.com/ – website of the Oxford Analytica Brief.

www.oxfam.org/en/ – website of Oxfam, UK.

www.twnside.org.sg/ – website of the Third World Network.

www.undp.org/ – website of the UNDP.

www.worldbank.org/ – website of the World Bank.

www.eldis.org/ – a gateway to development information on policy and research.

www.wdm.org.uk/ – website of the World Development Movement.

www.developmentgateway.org/ – website of the Development Gateway Foundation, a portal on development information.

There are also a number of interactive websites which allow you to map, visualise, calculate and/or correlate data on a wide range of issues pertaining to development. The three most useful in our view are:

http://globalis.gvu.unu.edu – interactive world atlas using UN data for human development, Millennium Development Goals etc. run by consortium supported by Norwegian Ministry of Foreign Affairs and Norwegian Development Agency (NORAD). Excellent up-to-date résumés of country characteristics.

www.gapminder.org – run by not-for-profit organisation based in Sweden. *Inter alia* allows for plotting of trends over time for specific countries of such as data as GNI per capita, education, and HIV/AIDS.

www.worldmapper.org – developed by Professor Danny Dorling, Geography, Sheffield University. Numerous maps on diverse range of development-related issues such as education, affordable drugs, terms of trade, slum growth, health, gender and so on.

Bibliography

Abel, Christopher and Lloyd-Sherlock, Peter (2000), 'Health policy in Latin America: themes, trends and challenges', in Peter Lloyd-Sherlock (ed.), *Healthcare Reform and Poverty in Latin America*, London: Institute of Latin American Studies, pp. 1–20.

Aboderin, Isabella (2006), 'African women and ageing: Nairobi, Beijing and the implications for African gender scholarship', *CODESRIA Bulletin*, 1 and 2, 23–5 (downloadable from www.codesria.org/Links/Publications/Journals/codesria_bulletin.htm).

Adepoju, Aderanti (ed.) (1997), *Family, Population and Development in Africa*, London: Zed.

Adepoju, Aderanti and Mbugua, Wariara (1997), 'The African family: an overview of changing forms', in Aderanti Adepoju (ed.), *Family, Population and Development in Africa*, London: Zed, pp. 41–59.

Afshar, Haleh and Dennis, Carolyne (eds) (1992), *Women and Adjustment Policies in the Third World*, Basingstoke: Macmillan.

Ahmed Obaid, Thoraya (2007), 'Healthy cities for the elderly', *Habitat Debate*, **13**(4), 14 (downloadable from www.unhabitat.org).

Alesina, Alberto and Dollar, David (2000), 'Who gives foreign aid to whom and why?', *Journal of Economic Growth*, **5**(1), 33–63.

Ambert, Cecile, Jassey, Katja and Thomas, Liz (2007), 'HIV, AIDS and urban development issues in sub-Saharan Africa. Beyond sex and medicines: why getting the basics right is part of the response!', report prepared for Division for Urban Development, Swedish International Development Agency, Stockholm (www.sida.se/sida/jsp/sida.jsp?d=118&a=30644&searchWords=hiv/aids%20urban%20development) (accessed 11 September 2007).

Annan, Kofi (2005), *In Larger Freedom: Towards Development, Security and Human Rights for All*, Report of the Secretary-General (A/59/2005), New York: United Nations (downloadable from daccessdds.un.org/doc/UNDOC/GEN/N05/270/78/PDF/N0527078.pdf?OpenElement).

Arimah, Ben (2007), 'The face of urban poverty: explaining the prevalence of slums in developing countries', paper presented at UNU-WIDER Workshop: 'Beyond the Tipping Point: Development in an Urban World', LSE, 18–20 October.

Armas, Henry (2007), *Whose Sexuality Counts? Poverty, Participation and Sexual Rights*, IDS Working Paper 294, Brighton: University of Sussex.

Association for Women's Rights in Development (AWID) (2007), *An Overview of the Paris Declaration on Aid Effectiveness and the New Aid Modalities*, Primer No. 1 (www.awid.org).

Asthana, Sheena (1994), 'Primary Health Care and Selective PHC: community participation in health and development', in David Phillips and Yola Verhasselt (eds), *Health and Development*, London: Routledge, pp. 182–96.

Atash, Farhad (2000), 'New towns and future urbanisation in Iran', *Third World Planning Review*, **22**(1), 67–86.

Athreya, Bama (2002), 'Women in the global economy', in Vandana Desai and Robert Potter (eds), *The Companion to Development Studies*, 1st edn, London: Arnold, pp. 342–6.

Baden, Sally (1993), *Gender and Adjustment in Sub-Saharan Africa*, Brighton: BRIDGE Report No. 8, Institute of Development Studies, University of Sussex (downloadable from www.ids.ac.uk/bridge/).

Bähre, Erik (2007), 'Reluctant solidarity: death, urban poverty and neighbourly assistance in South Africa', *Ethnography*, **8**(1), 33–59.

Baran, Paul A. (1957), *The Political Economy of Growth*, New York: Monthly Review Press.

Bardhan, Kalpana and Klasen, Stephen (1999), 'UNDP's gender-related indices: a critical review', *World Development*, **27**(6), 985–1010.

Barnett, Tony (2002), 'The social and economic impact of HIV/AIDS on development', in Vandana Desai and Robert Potter (eds), *The Companion to Development Studies*, London: Arnold, pp. 391–5.

Bayat, Asef and Denis, Eric (2000), 'Who is afraid of Ashwaiyyat? Urban change and politics in Egypt', *Environment and Urbanisation*, **12**(2), 185–99.

Bazoglu, Nefise and Mboup, Gora (2007), 'Do cities give the poor a better chance of survival?', *Habitat Debate*, **13**(4), 10 (downloadable from www.unhabitat.org).

Beales, Sylvia (2000), 'Why we should invest in older women and men: the experience of HelpAge International', *Gender and Development*, **8**(2), 9–18.

Beall, Jo and Fox, Sean (2007), *Urban Poverty and Development in the 21st Century: Towards an Inclusive and Sustainable World*, Oxford: Oxfam GB Research Report [Stock code 002P0392] (pdf version downloadable gratis, and free print copy available on request from www.oxfam.org).

Bebbington, Anthony (1999), 'Capitals and capabilities: a framework for analysing peasant viability, rural livelihoods and poverty', *World Development*, **27**(12), 2021–44.

Bebbington, Anthony (2003), 'Global networks and local developments: agendas for development geography', *Tijdschrift Voor Economische en Sociale Geografie*, **94**(3), 297–309.

Beck, Tony (1999), *Using Gender Sensitive Indicators*, London: Commonwealth Secretariat, Gender Management System Series (downloadable from www.thecommonwealth.org/gender).

Becker, Charles and Morrison, Andrew (1997), 'Public policies and rural–urban migration', in Josef Gugler (ed.), *Cities in the Developing World*, Oxford: Oxford University Press, pp. 88–105.

Bedford, Kate (2007), 'The imperative of male inclusion: how institutional context influences World Bank gender policy', *International Feminist Journal of Politics*, **9**(3), 289–311.

Beijard, Frans (1995), 'Rental and rent-free housing as coping mechanisms in La Paz, Bolivia', *Environment and Urbanisation*, **7**(2), 167–82.

Bell, Emma with Brambilla, Paola (2002), *Gender and Economic Globalisation: An Annotated Bibliography. Bibliography No. 12*, Brighton: Institute of Development Studies, 2002 (downloadable from www.bridge.ids.ac.uk/reports/BB12%20Globalisation.doc).

Benería, Lourdes and Roldán, Marta (1987), *The Crossroads of Class and Gender: Industrial Homework, Subcontracting and Household Dynamics in Mexico City*, Chicago, IL: University of Chicago Press.

Berger, Mark T. (2004), 'After the Third World? History, destiny and the fate of Third Worldism', *Third World Quarterly*, **25**(1), 9–39.

Berghäll, Outi (1998), 'The enabling concept: an unachievable ideal or a practical guide to action?', in Reino Hjerppe (ed.), *Urbanisation: Its Global Trends, Economics and Governance*, Helsinki: UNU/WIDER, pp. 107–20.

Berthélemy, Jean-Claude and Tichit, Ariane (2004), 'Bilateral donors' aid allocation decisions: a three-dimensional panel analysis', *International Review of Economics and Finance*, **13**(3), 253–74.

Bhana, Deevia (2007), 'Defining sexual rights (in marriage)', *Sexuality in Africa*, **4**(1), 3–6 (www.arsrc.org) (accessed 20 March 2008).

Bhatia, Mrigesh and Mossialos, Elias (2004), 'Health systems in developing countries', in Anthony Hall and James Midgely (eds), *Social Policy for Development*, London: Sage, pp. 168–204.

Binns, Tony (2008), 'Dualistic and unilinear concepts of development', in Vandana Desai and Robert Potter (eds), *The Companion to Development Studies*, 2nd edn, London: Hodder Arnold, pp. 81–6.

Blue, Ilona (1996), 'Urban inequalities in mental health: the case of São Paulo', *Environment and Urbanisation*, **8**(2), 91–9.

Boas, Morton (2008), 'Multilateral institutions and the developing world', in Vandana Desai and Robert Potter (eds), *The Companion to Development Studies*, 2nd edn, London: Hodder Arnold, pp. 547–550.

Boesten, Jelke (2007), 'Free choice or poverty alleviation? Population policies in Peru under Alberto Fujimori', *European Review of Latin American and Caribbean Studies*, **82**, 3–20.

Bradshaw, Sarah (2002), *Gendered Poverties and Power Relations: Looking Inside Communities and Households*, Managua: ICD, Embajada de Holanda, Puntos de Encuentro.

Bradshaw, Sarah (2008), 'From structural adjustment to social adjustment: a gendered analysis of conditional cash transfer programmes in Mexico and Nicaragua', *Global Social Policy*, **8**(2), 188–207.

Bradshaw, Sarah and Linneker, Brian (2003), *Challenging Women's Poverty: Perspectives on Gender and Poverty Reduction Strategies from Nicaragua and Honduras. CIIR-ICD Briefing*, London CIIR-ICD (downloadable from www.progressio.org.uk/shared_asp_files/uploaded files/%7B9F5D737B-0340-4C3E-95A8-87075EB3B85A%7D_wcp_Briefing_final.pdf).

Bradshaw, Sarah, Linneker, Brian and Zúniga, Rebeca (2002), 'Social roles and spatial relations of NGOs and civil society: participation and effectiveness post-Hurricane "Mitch"', in Cathy McIlwaine and Katie Willis (eds), *Challenges and Change in Middle America*, Harlow: Prentice Hall/Pearson, pp. 243–69.

Brandt, Willy (1980), *North–South: A Programme for Survival*, London: Pan.

Brock, Karen and McGee, Rosemary (eds) (2002), *Knowing Poverty: Critical Reflections on Participatory Research and Policy*, London: Earthscan.

Bromley, Ray (1997), 'Working in the streets of Cali, Colombia: survival strategy, necessity or unavoidable evil?', in Josef Gugler (ed.), *Cities in the Developing World: Issues, Theory and Policy*, Oxford: Oxford University Press, pp. 124–38.

Brown, Flor and Domínguez, Lilia (2007), *Determinants of Wage Differentials in the Maquila Industry in Mexico: A Gender Perspective, GEM-IWG Working Paper 07-6*, Utah: International Working Group on Gender, Macroeconomics and International Economics (downloadable from www.econ.utah.edu/genmac/WP/07-6.pdf).

Brown, Oli (2008), *Migration and Climate Change*, IOM Migration Research Series No. 31, Geneva: International Organisation for Migration (downloadable from www.iom.int),

Brydon, Lynne and Chant, Sylvia (1993), *Women in the Third World: Gender Issues in Rural and Urban Areas*, Reprinted edn, Aldershot: Edward Elgar.

Brydon, Lynne and Legge, Karen (1996), *Adjusting Society: The World Bank, the IMF and Ghana*, London: I.B. Tauris.

Budowksi, Monica (2002), 'Lone motherhood in Costa Rica: a threat for society or a chance for change?', in Christian Giordano and Andrea Boscoboinik (eds), *Constructing Risk, Threat, Catastrophe*, Fribourg: University Press Fribourg Switzerland, pp. 121–43.

Bulmer-Thomas, Victor (1996a), 'Conclusions', in Victor Bulmer-Thomas (ed.), *The New Economic Model in Latin America and its Impact on Income Distribution and Poverty*, Basingstoke: Macmillan, in association with the Institute of Latin American Studies, University of London, pp. 296–327.

Bulmer-Thomas, Victor (ed.) (1996b), *The New Economic Model in Latin America and its Impact on Income Distribution and Poverty*, Basingstoke: Macmillan, in association with the Institute of Latin American Studies, University of London.

Burgess, Rod (1982), 'Self-help housing advocacy: a curious form of radicalism', in Peter Ward (ed.), *Self-Help Housing: A Critique*, London: Mansell, pp. 58–97.

Burgess, Rod, Carmona, Marisa and Kolstee, Theo (eds) (1997), *The Challenge of Sustainable Cities*, London: Zed.

Burnell, Peter (2008), 'Foreign aid in a changing world', in Vandana Desai and Robert Potter (eds), *The Companion to Development Studies*, 2nd edn, London: Hodder Arnold, pp. 503–11.

Buvinic, Mayra and Gupta, Geeta Rao (1997), 'Female-headed households and female-maintained families: are they worth targeting to reduce poverty in developing countries?', *Economic Development and Cultural Change*, **45**(2), 259–80.

Camaiora, Ana Lucia (2007), 'Legalising property rights: unleashing the economic potential of the urban poor', *Habitat Debate*, **13**(2), 8 (downloadable from www.unhabitat.org).

Cardoso, Fernando Henrique (1995), 'Dependency and development in Latin America', in Stuart Corbridge (ed.), *Development Studies: A Reader*, Oxford: Blackwell, pp. 112–27.

Cardoso, Fernando Henrique and Faletto, Enzo (1979), *Dependency and Development in Latin America*, Berkeley, CA: University of California Press.

Carney, Diana (1998), 'Implementing the sustainable rural livelihoods approach', in Diana Carney (ed.), *Sustainable Rural Livelihoods: What Contribution Can We Make?*, London: DFID.

Chakravarty, Paula, Rani, Uma and Unni, Jeemol (2006), 'Decent work deficits in the informal economy: case of Surat', *Economic and Political Weekly* (Mumbai), **41**(21), 2089–97 (downloadable from www.epw.org.in).

Chambers, Robert (1995), 'Poverty and livelihoods: whose reality counts?', *Environment and Urbanisation*, **7**(1), 173–204.

Chant, Sylvia (1991), *Women and Survival in Mexican Cities: Perspectives on Gender, Labour Markets and Low-income Households*, Manchester: Manchester University Press.

Chant, Sylvia (1996), *Gender, Urban Development and Housing*, Publications Series for Habitat II, Vol. 2, New York: United Nations Development Programme.

Chant, Sylvia (1997a), *Women-headed Households: Diversity and Dynamics in the Developing World*, Basingstoke: Macmillan.

Chant, Sylvia (1997b), 'Women-headed households: poorest of the poor? Perspectives from Mexico, Costa Rica and the Philippines', *IDS Bulletin*, **28**(3), 26–48.

Chant, Sylvia (1998), 'Households, gender and rural–urban migration: reflections on linkages and considerations for policy, *Environment and Urbanisation*, **10**(1), 5–22.

Chant, Sylvia (1999), 'Informal sector activity in the Third World city', in Michael Pacione (ed.) *Applied Geography: An Introduction to Useful Research in Physical, Environmental and Human Geography*, London: Routledge, pp. 509–27.

Chant, Sylvia (2002a), 'Debate. Researching gender, families and households in Latin America: from the 20th into the 21st century', *Bulletin of Latin American Research*, **21**(4), 545–75.

Chant, Sylvia (2002b), 'Families on the verge of breakdown? Views on contemporary trends in family life in Guanacaste, Costa Rica', *Journal of Developing Societies*, **18**(2–3), 109–48.

Chant, Sylvia (2002c), 'Men, women and household diversity', in Cathy McIlwaine and Katie Willis (eds), *Challenge and Change in Middle America and the Caribbean*, Harlow: Pearson Education, pp. 26–60.

Chant, Sylvia (2003), *Female Household Headship and the Feminisation of Poverty: Facts, Fictions and Forward Strategies*, Gender Institute New Working Paper Series, Issue 9, London: London School of Economics (downloadable from eprints.lse.ac.uk/archive0000574).

Chant, Sylvia (2006), 'Re-thinking the "feminisation of poverty" in relation to aggregate gender indices', *Journal of Human Development*, **7**(2), 201–20.

Chant, Sylvia (2007a), *Gender, Generation and Poverty: Exploring the 'Feminisation of Poverty' in Africa, Asia and Latin America*, Cheltenham, UK and Northampton, MA, USA: Edward Elgar.

Chant, Sylvia (2007b), *Children in Female-Headed Households: Interrogating the Concept of an 'Inter-Generational Transmission of Disadvantage' with Particular Reference to The Gambia, Philippines and Costa Rica*, Gender Institute New Series Working Paper, Issue 19, London: London School of Economics (downloadable from www.lse.ac.uk/collections/genderInstitute/children.pdf).

Chant, Sylvia (2007c), *Gender, Cities, and the Millennium Development Goals in the Global South*, LSE Gender Institute, New Series Working Paper, Issue 21, London: London School of Economics (www.lse.ac.uk/collections/genderInstitute/pdf/CHANT%20GIWP.pdf).

Chant, Sylvia (2008a), 'The "feminisation of poverty" and the "feminisation" of anti-poverty programmes: room for revision?', *Journal of Development Studies*, **44**(2), 165–97.

Chant, Sylvia (2008b), 'The informal sector and employment', in Vandana Desai and Robert Potter (eds), *The Companion to Development Studies*, 2nd edn, London: Hodder Arnold, pp. 216–24.

Chant, Sylvia (2008c), *The Curious Question of Feminising Poverty in Costa Rica: The Importance of Gendered Subjectivities*, Gender Institute New Working Paper Series, Issue 22 (downloadable from www.lse.ac.uk/collections/genderInstitute/pdf/curiouschant.pdf).

Chant, Sylvia (2008d), 'Beyond incomes: a new take on the "feminisation of poverty"', *Poverty in Focus*, **13**, 26–7 (downloadable from www.undp.org/povertycentre.org/pub.ipcPovertyInFocus 13.pdf).

Chant, Sylvia and Gutmann, Matthew (2000), *Mainstreaming Men into Gender and Development: Debates, Reflections and Policy Experiences*, Oxford: Oxfam.

Chant, Sylvia and Gutmann, Matthew (2002), '" Men-streaming" gender? Questions for gender and development policy in the 21st century', *Progress in Development Studies*, **2**(4), 269–82.

Chant, Sylvia and McIlwaine, Cathy (1995), 'Gender and export manufacturing in the Philippines: continuity or change in female employment? the case of the Mactan Export Processing Zone', *Gender, Place and Culture*, **2**(2), 147–76.

Chant, Sylvia and Pedwell, Carolyn (2008), *Women, Gender and the Informal Economy: An Assessment of ILO Research and Suggested Ways Forward*, Geneva: ILO (downloadable from www.ilo.org/wcmsp5/groups/public/---dgreports/---dcomm/documents/publication/wcms_091 228.pdf).

Chant, Sylvia and Radcliffe, Sarah (1992), 'Migration and development: the importance of gender', in Sylvia Chant (ed.), *Gender and Migration in Developing Countries*, London: Belhaven, pp. 1–29.

Chant, Sylvia with Craske, Nikki (2003), *Gender in Latin America*, London: Latin America Bureau/New Brunswick, NJ: Rutgers University Press.

Chataway, Joanna and Allen, Tim (2000), 'Industrialisation and development: prospects and dilemmas', in Tim Allen and Alan Thomas (eds), *Poverty and Development into the 21st Century*, Oxford: Oxford University Press, pp. 509–32.

Chen, Martha Alter (2009), 'Informalisation of labour markets: is formalisation the answer?', in Shahra Razavi (ed.), *The Gendered Impacts of Liberalisation Policies: Toward 'Embedded' Liberalism?*, London/Geneva: Routledge/UNRISD Research on Social Development.

Chen, Martha Alter, Vanek, Joan and Carr, Marilyn (2004), *Mainstreaming Informal Employment and Gender in Poverty Reduction: A Handbook for Policy-makers and Other Stakeholders*, London: Commonwealth Secretariat (downloadable chapter by chapter from www.idrc.ca/en).

Chronic Poverty Research Centre (CPRC) (2005), *Chronic Poverty Report 2004–05*, Manchester: CPRC (downloadable from www.chronicpoverty.org/resources/cprc_report_2004-2005_contents.html).

Clark, Fiona and Laurie, Nina (2000), 'Gender, age and exclusion: a challenge to community organisations in Peru', *Gender and Development*, **8**(2), 80–88.

Clemens, Michael A., Kenny, Charles J. and Moss, Todd J. (2007), 'The trouble with the MDGs: confronting expectations of aid and development success', *World Development*, **35**(5), 735–51.

Collier, Jane, Rosaldo, Michelle and Yanagisako, Sylvia (1997), 'Is there a family? New anthropological views', in Roger Lancaster and Micaela di Leonardo (eds), *The Gender/Sexuality Reader*, New York: Routledge, pp. 71–81.

Collier, Paul and Hoeffler, Anke (2000), *Greed and Grievance in Civil War. World Bank Policy Research Working Paper No. 2355*, Washington, DC: World Bank (downloadable from http://econ.worldbank.org/external/default/main?menuPK=577939&pagePK=64165265&piPK=64165423&theSitePK=469382).

Comaroff, Jean (2007), 'Beyond bare life: AIDS, (bio) politics, and the neoliberal order', *Public Culture*, **19**(1), 197–219.

Commonwealth Secretariat (1995), *Commonwealth Plan of Action on Gender and Development*, London: Commonwealth Secretariat.

Connor, Stephen (2008), 'Managing health and disease in developing countries', in Vandana Desai and Robert Potter (eds), *The Companion to Development Studies*, 2nd edn, London: Hodder Arnold, pp. 413–17.

Conway, Dennis and Heyne, Nikolas (2008), 'Classical dependency theories: from ECLA to André Gunder Frank', in Vandana Desai and Robert Potter (eds), *The Companion to Development Studies*, 2nd edn, London: Hodder Arnold, pp. 92–6.

Corbridge, Stuart (1993), *Debt and Development*, Oxford: Blackwell.

Corbridge, Stuart (2008), 'Third World debt', in Vandana Desai and Robert Potter (eds), *The Companion to Development Studies*, 2nd edn, London: Hodder Arnold, pp. 508–11.

Cornia, Giovanni, Jolly, Richard and Stewart, Frances (eds) (1987),

Adjustment with a Human Face: Protecting the Vulnerable and Promoting Growth, Vol. 1, Oxford: Oxford University Press.

Cornwall, Andrea (2000), 'Missing men? Reflections on men, masculinities and gender in GAD', *IDS Bulletin*, **31**(2), 18–27.

Cornwall, Andrea (2003), 'Whose voices? Whose choices? Reflections on gender and participatory development', *World Development*, **31**(8), 1325–42.

Cornwall, Andrea and Jolly, Susie (2006), 'Introduction: sexuality matters', *IDS Bulletin*, **37**(5), 1–11.

Cornwall, Andrea and Molyneux, Maxine (eds) (2008), *The Politics of Rights: Dilemmas for Feminist Praxis*, London: Routledge.

Cornwall, Andrea and White, Sarah (2000), 'Men, masculinities and development: politics, policies and practice', *IDS Bulletin*, **31**(2), 1–6.

Cornwall, Andrea, Harrison, Elizabeth and Whitehead, Ann (2007), 'Introduction: feminisms in development: contradictions, contestations and challenges', in Andrea Cornwall, Elizabeth Harrison and Ann Whitehead (eds), *Feminisms in Development: Contradictions, Contestations and Challenges*, London: Zed, pp. 1–17.

Corrêa, Sonia (2008), 'Reproductive and sexual rights', in Vandana Desai and Robert Potter (eds), *The Companion to Development Studies*, 2nd edn, London: Hodder Arnold, pp. 385–90.

Corrêa, Sonia with Reichmann, Rebecca (1994), *Population and Reproductive Rights: Feminist Perspectives from the South*, London: Zed.

Coudouel, Aline, Hentschel, Jesko S. and Wodon, Quentin T. (2002), 'Poverty measurement and analysis', in Jeni Klugman (ed.), *PRSP Sourcebook*, Washington, DC: World Bank (downloadable from http://povlibrary.worldbank.org/files/5467_chap1.pdf).

Cowen, Michael P. and Shenton, Robert W. (1996), *Doctrines of Development*, London: Routledge.

Craig, David and Porter, Doug (2003), 'Poverty reduction strategy papers: a new convergence', *World Development*, **31**(1), 53–70.

Cueva Beteta, Hanny (2006), 'What is missing in measures of women's empowerment?', *Journal of Human Development*, **7**(2), 221–41.

D'Cruz, Celine and Satterthwaite, David (2005), 'Building homes, changing official approaches', *Poverty Reduction in Urban Areas Series, Working Paper 16*, London: International Institute for Environment and Development (downloadable from www.iied.org/pubs).

Datta, Kavita and Jones, Gareth (eds) (1999), *Housing and Finance in Developing Countries*, London: Routledge.

Datta, Kavita, McIlwaine, Cathy, Wills, Jane, Evans, Yara, Herbert, Joanna and May, Jon (2007), 'The new development finance or exploiting migrant labour? Remittance sending among low-paid migrant workers in London', *International Development Planning Review*, **29**(1), 43–67.

Davids, Tine and Driel, Francien van (2001) 'Globalisation and gender: beyond dichotomies', in Frans J. Schuurman (ed.), *Globalisation and Development Studies Challenges for the 21st Century*, London: Sage, pp. 153–75.

Davids, Tine and Driel, Francien van (2005), 'Changing perspectives', in Tine Davids and Francien van Driel (eds), *The Gender Question in Globalisation: Changing Perspectives and Practices*, Aldershot: Ashgate, pp. 1–22.

De Haan, Leo and Zoomers, Annelies (2005), 'Exploring the frontiers of livelihoods research', *Development and Change*, **36**(1), 27–47.

De Soto, Hernando (1989), *The Other Path: The Invisible Revolution in the Third World*, New York: Harper and Row.

Department for International Development (DFID) (2000a), *Eliminating World Poverty: Making Globalisation Work for the Poor*, White Paper on International Development, London: DFID.

Department for International Development (DFID) (2000b), *Poverty Elimination and the Empowerment of Women*, London: DFID (downloadable from www.dfid.gov.uk).

Department for International Development (DFID) (2006), *Making Governance Work for the Poor: A White Paper on International Development*, London: DFID (downloadable from www.dfid.gov.uk/pubs/files/whitepaper 2006/wp 2006foreword-preface-section1.pdf).

Desai, Vandana (2008), 'Role of non-governmental organisations (NGOs)', in Vandana Desai and Robert Potter (eds), *The Companion to Development Studies*, 2nd edn, London: Hodder Arnold, pp. 525–9.

Devereux, Stephen and Sabates-Wheeler, Rachel (2004), 'Transformative social protection', *IDS Working Paper 232*, Brighton: IDS.

Dijkstra, A. Geske and Hanmer, Lucia (2000), 'Measuring socio-economic gender inequality: toward an alternative to the UNDP Gender-related Development Index', *Feminist Economics*, **6**(2), 41–75.

Dodds, Klaus (2008), 'The Third World, developing countries, the South, poor countries', in Vandana Desai and Robert Potter (eds), *The Companion to Development Studies*, London: Hodder Arnold, pp. 3–7.

Douglass, Mike (2002), 'From global competition to cooperation for livable cities and economic resilience in Pacific Asia', *Environment and Urbanisation*, **14**(1), 53–68.

Drakakis-Smith, David (1987), *The Third World City*, London: Methuen.

Durand, Jorge and Massey, Douglas (1992), 'Mexican migration to the US: a critical review', *Latin American Research Review*, **27**(2), 3–42.

Easterly, William R. (2006), *The White Man's Burden: Why the West's*

Efforts to Aid the Rest have Done so Much Ill and so Little Good, Oxford: Oxford University Press.

Edwards, Michael (1982), 'The political economy of low-income housing', *Bulletin of Latin American Research*, **1**(2), 45–61.

Edwards, Michael (2004), *Civil Society*, Cambridge: Polity.

Edwards, Michael and Hulme, David (eds) (1995), *Non-Governmental Organisations: Performance and Accountability*, London: Earthscan.

Elliott, Jennifer A. (2008), 'Development as improving human welfare and human rights', in Vandana Desai and Robert Potter (eds), *The Companion to Development Studies*, 2nd edn, London: Hodder Arnold, pp. 40–45.

Elson, Diane (1989), 'The impact of structural adjustment on women: concepts and issues', in Bade Onimode (ed.), *The IMF, the World Bank and the African Debt, Volume 2: The Social and Political Impact*, London: Zed.

Elson, Diane (1992), 'From survival strategies to transformation strategies: women's needs and structural adjustment', in Lourdes Benería and Shelley Feldman (eds), *Unequal Burden: Economic Crisis, Persistent Poverty and Women's Work*, Boulder, CO: Westview, pp. 26–48.

Elson, Diane and Pearson, Ruth (1981), ' " Nimble fingers make cheap workers": an analysis of women's employment in Third World export manufacturing', *Feminist Review*, **7**, 87–107.

Environment and Urbanisation (2001a), Special issue produced by Shack Dwellers International, **13**(1), 1–294.

Environment and Urbanisation (2001b), 'Civil society in action', **13**(2), 1–276.

Environment and Urbanisation (2007a), 'Reducing risks to cities from disasters and climate change', **19**(1), 1–330.

Environment and Urbanisation (2007b), 'Finance for low-income housing and community development', **19**(2), 331–616.

Environment and Urbanisation (2008), 'Finance for housing, livelihoods and basic services', **20**(1), 1–304.

Escobar, Arturo (1995), *Encountering Development: The Making and Unmaking of the Third World*, Princeton, NJ: Princeton University Press.

Esplen, Emily (2007), *Women and Girls Living with HIV/AIDS: Overview and Annotated Bibliography*, Bibliography No. 18, Sussex: BRIDGE development-gender (downloadable from www.ids.ac.uk/bridge).

Esteva, Gustavo (1992), 'Development', in Wolfgang Sachs (ed.), *The Development Dictionary: A Guide to Knowledge as Power*, London: Zed, pp. 6–25.

Fernández-Kelly, Patricia (1983), *For We are Sold, I, and My People*, Albany, NY: State University of New York Press.

Fernández-Kelly, Patricia and Shefner, Jon (eds) (2006), *Out of the Shadows: Political Action and the Informal Sector in Latin America*, University Park, PA: Pennsylvania State University Press.

Folbre, Nancy (1991), 'Women on their own: global patterns of female headship', in Rita S. Gallin and Ann Ferguson (eds), *The Women and International Development Annual*, Vol. 2, Boulder, CO: Westview, pp. 69–126.

Fold, Niels and Wangel, Anne (1998), 'Sustained growth but non-sustainable urbanisation in Penang, Malaysia', *Third World Planning Review*, **20**(2), 165–77.

Frank, André Gunder (1967), *Capitalism and Underdevelopment in Latin America*, New York: Monthly Review Press.

Frank, André Gunder (1995), 'The Development of Underdevelopment', in Stuart Corbridge (ed.), *Development Studies: A Reader*, Oxford: Blackwell, pp. 27–37.

Friedman, Milton (1962), *Capitalism and Freedom*, Chicago, IL: University of Chicago Press.

Friedmann, John (1966), *Regional Development Policy: A Case Study of Venezuela*, Cambridge, MA: MIT Press.

Fritz, Verena and Menocal, Alina Rocha (2007), 'Developmental states in the new millennium: concepts and challenges for a new aid agenda', *Development Policy Review*, **25**(5), 531–52.

Furedy, Frank (1997), *Population and Development*, Cambridge: Polity.

Gardner, Katy and Lewis, David (1996), *Anthropology, Development and the Postmodern Challenge*, London: Pluto.

Geldstein, Rosa (1994), 'Working class mothers as economic providers and heads of families in Buenos Aires', *Reproductive Health Matters*, **4**, 55–64.

Gereffi, Gary (2005), *The New Offshoring of Jobs and Global Development: An Overview of the Contemporary Global Labor Market*, Geneva: ILO (downloadable from www.ilo.org/public/english/bureau/inst/download/spllect1.pdf).

Ghosh, Jayati (2009), 'Informalisation and women's workforce participation: a consideration of recent trends in Asia', in Shahra Razavi (ed.), *The Gendered Impacts of Liberalisation Policies: Toward 'Embedded' Liberalism?*, London/Geneva: Routledge UNRISD Research on Social Development.

Gideon, Jasmine (1998), 'The politics of social service provision through NGOs: a study of Latin America', *Bulletin of Latin American Research*, **17**(3), 303–22.

Gilbert, Alan (1995), 'Debt, poverty and the Latin American city', *Geography*, **80**(4), 323–33.

Gilbert, Alan (1998), *The Latin American City*, 2nd edn, London: Latin America Bureau.

Gilbert, Alan (2002), 'Housing policy and legal entitlements: survival strategies of the urban poor', in Christopher Abel and Colin Lewis (eds), *Exclusion and Engagement: Social Policy in Latin America*, London: Institute of Latin American Studies, University of London, pp. 303–30.

Gilbert, Alan (2003), *Rental Housing: An Essential Option for the Urban Poor in Developing Countries*, Nairobi: United Nations Centre for Human Settlements (downloadable from www.unhabitat.org).

Gilbert, Alan (2008a), 'The new international division of labour', in Vandana Desai and Robert Potter (eds), *The Companion to Development Studies*, 2nd edn, London: Hodder Arnold, pp. 186–91.

Gilbert, Alan (2008b), 'Housing the urban poor', in Vandana Desai and Robert Potter (eds), *The Companion to Development Studies*, 2nd edn, London: Hodder Arnold, pp. 257–61.

Gilbert, Alan and Gugler, Josef (1992), *Cities, Poverty and Development: Urbanisation in the Third World*, 2nd edn, Oxford: Oxford University Press.

Gilbert, Alan and Varley, Ann (1991), *Landlord and Tenant: Housing the Poor in Urban Mexico*, London: Routledge.

Goetz, Anne-Marie and Sandler, Joanna (2007), 'SWApping gender: from cross-cutting obscurity to sectoral security?', in Andrea Cornwall, Elizabeth Harrison and Ann Whitehead (eds), *Feminisms in Development: Contradictions, Contestations and Challenges*, London: Zed, pp. 161–73.

González de la Rocha, Mercedes (1988), 'Economic crisis, domestic reorganisation and women's work in Guadalajara, Mexico', *Bulletin of Latin American Research*, **7**(2), 207–23.

González de la Rocha, Mercedes (1994), *The Resources of Poverty: Women and Survival in a Mexican City*, Oxford: Blackwell.

González de la Rocha, Mercedes (2001), 'From the resources of poverty to the poverty of resources: the erosion of a survival model', *Latin American Perspectives*, **38**(4), 72–100.

González de la Rocha, Mercedes (2007), 'The construction of the myth of survival', *Development and Change*, **38**(1), 45–66.

Goodwin, Rick (1997), 'The other half of the sky: focused work on men and gender justice in Tamil Nadu, India', mimeo, London: Womankind Worldwide.

Gorman, Mark (1996), 'Older people and development: the last minority?', in Oxfam (ed.), *Development and Social Diversity*, Oxford: Oxfam, pp. 36–45.

Goulet, Denis (1971), *The Cruel Choice: A New Concept in the Theory of Development*, New York: Athenaeum.

Greenaway, David and Milner, Chris (2008), 'Trade and industrial policy in developing countries', in Vandana Desai and Robert Potter (eds), *The Companion to Development Studies*, 2nd edn, London: Hodder Arnold, pp. 196–200.

Greene, Margarita and Rojas, Eduardo (2008), 'Incremental construction: a strategy to facilitate access to housing', *Environment and Urbanisation*, **20**(1), 89–108.

Gupta, Geeta Rao (2006), 'Women and AIDS: from here, where?', inaugural lecture, LSEAIDS and DFID, London School of Economics, 9 October (www.lse.ac.uk/collections/LSEAIDS/pdfs/Gupta).

Gupta, Smita (2009), 'Women in India's National Rural Employment Guarantee Scheme', in Shahra Razavi (ed.), *The Gendered Impacts of Liberalisation Policies: Toward 'Embedded' Liberalism?*, London/ Geneva: Routledge/UNRISD Research on Social Development.

Gutmann, Matthew (2005), 'Scoring men: vasectomies and the totemic illusion of male sexuality in Oaxaca', *Culture, Medicine and Psychiatry*, **29**, 79–101.

Gutmann, Matthew (2007), *Fixing Men: Sex, Birth Control, and AIDS in Mexico*, Berkeley, CA: University of California Press.

Gwynne, Robert (2002), 'Export processing and free trade zones', in Vandana Desai and Robert Potter (eds), *The Companion to Development Studies*, 1st edn, London: Arnold, pp. 201–6.

Gwynne, Robert N. (2008), 'Free trade and fair trade', in Vandana Desai and Robert Potter (eds), *The Companion to Development Studies*, 2nd edn, London: Hodder Arnold, pp. 201–6.

Habitat Debate (2006), 'Cities – magnets of hope: a look at global migration problems', **12**(3), 1–24 (downloadable from www.unhabitat.org).

Habitat Debate (2007a), 'A look at the urban informal economy', **13**(2), 1–24 (downloadable from www.unhabitat.org).

Habitat Debate (2007b), 'Healthy cities', **13**(4), 1–24 (downloadable from www.unhabitat.org).

Hardon, Anita (1997), 'Reproductive rights in practice', in Anita Hardon and Elizabeth Hayes (eds), *Reproductive Rights in Practice: A Feminist Report on the Quality of Care*, London: Zed, pp. 3–14.

Hardon, Anita and Hayes, Elizabeth (eds) (1997), *Reproductive Rights in Practice: A Feminist Report on the Quality of Care*, London: Zed.

Hardstaff, Peter and Jones, Tim (2006), *Out of Time: The Case for Replacing the World Bank and IMF*, London: World Development Movement (downloadable from www.wdm.org.uk/resources/reports/debt/outoftime14092006.pdf).

Harms, Hans (1982), 'Historical perspectives in the practice and purpose of self-help housing', in Peter Ward (ed.), *Self-Help Housing: A Critique*, London: Mansell, pp. 17–53.

Harris, Olivia (1981), 'Households as natural units', in Kate Young, Carol Wolkowitz and Roslyn McCullagh (eds), *Of Marriage and the Market*, London: CSE Books, pp. 48–67.

Hart, Gillian (2001), 'Development critiques in the 1990s: culs de sac and promising paths', *Progress in Human Geography*, **25**(4), 649–58.

Hart, Keith (1973), 'Informal income opportunities and urban employment in Ghana', in Richard Jolly, Emanuel de Kadt, Hans Singer and Fiona Wilson (eds), *Third World Employment*, Harmondsworth: Penguin, pp. 66–70.

Hart, Keith (2007), 'Progress and evolution', *Habitat Debate*, **13**(2), 17–18 (downloadable from www.unhabitat.org).

Heintz, James (2006), *Globalisation, Economic Policy and Employment: Poverty and Gender Implications*, Employment Strategy Paper 2006/3, Employment Policy Unit, Employment Strategy Department, Geneva: ILO (downloadable from www.oit.org/public/english/employment/strat/download/esp 2006-3.pdf).

Heintz, James (2008), 'Poverty, employment and globalisation: a gender perspective', *Poverty in Focus*, **13** (January), 12–13 (www.undp-poverty-centre.org/pub/IPCPovertyInFocus 13.pdf) (accessed 15 January 2008).

Hewitt, Tom (2000), 'Half a century of development', in Tim Allen and Alan Thomas (eds), *Poverty and Development into the 21st Century*, Oxford: Oxford University Press, pp. 289–308.

Hicks, Douglas A. (1997), 'The inequality-adjusted Human Development Index: a constructive proposal', *World Development*, **25**(8), 1283–98.

Hirschman, Albert O. (1958), *The Strategy of Economic Development*, New Haven, CT: Yale University Press.

Hjerppe, Reino (ed.) (1998), *Urbanisation: Its Global Trends, Economics and Governance*, Helsinki: United Nations University, World Institute for Development Economics Research (downloadable from www.wider.unu.edu/publications).

Hoselitz, Bert F. (1952), *The Progress of Underdeveloped Areas*, Chicago, IL: University of Chicago Press.

Hoselitz, Bert F. (1995), 'Non-economic barriers to economic development', in Stuart Corbridge (ed.), *Development Studies: A Reader*, Oxford: Blackwell, pp. 17–27.

Howard-Grabman, Lisa (1996), ' "Planning together": developing community plans to address priority maternal and neonatal health problems in rural Bolivia', in Korrie de Koning and Marion Martin (eds), *Participatory Research in Health: Issues and Experiences*, London: Zed, pp. 153–63.

Hulme, David and Turner, Mark (1990), *Sociology and Development: Theories, Policies and Practices*, New York: Harvester Wheatsheaf.

Ilkkaracan, Pinar and Jolly, Susie (2007), *Gender and Sexuality: Overview Report*, Brighton: BRIDGE Development-Gender, University of Sussex.

Illich, Ivan (1997), 'Development as planned poverty', in Majid Rahnema and Victoria Bawtree (eds), *The Post-Development Reader*, London: Zed, pp. 94–101.

International Labour Organisation (ILO) (1972), *Employment, Incomes and Inequality: A Strategy for Increasing Productive Employment in Kenya*, Geneva: ILO.

International Labour Organisation (ILO) (2001), *Report of the Director General. Reducing the Decent Work Deficit – A Global Challenge*, Geneva: ILO.

International Labour Organisation (ILO) (2007), *Global Employment Trends Brief, January 2007*, Geneva: ILO.

International Organisation for Migration (IOM) (2005), *World Migration Report 2005*, Geneva: IOM (downloadable from www.iom.org).

Ishengoma, Esther (2007), 'Formalising informal firms: what can be done?', *Poverty in Focus*, 10, *Analysing and Achieving Pro-Poor Growth*, 16–17 (downloadable from www.undp-povertycentre.org/pub/IPC PovertyinFocus10.pdf).

Izazola, Haydea (2004), 'Migration to and from Mexico City 1995–2000', *Environment and Urbanisation*, **16**(1), 211–29.

Jackson, Cecile (1996), 'Rescuing gender from the poverty trap', *World Development*, **24**(3), 489–504.

Jackson, Cecile and Pearson, Ruth (eds) (1998), *Feminist Visions of Development: Gender Analysis and Policy*, London: Routledge.

Jauch, Herbert (2002), 'Export-processing zones and the quest for sustainable development: southern African perspectives', *Environment and Urbanisation*, **14**(1), 101–13.

Jenkins, Rhys and Pearson, Ruth (2001), 'Consensus or conflict: what's in a code?', *ID21 Insights*, Issue 35 (downloadable from www.id21.org/insights/insights 36/ insights-iss 36-art02.html).

Jenkins, Rob (2008), 'The emergence of the governance agenda: sovereignty, neoliberal bias and the politics of international development', in Vandana Desai and Robert Potter (eds), *The Companion to Development Studies*, 2nd edn, London: Hodder Arnold, pp. 516–19.

Jhabvala, Renana (2007), 'A bottom-up approach in India', *Habitat Debate*, **13**(2), 14 (downloadable from www.unhabitat.org).

Jodha, N.S. (1988), 'Poverty debate in India: a minority view', *Economic and Political Weekly*, **23**, 45–7.

Johnson, Stanley (1987), *World Population and the United Nations*, Cambridge: Cambridge University Press.

Johnson, Stanley (1995), *The Politics of Population: Cairo 1994*, London: Earthscan.

Jolly, Susie (2007), *Why the Development Industry Should Get Over its Obsession with Bad Sex and Start to Think About Pleasure*, Working Paper 283, Brighton: Institute of Development Studies (downloadable from www.ids.ac.uk).

Journal of Human Development (2006), 'Revisiting the Gender-related Development Index (GDI) and Gender Empowerment Measure (GEM)', Special issue, **7**(2), 145–290.

Jütting, Johannes P., Morrisson, Christian, Dayton-Johnson, Jeff and Dreschler, Denis (2006), *Measuring Gender (In)Equality: Introducing the Gender Institutions and Development Data Base (GID)*, Working Paper No. 247, Paris: OECD Development Centre (downloadable from www.oecd.org/dev/wp).

Kabeer, Naila (1994), *Reversed Realities: Gender Hierarchies in Development Thought*, London: Verso.

Kabeer, Naila (1999), 'Resources, agency, achievements: reflections on the measurement of women's empowerment', *Development and Change*, **30**, 435–64.

Kabeer, Naila (2003), *Gender Mainstreaming in Poverty Eradication and the Millennium Development Goals: A Handbook for Policy-makers and Other Stakeholders*, London: Commonwealth Secretariat.

Kabeer, Naila (2007), *Marriage, Motherhood and Masculinity in the Global Economy: Reconfigurations of Personal and Economic Life*, Working Paper 290, Sussex: Institute of Development Studies (downloadable from www.ids.ac.uk/ ids/bookshop).

Kabeer, Naila (2008), *Mainstreaming Gender in Social Protection for the Informal Economy*, London: Commonwealth Secretariat.

Kakwani, Nanak and Subbarao, Kalanidi (2005), *Ageing and Poverty in Africa and the Role of Social Pensions*, Working Paper 8, Brasilia: International Poverty Centre (downloadable from www.undp.org/ povertycentre).

Kiely, Ray (2008), 'Global shift: industrialisation and development', in Vandana Desai and Robert Potter (eds), *The Companion to Development Studies*, 2nd edn, London: Hodder Arnold, pp. 183–6.

Kiwala, Lucia (2005), 'Human settlements – a concern for women in the coming decade', *Habitat Debate*, **11**(1), 4–5 (downloadable from www. unhabitat.org).

Klak, Thomas (2008), 'World-systems theory: centres, peripheries and semi-peripheries', in Vandana Desai and Robert Potter (eds), *The*

Companion to Development Studies, 2nd edn, London: Hodder Arnold, pp. 101–6.

Klasen, Stephan (2006), 'UNDP's gender-related measures: some conceptual problems and possible solutions', *Journal of Human Development*, **7**(2), 243–74.

Klasen, Stephan (2007), 'Pro-poor growth and gender inequality: insights from new research', *Poverty in Focus, 10, Analysing and Achieving Pro-Poor Growth*, 5–6 (downloadable from www.undppovertycentre.org/pub/IPCPovertyinFocus10.pdf).

Krug, Etienne, Dahlberg, Linda, Mercy, James, Zwi, Antony and Lozano, Rafael (eds) (2002), *World Report on Violence and Health*, Geneva: World Health Organisation (downloadable from www.who.int/violence_injury_prevention/violence/world_report/en/full_en.pdf).

Kulczycki, Andrzej (2007), 'The abortion debate in Mexico: realities and stalled policy reform', *Bulletin of Latin American Research*, **26**(1), 50–68.

Kumar, Sunil (1996), 'Landlordism in Third World urban low-income settlements: a case for further research', *Urban Studies*, **33**(4–5), 753–82.

Kumar, Sunil (2001), *Social Relations, Rental Housing Markets and the Poor in Urban India*, London: LSE, Department of Social Policy (downloadable from www.siteresources.worldbank.org).

Larkin, Maureen (1998), 'Global aspects of health and health policy in Third World countries', in Ray Kiely and Phil Marfleet (eds), *Globalisation and the Third World*, London: Routledge, pp. 91–111.

Lawson, Victoria (2007), *Making Development Geography*, London: Hodder Arnold.

Le Billon, Philippe (2007), 'Geographies of war: perspectives on "resource wars"', *Geography Compass*, **1**(2), 163–82.

Lehmann, David (1997), 'An opportunity lost: Escobar's deconstruction of development', *Journal of Development Studies*, **33**(4), 568–78.

Lehmann, Volker and McClellan, Angela (2006), *Financing the United Nations*, Friedrich Ebert Foundation fact sheet, New York: Friedrich Ebert Foundation (downloadable from www.globalpolicy.org/finance/docs/2006/04factsheet.pdf).

Leone, Tiziana (2008), 'Population trends in developing countries', in Vandana Desai and Robert Potter (eds), *The Companion to Development Studies*, 2nd edn, London: Hodder Arnold, pp. 378–84.

Levy, Caren (1999), 'The relationships between policy approaches to development and to women and international agency policies', training handout, Gender Policy and Planning Programme, Development Planning Unit, University College London.

Lewis, David (2002), 'Non-governmental organisations: questions of performance and accountability', in Vandana Desai and Robert Potter (eds), *The Companion to Development Studies*, 1st edn, London: Hodder Arnold, pp. 519–23.

Lewis, David and Opoku-Mensah, Paul (2006), 'Moving forward research agendas on international NGOs: theory, agency and context', *Journal of International Development*, **18**, 665–75.

Lind, Amy (2002), 'Making feminist sense of neoliberalism: the institutionalisation of women's struggles for survival in Ecuador and Bolivia', *Journal of Developing Societies*, **18**, 228–58.

Lloyd-Sherlock, Peter (1997), *Old Age and Urban Poverty*, Basingstoke: Macmillan.

Lloyd-Sherlock, Peter (ed.) (2000), *Healthcare Reform and Poverty in Latin America*, London: Institute of Latin American Studies, University of London.

Lloyd-Sherlock, Peter (2002), 'Health, equity and social exclusion in Argentina and Mexico', in Christopher Abel and Colin Lewis (eds), *Exclusion and Engagement: Social Policy in Latin America*, London: Institute of Latin American Studies, University of London, pp. 172–88.

Londoño, Juan Luis and Frenk, Julio (2000), 'Structured pluralism: towards an innovative model for health system reform in Latin America', in Peter Lloyd-Sherlock (ed.), *Healthcare Reform and Poverty in Latin America*, London: Institute of Latin American Studies, pp. 21–56.

Longwe, Sara Hlupekile (1995), 'A development agency as a patriarchal cooking pot: the evaporation of policies for women's advancement', in Mandy MacDonald (comp.), *Women's Rights and Development*, Working Paper, Oxford: Oxfam, pp. 18–29.

Lopez-Claros, Augusto and Zahidi, Saadia (2005), *Women's Empowerment: Measuring the Global Gender Gap*, Geneva: World Economic Forum (downloadable from www.weforum.org).

Lugo, Jaire and Sampson, Tony (2008), 'E-informality in Venezuela: the "other path" of technology', *Bulletin of Latin American Research*, **27**(1), 102–18.

Manuel, George and Posluns, Michael (1974), *The Fourth World: An Indian Reality*, Toronto: Collier.

Marchand, Marianne and Parpart, Jane (eds) (1995), *Feminism/Postmodernism/ Development*, London: Routledge.

Marshall, Don D. (2008), 'The new world group of dependency scholars', in Vandana Desai and Robert Potter (eds), *The Companion to Development Studies*, 2nd edn, London: Hodder Arnold, pp. 96–101.

Maxwell, Simon (1999), *The Meaning and Measurement of Poverty*, London: ODI (downloadable from www.odi.org.uk/publications/poverty.html).

May, Jon, Wills, Jane, Datta, Kavita, Evans, Yara, Herbert, Joanna and

McIlwaine, Cathy (2007), 'Keeping London working: global cities, the British state and London's migrant division of labour', *Transactions of the Institute of British Geographers*, **32**(2), 151–67.

Mboup, Gora and Amuyunzu-Nyamongo, Mary (2005), 'Getting the right data: helping municipalities help women', *Habitat Debate*, **11**(1), 9 (downloadable from www.unhabitat.org).

McEwan, Cheryl (2001), 'Postcolonialism, feminism and development: intersections and dilemmas,' *Progress in Development Studies*, **1**(2), 93–111.

McEwan, Cheryl (2003), 'Material geographies and postcolonialism', *Singapore Journal of Tropical Geography*, **24**(3), 340–55.

McIlwaine, Cathy (1997), 'Vulnerable or poor? A study of ethnic and gender disadvantage among Afro-Caribbeans in Limón, Costa Rica', *The European Journal of Development Research*, **9**(2), 35–61.

McIlwaine, Cathy (1998a), 'Civil society and development geography', *Progress in Human Geography*, **22**(3), 415–24.

McIlwaine Cathy (1998b), 'Contesting civil society: reflections from El Salvador', *Third World Quarterly*, **19**, 651–72.

McIlwaine, Cathy (2002), 'Perspectives on poverty, vulnerability and exclusion', in Cathy McIlwaine and Katie Willis (eds), *Challenges and Change in Middle America*, Harlow: Prentice Hall/Pearson, pp. 82–109.

McIlwaine, Cathy (2007), 'From local to global to transnational civil society: re-framing development perspectives on the non-state sector', *Geography Compass*, **1**(6), 1252–81.

McIlwaine, Cathy (2008), 'Gender- and age-based violence', in Vandana Desai and Robert Potter (eds), *The Companion to Development Studies*, 2nd edn, London: Hodder Arnold, pp. 445–9.

McIlwaine, Cathy and Datta, Kavita (2003), 'From feminising to Engendering development', *Gender, Place and Culture*, **10**(4), 369–82.

McIlwaine, Cathy and Datta, Kavita (2004), ' " Endangered youth?" Youth, gender and sexualities in urban Botswana', *Gender, Place and Culture*, **11**(4), 483–511.

McIlwaine, Cathy and Moser, Caroline (2001), 'Violence and social capital in urban poor communities: perspectives from Colombia and Guatemala', *Journal of International Development*, **13**(7), 965–84.

McIlwaine, Cathy and Moser, Caroline (2003), 'Poverty, violence and livelihood security in urban Colombia and Guatemala', *Progress in Development Studies*, **3**(2), 113–30.

McIlwaine, Cathy and Moser, Caroline (2007), 'Living in fear: how the urban poor perceive violence, fear and insecurity', in Kees Koonings and Dirk Kruijt (eds), *Fractured Cities: Social Exclusion, Urban Violence and Contested Spaces in Latin America*, London: Zed, pp. 117–37.

McIlwaine, Cathy, Chant, Sylvia and Lloyd Evans, Sally (2002), 'Making a living: employment, livelihoods and the informal sector', in Cathy McIlwaine and Katie Willis (eds), *Challenges and Change in Middle America*, Harlow: Pearson, pp. 110–35.

McNay, Kirsty (2005), 'The implications of the demographic transition for women, girls and gender equality: a review of developing country evidence', *Progress in Development Studies*, **5**(2), 115–34.

Medeiros, Marcelo and Costa, Joana (2006), *Poverty Among Women in Latin America: Feminisation or Over-representation?*, Working Paper No. 20, Brasilia: International Poverty Centre (downloadable from www.undp-povertycentre. org).

Medeiros, Marcelo and Costa, Joana (2008), 'Is there really a "feminisation of poverty?" ', *Poverty in Focus*, **13**, 24–5 (www.undp-povertycentre.org/pub/ IPCPovertyInFocus 13.pdf).

Menzel, Ulrich (2006), 'Walt Whitman Rostow', in David Simon (ed.), *Fifty Key Thinkers on Development*, London: Routledge, pp. 211–17.

Miraftab, Faranak (1997), 'Flirting with the enemy: challenges faced by NGOs in development and empowerment', *Habitat International*, **21**(4), 361–75.

Miraftab, Faranak (2001), 'Risks and opportunities in gender gaps to access shelter: a platform for intervention', *International Journal of Politics, Culture and Society*, **15**(1), 143–60.

Mirchandani, Kiran (2004), 'Practices of global capital: gaps, cracks and ironies in transnational call centres in India', *Global Networks*, **4**(4), 355–73.

Mitlin, Diana (1997), 'Building with credit: housing finance for low-income households', *Third World Planning Review*, **19**(1), 21–50.

Mitlin, Diana, Hickey, Sam and Bebbington, Anthony (2007), 'Reclaiming development? NGOs and the challenge of alternatives', *World Development*, **35**(10), 1699–720.

Mitullah, Winnie (2007), 'Informality: the bedrock of African cities', *Habitat Debate*, **13**(2), 10 (downloadable from www.unhabitat.org).

Mohan, Giles, Brown, Ed, Milward, Bob and Zack-Williams, Alfred B. (eds) (2000), *Structural Adjustment: Theory, Practice and Impacts*, London: Routledge.

Mohanty, Chandra Talpade (1991), 'Under Western eyes: feminist scholarship and colonial discourses', in Chandra Mohanty, Ann Russo and Lourdes Torres (eds), *Third World Women and the Politics of Feminism*, Bloomington, IN: Indiana University Press, pp. 51- 80.

Molyneux, Maxine (1984), 'Mobilisation without emancipation?', *Critical Social Policy*, **4**(10), 59–75.

Molyneux, Maxine (2001), *Women's Movements in International Perspective: Latin America and Beyond*, Basingstoke: Palgrave.

Molyneux, Maxine (2006), 'Mothers at the service of the new poverty agenda: Progresa/Oportunidades, Mexico's conditional transfer programme', *Journal of Social Policy and Administration*, **40**(4), 425–49.

Molyneux, Maxine (2007), 'The chimera of success: gender ennui and the changed international policy environment', in Andrea Cornwall, Elizabeth Harrison and Ann Whitehead (eds), *Feminisms in Development: Contradictions, Contestations and Challenges*, London: Zed, pp. 227–40.

Montgomery, Mark, Stren, Richard, Cohen, Barney and Reed, Holly (2004), *Cities Transformed: Demographic Change and its Implications in the Developing World*, London: Earthscan.

Moore, Henrietta (1994), *Is There a Crisis in the Family?*, Geneva: United Nations Research Institute for Social Development, World Summit for Social Development, Occasional Research Paper 3 (downloadable from www.unrisd.org).

Morduch, Jonathan (2006a), 'Concepts of poverty', in UN (ed.), *Handbook on Poverty Statistics: Concepts, Methods and Policy Use*, New York: UN Statistics Division (downloadable from unstats.un.org/unsd/methods/poverty/chapter 21. htm).

Morduch, Jonathan (2006b), 'Poverty measures', in UN (ed.), *Handbook on Poverty Statistics: Concepts, Methods and Policy Use*, New York: UN Statistics Division (downloadable from http://unstats.un.org/unsd/methods/poverty/chapter 31. htm).

Morrison, Andrew, Raju, Dhushyanth and Sinha, Nistha (2008), 'Gender equality IS good for the poor', *Poverty in Focus*, **13** (January), 16–17 (www.undp-povertycentre.org/pub/IPCPovertyInFocus 13.pdf).

Moser, Annalise (2007), *BRIDGE Gender and Indicators: Overview Report*, Brighton: BRIDGE, Institute of Development Studies (downloadable from www.bridge.ids.ac.uk).

Moser, Caroline (1978), 'Informal sector or petty commodity production? Dualism or dependence in urban development', *World Development*, **6**(9/10), 1041–64.

Moser, Caroline (1992), 'Adjustment from below: low-income women, time and the triple role in Guayaquil, Ecuador', in Haleh Afshar and Carolyne Dennis (eds), *Women and Adjustment Policies in the Third World*, Basingstoke: Macmillan, pp. 87–116.

Moser, Caroline (1993), *Gender Planning and Development: Theory, Practice, Training*, London: Routledge.

Moser, Caroline (1998), 'The asset vulnerability framework: reassessing urban poverty reduction strategies', *World Development*, **26**(1), 1–19.

Moser, Caroline (2004), 'Urban violence and insecurity: an introductory roadmap', *Environment and Urbanization*, **16**(2), 3–16 (downloadable from eau.sagepub. com/content/vol16/issue2/).

Moser, Caroline (2007a), 'Asset accumulation policy and poverty reduction', in Caroline Moser (ed.), *Reducing Global Poverty: The Case for Asset Accumulation*, Washington, DC: Brookings Institute, pp. 83–103.

Moser, Caroline (ed.) (2007b), *Reducing Global Poverty: The Case for Asset Accumulation*, Washington, DC: Brookings Institute.

Moser, Caroline and McIlwaine, Cathy (2004), *Encounters with Violence in Latin America: Urban Poor Perceptions from Colombia and Guatemala*, London: Routledge.

Moser, Caroline and McIlwaine, Cathy (2006), 'Latin American urban violence as a development concern: towards a framework for violence reduction', *World Development*, **34**(1), 89–112.

Moser, Caroline and Moser, Annalise (2005), 'Gender mainstreaming since Beijing: a review of success and limitations in international institutions', *Gender and Development*, **13**(2), 11–22 (downloadable from http://dx.doi.org/10.1080/13552070512331332283).

Moser, Caroline, Tornqvist, Annika and van Bronkhorst, Bernice (1999), *Mainstreaming Gender and Development in the World Bank: Progress and Recommendations*, Washington, DC: World Bank.

Moßrucker, Harald (1997), 'Amerindian migration in Peru and Mexico', in Josef Gugler (ed.), *Cities in the Developing World: Issues, Theory and Policy*, Oxford: Oxford University Press, pp. 74–87.

Mukhopadhyay, Maitrayee (2007), 'Mainstreaming gender or "streaming" gender away: feminists marooned in the development business', in Andrea Cornwall, Elizabeth Harrison and Ann Whitehead (eds), *Feminisms in Development: Contradictions, Contestations and Challenges*, London: Zed, pp. 135–49.

Muller, Mike (2008), 'Free basic water – a sustainable instrument for a sustainable future in South Africa', *Environment and Urbanisation*, **20**(1), 67–87.

Munck, Ronaldo (2007), 'Global civil society: royal road or slippery path?', *Voluntas: International Journal of Voluntary and Nonprofit Organisations*, **17**, 325–32.

Myrdal, Gunnar (1957), *Economic Theory and Underdeveloped Regions*, London: Duckworth.

Neto, Frederico, Ha, Yejin and Weliwita, Amanda (2007), 'The urban informal economy: new policy approaches', *Habitat Debate*, **13**(2), 4–5 (downloadable from www.unhabitat.org).

Ofstedal, Mary Beth, Reidy, Erin and Knodel, John (2004), 'Gender differences in economic support and well-being of older Asians', *Journal of Cross-Cultural Gerontology*, **19**, 165–201.

Okunlola, Paul (2007), 'The informal economy in Lagos, Nigeria', *Habitat Debate*, **13**(2), 12 (downloadable from www.unhabitat.org).

Organisation for Economic Co-operation and Development (OECD) (2007), *Gender Equality and Aid Delivery: What Has Changed in Development Co-operation Agencies Since 1999?*, Paris: OECD (downloadable from www.oecd.org).

Organisation for Economic Co-operation and Development – Development Assistance Committee (OECD-DAC) (2007), *Aid in Support of Gender Equality and Women's Empowerment*, Paris: OECD (downloadable from www.oecd.org/dac/stats/crs).

Østergaard, Lise (1992), 'Health', in Lise Østergaard (ed.), *Gender and Development*, London: Routledge, pp. 110–34.

Overseas Development Institute [ODI] (2002), *Sovereignty and Global Governance*, London: ODI (downloadable from www.keysheets.org/red_13_sovereignty_and_global_gov.pdf).

Oxaal, Zöe with Baden, Sally (1997), *Gender and Empowerment: Definitions, Approaches and Implications for Policy*, BRIDGE Report No. 40, Brighton: University of Sussex, Institute of Development Studies (downloadable from www.ids.ac.uk/bridge/).

Oxfam (2006), *Kicking the Habit: How the World Bank and the IMF are Still Addicted to Attaching Economic Policy Conditions to Aid*, Briefing Paper No. 96, Oxford: Oxfam (downloadable from www.google.com/search?q=oxfam+briefing+paper+96&sourceid=mozilla-search&start=0&start=0&ie=utf-8&oe= utf-8).

Palmer, Ingrid (1992), 'Gender, equity and economic efficiency in adjustment programes', in Haleh Afshar and Carolyne Dennis (eds), *Women and Adjustment Policies in the Third World*, Basingstoke: Macmillan, pp. 69–83.

Pan-American Health Organisation (PAHO) (2003), *Gender Equity in Health*, Washington, DC: PAHO, Women, Health and Development Program (www.paho.org/genderandhealth) (accessed 13 November 2003).

Panos (2005), *Who's Richer, Who's Poorer? A Journalist's Guide to the Politics of Poverty Reduction Strategies*, London: Panos (downloadable from www.panos.org.uk/PDF/reports/prsptoolkit1.pdf).

Parnwell, Mike and Turner, Sarah (1998), 'Sustaining the unsustainable? City and society in Indonesia', *Third World Planning Review*, **20**(2), 147–63.

Parpart, Jane (1995), 'Deconstructing the development "expert": gender, development and the "vulnerable groups"', in Marianne Marchand and Jane Parpart (eds), *Feminism/Postmodernism/Development*, London: Routledge, pp. 221–43.

Parpart, Jane (2008), 'Rethinking gender and empowerment', in Vandana Desai and Robert Potter (eds), *The Companion to Development Studies*, 2nd edn, London: Hodder Arnold, pp. 355–9.

Parpart, Jane and Marchand, Marianne (1995), 'Exploding the canon: an introduction and conclusion', in Marianne Marchand and Jane Parpart (eds), *Feminism/Postmodernism/Development*, London: Routledge, pp. 1–22.

Patel, Tulsi (2008), 'Indigenous fertility control', in Vandana Desai and Robert Potter (eds), *The Companion to Development Studies*, 2nd edn, London: Hodder Arnold, pp. 390–95.

Pearson, Ruth (1998), ' " Nimble fingers": reflections on women and Third World industrialisation in the late twentieth century', in Cecile Jackson and Ruth Pearson (eds), *Feminist Visions of Development: Gender Analysis and Policy*, London: Routledge, pp. 171–88.

Pearson, Ruth (2007), 'Beyond women workers: gendering corporate social responsibility', *Third World Quarterly*, **28**(4), 731–49.

Pelling, Mark (2002), 'Dependency, diversity and change: towards sustainable urbanisation', in Cathy McIlwaine and Katie Willis (eds), *Challenges and Change in Middle America*, Harlow: Pearson, pp. 218–42.

Perrons, Diane (2004), *Globalisation and Social Change: People and Places in a Divided World*, London: Routledge.

Phillips, David and Verhasselt, Yola (eds) (1994a), *Health and Development*, London: Routledge.

Phillips, David and Verhasselt, Yola (1994b), 'Introduction: health and development', in David Phillips and Yola Verhasselt (eds), *Health and Development*, London: Routledge, pp. 3–32.

Pietilä, Hilkka (2007), *The Unfinished Story of Women and the United Nations*, NGLS Development Dossier 14, New York: UN Non-Governmental Liaison Service (downloadable from www.un.org or via www.siyanda.org).

Portés, Alejandro and Itzigsohn, José (1997), 'Coping with change: the politics and economics of urban poverty', in Richard Tardanico and Rafael Menjívar Larín (eds), *Global Restructuring, Employment and Social Inequality in Urban Latin America*, Miami: North-South Center, University of Miami, pp. 124–52.

Portés, Alejandro and Landolt, Patricia (2000), 'Social capital: promise and pitfalls of its role in development', *Journal of Latin American Studies*, **32**, 529–47.

Portés, Alejandro and Schauffler, Richard (1993), 'Competing perspectives on the Latin American informal sector', *Population and Development Review*, **19**(3), 33–60.

Potter, Robert (2008a), 'Theories, strategies and ideologies of development', in Vandana Desai and Robert Potter (eds), *The Companion to Development Studies*, 2nd edn, London: Hodder Arnold, pp. 67–71.

Potter, Robert (2008b), 'Global convergence, divergence and development', in Vandana Desai and Robert Potter (eds), *The Companion to Development Studies*, 2nd edn, London: Hodder Arnold, pp. 192–6.

Potter, Robert and Lloyd Evans, Sally (1998), *The City in the Developing World*, Harlow: Longman/Prentice Hall.

Potter, Robert, Binns, Tony, Elliott, Jennifer A. and Smith, David (2008), *Geographies of Development*, 3rd edn, Harlow: Pearson Education.

Power, Marcus (2003), *Rethinking Development Geographies*, London: Routledge.

Power, Marcus (2006), 'Anti-racism, deconstruction and "overdevelopment"', *Progress in Development Studies*, **6**, 24–39.

Power, Marcus (2008), 'Enlightenment and the era of modernity', in Vandana Desai and Robert Potter (eds), *The Companion to Development Studies*, 2nd edn, London: Hodder Arnold, pp. 71–5.

Pugh, Cedric (1997), 'The changing roles of self-help housing and urban policies, 1950–1996: experience in developing countries', *Third World Planning Review*, **19**(1), 91–109.

Radcliffe, Sarah (1991), 'The role of gender in peasant migration: conceptual issues from the Peruvian Andes', *Review of Radical Political Economy*, **23**(3–4), 148–73.

Radcliffe, Sarah (1992), 'Mountains, maidens and migration: gender and mobility in Peru', in Sylvia Chant (ed.), *Gender and Migration in Developing Countries*, London: Belhaven, pp. 30–48.

Rakodi, Carole (1999), 'A capital assets framework for analysing household livelihood strategies: implications for policy', *Development Policy Review*, **17**, 315–42.

Randriamaro, Zo (2006), *Gender and Trade, Overview Report*, Brighton: Institute of Development Studies (downloadable from www.bridge.ids.ac.uk/reports/CEP-Trade-OR.doc).

Rathgeber, Eva (1995), 'Gender and development in action', in Marianne Marchand and Jane Parpart (eds), *Feminism/Postmodernism/Development*, London: Routledge, pp. 204 20.

Razavi, Shahra (1999), 'Export-oriented employment, poverty and gender: contested accounts', *Development and Change*, **30**(3), 653–83.

Reddy, Sanjay (2008), 'Are estimates of poverty in Latin America reliable?', *One Pager*, 52, International Poverty Centre, Brasilia (downloadable from www.undo-povertycentre.org) (accessed 5 May 2008).

Reeves, Hazel and Baden, Sally (2000), *Gender and Development: Concepts and Definitions*, Brighton: BRIDGE Report No. 55, Institute of Development Studies, University of Sussex (downloadable from www.ids.ac.uk/bridge).

Richey, Lisa Ann and Ponte, Stefano (2006), *Better Red^{TM} Than Dead: 'Brand Aid', Celebrities and the New Frontier of Development Assistance*,

Working Paper No. 2006/26, Copenhagen: Danish Institute for International Studies (downloadable from www.diis.dk).

Rigg, Jonathan (2007), *An Everyday Geography of the Global South*, London and New York: Routledge.

Rigg, Jonathan (2008), 'The Millennium Development Goals', in Vandana Desai and Robert Potter (eds), *The Companion to Development Studies*, 2nd edn, London: Hodder Arnold, pp. 30–37.

Rist, Gilbert (1997), *The History of Development: From Western Origins to Global Faith*, London: Zed.

Roberts, Bryan (1991), 'The changing nature of informal employment: the case of Mexico', in Guy Standing and Victor Tokman (eds), *Towards Social Adjustment: Labour Market Issues in Structural Adjustment*, Geneva: International Labour Organisation, pp. 115 40.

Roberts, Bryan (1994), 'Informal economy and family strategies', *International Journal of Urban and Regional Research*, **18**(1), 6–23.

Roberts, Bryan (1995), *The Making of Citizens: Cities of Peasants Revisited*, London: Edward Arnold.

Roberts, J. Timmons and Bellone Hite, Amy (eds) (2007), *The Globalisation and Development Reader: Perspectives on Development Global Change*, Oxford: Blackwell.

Rodgers, Dennis (2004), ' " Disembedding" the city: crime, insecurity and spatial organisation in Managua, Nicaragua', *Environment and Urbanisation*, **16**(2), 113–24 (downloadable from http://eau.sagepub.com/content/vol16/issue2/).

Rodgers, Dennis (2007), ' " Each to their own": ethnographic notes on the economic organisation of poor households in urban Nicaragua', *Journal of Development Studies*, **43**(3), 391–419.

Roever, Sally (2007), 'Looking at the informal sector in Latin America', *Habitat Debate*, **13**(2), 15 (downloadable from www.unhabitat.org).

Rostow, Walt Whitman (1960), *The Stages of Economic Growth: A Non-Communist Manifesto*, Cambridge: Cambridge University Press.

Rowlands, Jo (1996), 'Empowerment examined', in Deborah Eade (ed.), *Development and Social Diversity*, Oxford: Oxfam, pp. 86–92 (downloadable from www.oxfam.org).

Royal Ministry of Foreign Affairs (1997), *A Strategy for Women and Gender Equality in Development Cooperation*, Oslo: Royal Ministry of Foreign Affairs.

Sachs, Jeffrey D. (2005), *The End of Poverty: How We Can Make It Happen in Our Lifetime*, New York: Penguin.

Safa, Helen (1998), 'Female-headed households in the Caribbean: sign of pathology or alternative form of family organisation?', *The Brown Journal of World Affairs*, **5**(2), 203–14.

Safa, Helen (2002), 'Questioning globalisation: gender and export processing in the Dominican Republic', *Journal of Developing Societies*, **18**(2–3),
11–31.

Saith, Ashwani (2006), 'From universal values to Millennium
Development Goals: lost in translation', *Development and Change*,
37(6), 1167–99.

Saith, Ruhi and Harriss-White, Barbara (1999), 'The gender sensitivity of
well-being indicators', *Development and Change*, **30**(3), 465–97.

Sapsford, David (2008), 'Smith, Ricardo and the world marketplace', in
Vandana Desai and Robert Potter (eds), *The Companion to Development
Studies*, 2nd edn, London: Hodder Arnold, pp. 75–81.

Sassen, Saskia (2002a), 'Locating cities on global circuits', *Environment and
Urbanisation*, **14**(1), 13–30.

Sassen, Saskia (2002b), 'Counter-geographies of globalisation: feminisation of survival', in Kreimild Saunders (ed.), *Feminist Post-Development
Thought*, London: Zed, pp. 89–104.

Sassen, Saskia (2006), *A Sociology of Globalisation*, London: W.W. Norton.

Satterthwaite, David (1997), 'Sustainable cities or cities that contribute to
sustainable development?', *Urban Studies*, **34**(10), 1667–91.

Satterthwaite, David (2005), 'The scale of urban change worldwide 1950–
2000 and its underpinnings', *Human Settlements Discussion Paper Series,
Theme: Urban Change-1*, London: International Institute for
Environment and Development (downloadable from www.iied.org/
pubs).

Satterthwaite, David (2007), *The Transition to a Predominantly Urban
World and its Underpinnings*, Human Settlements Discussion Paper
Series, Theme: Urban Change No. 4, London: International Institute for
Environment and Development (downloadable from www.iied.org/
pubs/).

Satterthwaite, David (2008), 'Urbanisation in low- and middle-income
nations', in Vandana Desai and Robert Potter (eds), *The Companion to
Development Studies*, 2nd edn, London: Hodder Arnold, pp. 237–43.

Satterthwaite, David, Huq, Saleemul, Reid, Hannah, Pelling, Mark and
Romero Lankao, Patricia (2007), *Adapting to Climate Change in Urban
Areas: The Possibilities and Constraints in Low- and Middle-income
Nations*, Human Settlements Discussion Paper Series, Climate Change
and Cities 1, London: International Institute of Environment and
Development (downloadable from www.iied.org/HS/publications.html).

Save the Children UK, HelpAge International and Institute of
Development Studies (2005), *Making Cash Count: Lessons from Cash
Transfer Schemes in East and Southern Africa for Supporting the Most
Vulnerable Children and Households*, Brighton: IDS (downloadable

from www.ids.ac.uk/UserFiles/File/poverty_team/MakingCashCount
final.pdf).

Schneider, Friedrich (2007), 'Measuring the informal economy', *Habitat Debate*, **13**(2), 19 (downloadable from www.unhabitat.org).

Schuurman, Frans (ed.) (2001), *Globalisation and Development Studies*, London: Sage.

Schuurman, Frans (2008), 'The impasse in development studies', in Vandana Desai and Robert Potter (eds), *The Companion to Development Studies*, 2nd edn, London: Hodder Arnold, pp. 12–16.

Sen, Amartya (1981), *Poverty and Famines*, Oxford: Clarendon Press.

Sen, Amartya (1985), *Commodities and Capabilities*, Helsinki: United Nations University, World Institute for Development Economics Research.

Sen, Amartya (1999), *Development as Freedom*, Oxford: Oxford University Press.

Sen, Gita (2008), 'Poverty as a gendered experience: the policy implications', *Poverty in Focus*, **13**, 6–7 (www.undp-povertycentre.org/pub/IPCPovertyInFocus 13.pdf) (accessed 15 January 2008).

Shetty, Prakash (2008), 'Malnutrition and nutrition policies in developing countries', in Vandana Desai and Robert Potter (eds), *The Companion to Development Studies*, 2nd edn, London: Hodder Arnold, pp. 399–403.

Sidaway, James D. (2008), 'Post-development', in Vandana Desai and Robert Potter (eds), *The Companion to Development Studies*, 2nd edn, London: Hodder Arnold, pp. 16–19.

Simon, David (ed.) (2006), *Fifty Key Thinkers on Development*, London: Routledge.

Simon, David (2007), 'Beyond antidevelopment: discourses, convergences, practices', *Singapore Journal of Tropical Geography*, **28**(2), 205–18.

Simon, David (2008), 'Neoliberalism, structural adjustment and poverty reduction strategies', in Vandana Desai and Robert Potter (eds), *The Companion to Development Studies*, 2nd edn, London: Hodder Arnold, pp. 86–92.

Singhanetra-Renard, Anchalee and Prabhudhanitisarn, Nitaya (1992), 'Changing socio-economic roles of Thai women and their migration', in Sylvia Chant (ed.), *Gender and Migration in Developing Countries*, London: Belhaven, pp. 154–73.

Sklair, Leslie (2002), *Capitalism, Globalisation, and its Alternatives*, 3rd edn, Oxford: Oxford University Press.

Smyke, Patricia (1994), *Women and Health*, London: Zed.

Smyth, Ines (1994), *Population Policies: Official Responses to Feminist Critiques*, Global Governance Discussion Paper 14, London: London School of Economics.

Spivak, Gayatri Chakravarty (1988), 'Can the subaltern speak?', in Cary Nelson and Lawrence Grossburg (eds), *Marxism and the Interpretation of Cultures*, Basingstoke: Macmillan, pp. 271–313.

Spronk, Rachel (2008), 'Beyond pain, towards pleasure in the study of sexuality in Africa', *Sexuality in Africa*, **4**(3), 3–8 (downloadable from www.arsrc.org).

Standing, Guy (1989), 'Global feminisation through flexible labour, *World Development*, **17**(7), 1077–95.

Standing, Guy (1991), 'Structural adjustment and labour market policies: towards social adjustment?', in Guy Standing and Victor Tokman (eds), *Towards Social Adjustment: Labour Market Issues In Structural Adjustment*, Geneva: International Labour Organisation, pp. 5–51.

Standing, Guy (1999), 'Global feminisation through flexible labour: a theme revisited', *World Development*, **27**(3), 583–602.

Standing, Hilary (2007), 'Gender, myth and fable: the perils of mainstreaming in sector bureaucracies', in Andrea Cornwall, Elizabeth Harrison and Ann Whitehead (eds), *Feminisms in Development: Contradictions, Contestations and Challenges*, London: Zed, pp. 101–11.

Stephens, Carolyn and Harpham, Trudy (1992), 'Health and environment in urban areas of developing countries', *Third World Planning Review*, **14**(3), 267–82.

Stiglitz, Joseph E. (1999), 'The World Bank at the millennium', *The Economic Journal*, **109**(459), 577–97.

Stiglitz, Joseph E. (2002), *Globalisation and its Discontents*, New York: W.W. Norton.

Stockholm International Peace Research Institute (SIPRI) (2007), *SIPRI Yearbook 2007*, Oxford: Oxford University Press (downloadable from: http:// yearbook2007.sipri.org/).

Structural Adjustment Participatory Review International Network (SAPRIN) (2004), *Structural Adjustment: The SAPRI Report: The Policy Roots of Economic Crisis, Poverty and Inequality*, London: Zed (also available on www.saprin.org/SAPRI_Findings.pdf).

Subrahmanian, Ramya (2007), 'Making sense of gender in shifting institutional contexts: some reflections on gender mainstreaming', in Andrea Cornwall, Elizabeth Harrison and Ann Whitehead (eds), *Feminisms in Development: Contradictions, Contestations and Challenges*, London: Zed, pp. 112–21.

Szirmai, Adam (1997), *Economic and Social Development*, New York: Prentice Hall.

Tacoli, Cecilia (2002), *Changing Rural–Urban Interactions in Sub-Saharan Africa and their Impact on Livelihoods: A Summary*, Rural–Urban Interactions and Livelihood Strategies Working Paper 7, London:

International Institute for Environment and Development (download-able from www.iied.org).

Tacoli, Cecilia (ed.) (2006), *The Earthscan Reader in Rural–Urban Linkages*, London: Earthscan.

Tannerfeldt, Göran and Ljung, Per (2006), *More Urban, Less Poor*, London: Earthscan.

Taylor, Peter Doel, Marcus, Hoyler, Michael, David Walker and Beaverstock, Jonathan (2000), 'World cities in the Pacific Rim: a new global test of regional coherence', *Singapore Journal of Tropical Geography*, **21**(3), 233–45.

Thirlwall, A.P. (2008), 'Development as economic growth', in Vandana Desai and Robert Potter (eds), *The Companion to Development Studies*, 2nd edn, London: Hodder Arnold, pp. 37–40.

Thomas, Alan (2000a), 'Meanings and views of development', in Tim Allen and Alan Thomas (eds), *Poverty and Development into the 21st Century*, Oxford: Oxford University Press, pp. 23–48.

Thomas, Alan (2000b), 'Poverty and the "end of development"', in Tim Allen and Alan Thomas (eds), *Poverty and Development into the 21st Century*, Oxford: Oxford University Press, pp. 3–22.

Thomas, Alan and Allen, Tim (2000), 'Agencies of development', in Tim Allen and Alan Thomas (eds), *Poverty and Development into the 21st Century*, Oxford: Oxford University Press, pp. 189–216.

Thomas, Caroline (1999), 'Where is the Third World now?', *Review of International Studies*, **25**, 225–44.

Thomas, J.J. (1995), *Surviving in the City: The Urban Informal Sector in Latin America*, London: Pluto.

Thomas, J.J. (1996), 'The new economic model and labour markets in Latin America', in Victor Bulmer-Thomas (ed.), *The New Economic Model in Latin America and its Impact on Income Distribution and Poverty*, Basingstoke: Macmillan, in association with the Institute of Latin American Studies, University of London, pp. 79–102.

Tokman, Victor (1991), 'The informal sector in Latin America: from under-ground to legality', in Guy Standing and Victor Tokman (eds), *Towards Social Adjustment:Labour Market Issues in Structural Adjustment*, Geneva: International Labour Organisation, pp. 141–57.

Touray, Isatou (2006), 'Sexuality and women's sexual rights in The Gambia', *IDS Bulletin*, **27**(5), 77–83.

Tsikata, Dzodzi (2007), 'Announcing a new dawn prematurely? Human rights feminists and the rights-based approaches to development', in Andrea Cornwall, Elizabeth Harrison and Ann Whitehead (eds), *Feminisms in Development: Contradictions, Contestations and Challenges*, London: Zed, pp. 214–26.

Tsikata, Dzodzi (2009), 'Informalisation, the informal economy and urban women's livelihoods in sub-Saharan Africa since the 1990s', in Shahra Razavi (ed.), *The Gendered Impacts of Liberalisation Policies: Toward 'Embedded' Liberalism?*, London/Geneva: Routledge/UNRISD Research on Social Development.

Turner, John F.C. (1970), 'Barriers and channels for housing development in modernising countries', in William Mangin (ed.), *Peasants in Cities*, Boston, MA: Houghton Mifflin, pp. 1–19.

Turner, J.F.C. (1972), 'Housing as a verb', in John F.C. Turner and Robert Fichter (eds), *Freedom to Build*, New York: Macmillan, pp. 148–75.

Turner, J.F.C. (1976), *Housing by People*, London: Marion Boyars.

Turner, John F.C. (1982), 'Issues in self-help housing', in Peter Ward (ed.), *Self-Help Housing: A Critique*, London: Mansell, pp. 99–103.

Tvedt, Terje (2006), 'The international aid system and the non-governmental organisations: a new research agenda', *Journal of International Development*, **18**, 677–90.

Ugalde, Antonio, Homedes, Nuria and Zwi, Anthony (2002), 'Globalisation, equity and health in Latin America', in Christopher Abel and Colin Lewis (eds), *Exclusion and Engagement: Social Policy in Latin America*, London: Institute of Latin American Studies, University of London, pp. 151–71.

Undie, Chi-Chi and Benaya, Kabwe (2006), *The State of Knowledge on Sexuality in Africa: A Synthesis of the Literature*, APHRC Working Paper No. 24, Nairobi: African Population and Health Research Centre (www.aphrc.org) (downloaded 20 March 2008).

Unger, Alon and Riley, Lee W. (2007), 'Slum health: from understanding to action', *PLoS Medicine*, **4**(10), 1561–66 (e295) (downloadable from www. plosmedicine.org).

United Nations (UN) (1997), *Report of the Economic and Social Council for 2007*, A/52/3, New York: UN.

United Nations (UN) (2000), *The World's Women 2000: Trends and Statistics*, New York: UN (downloadable from http://unstats.un.org/ demographic/ products/indwm).

United Nations (UN) (2005), *Demographic Yearbook 2002*, New York: UN.

United Nations (UN) (2006a), *Demographic Yearbook 2003*, New York: UN.

United Nations (UN) (2006b), *Progress of the World's Women 2005: Progress in Statistics*, New York: UN (downloadable from www.un.org).

United Nations (UN) (2007), *The Millennium Goals Report 2007*, New York: UN (downloadable from http://mdgs.un.org/unsd/mdg/ Resources/ Static/Products/ Progress 2007/UNSD_MDG_Report_2007e.pdf).

United Nations AIDS (UNAIDS) (2006), *2006 Report on the Global AIDS Epidemic: Executive Summary*, Geneva: UNAIDS (downloadable from http://www.data.unaids.org/pub/GlobalReport/2006/2006_GR-Executive Summary_en.pdf).

United Nations AIDS (UNAIDS) (2007), *AIDS Epidemic Update*, Geneva: UNAIDS/WHO (downloadable from www.unaids.org/en/HIV_data/2007EpiUpdate/default.asp).

United Nations Centre for Human Settlements (UNCHS Habitat) (1996), *An Urbanising World: Global Report on Human Settlements 1996*, Oxford: Oxford University Press.

United Nations Centre for Human Settlements (UNCHS Habitat) (2001), *Cities in a Globalising World: Global Report on Human Settlements 2001*, London: Earthscan (downloadable from www.unhabitat.org).

United Nations Children's Fund (UNICEF) (2007), *State of the World's Children 2007: Women and Children: The Double Dividend of Gender Equality*, UNICEF: New York (downloadable from http://www.unicef.org).

United Nations Development Fund for Women (UNIFEM) (2002), *Progress of the World's Women 2002*, Vol. 2, New York: UNIFEM.

United Nations Development Fund for Women (UNIFEM) (2006), *Progress of the World's Women 2005: Women, Work and Poverty*, New York: UNIFEM (downloadable from www.un-ngls.org/women-2005.pdf).

United Nations Development Programme (UNDP) (1995), *Human Development Report 1995*, New York: Oxford University Press (downloadable from www.undp.org).

United Nations Development Programme (UNDP) (1997), *Human Development Report 1997*, Oxford: Oxford University Press.

United Nations Development Programme (UNDP) (2000), *Human Development Report 2000*, Oxford University Press, New York (downloadable from www.undp.org).

United Nations Development Programme (UNDP) (2001), *Human Development Report 2001: Making New Technologies Work for Human Development*, New York: Oxford University Press (downloadable from www.undp.org).

United Nations Development Programme (UNDP) (2003), *Human Development Report 2003*, New York: Oxford University Press (downloadable from www.undp.org).

United Nations Development Programme (UNDP) (2005), *Human Development Report 2005*, Oxford University Press, New York (downloadable from www.undp.org).

United Nations Development Programme (UNDP) (2006), *Human Development Report 2006*, Oxford University Press, New York (downloadable from www.undp.org).

United Nations Fund for Population Activities (UNFPA) (2007), *State of the World's Population 2007: Unleashing the Potential of Urban Growth*, New York: UNFPA (downloadable from www.unfpa.org).

United Nations-Habitat (UN-Habitat) (2004), *Urban Land for All*, Nairobi: UN-Habitat (downloadable from www.unhabitat.org).

United Nations-Habitat (UN-Habitat) (2006), *State of the World's Cities 2006/7, The Millennium Development Goals and Urban Sustainability: 30 Years of Shaping the Habitat Agenda*, London: Earthscan.

United Nations Millennium Project (UNMP), Task Force on Education and Gender Equality (TFEGE) (2005), *Taking Action: Achieving Gender Equality and Empowering Women*, London: Earthscan (also downloadable from www.unmillenniumproject.org/documents/gender).

United Nations Research Institute for Social Development (UNRISD) (2005), *Gender Equality: Striving for Justice in an Unequal World*, Geneva: UNRISD (downloadable from www.unrisd.org).

United Nations Statistics Division (UNSD) (2005), *Special Report of the World's Women 2005: Progress in Statistics. Focusing on Sex-disaggregated Statistics on Population, Births and Deaths*, New York: UNSD, Department of Social and Economic Affairs (downloadable from www.ops.oms.org).

Unwin, Tim (2008), 'Conflict, development and aid', in Vandana Desai and Robert Potter (eds), *The Companion to Development Studies*, 2nd edn, London: Hodder Arnold, pp. 450–53.

Vaa, Mariken (2000), 'Policy after political transition: the case of Bamako', *Environment and Urbanisation*, **11**(2), 27–34.

Van Donk, Mirjam (2006), '"Positive" urban futures in sub-Saharan Africa: HIV/AIDS and the need for ABC (A Broader Conceptualisation)', *Environment and Urbanisation*, **18**(1),155–75.

Van Grunsven, Leo (1998), 'The sustainability of urban development in the SIJORI growth triangle', *Third World Planning Review*, **20**(2), 179–201.

Van Naerssen, Tom and Barten, Françoise (1999), 'Healthy Cities in Developing Countries: A Programme of Multilateral Assistance', in David Simon and Anders Närman (eds), *Development as Theory and Practice*, Harlow: Longman, pp. 230–46.

Van Rooy, Alison (2008), 'Strengthening civil society in developing countries', in Vandana Desai and Robert Potter (eds), *The Companion to Development Studies*, 2nd edn, London: Hodder Arnold, pp. 520–25.

Van Vliet, Willem (2002), 'Cities in a globalising world: from engines of growth to agents of change', *Environment and Urbanisation*, **14**(1), 31–40.

Varley, Ann (1987), 'The relationship between tenure legalisation and housing improvement: evidence from Mexico City', *Development and Change*, **18**, 463–81.

Varley, Ann (1993), 'Gender and housing: the provision of accommodation for young adults in three Mexican cities', *Habitat International*, **17**(4), 13–30.

Varley, Ann (2008), 'Gender, families and households', in Vandana Desai and Robert Potter (eds), *The Companion to Development Studies,* 2nd edn, London: Hodder Arnold, pp. 346–51.

Varley, Ann and Blasco, Maribel (2000), 'Intact or in tatters? Family care of older women and men in urban Mexico', *Gender and Development*, **8**(2), 47–55.

Velasco, Andrés (2002), 'The dustbin of history: dependency theory', *ForeignPolicy.com* (downloadable from www.foreignpolicy.com/Ning/archive/archive/133/dustbin.pdf)

Vera-Sanso, Penny (2006), 'Experiences in old age: a South Indian example of how functional age is socially structured', *Oxford Development Studies*, **34**(4), 457–72.

Vernego, Matias (2006), 'Technology, finance, and dependency: Latin American radical political economy in retrospect', *Review of Radical Political Economics*, **38**(4), 551–68.

Von Hayek, Friedrich (1978), *New Studies in Philosophy, Politics and Economics*, Chicago, IL: University of Chicago Press.

Wade, Robert Hunter (2002), 'US hegemony and the World Bank: the fight over people and ideas', *Review of International Political Economy*, **9**(2), 215–43.

Wallerstein, Immanuel (2004), *World-Systems Analysis: An Introduction*, Durham, NC: Duke University Press.

Wangari, Esther (2002), 'Reproductive technologies: a Third World feminist perspective', in Kriemild Saunders (ed.), *Feminist Post-Development Thought*, London: Zed, pp. 298–312.

White, Howard (2008), 'The measurement of poverty', in Vandana Desai and Robert Potter (eds), *The Companion to Development Studies*, 2nd edn, London: Hodder Arnold, pp. 25–30.

Whitman, Jim (2008), 'The role of the United Nations in developing countries', in Vandana Desai and Robert Potter (eds), *The Companion to Development Studies*, 2nd edn, London: Hodder Arnold, pp. 555–9.

Wield, David and Chataway, Joanna (2000), 'Unemployment and making a living', in Tim Allen and Alan Thomas (eds), *Poverty and Development into the 21st Century*, Oxford: Oxford University Press, pp. 99–124.

Willis, Katie (2002), 'Open for business: strategies for economic diversification', in Cathy McIlwaine and Katie Willis (eds), *Challenges and Change in Middle America*, Harlow: Pearson, pp. 136–58.

Willis, Katie (2005), *Theories and Practices of Development*, London and New York: Routledge.

Willis, Katie (2008), 'Migration and transnationalism', in Vandana Desai and Robert Potter (eds), *The Companion to Development Studies*, 2nd edn, London: Hodder Arnold, pp. 212–16.

Willis, Katie and Yeoh, Brenda (eds) (2000), *Gender and Migration*, Cheltenham, UK and Northampton, MA, USA: Edward Elgar.

Women's Environment and Development Organisation (WEDO) (2005), *Beijing Betrayed: Women Worldwide Report that Governments have Failed to Turn the Platform into Action*, New York: WEDO (downloadable from www.wedo.org/ library.aspx?ResourceID=31).

Woodford-Berger, Prudence (2007), 'Gender mainstreaming: what is it (about) and should we continue doing it?', in Andrea Cornwall, Elizabeth Harrison and Ann Whitehead (eds), *Feminisms in Development: Contradictions, Contestations and Challenges*, London: Zed, pp. 122–34.

World Bank (1990), *World Development Report 1990*, New York: Oxford University Press.

World Bank (1993), *Housing: Enabling Markets to Work*, Washington, DC: World Bank.

World Bank (1994), *World Development Report 1994*, New York: Oxford University Press.

World Bank (1996), *World Development Report 1996*, New York: Oxford University Press.

World Bank (2000), *World Development Report 2000/2001*, New York: Oxford University Press.

World Bank (2005), *Issues and Options for Improving Engagement Between the World Bank and Civil Society Organizations*, Washington, DC: World Bank (downloadable from http://siteresources.worldbank.org/CSO/Resources/Issues_and_Options_PUBLISHED_VERSION.pdf).

World Bank (2006), *Gender Equality as Smart Economics: A World Bank Group Gender Action Plan (Fiscal Years 2007–10)* (http://siteresources.worldbank.org/INTGENDER/Resources/GAPNov2.pdf) (accessed 4 May 2008).

World Bank (2007a), *Global Monitoring Report 2007: Confronting the Challenges of Gender Equality and Fragile States*, Washington, DC: World Bank (downloadable from http://www.worldbank.org).

World Bank (2007b), *Healthy Development: The World Bank Strategy for Health, Nutrition and Population Results*, Washington DC: World Bank (downloadable from http://www.worldbank.org).

World Bank (2008), 'Gender equality as smart economics: World Bank Group gender action plan. First year progress report (January 2007–January 2008)', Mimeo, Washington, DC: World Bank.

World Health Organisation (WHO) (2001), *World Health Report 2001*.

Mental Health: New Understanding, New Hope, Geneva: WHO (downloadable from www.who.org).

World Health Organisation (WHO) (2004), *Progress in Reproductive Health Research, No. 67*, Geneva: WHO (www.who.int/reproductive-health/hrp/progress/67.pdf).

Wright, Melissa W. (2006), *Disposable Women and Other Myths of Global Capitalism*, London and New York: Routledge.

Wroe, Martin and Doney, Malcolm (2005), *The Rough Guide to a Better World*, London: Rough Guides (downloadable from www.dfid.gov.uk/pubs/files/rough-guide/better-world.pdf).

You, Nicholas (2007), 'Cities, climate change and global health', *Habitat Debate*, **13**(4), 4–5 (downloadable from www.unhabitat.org).

Zhang, Heather Xiaoquan and Locke, Catherine (2004), 'Interpreting reproductive rights: institutional responses to the agenda in the 1990s', *Public Administration and Development*, **24**, 41–50.

Zuckerman, Elaine (2002), '"Engendering" poverty reduction strategy papers (PRSPs): the issues and the challenges', *Gender and Development*, **10**(3), 89–94 (downloadable from www.genderaction.org/images/Oxfam%20Gender&Devt%20Journal%20Article-EZ%20PRSPs.pdf).

Zuckerman, Elaine (2007), 'Critique: gender equality as smart economics: World Bank Group Gender Action Plan (GAP) (Fiscal years 2007–10)', mimeo, Washington, DC: GenderAction (www.genderaction.org) (accessed 2 May 2008).

Index

abortion 74–5, 268
accountability 288, 293
accounts, national 15, 190
accumulation 30, 37, 182, 203
ACTIONAID 74
actors
  civil society 295–305
  development 2, 281–305
  non-state 56
ADHD (Attention Deficit
    Hyperactivity Disorder) 54
adoption 236, 278
advanced economies 65, 77–8, 116,
    205, 225, 257, 260
advocacy 295, 302
Afghanistan 46, 55–6, 58
Africa 2, 8, 11, 22, 41, 56, 60, 67, 72,
    74–5, 80, 85–6, 91, 93, 97, 101,
    103–5, 115–16, 119, 132, 151,
    196–7, 244, 253, 265–6, 268, 279,
    287
Africans 21, 35, 46, 58, 75, 77, 86, 115,
    198, 201, 243, 278, 284, 286
ageing 3, 64, 76–8, 80, 92, 238,
    265
agencies
  bilateral 289
  development 45, 108, 129, 151, 220,
      232, 281–2, 289, 306
  donor 292, 294, 305
  law enforcement 60
  multilateral 281–2, 285, 290
  non-governmental 151
  UN, see UN (United Nations)
agricultural economies 136
agriculture 29, 34, 90, 190
aid 13, 22, 30, 38, 81, 129, 153, 200,
    221, 234, 276, 281–2, 287–94, 296,
    301, 306
aid delivery 293, 306
AIDS (Acquired Immunodeficiency
    Syndrome) 4, 20, 58, 67, 70, 74–5,

77–8, 195, 197, 199, 201, 241,
    255–9, 262–4, 268, 270–71, 278,
    280, 304; see also HIV
alcoholism 183
Algeria 168, 293
alienation 5, 262
Amazonia 288
America, Middle 208
America, North 52, 66, 97, 99, 114, 258
amoebiasis 259
anaemia 268
ANGO (advocacy-oriented non-
    governmental organisation) 296,
    298
Angola 58, 102
Annan, Kofi 236, 285
anti-natalist agendas 68
Argentina 36–7, 52, 78, 81, 100, 103–4,
    120, 138–9, 158, 167, 170, 245,
    260–61
Armenia 104
ART (Anti-Retroviral Therapy) 203,
    278, 280, 305
ascariasis 259
ASEAN (Association of Southeast
    Asian Nations) 11
Asia
  East 23, 36, 51, 66, 71, 77, 114, 116,
      138, 151, 196–7, 208, 244, 257,
      266, 287
  central 66, 119, 216, 244, 287
  in general 8, 11, 56, 66, 74, 80, 87,
      93, 97, 105, 115, 119, 132, 141,
      145–6, 151, 155, 166, 196–8,
      216, 244, 253, 266, 273, 287
  Northeast 10
  south 38, 66, 71, 81, 86, 113–14, 116,
      138, 196–8, 208, 216, 245, 257,
      266, 271, 287
  southeast 23, 37, 81, 85–6, 104, 138,
      146, 150, 158, 244, 249, 266
  west 23, 81, 244

Mexico 11, 35–7, 40, 49, 54, 74, 78,
    81–2, 87–8, 91, 94, 100–101, 103,
    107, 117, 138, 141, 145, 147–8,
    168, 181–3, 237, 245–6, 253, 260
MHT (Gujarat Mahila Housing
    SEWA Trust) 300
microenterprises 169, 178
middle classes 55, 117, 301
Midgely, James 279
MIGA (Multilateral Investment
    Guarantee Agency) 286
migration 80–91
    duration of 82
    effects of 81–92
    gender selective 84, 86–9
    international 81, 84, 247–9, 181, 265,
        304
    labour 247
    major patterns of 91
    permanent 265
    rural–urban 3, 64, 82, 86, 88, 90, 92,
        101, 106–7, 124, 167
    temporary 82
    theory 82–4
    urban policy, implications of 92
    young people's 85
mining 281
minorities 11, 57, 166, 194, 199
MNC (multinational corporation or
    company) 140, 143–7, 151
mobilisation
    of assets 193
    community 262
    mass 300
mobility 64, 80–91, 148, 242
models
    core–periphery 28
    demographic transition 65
    epidemiological transition 258
    neo-classical 83, 137
    neo-Marxian 83
    segmented 273
    transition 65–7, 257–8
modernisation 3, 25–32, 34, 38–9,
    49–50, 54, 61, 101, 241–2
modernisation theory 25–7, 31–2, 34,
    38–9, 50, 53–4
modernity 28, 49, 260
Molyneux, Maxine 183, 224–5, 232,
    234

MONGO (my own non-governmental
    organisation) 296
Mongolia 10
monitoring 47, 152, 208, 219, 230–31,
    283, 285, 294, 303
monopolies 39
morbidity 200, 257–8, 265
Morocco 72, 115, 120, 168, 251
mortality 16, 20, 43, 66, 101, 167, 256,
    260–61, 266, 276–7
Moser, Caroline 59–61, 172, 178–9,
    182, 193–5, 199, 201, 203, 212,
    217, 219, 223–5, 227, 230–31, 236
motherhood 69, 250
mothers 75, 88–9, 181, 224, 233–4,
    240, 246, 262, 267
Mozambique 8, 46, 71, 87, 115
multilaterals 136–7, 200, 281–2, 284–5,
    288–90, 292–4, 302, 304–5
multinationals 31, 104, 140, 143,
    146–7, 151, 154
Myrdal, Gunnar 28, 50

NAFTA (North American Free Trade
    Agreement) 11, 54
Nairobi 94, 102, 134, 184, 221, 227
NAM (Non-Aligned Movement) 7, 11
Namibia 87, 104, 132, 169, 256
NASVI (National Association of
    Street Vendors of India) 300
National Slum Dwellers Federation
    131
NATO (North Atlantic Treaty
    Organisation) 7
needs 1, 16, 21, 41, 47, 55, 71–5, 83, 85,
    108, 114, 151, 178, 187, 189–90,
    200, 223–5, 229, 231, 251, 258,
    267, 276–7, 279, 288, 299, 302,
    305
neighbourhoods 1, 52, 59, 114, 134,
    261
neo-classical equilibrium approach 38,
    50, 82–3, 137
neo-liberalism 22, 38–48, 61, 140, 151,
    283
Nepal 49
Netherlands 104, 290–91
networks
    criminal 58, 60
    family 88